Lincoln

PROFILES IN POWER

General Editor: Keith Robbins

Lincoln

Richard J. Carwardine

To Dennis,

with very best wishes

Richard Carwardine
June 2008

PEARSON
Longman

PEARSON EDUCATION LIMITED

Head Office:
Edinburgh Gate
Harlow CM20 2JE
Tel: +44 (0)1279 623623
Fax: +44 (0)1279 431059

London Office:
128 Long Acre
London WC2E 9AN
Tel: +44 (0)20 7447 2000
Fax: +44 (0)20 7447 2170
Website: www.history-minds.com

First published in Great Britain in 2003

The rights of Richard J. Carwardine to be identified as Author
of this Work has been asserted by him in accordance
with the Copyright, Designs and Patents Act 1988.

ISBN 0 582 03279 2

British Library Cataloguing in Publication Data
A CIP catalogue record for this book can be obtained from the British Library

Library of Congress Cataloging in Publication Data
A CIP catalog record for this book can be obtained from the Library of Congress

10 9 8 7 6 5 4 3 2 1

Typeset by Graphicraft Limited, Hong Kong
Printed and bound in Malaysia

The Publishers' policy is to use paper manufactured from sustainable forests.

In memory of Peter Parish, Robert Parry and Brian Stevens

CONTENTS

CONTENTS

List of Abbreviations

ALP — Abraham Lincoln Papers, Library of Congress

CW — Roy P. Basler et al., eds, *The Collected Works of Abraham Lincoln* (9 vols, New Brunswick, NJ: Rutgers University Press, 1953–55)

DJH — Michael Burlingame and John R. Turner Ettlinger, eds, *Inside Lincoln's White House: The Complete Civil War Diary of John Hay* (Carbondale, IL: Southern Illinois University Press, 1997)

Donald — David Herbert Donald, *Lincoln* (New York: Simon and Schuster, 1995)

Herndon's Lincoln — William H. Herndon and Jesse W. Weik, *Herndon's Life of Lincoln: The History and Personal Recollections of Abraham Lincoln as Originally Written by William H. Herndon and Jesse W. Weik with an Introduction and Notes by Paul M. Angle* (Cleveland, OH and New York: The World Publishing Company, 1942)

HI — Douglas L. Wilson and Rodney O. Davis, eds, *Herndon's Informants: Letters Interviews, and Statements about Abraham Lincoln* (Urbana and Chicago, IL: University of Illinois Press, 1998)

Lincoln's Journalist — Michael Burlingame, ed., *Lincoln's Journalist: John Hay's Anonymous Writings for the Press, 1860–1864* (Carbondale, IL: Southern Illinois University Press, 1999)

Lincoln Observed — Michael Burlingame, ed., *Lincoln Observed: Civil War Dispatches of Noah Brooks* (Baltimore, MD: Johns Hopkins University Press, 1998)

N&H — John G. Nicolay and John Hay, *Abraham Lincoln: A History* (10 vols, New York: The Century Co., 1890)

Nicolay, *Oral History* — Michael Burlingame, ed., *An Oral History of Abraham Lincoln: John G. Nicolay's Interviews and Essays* (Carbondale, IL: Southern Illinois University Press, 1996)

RWAL   Don E. Fehrenbacher and Virginia Fehrenbacher, comps and eds, *Recollected Words of Abraham Lincoln* (Stanford, CA: Stanford University Press, 1996)

Note on the text

I have aimed to reproduce all quoted material as it is in the cited source, though I have occasionally made minor alterations to punctuation. Unless I have indicated otherwise, italics in quoted material represents emphasis in the original text. I have avoided the use of '*sic*' to indicate errors.

Preface

Abraham Lincoln understood the value of a well-judged disclaimer, so it may be as well to begin by stating what this book does not purport to be. It is not a personal biography of the United States' sixteenth president. Rather, it is a study of Lincoln's political career and, in the spirit of the series for which it was commissioned, one which explores the sources and characteristics of his political authority, both before and after he won national recognition.

To study Lincoln involves peering through a veil of myth and iconography. Any president who successfully steers a nation through a civil war can expect to be decked with the victor's laurels, but in Lincoln's case garlands for the Union's Saviour and Great Emancipator have been interwoven with wreaths for its First Martyr. The nature and timing of Lincoln's death, personal and public tragedy though it was, proved perfect for his historical canonization. Legions of Lincoln scholars have recognized this, of course, and have tussled to reveal the enigmatic human being and unvarnished politician encased within the marble figure of national memory. After all, the Union's war president was scarcely a revered national hero at the time: even the loyal press – impatient, anxious and occasionally despairing – often questioned his wisdom and suitability for the job. Yet Lincoln still emerges, in so much that is written about him and the wartime Union, as a wholly – even unaccountably – exceptional figure. The remedy does not lie in gratuitous debunking: Lincoln was indeed a talented politician who rose beyond expectation to the supreme challenge of his office. But the key to understanding his rise to power and his achievement as president is to place him firmly into the setting in which he operated and to recognize the external sources of his authority, as much as his own endowments.

In mid-nineteenth-century America, the world's first mass participatory democracy, political success derived from the effective interplay of three elements: personal drive, the force of public opinion, and the organizing machinery of the political party and other networks of communication. As a peacetime politician and then as the only United States president to face the challenge of a civil war, Lincoln's great achievement was to set ambitious but realizable political goals; to fathom the thinking of ordinary citizens and to reach out to them with uncommon assurance; and to hone impressive skills as a manager of the often unstable and fractious elements that made up the political parties to which he belonged. In what follows I have given particular emphasis to each of these elements, but within a largely narrative framework which recognizes that Lincoln's words and actions, and those for whom they were intended, need to be understood within specific and changing contexts.

It seemed to many who watched Lincoln at first hand in Illinois and Washington that his special talent lay in his feel for opinion and in establishing a rapport with the public at large. One young Springfield lawyer, convinced that Lincoln was privately 'a radical – fanatically so', deemed that his strength lay in his never going 'beyond the People'. For George Baker, a clerk in the State Department, the president's success 'consisted very much in the confidence and respect he won from the people. Other wiser, greater and as good men might not have won this and then all would have been lost in some of our great crises.'[1] But public opinion in Illinois and the wider Union comprised many ideological and cultural strands. Understanding 'the people' meant comprehending pluralism. A common theme in what historians have written about Lincoln is the skill with which he made himself attractive, or at least indispensable, to a broad range of conservative, moderate and radical elements within – successively – the Whig party, the antebellum Republican coalition and the wartime Union. Less well appreciated is his remarkable success in reaching out to what was the most powerful of all the era's subcultures, evangelical Protestantism. Mainstream evangelicals did much to shape the style, substance and rhetoric of the mass participatory politics that reached their maturity in America at about the same time that Lincoln arrived at his. In antebellum Illinois, as elsewhere, the political faultlines commonly coincided with religious and ethnic ones. Alert to the power of religious opinion, Lincoln fused appeals to Protestant millennialism and Enlightenment rationalism. The orthodox Protestantism which underpinned the ethical stance of Republicans and much of the wartime Union coalition, and which flourished in New England and its 'Yankee' diaspora, was not Lincoln's religious faith. But he shrewdly harnessed the power of the most politically influential and energetic members of that constituency, both to win the presidency and to rally support behind his national vision and the war's purposes.

Half this study addresses Lincoln's pre-presidential career. The first chapter explores the roots of Lincoln's political ambition, examining his early life, the sources of his ideas, his alienation from the land, his seizing of the opportunities offered by the emerging market economy, and his evolution by 1840 into a leading Illinois Whig. His effectiveness in state politics and his election to the US Congress, where he served from 1847 to 1849, signaled his political ability, but only hinted at the more serious and morally engaged figure that re-entered politics in 1854 after the repeal of the Missouri Compromise opened the door to slavery's westward expansion into Kansas–Nebraska. Establishing the philosophical sources of that moral engagement demands a discussion of Lincoln's evolving religious views.

Chapter two examines how during the mid-1850s Lincoln became a chief beneficiary of the swirling public opinion that, acting as the arbiter of political power, destabilized the old parties and opened the door to realignment. Through several seasons of public speaking Lincoln's steady advocacy of an antislavery argument did much to shape public sentiment and to effect the displacement of the Whigs by a broader-based Republican party that aspired to national power. Within the mix of ideological, ethnic and religious loyalties amongst Illinois voters, Yankee influence came to preponderate through the decade. In his debates in 1858 with his great rival, United States Senator Stephen A. Douglas, Lincoln earnestly sought to harness antislavery religious sensibilities not only in the Yankee-dominated settlements but as widely as possible across the state, and showed his grasp of the dynamics of the emergent mass democracy that made America politically unique.

Two years after Lincoln's narrow defeat at Douglas's hands, the power of a crusading party unlocked the door of the presidency. In the interplay of the elements shaping Lincoln's antebellum career, it was the operations of party which did most to bring about his remarkable political ascent in 1860. Chapter three shows how his winning the presidential nomination demanded the confidence of a Republican organization whose national leadership had several other names from which to choose. Once selected, Lincoln's reaching office was almost completely dependent upon his party's exertions. Party organizations were essential to effective campaigning, their controls over patronage providing the necessary levers of discipline and unity. The chapter examines the posture of a party that was an institutional and philosophical amalgam. Economic interest and bitter anti-southern feeling were important elements of the Republican mix. Equally important, the party was an expression of the reform-minded, optimistic Protestant evangelicalism unleashed by the religious movement known as the Second Great Awakening. Lincoln's candidacy served its purposes well, for in his blend of constitutional conservativism and high-minded, even Yankee-style, moralism, they had a champion behind whom both pragmatic coalition-builders and high-minded crusaders could enthusiastically rally.

The fourth chapter examines Lincoln's response to the challenge of exercising influence and power during the year or so between his election and early 1862. During the three phases of this period – as president-elect, as president during the uneasy peace before Sumter, and as a war leader – Lincoln showed those signs of anxiety and uncertainty only to be expected in someone lacking executive experience and facing a uniquely daunting challenge. Still, what gave coherence and continuity to his political course throughout this momentous year were three elements essential to Union victory and his own political survival. First, he kept an undeviating focus on the permanence of the Union. Secondly, he instinctively understood the strategic essentials: limiting secession and maximizing support in the border region; blockading the South; and preventing the internationalizing of the conflict. Thirdly, he engaged with and nourished a cross-party, broad-based popular patriotism.

Chapter five concerns Lincoln's political purposes and their evolution from restoring the pre-war Union to embracing emancipation. Lincoln's assault on slavery was born of pragmatism and sustained by his evolving ideas of divine as well as human purposes. He defended emancipation as an essential means of preserving the Union and mortally wounding the Confederacy. But it became an end in itself, something without which the Union was scarcely worth saving and toward which God's own plan appeared to be driving him. Emancipation raised unavoidable questions about the place of the ex-slave and African American in the nation's life, issues on which Lincoln and the more radical Republicans found themselves at odds as they fashioned their policies on the reconstruction of the Union. By the end of his life Lincoln was contemplating votes for educated freedmen; he had traveled a long way from the defense of the racial *status quo* that he had mounted as an antebellum aspirant for political office.

The instruments of Lincoln's presidential power provide the focus of chapter six. Much of that authority derived from a strong-arm use of the law and the military: charges of coercion and dictatorship were not without some foundation in fact. But Lincoln's achievement in holding the Union together and in enjoying the unique experience of being re-elected president during a bloody civil war derived less from coercion than from his ability to harness the surges of Union patriotism that flowed through three essentially 'voluntary' organizations: his party, the Union army, and the religious-philanthropic bodies of the North. Republican/Union party leaders, most notably the state governors and the editorial corps, mobilized massive and sustained support for the war; the army, whatever loyalty it had once felt for general-in-chief George McClellan, evinced even more for 'Father Abraham'; organized Protestantism provided the president with a ready-made and devoted network of speakers and fundraisers. The outcome of the 1864 presidential election plainly revealed Lincoln's success in nurturing and sustaining Unionism in each of these domains.

Active in life, Lincoln passively exerted further power in death, as his transformation into a Christ-like martyr, slain on Good Friday, gave a new layer of sanctification to American nationalism. As they mourned his assassination Americans read into their bereavement a millennial promise that fused the sacred all the more powerfully with the secular. The book's conclusion notes how the nationhood preserved by Unionists through the Civil War now yielded an enhanced and ambitious patriotism quite unlike any that the country had known before.

*

Many elements of the inner Lincoln, including his personal faith and key questions about his motivation and evolving political ambitions, necessarily remain a puzzle. Lincoln wrote with arresting precision and clarity, but he kept no diary or private journal. Only reluctantly did he proffer a few, spare autobiographical sketches. Though he was an indefatigable conversationalist, could be excellent company and dominated gatherings through his story-telling, even his near friends encountered reticence and secrecy, and most judged that he 'never told all he felt'. Discretion in politically sensitive matters, including racial issues, marked his handling of men and measures. Norman Judd, one of his closest associates, stated bluntly, 'Lincoln never told mortal man his purposes – Never.'[2] We are left reflecting that the Great Emancipator's enduring hold over the historical imagination may owe almost as much to his enigmatic features as to the reality of his achievements and to his tragic end.

Even so, questions about Lincoln's private political reflections, moral convictions and religious understanding must be addressed, particularly if it is true – as some scholars have convincingly argued[3] – that he took ideas seriously: Lincoln had a pragmatic streak but he by no means lacked philosophical moorings. Some answers to hard questions can be gleaned from the galaxy of first-hand recollections left by family, friends, professional associates, and acquaintances. In recent years reprinted memoirs – variable in reliability and usefulness, and including at least one grotesque fabrication – have cascaded from the presses. A cluster of works marked by superb editorial scholarship deserve particular note: Douglas L. Wilson and Rodney O. Davis's fine edition of the reminiscences accumulated by Lincoln's law partner, William Herndon; Michael Burlingame's several volumes of materials written or prompted by the president's personal secretaries; and Don and Virginia Fehrenbacher's comprehensive collection of Lincoln's attributed remarks. These works, together with the magnificent electronic edition of the Lincoln Papers in progress at the Library of Congress and the equally impressive documentary collection of the Lincoln Legal Papers, show that however much historical writing remains an individual effort it inevitably depends on the assembled efforts of many others.

I am grateful to the University of Illinois Press and the editor of the *Journal of the Abraham Lincoln Association* for granting permission to reprint material from 'Lincoln, Evangelical Religion, and American Political Culture in the Era of the Civil War' (vol. 18: Winter 1997). I am pleased to acknowledge the invaluable assistance of grants from the University of Sheffield Research Fund and of a research leave award from the Humanities Research Board of the British Academy. I also extend my sincere thanks to those whose personal kindness and scholarly assistance have helped bring this book to completion. Thomas F. Schwartz, as secretary of the Abraham Lincoln Association and as state historian of Illinois, did much at a critical stage to boost the confidence of a fledgling Lincolnian. I am grateful to him and Cathy Schwartz for their generosity. William E. Gienapp's superlative work on the early Republican party and long years of friendship have been an inspiration. Kim Bauer, Cheryl Pence and Cheryl Schnirring at in the Illinois State Historical Library archives, David Himrod at the Garrett-Evangelical Theological Seminary Library in Evanston, and the staff of the Chicago Historical Society could not have been more helpful. Mark A. Noll, Constance Rajala, Hope and Bill Rajala, and William R. Sutton in various important respects eased my visits to Illinois. Nigel Williamson assisted in all sorts of ways with information technology. Sally Wiseman was an impeccable research assistant. I owe special thanks to Robert Cook, Patrick Renshaw, Adam Smith, and Linda Kirk for giving the text a close reading and for their thoughtful suggestions and criticisms. Peter Parish, friend and guide, would have read it, too, had not his untimely death removed him from the cluster of British nineteenth-century American historians which he led with such distinction. Finally, I must thank Keith Robbins, not only for asking me to write this book, but for waiting so long and so uncomplainingly for me to complete it.

Chapter One

Inner Power: Lincoln's Ambition and Political Vision, 1809–54

It is tempting to treat Abraham Lincoln's progress to national visibility and power as an instance of dramatic transfiguration: the story of how, during the mid-1850s, a moderately successful provincial politician – after some two decades of conventional party organizing, stump speaking and periodic legislative service, including a largely unremarkable two-year term in Washington – successfully seized his chance to play out politics on a larger stage, extend his moral reach and win national recognition. It is a plausible interpretation. It properly reflects the sense of increased seriousness and maturity which Lincoln's contemporaries saw in him after 1854, a watershed year in national politics, and it serves as a healthy antidote to the biographical pietism that too easily detects in every footstep of the younger Lincoln the marking out of a course to greatness.

The burden of what follows, however, is that in important ways Lincoln's route to political power was characterized by continuity. His inner drive, personal qualities and political ideas were scarcely fashioned *de novo* in mid-career. The desire for political distinction, which so clearly propelled him from 1854, was no new appetite. His ambition – and particularly his hunger for public recognition – had been evident from his young manhood in the early 1830s. Equally, the essential elements of Lincoln's social and moral project remained constant over time: the construction of an enterprising, commercially prosperous nation in which, under the equal operation of the laws, each and every citizen would enjoy both the right to rise and the education needed to seize the opportunities presented by a fluid and expanding society. This Union, built on the philosophical foundations of the Declaration of Independence, was inevitably compromised by the persistence of slavery: Lincoln's conviction that the South's 'peculiar institution' was both morally repugnant and economically unjust had long been a feature of his thought. What changed during the 1850s was less Lincoln's vision than the evolving challenge to it from national events. His speeches in response to the Kansas–Nebraska Act of 1854 sprang out of well-established elements in his thought.

The Lincoln of this period did indeed evince a new seriousness in tone and a sharper moral edge. This seems to have been related to a greater thoughtfulness about religion. Although the church-going and scripture-quoting Lincoln of the 1850s was no orthodox Trinitarian Christian, he had evidently moved away from the skepticism, even iconoclasm, of his youth. But here too there is evidence of continuity in his thought, as a seam of fatalism, shaped by the strict Calvinist milieu of his upbringing, repeatedly surfaced in his private conversations and in his ideas about the course of history.

Ambition

Unquenchable ambition was a valuable if not essential commodity for candidates pursuing political office in the rough and tumble of the world's first mass democracy. Though his antebellum contemporaries have bequeathed us widely divergent views about the private Abraham Lincoln, those who knew him well were at least agreed over one thing: his passionate yearning to make a mark. His Illinois neighbors and fellow lawyers largely shared the view of his partner, William Herndon, that Lincoln was 'the most ambitious man in the world'. He was particularly fascinated by Shakespeare's depiction of Richard III, Macbeth and Claudius, all preternaturally ambitious characters. According to Sophie Hanks, his cousin, 'Abe always had a natural idea that he was going to be something.'[1]

A degree of mystery surrounds the sources of that inner drive toward political recognition. We can be sure that it was related to Lincoln's earnest desire to improve himself. But that, too, is not so simply accounted for, though the pointers may seem obvious. Extreme material hardship marked his childhood. The family left Kentucky when he was seven, Lincoln's father having failed to establish himself as an independent farmer in a slave state blighted by insecure land titles. Lincoln's own dispiriting memories included the rain washing away the pumpkin seed he had planted through a day of back-breaking labor. Migration to Indiana, in 1816, meant the taming of the wilderness, the threat of wild beasts, and the wielding of axes to clear the land. It meant the death of his mother, Nancy, from consuming the milk of cows that had grazed on poisonous white snakeroot. It meant a farming regimen which allowed few opportunities for formal education and intellectual growth: the periods of Lincoln's own schooling, scattered across several winters, amounted to less than twelve months in all. Together these elements may seem more than adequate explanation for Lincoln's aversion to the farmer's life and his snatching every opportunity for reading and mental activity. But poverty, drudgery, loneliness and rural wildness need not of themselves breed enterprise and aspiration, as his own father's outlook made only too clear. Thomas Lincoln's straitened circumstances and total lack of education seem to have fused with his Separate Baptist faith – a strict Calvinism – to fashion a fatalistic, easy-going acceptance of a near-subsistence, rustic lot quite characteristic of border-state southerners of his time. Lincoln himself remarked that the ill-qualified teachers of the so-called 'blab schools' did 'absolutely nothing to excite ambition for education'. What then was it that prompted his drive for self-improvement, what his White House secretaries described as his 'fixed and inflexible will to succeed'?[2]

We can only speculate, for the intensely private Lincoln offered few clues. Part of the explanation may lie quite simply in natural endowment: Lincoln himself believed that his mother was the illegitimate daughter of Lucy Hanks and 'a well-bred', 'broad-minded' Virginian planter, to whom he attributed his own mental attributes and ambitious striving.[3] Also significant may have been the influence of his stepmother, Sarah Bush Johnston, whose marriage to Thomas Lincoln in 1819, the year after Nancy Lincoln's death, brought spruceness, good order, and even a degree of luxury to the family's Indiana cabin. She evidently acted as a counterbalance to her husband, whose uneasy and even antagonistic relationship with his son reflected their temperamental incompatibility and his exasperation at Lincoln's reading and intellectual aspirations. The young Abraham certainly cherished Sarah's encouragement and affection, which contrasted with his father's efforts to rent out his services and, indirectly if not deliberately, thwart his studies.

Lincoln was legally required to remain obedient to his father and stay at home until he was twenty-one. He felt, but resisted, the temptation to run away. He even deferred the moment of leave-taking until he had assisted the family's removal, by pioneer wagon, to the fertile soil of Macon County in central Illinois, cleared and fenced the ground, and seen them through their first, harsh, isolated winter. But in the spring of 1831 he left home to take a flatboat of goods to New Orleans for Denton Offutt, a local entrepreneur. It marked a critical turning point in Lincoln's journey of self-improvement. His companions – his cousin, John Hanks, and stepbrother, John D. Johnston – soon returned to a life of farming, but Lincoln would never go back. He subsequently saw little of, and wanted little to do with, his father. Even when he knew that Thomas was near to death, in 1851, Lincoln asked his stepbrother to tell him 'that if we could meet now, it is doubtful whether it would not be more painful than pleasant'.[4] He invited none of his family to the ceremony when he married the refined Mary Todd. His separation from them signaled his repudiation of rural life.

In July 1831 Lincoln settled in New Salem, an aspiring, commercial hamlet set on the cliff above the Sangamon river, where Offutt had promised to employ him as a clerk on his return from New Orleans. With water-powered mills, artisan shops, general stores, a tavern and a population of about a hundred, the village had grown impressively from nothing in just two years. Its future growth would depend on its ability to develop navigable waterway links between its surrounding country-side and eastern and southern towns. During his six years' residence there Lincoln pursued a variety of occupations, following no particular blueprint, but in each case able to exploit and enhance his reputation as an agreeable young man of dependable, ingenious and persevering habits. When, as Lincoln put it, Offutt's overblown schemes 'petered out', he lost his job as store clerk and mill manager, but was temporarily rescued from joblessness by the outbreak of the Black Hawk War, which followed the attempt of Saux and Fox Indians to reoccupy their old lands east of the Mississippi: he served as a militia captain but saw no fighting. Then he considered the blacksmith's trade, for which he had the physique but not the appetite, before seizing the chance to buy (jointly, with William F. Berry, and on credit) one of the village's general stores. It was a mistake: the business 'winked out', a consequence of the stuttering growth of New Salem, and left Lincoln with Berry's worthless notes and the moral obligation of paying off what he called 'the national debt'.[5] He was able to make a little money through splitting fence rails before his friends successfully interceded to secure him the office of postmaster. The position was not burdensome, but neither did it provide a living. When the new county surveyor, John Calhoun, asked him to become his assistant, he accepted a job for which he had no training but much aptitude, and whose fees allowed him to start meeting his debts.

Lincoln's escape from a life of common laboring owed much to his conscientious attempts to improve his mind. He read widely and purposefully. In his early years his books had been restricted to his classroom texts and those his stepmother had brought with her to Indiana, notably the Bible, John Bunyan's *Pilgrim's Progress*, Defoe's *Robinson Crusoe*, *Aesop's Fables*, Parson Weems's *Life of George Washington*, and Benjamin Franklin's *Autobiography*. These were many times re-read. (His cousin recalled how, at the end of the farming day, Lincoln would take a piece of cornbread and a book, and 'sitting on his shoulder-blades', 'cock his legs up as high as his head, and read'.)[6] As storekeeper and post-master in New Salem he now had time to indulge his love of poetry, broaden his grasp of political philosophy, immerse himself in the news-papers that passed through his office, and engage in strenuous study. His self-discipline impressed his neighbors. At his Indiana fireside he had nightly scribbled essays and arithmetical exercises on a wooden shovel, then shaved off the evidence and started again. Now he showed the same appetite for mental drill in his study of Kirkham's *English Grammar*, a copy of which he had walked miles to secure. Teaching himself the principles of surveying, which called for a grasp of geometry, trigonometry and logarithms, demanded even greater application.

Though some described the pre-Illinois Lincoln as 'lazy', alluding to his frustration with physical work, they missed his natural industriousness, and his mental energy and toughness. Lincoln's flight from the land had nothing to do with indolence and all to do with self-fulfillment. He was deeply impatient of sloth. 'The leading rule' for men of all callings, he later wrote, 'is diligence. Leave nothing for tomorrow which can be done today.' When his stepbrother, to whom he often lent money, sought to borrow more, he offered a sharp reprimand: 'You are not *lazy*, and still you *are* an *idler*. I doubt whether since I saw you, you have done a good whole day's work, in any one day.... This habit of uselessly wasting time, is the whole difficulty; and it is vastly important to you, and still more to your children that you should break this habit.' When later asked by a prospective law student how to succeed, Lincoln replied, 'Work, work, work, is the main thing.' Effort and endeavor were not only good in themselves but the means to financial self-sufficiency. Not that Lincoln was driven by the desire for wealth alone: money was important as the route to bourgeois civility, not as an end in itself. Years later David Davis reminisced that Lincoln, even when he enjoyed a good income from his practice of law, maintained 'simple and unostentatious habits', kept his charges low, since few of his clients were rich, and showed no interest in accumulating a fortune.[7] Unlike most of the Illinois political elite in the 1850s, he largely resisted the lure of land speculation.

In Lincoln's ambitious striving there was something of the temper of the New England Puritan, a 'Yankee' blend of self-discipline, character-building and initiative, though he did not subscribe to the moral coercive-ness shared by many of that breed. His celebration of enterprise and individual effort had much more in common with the advancing tide of 'modern', or Arminianized, Calvinism, and its preoccupation with human responsibility, than with traditional, rural predestinarianism. Significantly, he disliked alcohol, which left him feeling 'flabby', and tobacco: these ubiquitous elements of frontier life threatened the individual's self-control and self-reliance. Though he retained a natural humility and many of the badges of his rural origins – his accent and turn of phrase, his physical strength, his earthy humor and story-telling – he found many other features of frontier primitivism repugnant. Lincoln hated cruelty to animals, disliked hunting, would not use a gun, and had no respect for revivalist religion's raw emotionalism and theological oversimplifications.

The possibility of self-fulfillment through a career in politics struck Lincoln early on, though exactly when is not certain. As well as the *Life of George Washington*, his youthful reading included William Scott's *Lessons in Elocution*. During his limited schooling in Indiana he wrote essays on politics and entertained his fellow pupils with his efforts at public speaking and story-telling. He was a regular reader of the political press well before he left for Illinois, and not long after his arrival he delivered an impromptu speech in Decatur, during the campaign for the state legislature. Two years later, only twenty-three, and impressing his New Salem neighbors with his integrity, forceful mind and folksy charm, he was urged by several men of influence, including the justice of the peace and the president of the debating society, to run for the legislature himself.

In Lincoln they saw a popular, confident young man who they knew was determined to foster New Salem's commercial interests, notably by securing government support for improved and cheaper river transportation. Setting out his stall in an election statement, Lincoln advocated low-interest credit, better navigation and educational opportunity as the means of fostering an industrious, enterprising and moral community.[8] In this he implicitly allied himself with the stance of the embryonic Whig party and the economic program of the national political leader whom he admired above all others, Henry Clay. But he chose to avoid any direct reference to national issues and politics, probably because of the popularity which Clay's rival for the White House, the incumbent Democratic president, Andrew Jackson, enjoyed locally and throughout the western states.

Soon after declaring his candidacy the Black Hawk War provided Lincoln with heartening evidence of his local popularity, for the men of his volunteer company elected him captain; nearly thirty years later he would declare this 'a success which gave me more pleasure than any I have had since'. Three months' war service left him little time for campaigning in the elections for the state Assembly but he made a few speeches and did himself no harm. Judge Stephen T. Logan encountered him for the first time, and though considering him 'gawky, and rough-looking' ('his pantaloons didn't meet his shoes by six inches'), he was much impressed by the novelty with which Lincoln set out his ideas: 'He had the same individuality that he kept through all his life.'[9] Lincoln won almost all the votes of New Salem village, but was not well enough known across the electoral district to prevent the disappointment of defeat.

That defeat did not dent his ambition or self-confidence. He had gained experience, as well as the friendship of Logan and other leading Whigs, including the urbane John Todd Stuart of Springfield. Running again in 1834, when thirteen candidates contested four legislative places, Lincoln was this time elected, and stepped into a new world. He bought a suit on borrowed money and, encouraged by Stuart, who lent him books and overcame the young man's reservations about his inadequate education, turned to the study of law. The legislative session ending in February, Lincoln spent much of 1835 mastering Blackstone's *Commentaries* and other legal texts by the same means he had acquired his knowledge of surveying: studying alone and, in his own words, going 'at it in good earnest'.[10] Impressively, within two years he was equipped to take the oath of admission to the Illinois bar. He rode out of New Salem for good in April 1837, heading the short distance to Springfield, the Sangamon County seat and a raw, bustling town of 1,500 inhabitants, where Stuart had offered him a partnership. A law practice was the ideal complement to a career in politics. It provided not only a livelihood and the technical grasp needed for the drafting of legislation, but offered a valuable social network and – since litigation was relatively uncomplicated – considerable time for public political conversation and debate, in front of curious and admiring onlookers.

At Vandalia, the state capital, Lincoln remained largely inconspicuous through his first term of office, listening, observing and quietly impressing. After his re-election in 1836 the Sangamon County Whig delegation, known as the 'Long Nine' since each was over six feet tall, made him their floor leader out of respect for his parliamentary skills, a confidence fully repaid by his masterly handling of the bill to move the state capital to Springfield. Two more terms, from 1838 and 1840, further enhanced his confidence and reputation. He led the Whigs in the House, and was twice candidate for speaker, on one occasion failing by just a single vote. Though he chose not to stand for re-election at the end of his fourth term, this did not signal the end of political ambition, nor did his refusing (in 1841, and again in 1844) to be run as a candidate for governor. Rather, it showed a clear-headed realism. In the Illinois legislature he had shown his political mastery and had nothing further to prove, while in a Democrat-controlled state a Whig could not seriously expect to win the governorship. He may have had the idea of running for the state Senate, but if so it came to nothing. More significantly, he was chosen as a Whig 'presidential elector' for the campaign of 1840, when he stumped the state for the party's nominee, William Henry Harrison, and once more in 1844, when he traveled even further afield on behalf of his 'beau ideal of a statesman', Henry Clay. This gave him experience of, as well as an appetite for, politics on a larger stage. Lincoln may already have had his sights fixed on the United States Congress when he finally left the state Assembly in 1841. It is certain that when John Todd Stuart revealed that he did not intend to seek re-election as congressman in 1843, Lincoln was determined to throw his hat into the ring.[11]

The newly formed Seventh Congressional District embraced the areas of greatest Whig strength in the state. Whoever won the Whig nomination would surely go on to win the congressional election. The District also boasted many of the ablest Whig leaders. Lincoln's hunger for his party's nomination was obvious, and he worked energetically for support. He told a fellow lawyer, Richard S. Thomas: 'if you should hear any one say that Lincoln don't want to go to Congress, I wish you . . . would tell him you have reason to believe he is mistaken. The truth is, I would like to go very much.' When his great friend and glittering rival, Edward D. Baker, instead won the support of the Sangamon County Whigs, Lincoln was bitterly upset. As one of the delegates appointed to carry that endorsement to the District convention, he considered himself ' "fixed" a good deal like a fellow who is made groomsman to the man what has cut him out, and is marrying his own dear "gal".'[12] He did nothing to hinder Baker's nomination but sought equally to prevent any drifting away of his own support in the counties where he was strong. When the delegates met, at Pekin in May 1843, both men suffered disappointment, losing out to the gifted and equally ambitious John J. Hardin of Jacksonville. But Lincoln usefully secured the adoption of a resolution which in effect limited Hardin to a single congressional term in Washington, to be followed by Baker. It implicitly left open the possibility of his own nomination two elections on. Even so, the depth of Lincoln's disappointment may be measured by what looked like a rare act of vengeance, his refusal to cast a ballot for Hardin when election day arrived.

As hoped, Baker took the Seventh District in 1844. Lincoln, his own ambitions bound up in the outcome, earnestly supported him. But the real test of Lincoln's mettle and single-mindedness would lie in the next contest. He began to make moves in September 1845, almost a year before polling day. Securing from Baker a promise that he would not run against him, Lincoln visited Hardin, who would make no such pledge. Six months of political fencing followed, during which Lincoln kept the initiative, thanks essentially to his use of the Pekin agreement of 1843 and the argument that 'Turn about is fair play'.[13] By not running in 1844 Hardin had appeared to endorse the idea of 'rotation of office', though he now denied it and declared the principle anti-republican.[14] Many of the party's leaders thought well of the Jacksonville Whig, but some had already committed themselves to Lincoln before Hardin had declared his interest. Lincoln's made delicate and effective use of the press, especially in Sangamon and the pivotal northern counties, and encouraged the idea that Hardin be run for governor, not Congress. Outflanked, Hardin charged Lincoln with impropriety and 'maneuvering' in pursuit of the nomination. Striving to control his temper, Lincoln managed, crucially, to keep the worst of their differences from the press. Hardin withdrew from the field as precinct and county conventions endorsed the growing view 'that it is Abraham's turn now'.[15]

After this strenuous struggle for the party nomination, Lincoln's battle with the Democratic candidate, Peter Cartwright, was rather a low-key affair. Lincoln did not take victory over the famed Methodist preacher for granted, but in the event Cartwright, though a scourge of Calvinists, total immersionists and backsliders, proved no match for the Whigs. Lincoln was carried to Washington by a handsome majority. However, as he told his friend Joshua Speed, his electoral success had 'not pleased me as much as I expected', and his term in Congress, rather than a springboard for achieving a national reputation, proved anticlimactic and largely undistinguished. Even so, Lincoln would happily have sought a second term had it not been for the principle of rotation in office. He had declared at the outset that he would not stand again, 'more from a wish to deal fairly with others . . . than for any cause personal to myself'; he could not go back on his 'word and honor', unless 'it should so happen that nobody else wishes to be elected'.[16] With elective office thus closed off he was induced, reluctantly at first, to seek the most prestigious patronage appointment available to aspiring Illinoisans: commissioner of the General Land Office. When the new Whig administration of President Zachary Taylor instead awarded the job to Justin Butterfield, an able land lawyer from Chicago, who unlike himself had done little to secure the president's victory, Lincoln was bitterly disappointed. In the right hands – his own – he believed the post and the patronage it controlled could be the ideal means of building a stronger Whig machine in a state where Democrats, the majority party, dominated the presidential and gubernatorial races. An opportunity to benefit the most ambitious leaders of Whiggery had been lost. When offered the governorship of Oregon Territory by way of compensation, Lincoln declined what he (and his wife) judged a political dead-end.

Lincoln's return to the law in 1849, by now in partnership with William Herndon, marked the beginning of a period of relative withdrawal from politics that ended only in 1854. The degree of that withdrawal and the significance of those mid-life years for Lincoln's personal development are contested. Lincoln himself later wrote that at this time he 'practiced law more assiduously than ever before' and 'was losing interest in politics', and that by 1854 'his profession had almost superseded the thought of politics in his mind'. He did not demur when in 1860 he read in William Dean Howells's campaign biography that after 1849 'ambition could not tempt him'. He declined suggestions that he should run once more for Congress or the state legislature, and even missed some landmark political meetings. But there is no reason to believe that Lincoln had stopped yearning for public distinction. These were years marked by periods of deep introspection and depression, and by nightmares. We can only speculate on the sources of his unhappiness, but it may have had to do with his sense of failure. Herndon noted that on his return from Congress 'he despaired of ever rising again in the political world'. Compared with his long-standing rival, Stephen A. Douglas, a comet in the Democratic firmament, his career remained stubbornly terrestrial. But he did not write himself off politically. He continued in party management. He worked as a national committeeman and campaign speaker for the Whigs' presidential candidate, Winfield Scott, in 1852. He delivered eulogies on the deaths of Zachary Taylor and Henry Clay. If the political opportunity were there to be seized, as would become the case in 1854, he had not lost the ambition to seize it.[17]

Why did Lincoln's unresting ambition find its particular expression in the search for political office? In this, as in other questions about him, speculation has to decorate fact. It was not an odd choice of career: the most well-traveled route to distinction in the developing western states was not business but politics, and its handmaid, the law. At a prosaic level, political office provided a livelihood for a debt-ridden young man who possessed no formal qualifications, but had self-confidence, a clear head for analysis, and a proper estimate of his talent for public speaking. In due course Mary Todd Lincoln, fiercely political, played a role, certainly in urging Lincoln on to higher political achievement and perhaps in shaping a sometimes discordant domestic environment from which he

sought relief; but Lincoln's political career and ambitions were well established long before she entered his life. We can be certain that Lincoln,
who had a natural humility, was not attracted to political leadership by
megalomania or a 'cheap desire to lord it over others'. He warned against
tyrants in his speech at the Young Men's Lyceum in Springfield in January
1838, but it takes a special kind of historical contortionism to read this
as a confession of sinister designs. During his later years, Lincoln may
have looked to political achievement as a way of transcending death,
but as a young man the psychological imperative may have lain in an
urge to repair the damage that his early years' rusticity, educational
deficiencies and 'emotional malnutrition' inflicted on his self-esteem. He
was possibly embarrassed by his marks of physical eccentricity: his
remarkable height, long arms and general ungainliness. Politics may
have promised acceptance and affirmation. In his first ever campaign
address, to the voters of his county in 1832, he wrote, 'Every man is said
to have his peculiar ambition. . . . I have no other so great as that of being
truly esteemed of my fellow men, by rendering myself worthy of their
esteem.'[18]

Political vision

Behind Lincoln's appetite for political power lay much more than the
drive for personal recognition. His ambition was nourished by a vision of
what the nation should be. Lincoln issued no early, comprehensive statement of political faith but his election addresses and his performance in
state and national legislatures offered what amounted to a largely consistent political program, reflecting a clear philosophy and ethical stance.
At its heart was a belief in meritocracy, in the right of all individuals,
through their industry, enterprise and self-discipline, to rise in an increasingly market-oriented society. Essential to his hopes for the poor were
the nation's economic development and material advance. These were
to be promoted and nurtured by an interventionist, forward-looking
government, doing 'for a community of people, whatever they need to
have done, but can not do, *at all*, or can not, *so well do*, for themselves –
in their separate, and individual capacities'.[19] The logic of Lincoln's economic thought was a social and moral order at odds with slavery. It was
an order whose well-being, he believed, was protected and enhanced by a
Union of states loyal to the Founders' vision of republican liberty.

Well before the family trekked from Indiana, Lincoln's experience of
personal struggle had fused with the political prescriptions he read in the

Louisville Journal and other anti-Jacksonian newspapers to give definition to his thought. In Henry Clay's 'American System' – comprising a
national bank, a protective tariff, and better roads and waterways ('internal
improvements') for transporting goods – Lincoln identified the essential
means of the young Republic's economic development. Taken as a whole,
the program of the emerging Whig party would speed the transition
from a subsistence to a market economy and draw ever more farmers
and mechanics into the newly emerging commercial and industrial order.
When Lincoln arrived in central Illinois he saw in the richness of the
soil, the abundance of the state's natural resources and the burgeoning immigration of southern-born and Yankee settlers the potential for
formidable growth. His earliest political speech, at Decatur, dwelt on the
need for improved water-borne transportation. In his first bid for office,
two years later, the main burden of his address to Sangamon County's
electors was the need to improve the region's poor communications: how
else could they sell their surplus meat and cereals, and acquire the manufactured goods they needed? Presenting himself as a knowledgeable river
pilot and adopting a tone of financial prudence, Lincoln commended the
plan of clearing the Sangamon river, by which New Salem's commercial
future might be assured.[20]

Over the next decade ambitious internal improvements sat at the heart
of Lincoln's political agenda, the means by which he expected Illinois as
a whole to achieve new levels of prosperity, increase its land values and
pull in new settlers. He told Joshua Speed he wanted to be 'the DeWitt
Clinton of Illinois': the New York state governor's celebrated Erie Canal
could surely be cloned further west.[21] The special session of the state
legislature during the winter of 1835–36 proved a watershed. Legislators,
faced with a plan to build the Illinois–Michigan Canal, to link the Mississippi with the Great Lakes, the Erie Canal and the Atlantic, authorized a
$500,000 loan. Previously Lincoln had called for such projects to be sup-
ported by federal aid, raised by the sale of public lands; others had
insisted on private funding alone. Now, carried along on the swelling
speculative tide of the 1830s and alert to the grandiose projects underway
in other states, and with private capital unforthcoming, they not only
agreed to the principle of state-level funding, but in the subsequent
Assembly sanctioned a massive railroad and river scheme to supplement
the Canal project. Two trunk roads, six spurs and a variety of smaller
projects – intended to secure the broadest possible base of political support – elicited a government loan of over $10 million. All was agreed
without detailed estimates or proper surveys. Roads would not only be run
at a debt-clearing profit, but would increase the price of land, allowing

the state to sell off its domain, not least to foreign capitalists. As the party with most of the votes in the Assembly, the Democrats (notably Stephen A. Douglas) were the prime legislative movers, but Lincoln, the Whig leader, and his Sangamon colleagues gave support at every turn.

Then came the financial panic of 1837, the collapse of land sales, falling prices and wages, and bankruptcies. The so-called Illinois System shuddered as revenues fell. Lincoln, determined to prevent its collapse, considered new ways of financing it. In particular, he came up with an imaginative if unrealistic plan to buy all federally-owned land in the state at a discount and sell it at a profit to settlers, using the proceeds to pay off the debt: he secured the Assembly's support but Washington was not interested. He also endorsed a graduated land tax, to replace the current levies, which were quite unrelated to land values. He thought the measure would be acceptable to the people 'because it does not increase the tax upon the "*many poor*" but upon the "*wealthy few*"'. The Illinois public, however, facing a deepening depression in 1839, turned increasingly against the System, and many previous political supporters jumped ship. Lincoln, though, remained steadfast, steeled by economic conviction and a sense of moral obligation. Even when it was plain that the plan must sink, he persisted in trying 'to save something to the State, from the general wreck', particularly the Canal project. But he failed to convince the vast majority of legislators, who knew their constituents had no stomach for adding to the state's financial obligations. It would take Illinois forty years to pay off the debt on a project of which almost nothing except the Canal was saved.[22]

Lincoln's advocacy of internal improvements was interwoven with his staunch defense of banks. Like Clay, he championed federal control of the banking system. However, after President Jackson's successful assault on the national bank, the Bank of the United States, Lincoln put the banking needs of his state before party loyalty. When Illinois legislators considered the incorporation of the State Bank in 1835 Lincoln cast his vote with pro-bank Democrats to secure what he judged an essential mechanism of the new capitalist order. A well-regulated bank would provide a sound, elastic currency, protecting the public against the extreme prescriptions of the hard-money men on one side and the paper infla-tionists on the other; it would be a safe depository for public funds and provide the credit mechanisms needed to sustain state improve-ments; it would bring an end to extortionate money-lending. These advantages, he believed, would benefit all Illinoisans. While nostalgic agrarians, mainly hard-money Democrats, saw banks as a symbol of an avaricious new order, serving only politicians, bankers and their rich friends, Lincoln was convinced that the 'honest . . . farmer and mechanic' benefited as much as the plutocrat. In a speech to the Illinois House in January 1837, responding to the anti-bank forces' call for an investigation into the management of the Springfield corporation, Lincoln deftly represented the attack on the bank as 'exclusively the work of politicians; a set of men who have interests aside from the interests of the people, and who, to say the most of them, are, taken as a mass, at least one long step removed from honest men. I say this with the greater freedom because, being a politician myself, none can regard it as personal.' By contrast, ordinary Illinoisans found no fault in the Bank. 'It has doubled the prices of the products of their farms,' he claimed (with more political than economic acuity), 'and filled their pockets with a sound circulating medium.'[23]

Westerners' animus against bankers turned more deadly when the banks suspended specie payments after the panic of 1837 and when temporary resumption was succeeded by a further suspension in 1839. Lincoln fought as tenaciously to defend the State Bank as he did the improvements scheme, whose fate was bound up with the credit system. But the further devaluation of its paper, mortgage foreclosures and the calling in of loans only reduced its political chances. The Democrats sought to make the Bank resume specie payments to its suffering noteholders. Lincoln and the pro-Bank Whigs knew as well as their enemies that compulsory resumption could prove mortal, for the insatiable specie demands of all the western states would devour its coin. A moment of embarrassing theater offered a measure of Lincoln's determination. To stop the Democrats prematurely adjourning the House, which would bring to an end the period of suspended specie payments agreed by the previous Assembly, Whigs stayed away to prevent a quorum. Lincoln and a few colleagues watched as the arrival of halt and lame Democrats made the body quorate. To take the numbers under the voting threshold again, the clutch of Whigs tried to leave. When the doorkeeper prevented their exit, they jumped out of the window. But their presence had been recorded. Adjournment, credit resumption and Democratic ridicule followed. Lincoln, the respecter of law and constitutional order, who 'deprecated everything that savored of the revolutionary', always regretted the action.[24]

This was not Lincoln's last effort for the State Bank but he could be in little doubt about the strength of popular prejudice agains the banking system. The electoral experience of 1840 offered little en ouragement. Much of the Whig effort for William Henry Harrison in the effervescent Log Cabin campaign aimed to cloak not delineate policy positions, but

Lincoln, by contrast, set out to address and clarify a substantive issue: federal banking. In speech after speech, he tirelessly argued that a national bank would be a better fiscal agent for the Washington government than the system of independent federal depositories proposed by Jackson's Democratic successor, Martin Van Buren. Despite a few populist touches, he took a reasoned and technical, if essentially derivative, approach, stressing the hazardous, deflationary impact of the reduced money supply that would follow the Democrats' scheme, the disabling effect on the purchasing power of poor farmers and laborers, and the superiority of a central bank in maintaining 'a sound and uniform state of currency'. Lincoln's paltry reward for taking banks seriously, however, was defeat for the Whig ticket of presidential electors, as well as a drop in his own personal vote for re-election to the Assembly.[25]

The State Bank finally failed in 1842. But neither that nor the clattering debris of the Illinois System could shake Lincoln's faith in the potential of the credit system and the 'transportation revolution' to transform the lives and hopes of ordinary Americans. He blamed not a flawed Whig vision for the hard times after 1837, but the misguided policies of the national administrations. Even so, by 1843 improvements and banking had become electoral liabilities. When setting out the Whigs' stall, in his 'Address to the People of Illinois' and in his campaign speeches in 1844, he gave priority instead to the third element of the presidential candidate's American System: the protective tariff.

Once more Lincoln's preoccupation with American economic development and opening doors of individual advancement shines through. So, indeed, does his deeper commitment to the commercial-industrial future than to the agrarian past and present. Tariff walls would encourage nascent and potential manufacturing industries, whose growth would provide Americans with cheaper goods and whose employees would increase domestic demand for agricultural produce, to the benefit of farmers. Lincoln the political campaigner of 1843–44 gave his arguments a populist, even chauvinist, spin. As a revenue-raising measure, the tariff, he maintained, was cheaper than the proposed alternative, a direct tax system, which would cover the land 'with assessors and collectors, going forth like swarms of Egyptian locusts, devouring every blade of grass and other green thing'. It was chiefly the foreign manufacturer who suffered from tariff duties, along with the wealthy consumer of foreign luxuries ('those whose pride, whose abundance of means, prompt them to . . . strut in British cloaks, and coats, and pantaloons'). The ordinary farmer, on the other hand, 'who never wore, nor never expects to wear, a single yard of British goods in his whole life', would benefit.[26]

A writer to the Democratic *Illinois State Register* drolly represented Lincoln as floundering when he was asked why the 'high pressure tariff made every thing . . . cheaper' for the farmer. Lincoln probably judged it a palpable hit: after the election he took stock, read more deeply (notably the writings of the high protectionist Henry C. Carey) and conceded, in a set of private notes, that the burden of the tariff was equally felt by the consumer, the producer and the merchant. Even so, Lincoln argued, the policy of protection was the one best placed to achieve what he saw as 'a most worthy object of any good government', namely to secure 'to each labourer the whole product of his labour, or as nearly as possible'. Scripture fused with classical economics (the labor theory of value) to persuade Lincoln that it was 'wrong' to tolerate economic arrangements where '*some* have laboured, and *others* have, without labour, enjoyed a large proportion of the fruits'. Only '*useful* labour' deserved reward; '*useless* labour', which included the unnecessary transporting of cotton, wool, iron and other American raw materials to overseas markets and their return as manufactured goods, was a 'heavy pensioner' upon it. Removing protection would increase the parasitic impediments to righteous labor and proportionately 'must produce want and ruin among our people'.[27]

Lincoln's own experience of getting on in life tended rather to sharpen than to blur his meritocratic vision, though the process was complex. He was subject to various influences which, unrestrained, could have estranged him completely from the constituency of farmers and ordinary folk on whom his political progress depended. In association first with John T. Stuart and then with Stephen T. Logan, perhaps the foremost lawyer in the county, he sharpened his professional skills, won prestige on the judicial circuit, and acquired financial stability and status. Marriage to Mary Todd in 1842, connecting him with one of eastern Kentucky's most glittering families, confirmed his ascent into the respectable middle class. He paid off his debts and moved with his wife and infant son from rented accommodation into a modest house of their own, one which ten years later they were able to develop into one of the most substantial and handsome houses in Springfield. Through his law practice and political standing, Lincoln the solid burgher became the associate of bankers, large landowners, cattle kings, speculators and the professional elite. His determination to meet the interest on the growing state debt after 1836 led him to subordinate the interests of pioneers and ordinary working men, who wanted cheap land and low taxes, to the needs of the creditor class and the developers of public works. By endorsing the policies of distribution (of the proceeds of the public domain) and increased taxation, and by defending the State Bank, he exposed himself to the charge of turning his back on his own kind. When he contended for the Whig nomination for the congressional seat in 1843 he discovered that, whatever his circumstances when he arrived in the state (a 'friendless, uneducated, penniless boy, working on a flatboat – at ten dollars per month') he was now 'put down . . . as the candidate of pride, wealth, and arristocratic family distinction'.[28]

But we misunderstand Lincoln's Whiggery if we judge it to have been driven mainly by a concern to defend the rich and propertied. He may have fled rusticity himself, but he did not lose his feel for the concerns of ordinary country-dwellers. He knew their make-up well enough to take an early stand against a cattle-breeding and enclosure measure (the 'Little Bull Law') that made good economic sense but disadvantaged the poorer farmer. Most of his early legal cases related to land issues – including debt, disputes over titles, trespass, mortgage foreclosures, property seizure – and most of his clients were common folk, whom he charged only moderate fees. He could make fun of bucolic speech, as he did in his pseudonymous contribution to the local Whig paper, 'Letter from the Lost Townships', but this was more an exercise in affectionate humor than patronizing contempt. His capacity for empathetic understanding of those beyond the charmed circle of bourgeois success was never more clearly set out than in his address to Springfield's Washingtonian temperance reformers in 1842: he warned his respectable, middle-class audience against censoriousness and affirmed his view that 'if we take habitual drunkards as a class, their heads and their hearts will bear an advantageous comparison with those of any other class'. Lincoln's concern, whether in the case of reformed town drunks or modest farmers, was to respect their aspirations toward self-improvement and a decent living that he knew to be the motors of his own life. Unlike a number of his fellow Whigs, members of a defensive social elite anxious in the face of democratic upheaval, Lincoln was moved less by questions of class than by a wish to widen opportunities for individual fulfillment through economic transformation.[29]

The institution of slavery, though negating the meritocratic society he prized, remained very much on the periphery of Lincoln's field of vision during his years of state-level politics. Even so, the main elements of his opposition to the South's peculiar institution were already in place before he stepped into the national arena. His first recorded statement on the subject was a response to a set of resolutions on abolitionism and slavery which the Illinois Assembly had endorsed in January 1837. Though a free state, Illinois felt powerfully the influence of its southern-born settlers, the largest element of the population in its early years: they very much shaped its stance on racial issues, failing narrowly to introduce slavery in the early 1820s, but ensuring that a system of indenture and restrictive 'Black Laws' controlled the relatively small population of free blacks. While resisting the request of some slave states that abolitionism be suppressed by law, the Assembly readily affirmed its strong disapproval of abolitionist societies and doctrines, and declared that 'the right of property in slaves is sacred to the slaveholding States by the Federal Constitution'. A few weeks later Lincoln and Dan Stone, a fellow Whig lawyer from Springfield, presented a protest to the House. Its significance derives not from their view of slaveholders' rights, for the two Sangamon representatives occupied the same constitutional ground as their fellow assemblymen. Rather it lies in the nuanced difference between the Assembly's direct assault on abolitionist teaching itself and Lincoln's statement 'that the *promulgation* of abolition doctrines tends rather to increase than to abate its [slavery's] evils'. It lies in the more positive emphasis Lincoln gives to the constitutional authority of Congress over the future of slavery in the District of Columbia. It lies most of all in his unequivocal insistence 'that the institution of slavery is founded on both injustice and bad policy'.[30]

Lincoln in later years often reflected on his antislavery disposition. 'I am naturally antislavery', he wrote in 1864. 'If slavery is not wrong, nothing is wrong. I can not remember when I did not so think, and feel.' That moral abhorrence may have been absorbed from his parents and stepmother, whose aversion to slavery is well authenticated, and whose church fellowship with antislavery Baptists only underscored their revulsion. After spending the first seven years of his life in a slaveholding county, Lincoln's subsequent acquaintance with the institution would have been mostly random and intermittent. He would have seen large concentrations of slaves and stark examples of slave-trading on his two trips by flatboat to New Orleans in 1828 and 1831. On the second of these, according to his cousin John Hanks, the sight of 'Negroes Chained – maltreated – whipt & scourged . . . ran its iron in him then & there'. On trips to Kentucky to visit friends or his wife's family he probably saw the paraphernalia of slave-selling at Lexington. In 1841 he certainly made a steamboat journey down the Ohio from Louisville in the company of a dozen chained slaves, 'strung together precisely like so many fish upon a trot-line'. Some have contrasted the earnest intensity with which Lincoln later referred to this experience ('That sight was a continual torment to me', he recalled in 1855) with the tolerant, even amused, acceptance he is judged to have shown at the time, when writing to Mary Speed. But in fact that earlier letter also alludes to the violent sundering of slave families, the perpetuity of their condition, and the 'ruthless and unrelenting' cruelty to which they were exposed; its detachment, if such it is, lies in its near-anthropological reflection on the slaves' apparent cheerfulness in the face of these horrors and in its endorsement of the theological truth that ' "God tempers the wind to the shorn lamb," or in other words, that He renders the worst of human conditions tolerable'.[31]

We of course distort the words of the younger Lincoln if we try to read them simply as a prologue to Emancipation, but neither should we set aside the recollections of several acquaintances confirming the tenacity with which, from his earliest years, he held that slavery was an offense against justice and sound policy. The horrors perpetrated by slave-traders and inhumane plantation overseers helped shape his repugnance. But so too did that understanding of economic morality that guided his thinking more generally. Slavery stifled individual enterprise, discouraged self-discipline, and sustained a fundamental inequality: depriving human beings of the just rewards of their labor. Lincoln the protectionist, alert to justice for the laborer, was the same Lincoln who, at about the same time, sarcastically told Ward Hill Lamon, 'you Virginians shed barrels of perspiration while standing off at a distance and superintending the work your slaves do for you. It is different with us. Here it is every fellow for himself, or he does n't get there.'[32]

The elements of Lincoln's antislavery posture were essentially in place before he left for Washington in 1847: moral repugnance at the institution, sympathy for the slave, respect for the protection the federal constitution afforded slavery, commitment to preserving social order, belief in the essential goodwill of the southern slaveholder, and the need for common, gradual action by North and South on a problem for which they shared responsibility. His two sessions as congressman effected no fundamental change in his views, but a novel environment and the current of events brought his antislavery vision into sharper focus. In a city a quarter of whose population was black, and which included 2,000 slaves, he could not avoid encountering some of the bleakest features of the peculiar institution: the auction block and the trading warehouse. Lincoln shared his lodgings with several other Whig representatives, including Joshua Giddings from Ohio's Western Reserve, the most luminously antislavery of all congressmen. Here, in Mrs Sprigg's boarding house, the meatiest conversations addressed the main questions before the Thirtieth Congress: the resolution of the conflict with Mexico, the organization of the ceded territories, and a variety of other slavery-related issues.

Within three weeks of arriving in Washington Lincoln introduced a series of resolutions bearing on the outbreak of the Mexican War, a conflict which he and most Whig representatives believed had been 'unnecessarily and unconstitutionally begun' by President James K. Polk's Democratic administration to secure more territory for slavery.[33] The resolutions required the president to prove his claim that the 'spot' where Mexicans in 1846 had first shed the blood of United States citizens was in fact American soil, and not, as anti-war Whigs believed, a Mexican settlement. Lincoln soon followed this up with a long speech in the House surmising that a disingenuous president was 'deeply conscious of being in the wrong – that he feels the blood of this war, like the blood of Abel, is crying to Heaven against him'. No doubt part of Lincoln's purpose here was to impress his congressional colleagues. No doubt it was also, with the presidential election of 1848 on the horizon, to secure an advantage for his party (with the bloodiest fighting now over, Whigs would be less vulnerable to accusations of disloyalty). But Lincoln's earnestness, even biblical fervor, in pressing the charges sprang, too, from a determination to expose what he privately described as 'a foul, villainous, and bloody falsehood'. It sprang from his conscientious objection to unprovoked aggression against a feeble neighbor for territorial gain. Though he pragmatically accepted the Mexican cession, he continued to stress that Whigs, the champions of intensive cultivation of the social order, 'did not believe in enlarging our field, but in keeping our fences where they are and cultivating our present possession, making it a garden, improving the morals and education of the people, devoting the administration to this purpose'.[34]

The final strand in Lincoln's concern was what the war might mean for the future of slavery. In 1845 he had written that while it was 'a paramount duty of us in the free states, due to the Union of the states, and perhaps to liberty itself (paradox though it may seem) to let the slavery of the other states alone', it was 'equally clear, that we should never knowingly lend ourselves directly or indirectly, to prevent that slavery from dying a natural death – to find new places for it to live in, when it can no longer exist in the old'. Yet he did not then insist on treating new territory as the life blood of the slave system. He had no enthusiasm for the annexation of Texas by the United States that same year but his opposition was low-key compared with the strident warnings of abolitionists who denounced it as the diabolical enterprise of an expansionary 'slave power'. He did not then see 'very clearly . . . how the annexation would augment the evil of slavery', given that 'slaves would be taken there in about equal numbers', whether or not the territory were annexed. He did, though, recognize that as a new member of the Union Texas might become the home of American slaves who might otherwise have been freed: 'To whatever extent this may be true, I think annexation an evil.' At the outbreak of the Mexican War, Lincoln remained unimpressed when the abolitionists who made up the tiny Liberty party renewed their warnings against a slave power conspiracy. As a congressman, however, he could not duck the question of slaveholders' rights in whatever land might be acquired from Mexico. This had been repeatedly and acrimoniously addressed through the Twenty-Ninth Congress (1845–47), ever since David Wilmot of Pennsylvania had, in August 1846, introduced his proposed ban on slavery in any acquisition. Lincoln was friendly with southern Whigs (and would indeed support a slaveholding presidential candidate in 1848), but he consistently lined up to vote with the advocates of the Wilmot Proviso – though his later claim to have done so 'at least forty times' was surely an exaggeration. He had come to see that to stop slavery 'finding new places to live in' meant adopting a hard-line, 'free-soil' stance.[35]

Though Lincoln took quite a low profile in the debates over slavery's expansion, he was not reticent on all slavery-related issues. His most salient contribution was his proposal for a bill to abolish slavery in the District of Columbia. Its features were entirely consistent with the stand he had taken in the Illinois Assembly in 1837 and aimed to achieve an accommodation between antislavery and southern members. All children born to slave mothers after New Year's Day 1850 would be free, but would serve apprenticeships. Unlike the more radical proposals of representative Daniel Gott, Lincoln's bill would require federal cash compensation for owners who manumitted their existing slaves. To mollify slaveholders who feared that a free Washington would act as a magnet for runaways, Lincoln called for the local authorities 'to provide active and efficient means to arrest, and deliver up to their owners, all fugitive slaves escaping into said District'. The whole plan depended on a referendum of the municipality's white voters. Lincoln was initially hopeful: he had privately consulted prominent citizens of the District and possessed an ally in Giddings, who believed it was 'as good a bill as we could get at this time'.[36] But once the scheme's particulars were made public, it lost the promised support of Washington's mayor and brewed up a fatal mix of abolitionist contempt and pro-slavery fears. Lincoln decided not to introduce his bill.

While Lincoln's congressional experience was working to crystallize his antislavery thought, developments in his native state worked to the same end. Lincoln warmly embraced the plan of gradual emancipation put before the Kentucky constitutional convention of 1849. The scheme's advocates included his father-in-law, Robert S. Todd, as well as his great hero, Henry Clay. The state's non-slaveholding whites were almost twenty times as numerous as slaveholders, but the plan proved thoroughly unpopular amongst all classes. Lincoln, recalled an Illinois colleague, was deeply disturbed by the enthusiasm for slavery amongst a new generation of Kentuckians, 'the thoughtless and giddy headed young men who looked upon work as vulgar and ungentlemanly'. He highlighted these changing southern perceptions when he spoke to mark Clay's death in 1852. The wise Kentucky statesman, he said, 'ever was, on principle and in feeling, opposed to slavery' but, like most white southerners, he had regretfully tolerated it, for he could not see 'how it could be at *once* eradicated, without producing a greater evil, even to the cause of human liberty itself'. Now, though, to Lincoln's alarm, 'an increasing number of men', by no means restricted to the states' rights eccentrics of South Carolina, 'for the sake of perpetuating slavery, are beginning to assail and to ridicule the white-man's charter of freedom – the declaration that "all men are created free and equal".'[37]

Lincoln's attention here to the question of slavery – unusual amongst the avalanche of orations prompted by Clay's death – shows how far the issue had moved up his political agenda. That speech, significantly, provides us with his first serious discussion of colonization as a means of tackling a problem he then judged intractable, perhaps insoluble. Clay had staunchly supported the American Colonization Society from its organization in 1816, serving as its president for many years. Its plan of voluntarily 'returning' African Americans to their 'native' continent was regarded by the most radical opponents of slavery as a cruel deception designed not to weaken the slaves' shackles but, by removing the troublesome free black population from the South, to tighten them. At the same time the Society was the target of the suspicion and outright hostility of many planters, especially in the Deep South, who regarded it as an abolitionist front. In truth, it was a philosophical hybrid, attracting both racist deportationists and genuine humanitarians. Clay straddled the two positions. Lincoln himself chose to emphasize the moral grandeur of the scheme and its potential for redeeming a guilty nation, an affronted race and the African continent. He spoke as a prophet: 'Pharaoh's country was cursed with plagues, and his hosts were drowned in the Red Sea for striving to retain a captive people who had already served them more than four hundred years. May like disasters never befall us!' A gradualist, socially responsible scheme, colonization offered the best, if uncertain, means of 'freeing our land from the dangerous presence of slavery; and . . . restoring a captive people to their long-lost father-land'. Like many, Lincoln over-estimated the enthusiasm of blacks themselves and underestimated the obstacles to success. In time, logic and experience would lead Lincoln to see the illusion on which colonization was built. But for the moment he was a believer and took on a managing role with the Illinois State Colonization Society in the 1850s. It was a faith rooted as much in ethical concern as in self-deception.[38]

Lincoln saw slavery as a chronic blight on the essential purpose of the American Union, namely to perpetuate the 'political edifice of liberty and equal rights' bequeathed by the republic's architects. As we have seen, his vision of the Union operated at a more materialistic level, too: it would be the means of fulfilling the unique potential of what he described in 1838 as 'the fairest portion of the earth, as regards extent of territory, fertility of soil, and salubrity of climate'. But the physical grandeur and material endowments of the United States were mainly to be seen as adjuncts to the moral magnificence of the nation's free institutions. Thus he praised Clay's motives in seeking 'the prosperity of his countrymen . . . chiefly to show to the world that freemen could be prosperous'. With an intensity far removed from his chill feelings towards his own father, Lincoln revered the nation's founders for fashioning a political system which conduced 'more essentially to the ends of civil and religious liberty, than any of which the history of former times tells us'. The Declaration of Independence, with its philosophical celebration of equality and liberty, and the federal Constitution, the legal guarantor of those principles, were measures of American uniqueness. '*Most governments* have been based, practically, on the denial of equal rights of men . . . ; *ours* began, by *affirming* those rights. *They* said, some men are too *ignorant*, and *vicious*, to share in government. Possibly so, said we; and, by your system, you would always keep them ignorant, and vicious. We proposed to give *all* a chance; and we expected the weak to grow stronger, the ignorant, wiser; and all better, and happier together.' Lincoln attributed to the American Union a special role in world history, the duty of acting as a beacon of freedom to all. Sharing Clay's view that the Union was 'the world's best hope', he interpreted the European nationalist movements of the mid-nineteenth century – in Hungary, Ireland, France and Germany – as part of 'the general cause of Republican liberty'. At the same time, he saw the impurities in the American example: through the persistence of slavery, the ideals of the Fourth of July were inevitably compromised. If he was unable to imagine the process by which slavery might be uprooted, his vision for his country demanded there be no further erosion of the Jeffersonian credo that all men were created equal, and no interference with the natural process by which slavery would die 'a natural death'.[39]

Moral crisis: 1854

The year 1854 was both a watershed in antebellum politics and the defining passage of Lincoln's pre-presidential public life. Stephen A. Douglas's Nebraska bill, by repealing the restrictions of the Missouri Compromise of 1820, dramatically opened up to slavery the northern portion of the Louisiana Purchase, an area of several million acres which for a generation had been regarded as forever free. The spectacular public storm over the Kansas–Nebraska Act, and the subsequent settlement of Kansas territory, had profound consequences for both Whigs and Democrats, repercussions which will be addressed in the next chapter. For Lincoln himself the Nebraska bombshell represented both a threat and an opportunity.

Lincoln later reflected that he was 'losing interest in politics when the repeal of the Missouri Compromise aroused me again'. As a summary this was accurate enough. The electoral off-years of 1851 and 1853, a dispiriting Whig presidential campaign in 1852, the relative abeyance of issue politics, and the demands of his law practice all helped to blunt the edge of his political appetite; but by the end of 1854 he had established himself as one of the leaders of the anti-Nebraska movement in Illinois and had been returned as a Whig to the state legislature. What Lincoln's statement does not explain, though, is why it took him several months to speak out against something which, by his own account, had left him 'astounded' and 'thunderstruck'. The bill was introduced in January, prompted immediate and concerted opposition from Salmon P. Chase, Joshua Giddings and other free-soil radicals inside and outside Congress, and was signed by Douglas's fellow-Democrat, President Franklin Pierce, on 30 May. All this time Lincoln was publicly silent. He remained so throughout the summer months, even as the free states resounded with calls for cross-party alliances to defeat the Pierce administration's forces in the fall elections. Only in late August did he take up the issue, campaigning for the re-election of his district's Whig congressman, Richard Yates.[40]

Why was Lincoln slow to take a public stand? Cynics might attribute his reticence to political calculation, self-interest and opportunism: the shrewd politician may have been coolly waiting to see how opinion moved before committing himself.[41] But there are more compelling, less shallow explanations. In the earlier part of the year Lincoln had been preoccupied with one of the most important and demanding legal cases of his career, acting for the Illinois Central Railroad before the state's Supreme Court. Thereafter, in spring and early summer, he had had more opportunity to speak out but no formal public position or platform from which to do so, and this at a time when the early opposition to Douglas in the state lacked coherence. Possibly, too, the naturally cautious Lincoln saw additional reason to be wary in the face of emergent nativism – that is, native-born Americans' organized hostility to immigrant arrivals. Swelling numbers of foreign-born workers worked to loosen Illinois political anchorages in 1854. Lincoln was no xenophobe, but hesitancy was a realistic response to an unpredictable movement whose enthusiasts included some of his close political friends.

By temperament Lincoln favored careful reflection, not impulsive action. His circumstances now allowed him to follow a course of listening, reading and thinking. Lincoln's opponents would later write disparagingly of his 'mousing about the libraries' in the statehouse.[42] By the time he threw himself into the campaign, and then agreed to run for the legislature, his arguments were already well formulated. He delivered a number of speeches before engineering, early in October, what was in effect a joint debate with Douglas at Springfield. On an uncomfortably sticky afternoon, his three-hour address deeply impressed, even excited, a large audience in the hall of the House of Representatives. His words were not reported verbatim but he later made available for state-wide circulation a full transcript of what was essentially the same text, his speech at Peoria on 16 October.[43] Its intellectual quality, moral force and rhetorical power made it the greatest speech of his political career to date, and its qualities provide their own argument that his campaign utterances were prompted by something more than political opportunism or convenience. The 'Peoria speech' contained most of the essential elements of his public addresses over the next six years.

What most thrilled Lincoln's hearers, including radical antislaveryites who had not previously considered him a kindred spirit, was the moral and philosophical clarity with which he identified the larger issues at stake in the repeal of the Missouri Compromise. As well as engaging in a Union-threatening piece of political perfidy, Lincoln argued, Douglas and his allies had reversed the 'settled policy' of the republic at a stroke. The new nation had followed Thomas Jefferson's lead in excluding slavery from the territories of the Old Northwest, and in 1820 the terms of that exclusion had been applied again within the northern portion of the Louisiana Purchase. No other policy would have been consistent with the principles of natural rights, human equality and political freedom laid out in the Virginian's Declaration of Independence. Douglas's novel principle of 'popular sovereignty', by contrast, assumed a moral neutrality toward slavery, leaving it to local communities to decide the issue for themselves – not with reference to the principles of civil liberty but in line only with material self-interest. His claim that the repeal of the Missouri Compromise had established 'the sacred right of self-government' ran aground on the rocks of negro manhood: 'if the negro *is* a man, is it not to that extent, a total destruction of self-government, to say that he too shall not govern *himself*? When the white man governs himself that is self-government; but when he governs himself, and also governs *another* man, that is *more* than self-government – that is despotism. If the negro is a *man*, why then my ancient faith teaches me that "all men are created equal;" and that there can be no moral right in connection with one man's making a slave of another.' Describing Jefferson's Declaration as the 'sheet anchor of American republicanism', Lincoln insisted that no man was 'good enough to govern another man, *without that other's consent'*.

Douglas might proclaim a moral indifference toward slavery, Lincoln explained, but this posture masked his and his allies' 'covert *real* zeal' for its spread; the fraudulent, 'lullaby' argument, that climate and natural conditions made the new territories unsuitable for slavery, diverted attention from 'the great Behemoth of danger' threatened by slavery's extension; the 'first few' having once fixed slavery in Nebraska, 'the subsequent many' would find it hard to be rid of it. This was the closest Lincoln got to employing what was one of the most powerful themes of anti-Nebraska agitation, the maneuverings of a conspiratorial southern 'slave power'. Instead, his emphasis lay on the stark ethical choices which now confronted the nation. The Nebraska Act, by putting slavery 'on the high road to extension and perpetuity', endangered the moral foundations of the republic. It gave the peculiar institution new status; it assumed 'that there CAN be MORAL RIGHT in the enslaving of one man by another'. But, observed Lincoln, slavery in reality 'is founded in the selfishness of man's nature – opposition to it, [in] . . . his love of justice. These principles are an eternal antagonism.' With a preacher's scorn he scoffed at the folly of the Nebraska men: 'Repeal the Missouri compromise[,] . . . repeal the declaration of independence . . . [but] you still can not repeal human nature. It still will be the abundance of man's heart, that slavery extension is wrong.'

In emphasizing the ethical polarities of slave and free societies, and by implication their incompatibility, Lincoln had set at least one foot on radical ground. He stood close to the position he would adopt explicitly in a private letter to George Robertson the following year: 'Our political problem now is "Can we, as a nation, continue together *permanently – forever* – half slave, and half free?"' His most celebrated formulation of that question lay a few years off, to be posed in the celebrated 'House Divided' speech, but the intellectual framework that supported it had been fashioned in his election addresses of 1854.

It must be said that those speeches by no means marked a complete break with Lincoln's political past. Their radicalism was qualified by persisting elements of conservative Whiggery. The lawyer who in 1847 had defended a Kentucky slaveowner – Robert Matson – in his attempt to secure the return from Illinois of his runaway slaves, and who had no doubt of the legitimacy of the harsh Fugitive Slave Law of 1850, continued to emphasize the constitutional rights of southern slaveholders. Dismantling slavery presented intractable problems: 'If all earthly power were given to me,' he confessed, 'I should not know what to do, as to the existing institution.' He reiterated his support for colonization and other gradual, voluntary means of the removal of slavery. He refused to entertain political and social equality for free blacks: 'My own feelings will not admit of this; and if mine would, we well know that those of the great mass of white people will not.' Earnestly, he stressed his own devoted Unionism and his lack of prejudice against the people of the South. Entrapped by circumstances not of their own making, they deserved sympathy for their virtual impotence in the face of an entrenched institution.

Lincoln founded his tolerant, encompassing nationalism, however, not on moral concessions to slaveholding but on a conviction that most southerners, in continuing to hold firm to the principles of the Declaration of Independence, shared his own view of slavery as a 'monstrous injustice'. He was sure that '[t]he great majority, south as well as north, have human sympathies, of which they can no more divest themselves than they can of their sensibility to physical pain. These sympathies in the bosoms of the southern people, manifest in many ways, their sense of the wrong of slavery, and their consciousness that, after all, there is humanity in the negro.' This allowed him to build to a rhetorical and moral climax, in which he called on all Americans, 'south, as well as north', to resist the spirit of Nebraska and re-energize 'the spirit of seventy-six'. In language that paralleled the spiritual warnings, cosmic meanings and millennialist hopes of the salvationist preacher, Lincoln once more stressed the moral incompatibility of the principles at stake, and urged that Americans 'repurify' their soiled 'republican robe' by rededicating themselves to Jefferson's principles and practice. 'If we do this, we shall not only have saved the Union; but we shall have so saved it, as to make, and to keep it, forever worthy of the saving. We shall have so saved it, that the succeeding millions of free happy people, the world over, shall rise up, and call us blessed, to the latest generations.'

Lincoln's outrage and moral earnestness over the Nebraska issue surprised many in his audiences, who were expecting less serious-ness and history, and more anecdotes. This new-found authority has prompted historians to dramatize the change from the Lincoln of 1849, the clever but essentially provincial and 'self-centered' politician, to the powerful, broad-horizoned statesman of the anti-Nebraska struggle. Michael Burlingame, drawing on Jungian psychology, sees Lincoln's new seriousness and enhanced stature as the product of a mid-life crisis, a time when he spent hours brooding on his modest achievements in law and politics, and on the legacy he would leave.[44] Certainly, Lincoln in his early forties had good reason to take stock of his life, as the deaths of his father and, more poignantly, of his son Eddie prompted a heightened sense of his own mortality. These were years, too, when he successfully mastered Euclidean logic, a quintessential act of self-improvement that would leave its mark on all of his subsequent oratory. In the strains of the Peoria speech we hear the voice of a man who had without doubt matured during his five years beyond the political mainstream.

Yet Lincoln's 'transformation' need hardly surprise us. His assault on Douglas and the Democratic administration sprang naturally from well-established elements in his thought. To the Whiggish respecter of law and precedent, one who had urged in his landmark Lyceum speech that reverence for the laws should become 'the *political religion* of the nation', the Nebraskaites had perpetrated a statutory violation; to the proponent of economic progress and the intensive cultivation of the American west, the Act was a blow against self-improving, independent laborers. Most of all, the measure presented a potent moral challenge to a man who had held a life-long conviction that slavery was a wrong, tolerable only because it was slowly stumbling to a natural death. Lincoln saw the repeal of the Missouri Compromise threatening to revive an otherwise doomed institu-tion; no morally responsible citizen could passively watch this reversal of the nation's ethical direction. From Lincoln's perspective, the real trans-formation of these years was not in his own moral calculus, but in the nation's leaders.

The religious roots of moral power

Lincoln's most intimate friend, Joshua Speed, wrote of his fellow Kentuckian, 'Unlike all other men there was an entire harmony between his public and private life. He must believe that he was right and that he had truth and justice with him or he was a weak man. But no man could be stronger if he thought that he was right.' Likewise, Joseph Gillespie, another long-standing, shrewd and trusted friend, considered Lincoln's powerful sense of justice the essential key to his colleague's actions. '[T]he sense of right & wrong was extremely acute in his nature', he recalled. 'He was extremely just and fair minded. He was as gentle as a girl and yet as firm for the right as adamant.' Gillespie located Lincoln's earnest hostility to slavery and to the Nebraska bill – 'about the only public question on which he would become excited' – in an affront to his sense of justice.[45]

Lincoln's succinct formulation, 'if slavery is not wrong, nothing is wrong', may have owed something to a New Haven Congregationalist minister, Leonard Bacon, whose essays on slavery, published in 1846, used similar phraseology and had found their way to Springfield.[46] That Lincoln appears to have acknowledged this debt to a Yankee clergy-man, and that a deep ethical conviction marked the period of his re-engagement with serious politics, inevitably raises the issue of the religious sources of that moral concern. It is a question more easily put than answered. Lincoln made no public statement of personal faith in the 1850s and many of those close to him had no idea about his private views. Judge David Davis, in whose company Lincoln spent many hours on the Eighth Judicial Circuit, considered him 'the most reticent – Secretive man I Ever Saw – or Expect to See', and thought it absurd that any but rare intimates should claim to have known his mind.[47] Those who, after Lincoln's death, did profess to fathom him were scarcely dis-interested parties, and their unseemly tussle for his soul leaves us chary about accepting their conflicting judgments at face value.

When Lincoln's first biographer, Josiah Holland, poured him into the mold of a Christian president, a disbelieving William Herndon found the outcome unrecognizable as the man with whom he had practiced law. He set about interviewing those who might be in a position to know, and in a series of lectures denied there were any Christological elements in Lincoln's spiritual thought. Still, few religious traditions have subsequently failed to embrace him. Friends have pointed to his Virginia Quaker for-bears, Baptists to his parents' faith, Methodists to a supposed conversion at a camp-meeting, Catholics to a surreptitious joining of their Church, and Presbyterians to a public attendance at theirs. Masons, Unitarians and Universalists have each clasped him to their bosoms. Following the visits of two or three mediums to the wartime White House, the Spiritualists claimed him as one of theirs, though Lincoln himself was facetiously dismissive, remarking that the contradictory voices of the spirits at these seances reminded him of his Cabinet meetings.[48]

If such chauvinism befogs rather than illuminates the inner Lincoln, it is equally true that the themes of Lincoln the shrewd pragmatist and political manager have, with a few honorable exceptions, tended to obscure the reflective Lincoln, a politician capable of serious thought about ultimate matters. Yet in the course of his adult life Lincoln faced the traumas of courtship and a broken engagement, embarked on an uncertain marriage, suffered the painful loss of two young sons and confronted the carnage of a fratricidal war. It would have been strange indeed had a man so given to introspection not added new layers to his understanding of the meaning of life and death. If, as Gillespie judged, he was not given particularly to metaphysical speculation, Lincoln's old New Salem friend, Isaac Cogdal, was surely right when he asserted that 'his mind was full of terrible enquiry – and was skeptical in a good sense'. Speed was sure that over the years Lincoln 'was a growing man in religion', advancing from religious skepticism in the 1830s to serious Christian inquiry in the White House. Though James Matheny suggested that the only change to occur was in Lincoln's greater discretion, not his views, which Matheny thought remained skeptical (at least up to 1861), there are reasonable grounds for believing that the mature Lincoln of the 1850s was more receptive to Protestant orthodoxy than he had been twenty years earlier.[49] Then the essential elements of Lincoln's religious outlook surely contributed to the new tone and substance of his speeches following his return to politics in 1854. For the first time he devoted whole speeches to the question of slavery, including its corrosive effect on individual enterprise and aspiration, and found a moral edge for which political opportunism provides only the shallowest of explanations.

Lincoln's earliest experience of religion came, naturally enough, through his parents. As 'hard-shell' Baptists, members of the Little Mount Separate Baptist Church, they subscribed to a predestinarian, hyper-Calvinist system of beliefs: these included 'election by grace before the world began'; missionary work was an act of presumption against the Almighty, who needed no assistance to achieve His foreordained plan. When Thomas Lincoln moved to Indiana and remarried, he and his wife eventually joined the Pigeon Creek Baptist Church, Thomas becoming a leading man amongst the 'Separates' in the new state. It was a milieu of unlettered preachers and few books. Abraham generally attended church meetings but, unlike his sister, who was admitted to membership, he made no profession of faith. 'Abe had no particular religion – didnt think of that question at the time, if he ever did', his stepmother, Sarah Bush Johnston, recalled. 'He never talked about it.'[50]

The Kentucky and Indiana years left Lincoln with a mixed legacy of belief. Negatively, he can have found little to celebrate in the particular rigidities and exclusiveness of a strict Baptist creed, nominally Calvinist, but one that Calvin himself would barely have recognized. He had no time for the inter-sectarian rivalries and theological brawling, especially between Baptists and Methodists, that marked the developing West. It was here that were sown the seeds of his aversion to church creeds and his skepticism about 'the possibility, or propriety, of settling the religion of Jesus Christ in the models of man-made creeds and dogmas'. He saw little to admire in the religious 'enthusiasm' of frontier revivalism, and was more likely to parody and deride the physical and mental gymnastics of uneducated hell-fire preachers than to respect them. There was a typical mix of irony and humor in his remark, 'when I hear a man preach, I like to see him act as if he were fighting bees!'[51]

At the same time, Lincoln held on to much of what he had learnt in his early experience of religion. Not least, Lincoln's commonly-noted fatalism, which he never shed, reflects the continuing legacy of his high Calvinist upbringing. Equally influential were the handful of books that he read over and over. These included such standards of the English Nonconformist tradition as Bunyan's *Pilgrim's Progress* and Watts's hymns, works whose simplicity and strength of language effected an unmeasurable but undoubted influence on Lincoln's own prose, at its best spare and taut. Above all, he encountered the King James Bible. Through his mother's teaching and his own study he acquired a command of the Scriptures which would continue to impress observers and inform his rhetoric throughout his life. His stepmother, seeking to puncture overblown claims about Lincoln's early piety, noted that 'Abe read the bible some, though not as much as said: he sought more congenial books'. But the habit of scripture-reading was established and thereafter not lost. Allied to his formidable memory ('My mind is like a piece of steel, very hard to scratch anything on it and almost impossible after you get it there to rub it out', he once explained), his close acquaintance with the Bible gave him a formidable weapon for use on audiences steeped in the Scriptures, whether in set-piece speeches or on informal occasions.[52] An Illinois minister, seeing Lincoln in the street regaling a gathering of citizens with a sequence of anecdotes, remarked as he passed, 'Where the great ones are there will the people be.' Quickly Lincoln replied, 'Ho! Parson a little more Scriptural; "Where the carcass is there will the eagles be gathered together."'[53]

To know the Bible well is not necessarily to consider it inspired. Dennis Hanks, a cousin who lived with the family in the Indiana years, questioned whether Lincoln really believed in it, and there is barely any doubt that during the 1830s, as a young man in New Salem and Springfield, Lincoln openly contested its authority. Like others in his circle, he read Tom Paine's *Age of Reason* and Constantin de Volney's *Ruins*, and found in their critique of Christianity and the Scriptures, and in their pursuit of a rational theology, much to satisfy his logical, inquiring mind. As an aspiring lawyer, he clearly warmed to their testing of the Bible by the rules of evidence, and to their use of reason and ridicule to expose its contradictions. At the same time he evinced a strong partiality for the caustic, witty poetry of another religious skeptic, Robert Burns, and delighted in his mocking satire on Calvinist self-righteousness, 'Holy Willie's Prayer'.[54]

Amongst his circle in New Salem, and then in Springfield as the junior partner of John Stuart, Lincoln had a reputation as 'an infidel'. We need not dismiss as unfounded (as have some of his champions) the claim that Lincoln wrote an essay questioning the Bible as divine revelation but that New Salem friends made him burn it to prevent damage to his public career: the story is of a piece with what else we know of his views at this time and was later conceded by several of his circle. James Matheny recalled that his father, a Methodist preacher, though 'loving Lincoln with all his soul[,] hated to vote for him' in the mid-1830s because of the taint of unbelief. Matheny himself, friendly with Lincoln in the Springfield office, told how he had heard Lincoln 'call Christ a bastard', how he 'would talk about Religion – pick up the Bible – read a passage – and then Comment on it – show its falsity – and its follies on the grounds of Reason – would then show its own self made & self uttered Contradictions and would in the End – finally ridicule it'. Stuart, too, thought Lincoln's unorthodoxy 'bordered on atheism'. He 'went further against Christian beliefs – & doctrines & principles than any man I ever heard: he shocked me – . . . Lincoln always denied that Jesus was the . . . son of God as understood and maintained by the Christian world.'[55]

Lincoln was in fact no more of an atheist than Paine, who, despite his popular reputation, had not launched an assault on all religion. Even in his New Salem period Lincoln believed in a Creator. Isaac Cogdal, while conceding the existence of Lincoln's essay denying the inspiration of Scripture, insisted that his friend 'believed in God – and all the great substantial groundworks of Religion'. But this was not a quixotic God who would act on impulse or anger. Cogdal, claiming to have often discussed religion with Lincoln between 1834 and 1859, considered him 'a Universalist tap root & all in faith and sentiment', someone who could not subscribe to the orthodox Calvinist belief in hell and endless punishment. Corroborative evidence comes from Mentor Graham, who gave

Lincoln some instruction at New Salem and who recalled reading a manuscript that Lincoln gave him in defense of universal salvation. Denying that 'the God of the universe' would ever become 'excited, mad, or angry', Lincoln 'took the passage, "As in Adam all die, even so in Christ shall all be made alive,"' to contradict the theory of eternal damnation. It is unlikely that Lincoln was here endorsing the Christian doctrine of atonement, but rather affirming the case for a Creator who operated according to the maxims of justice and rationality in His dealings with humankind.[56]

Lincoln's personal and religious circumstances in Springfield worked to refine and reshape his opinions. For the first time he belonged to a community that numbered educated, college-trained ministers, settled pastors capable of engaging intelligently with unorthodox opinion. Hesitant at first about attending any of the city's fashionable churches, Lincoln, after his marriage to Mary Todd, became an occasional worshipper at the Episcopal church. When their three-year-old son Eddie died in 1850, the family switched their allegiance to the First Presbyterian Church, whose Old School pastor, James Smith, had conducted the funeral ceremony. Mary entered into full membership, and the Lincolns rented a pew (though Lincoln himself would be by no means the most regular of attenders: he had, as one friendly commentator politely put it, 'western and not puritan views' of Sabbath observance). Smith was an intellectual Scot familiar with the works of Paine, Volney and other freethinkers. In *The Christian's Defense*, a substantial work of theology, Smith deployed rational argument and the evidence of historical and natural sciences to plead the cause of orthodox Christianity. He gave a copy of his book to Lincoln, whose home on Eighth and Jackson he quite regularly visited, and who, Smith maintained, gave the arguments on both sides 'a most patient, impartial and Searching investigation'. It was not Lincoln's only reading on the issues of faith and reason. He gave a close examination to Robert Chambers's *Vestiges of the Natural History of Creation* (1844), an analysis of Christianity and evolutionary science; Herndon and Jesse Fell lent him the writings of liberal theologians.[57]

In consequence, according to Smith, Lincoln avowed 'his belief in the Divine Authority and the Inspiration of the Scriptures'. Ninian Edwards, remembered Lincoln, his brother-in-law, declaring that thanks to his dialogues with his pastor 'I am now convinced of the truth of the Christian religion'. Several of Lincoln's acquaintances maintained that in the late 1850s he had professed his belief in the atonement of Christ for the final salvation of all men. This was the Methodist Jonathan Harnett's recollection of a discussion in Lincoln's office in 1858, when Lincoln had said 'that Christ must reign supreme, high over all, The Saviour of all'. Isaac Cogdal, a Universalist, recalled a similar, perhaps the same, meeting 'in 1859' at which Lincoln declared 'that all that was lost by the transgression of Adam was made good by the atonement: all that was lost by the fall was made good by the sacrifice'. A colleague on the judicial circuit, John H. Wickizer, considered Lincoln 'very liberal in his views', but he added, 'I think he believed in "Jesus Christ, and him crucified"'. It is, then, quite possible that Lincoln's intellectual development within a Presbyterian institutional framework in Springfield made him much more receptive to the idea of the inspiration of Scripture. It is also possible that he had embraced a more Christological theology, now using the terms 'Lord' and 'Saviour' in more than just a humanist sense.[58]

It is possible, but the weight of evidence is against it. In a rare moment of private openness, during his father's last days in 1851, Lincoln asked his stepbrother John Johnston to tell Thomas Lincoln 'to remember to call upon, and confide in, our great, and good, and merciful Maker; who will not turn away from him in any extremity. He notes the fall of a sparrow, and numbers the hairs of our heads; and He will not forget the dying man who puts his trust in Him.' Johnston should say that, were his father to die, 'he will soon have a joyous [meeting] with many loved ones gone before; and where the [rest of] us, through the help of God, hope ere long [to join] them'.[59] The statement confirmed Lincoln's faith in an omnipotent and kindly Creator, but significantly there is no Christology. If there is anything theologically striking about it, it is in its allusion to an afterlife. Although this was not an unequivocal statement of personal belief, it put Lincoln closer to orthodoxy than in his New Salem days, when he had allegedly declared, 'It isn't a pleasant thing to think that when we die that is the last of us.'[60]

The balance of testimony in fact points to Lincoln inclining toward essentially Unitarian, not Trinitarian, beliefs in the 1850s. Jesse Fell, a Bloomington lawyer and liberal Christian who had 'repeated Conversations' with Lincoln on religious subjects over a period of two decades, argued forcefully that during Lincoln's Springfield years, 'whilst he held many opinions in common with the great mass of Christian believers, he did not believe in what are regarded as the orthodox or evangelical views of Christianity'. Accepting that Lincoln might have changed his outlook during his presidency, Fell was sure that throughout the time of their friendship his views put him 'entirely outside the pale of the Christian Church': 'On the inate depravity of Man, the character & office of the great head of the Church, the atonement, the infallibility of the written revelation, the performance of myricles, the nature & design of present

& future rewards & punishments . . . and many other Subjects, he held opinions . . . utterly at variance with what are usually taught in the Churches.' In the mid-1850s they discussed at length the Unitarianism of William E. Channing and Theodore Parker, both of whose works Lincoln read and admired. Without subscribing to everything they argued, Lincoln warmed to their liberalism and rationality. 'His religious views were eminantly practical,' Fell insisted, 'and are Sumed up on these two propositions, "the Fatherhood of God, and the Brotherhood of Man".'[61]

Lincoln's son Robert wrote that he knew nothing 'of Dr Smith's having "converted" my father from "Unitarian" to "Trinitarian" belief': he had never heard Lincoln speak of it. John Stuart went further. He told William Herndon that Smith had 'tried to Convert Lincoln from Infidelity so late as 1858 and Couldn't do it'. Listening for Lincoln's authentic voice in the recollections of his friends and acquaintances of this time, we perhaps hear it most clearly through James W. Keyes, a Springfield tailor. Lincoln, he said, gave as his reason for believing in an omnipotent Creator 'that in view of the Order and harmony of all nature . . . , it would have been More miraculous to have Come about by chance, than to have been created and arranged by some great thinking power'. As for the theory that 'Christ is God, or equal to the Creator[,] he said [it] had better be taken for granted – for by the test of reason all might become infidels on that subject, for evidence of Christs divinity Came to us in somewhat doubtful Shape – but that the Sistom of Christianity was an ingenious one at least – and perhaps was Calculated to do good'. This wary and qualified formulation of belief has an authentic Lincolnian ring to it.[62]

Whether or not Lincoln moved closer intellectually to a conventional Trinitarian Christian stance during these years, all were agreed that he was not, in Mary Todd Lincoln's words 'a technical Christian'; he had, she said, 'no hope – & no faith in the usual acceptation of those words'. His neighbors knew this too. One of his warmest evangelical supporters in Springfield, the New School minister Albert Hale, was saddened that Lincoln was not 'born of God'. Most, though, were adamant that he was '*naturally* religious', whatever his shortcomings over ceremonials and creeds. 'He would ridicule the Puritans, or swear in a moment of vexation; but yet his heart was full of natural and cultivated religion', insisted one of his closest associates, Leonard Swett. Judged 'by the higher rule of purity of conduct, of honesty of motive, of unyielding fidelity to the right and acknowledging God as the Supreme Ruler, then he filled all the requirements of true devotion and love of his neighbor as himself'. Even those who doubted his piety found it hard to question the moral integrity and private behavior of a man known not to drink, smoke or gamble.[63]

On one feature of Lincoln's thought there was no disagreement. Lincoln described himself as a life-long fatalist, and none demurred. 'What is to be will be', he told congressman Isaac Arnold. 'I have found all my life as Hamlet says: "There's a divinity that shapes our ends, Rough-hew them how we will."' Mary Todd heard that formulation many times, for as she confirmed to Herndon, Lincoln's 'maxim and philosophy was – "What is to be will be and no cares of ours can arrest the decree"'. Not that Herndon needed reminding. He recalled many conversations about predestination in which Lincoln had asserted that 'all things were fixed, doomed in one way or the other, from which there was no appeal' and that 'no efforts or prayers of ours can change, alter, modify, or reverse the decree'. Lincoln often told his law partner that he had a foreboding of 'some terrible end', but when Joseph Gillespie and others urged him to take precautions against assassination, he took a fatalistic view. 'I will be cautious', he told an anxious acquaintance shortly before his final departure from Springfield, 'but God's will be done. I am in his hands . . . and what he does I must bow to – God rules, and we should submit.'[64]

The predestinarian ethos of Lincoln's hyper-Calvinist, Baptist upbringing undoubtedly molded this view of fate: throughout his life he would allude to the determining power of 'Divine Providence', 'the Divine Being' and 'the providence of God'. This was a God, he told Isaac Cogdal, that 'predestined things – and governed the universe by Law – nothing going by accident'. Lincoln's determinism, though, had more secular roots. According to Herndon, Lincoln believed that all conscious human action was shaped by 'motives' – that is, self-interested, rational and predictable responses to surrounding conditions 'that have somewhat existed for a hundred thousand years or more'. There was thus no freedom of the will: as Lincoln put it in an election handbill of 1846, explaining his belief in the 'Doctrine of Necessity', he had found persuasive the idea 'that the human mind is impelled to action, or held in rest by some power, over which the mind itself has no control'. Defensively, Lincoln stressed that this was an opinion consistent with religious faith, as 'held by several of the Christian denominations', but as Allen Guelzo has shrewdly observed, there were non-religious influences working here, too, including Benthamite utilitarianism, as mediated by American legal reformers. Lincoln's views on motives, interests, and the lack of freedom of the moral will powerfully resembled Jeremy Bentham's. Whatever their sources, Lincoln's views were anathema to many mainstream Christians – Methodists and 'Arminianized' Calvinists – who viewed the 'doctrine of necessity' as a Godless creed that denied moral responsibility. Lincoln, though, continued mainly to present his deterministic faith in a religious language that invoked an all-controlling God.[65]

This hybrid religious faith, with its rationalist, Universalist, Unitarian, fatalist, but only residually Calvinist elements, helped shape Lincoln's approach to slavery as a morally-charged political issue. The Declaration of Independence, in which he rooted his arguments during the 1850s, was for Lincoln more than a time-bound expression of political grievance. It was a near-sanctified statement of universal principles, and one that squared with essential elements of his personal faith: belief in a God who had created all men equal and whose relations with humankind were based on the principles of justice. Lincoln found the scriptural basis for the Declaration in the book of Genesis: if humankind were created in the image of God, then 'the justice of the Creator' had to be extended equally 'to *all* His creatures, to the whole great family of man'. As he told an audience at Lewistown, Illinois, the Founders had declared that 'nothing stamped with the Divine image and likeness was sent into the world to be trodden on, and degraded, and imbruted by its fellows'. In setting down the Declaration's self-evident truths, they had provided a basis for resistance 'in the distant future' to a 'faction' or 'interest' determined to argue that 'none but rich men, or none but white men, were entitled to life, liberty and the pursuit of happiness'. Sustain that document and you ensured that 'truth, and justice, and mercy, and all the humane and Christian virtues . . . [would] not be extinguished from the land'.[66]

Lincoln's use of the Bible in the struggle over slavery was driven by conviction, not expediency. As Herndon recognized, whether or not Lincoln believed in the divine inspiration of Scripture, 'he accepted the practical precepts of that great book as binding alike upon his head and his conscience'; late in life he described it as the means of distinguishing right from wrong. Not that Lincoln brandished the Bible as an all-purpose antislavery manual, but he was clear enough where its principles led: ' "*Give* to him that is needy" is the christian rule of charity; but "Take from him that is needy" is the rule of slavery.' He was wryly scornful of those southern divines like the Presbyterian Frederick A. Ross, who had constructed a proslavery theology that concluded, as he put it, that 'it is better for *some* people to be slaves; and, in such cases, it is the Will of God that they be such'. But how was God's will to be established? Suppose Ross had a slave named Sambo. To the question 'Is it the Will of God that Sambo shall remain a slave, or be set free?' God gives no audible answer and the Bible, his revelation, 'gives none – or, at most, none but such as admits of a squabble, as to its meaning'. But the fact that the question was to be resolved by Dr Ross, who 'sits in the shade, with gloves on his hands, and subsists on the bread that Sambo is earning in the burning sun', gave little confidence that he would 'be actuated by that perfect impartiality, which has ever been considered most favorable to correct decisions'.[67]

God's words to Adam, 'In the sweat of thy face shalt thou eat bread', provided Lincoln with a text for his theology of labor: that is, the burden of work, the individual's duty to engage in it, and his moral right to enjoy the fruits of his labor.[68] Equally, God's arrangement of the human form was an expression of that theology and offered a physical argument for giving blacks the education and path to self-improvement which slavery denied them: 'as the Author of man makes every individual with one head and one pair of hands, it was probably intended that heads and hands should cooperate as friends; ... that that particular head, should direct and control that particular pair of hands[;] ... that each head is the natural guardian, director, and protector of the hands and mouth insepar-ably connected with it; and that being so, every head should be cultivated, and improved, by whatever will add to its capacity for performing its charge'. Joseph Gillespie recorded the animation and almost Puritan earnestness with which Lincoln discussed the need to challenge slavery's moral and social evils: ostentatious wealth, enervating leisure and a view of labor as 'vulgar and ungentlemanly'. Slavery 'was a great & crying injustice [and] an enormous national crime': the country, he told Gillespie, 'could not expect to escape punishment for it'. Surfacing here in Lincoln's thought was the Calvinist view of the political nation as a moral being. God punished wicked nations for their sins, just as he punished delin-quent individuals.[69]

Punishment would bring reformation and progress: Lincoln, explained Leonard Swett, expected the 'ultimate triumph of right, and the over-throw of wrong'. Here we see again Lincoln's idea of destiny and his view that the universe followed a course fixed by divine laws. 'He believed the results to which certain causes tended, would surely follow; he did not believe that those results could be materially hastened or impeded', wrote Swett. 'His whole political history, especially since the agitation of the Slavery question, has been based upon this theory.'[70] It was a theory that threw up two areas of paradox in his thought and practice toward the peculiar institution.

First, his scorn for the argument that slavery was good for people ('As a *good* thing, slavery is strikingly perculiar, in this, that it is the only good thing which no man ever seeks the good of, *for himself*') stopped short of full-blown censure of slaveholders, or malice toward them. Believing that people are the product of their circumstances, that environments trap them into unbreakable habits and prompt actions according to the laws of motive, Lincoln was remarkably free from hate. Southerners did no more and no less than the people of the free states would have done had their positions been reversed. Moral opprobrium was inappropriate. 'No man was to be eulogized for what he did or censured for what he did not do or did do', Herndon explained. 'I never heard him censure anyone but slightly, nor' – Jefferson and Clay excepted – 'eulogize any'.[71]

Further, if Lincoln really did believe 'that what was to be would be inevitably', and that slavery was a doomed institution, why did he so energetically engage in efforts to prevent its spread? Those who have alluded to the essential 'passivity' of Lincoln's nature have used a misleading term: he may have been fatalistic, but he was also ambitious, enterprising, and determined. He was scarcely inert politically. How, then, does one square the circle? First, we should note that even those who made much of this trait in Lincoln were quick to caution against a picture of blind belief in destiny. As Herndon himself explained, 'his fatalism was not of the extreme order like the Mahometan idea of fate'; Lincoln conceded that 'the will to a very limited extent, in some fields of operation, was somewhat free'. Humans had the capacity to 'modify the environments' which shaped them. Secondly, as Joseph Gillespie shrewdly observed, Lincoln yoked a belief in foreordained *instrumentality* with his faith in predestined ends, 'and therefore he was extremely diligent in the use of means'. As Lincoln told a newly-married Joshua Speed, 'I believe God made me one of the instruments of bringing your Fanny and you together, which union, I have no doubt He had fore-ordained.' This was how he stood in regard to the agitation over slavery, which from the first, according to Swett, he expected to succeed and so 'acted upon the result as though it was present from the beginning'. Much later, as president, he not only trusted deeply in God's purpose to save the Union but, in Gillespie's judgment, concluded 'that he himself was an instrument fore-ordained to aid in the accomplishment of this purpose as well as to emancipate the slaves'.[72]

The fatalist and activist were thus fused in Lincoln, who was in this respect a by no means unique historical figure. As Allen Guelzo has remarked, the doctrine of inevitability has often generated a psychological imperative to action, for instance amongst Puritan revolutionaries or the disciples of Marx and Lenin. In Lincoln's case we may have a sense of paradox, but his views were not absurdly self-contradictory. Driven by a clear understanding of the Union's purpose, by a view of slavery as a doomed aberration in an enterprising, egalitarian society,

24 Joseph Gillespie, quoted in N&H, 1:158–62.

25 Paul Simon, *Lincoln's Preparation for Greatness: The Illinois Legislative Years* (University of Oklahoma Press, 1965; repr. Urbana, IL: University of Illinois Press, 1971), 263–4; Boritt, *Lincoln and the Economics of the American Dream*, 56–7; *CW*, 1:159–79, 237–8.

26 *CW*, 1:309–13, 334–5.

27 *CW*, 1:334, 407–16; Donald, 110; Olivier Fraysse, *Lincoln, Land, and Labor, 1809–1860*, trans. Sylvia Neely (Urbana, IL: University of Illinois Press, 1994), 101.

28 *CW*, 1:320.

29 *CW*, 1:271–9, 291–7; *Herndon's Lincoln*, 206–7.

30 *CW*, 1:74–5 (emphasis added).

31 *CW*, 1:260, 2:320, 4:62, 7:281; Burlingame, *Inner World*, 25; *HI*, 457.

32 Ward Hill Lamon, *Recollections of Lincoln, 1847–1865*, ed. Dorothy Lamon Teillard (Lincoln, NB: Bison Books, 1994; repr. from the 2nd edn of 1911), 15.

33 The words of the Whig-supported Ashmun amendment. Donald W. Riddle, *Congressman Abraham Lincoln* (Westport, CT: Greenwood Press, 1979), 1, 42.

34 *CW*, 1:420–2, 431–42, 457; 2:4.

35 *CW*, 1:347–8.

36 *CW*, 2:20–2; Giddings' diary, 11 Jan. 1849, in N&H, 1:286.

37 *HI*, 183; *CW*, 2:130.

38 *CW*, 2:131–2.

39 *CW*, 1:108, 347; 2:62, 115–16, 126, 222.

40 *CW*, 2:226–7; 3:551–2.

41 This is the implication of Riddle, *Congressman Abraham Lincoln*, 246–9.

42 N&H, 1:376.

43 *CW*, 2:247–83.

44 Burlingame, *Inner World*, 1–56.

45 *HI*, 183–4, 499, 507.

46 Bacon wrote: 'If those laws of the southern states, by virtue of which slavery exists there, and is what it is, are not wrong – nothing is wrong.' His uncle taught in Springfield. Leonard Bacon, *Slavery Discussed in Occasional Essays, from 1833 to 1846* (New York, 1846), x; Theodore Davenport Bacon, *Leonard Bacon: A Statesman in the Church* (New Haven, CT: Yale University Press, 1931), 269–73.

47 *HI*, 348.

48 William E. Barton, *The Soul of Abraham Lincoln* (New York: George H. Doran Company, 1920), 225–43.

49 *HI*, 156, 441, 476, 505, 521, 576–7.

50 *HI*, 107, 215, 233, 455; Allen C. Guelzo, 'Abraham Lincoln and the Doctrine of Necessity', *Journal of the Abraham Lincoln Association*, 18 no. 1 (Winter 1997), 66–7.

51 William J. Wolf, *The Almost Chosen People: A Study of the Religion of Abraham Lincoln* (Garden City, NY: Doubleday, 1959), 50–1, 74–5; *RWAL*, 457.

52 *HI*, 37, 40–1, 76, 106–7, 499.

53 *HI*, 573 (spelling corrected). Lincoln's text was Luke xvii 37.

54 *HI*, 106; Douglas L. Wilson, *Honor's Voice: The Transformation of Abraham Lincoln* (New York: Alfred A. Knopf, 1998), 73–80. Burns's poem includes the stanza: 'O Thou that in the Heavens does dwell, / Wha, as it pleases best Thysel, / Sens ane to Heaven an' ten to Hell / A' for Thy glory, / And no for onie guid or ill / They've done before Thee!'

55 *HI*, 24, 61–2, 432, 441, 472, 576–7; Walter B. Stevens, *A Reporter's Lincoln*, ed. Michael Burlingame (Lincoln, NB: University of Nebraska Press, 1998), 11–12; Wilson, *Honor's Voice*, 81–3. Matheny subsequently retracted some of his statements, but not those relating to Lincoln's religion in his younger days. Barton, *Soul of Abraham Lincoln*, 320–1.

56 *HI*, 441. Fehrenbacher casts doubt on Cogdal's reliability. *RWAL*, 110–11.

57 *HI*, 549; *Herndon's Lincoln*, 354.

58 *HI*, 516, 547; Barton, *Soul of Abraham Lincoln*, 324, 348–9.

59 *CW*, 2:97.

60 Stevens, *A Reporter's Lincoln*, 12.

61 *HI*, 578–80.

62 *HI*, 360, 464, 524, 576.

63 Nicolay, *Oral History*, 95–6; *HI*, 167–8, 358, 360, 453, 516.

64 Isaac N. Arnold, *The Life of Abraham Lincoln* (Chicago, IL: McClurg & Company, 1884), 81; *HI*, 185, 358, 360, 426; Emanuel Hertz, *The Hidden Lincoln: From the Letters and Papers of William H. Herndon* (New York: Blue Ribbon Books, 1940), 167.

65 *HI*, 441; Hertz, *The Hidden Lincoln*, 142, 167–8, 265–6, 407–8; *CW*, 1:382; Guelzo, 'Abraham Lincoln and the Doctrine of Necessity', 57–81.

66 *CW*, 2:544–7.

67 *Herndon's Lincoln*, 360; *CW*, 3:204–5.

68 *CW*, 1:411–12 (Genesis iii 19).

69 *CW*, 3:479–80; *HI*, 183–4, 441.

70 *HI*, 162, 167–8, 441.

71 *CW*, 3:205; Hertz, *The Hidden Lincoln*, 266.

72 Hertz, *The Hidden Lincoln*, 265–7; *HI*, 162, 506; *CW*, 1:289.

73 Guelzo, 'Abraham Lincoln and the Doctrine of Necessity', 79.

Chapter Two

The Power of Opinion: Lincoln, the Illinois Public, and the New Political Order, 1854–58

Through the novel system of participatory democracy that evolved during the first half of the nineteenth century, ordinary Americans came to wield real political influence. By later standards, of course, it was a restrictive and discriminatory system, for it denied the formal vote to women and most non-whites. Yet, measured against the practice of other political communities of the time, universal white manhood suffrage represented a radical new departure, one which seemed to herald the rule of the common man. When introduced, it demanded a revolution in thinking by the republic's elite, many of them heirs of their eighteenth-century political world where authority was synonymous with property and intellect. Some, lamenting the empowerment of the poor and unlettered, failed to adapt to the altered reality, but most politicians proved quick to develop new devices to deal with the challenge of the 'sovereign crowd'.

Of these, the most significant was the mass-based political party. For Martin Van Buren, Thurlow Weed and other astute professionals, party conventions, platforms and networks provided a way of managing, channeling, mediating, and possibly even manipulating, public opinion. By the 1830s and 1840s disciplined, organized and recognizably modern parties had taken root in almost every part of the American Union and were intended to endure. Within what historians have termed the Jacksonian or second 'party system' most voters were either Whigs or Democrats.[1] Even so, popular insurgency and the turbulence of democratic politics meant that the party managers' control was often tenuous and never complete. In a system of almost constant electioneering unresponsive candidates would be beached if they neglected shifts in popular tides and currents. Though shrewd managers acknowledged the need to respect public opinion, they contended with parties which, as coalitions of diverse interests, were often unstable. As well as articulating the material aspirations of ordinary people, politicians had to respond to prejudices and loyalties that frequently cut across the lines drawn by simple economic interest. In particular, they had to contend with the ethnic and religious hostilities of a heterogeneous, growing electorate, and the increasing inter-sectional animus that poisoned North–South relations in the quarter century before the Civil War.

The truth that in a mass democracy voters could be the ultimate arbiters of political power shone with dazzling clarity in the 1850s. The framework of the system within which politics had been conducted for twenty years buckled and then collapsed under the weight of popular revolt against the established parties. Native-born Americans, fearing the effects of mass immigration from Ireland and Germany, called for tough naturalization laws, stiff controls on the sale and consumption of alcohol, and the stout defense of Protestantism, especially in schools. When neither Democrats (the long-standing friends of the immigrant) nor Whigs (once sensitive to the anxieties of native-born voters but now fearful of offending a huge foreign-born constituency) moved energetically against rum and Romanism, hundreds of thousands of nativists jumped ship for a new vessel dedicated to the protection of the republic. Secretive and localized in its origins and structure, the Know Nothing or 'American' party was initially a classic 'bottom-up' political movement.

Insurgent nativism alone might have been enough to deliver the death-blow to the mid-century party system. As it was, the established parties had also to contend with widespread popular distrust of their policies over slavery in the United States territories (those parts of the national domain that had yet to be admitted into full statehood). During the protracted political crisis from 1846 to 1850 a groundswell of 'free-soil' opinion – opposed to the spread of slave labor into the federal territories – worked to erode support for the two main parties in the North, while a surge of proslavery radicalism upset the political balance in parts of the lower South. The political settlement of 1850 appeared to restore broad public faith in the major parties, but the suspicion that both had a rogue element capable of undermining their popular credibility proved only too well-founded during the storm over Nebraska. A revolt of southern voters against a Whig party tainted by antislavery radicalism was paralleled by a haemorrhage of northern anti-Nebraska men from Stephen Douglas's apparently proslavery Democrats. The party system of the Jacksonian era lay in ruins.

Lincoln entered the political arena in the early 1830s, when the distinct-ive elements of American participatory democracy had clearly, if not definitively, emerged, and the first two decades of his public career coin-cided more or less precisely with the maturing of a mass democratic system. He lived in a society in which his fellow citizens came to accept and encourage boisterous electioneering, theatrical campaigns, unrationed oratory and the vivid polemics of local newspaper editors. It was a world in which men turned out to vote in proportions rarely matched by Americans before or since. Lincoln possessed a natural aptitude for the new politics: as a stump speaker he felt at ease with himself and, mostly, with the voters he addressed. He also had a clear view about the role and responsibilities of the republican citizen, as well as the duties of democratic leaders towards 'the people' – that is, whether politicians should lead or follow, teach or take instruction, act as pedagogue or demagogue. These issues – together with an analysis of Lincoln's personal power over his audience and his alertness to the cultural and sectional faultlines within the Illinois electorate – form the substance of the discussion that immediately follows.

This will act as a prelude to examining Lincoln's political career from the Nebraska watershed of 1854 to his celebrated debates with Stephen Douglas in 1858. Lincoln never felt the politically destabilizing power of public opinion more intensely during his Illinois career than in the mid-1850s, when the state's popular revolt over Kansas–Nebraska seriously wounded the Democrats, while the concerns of nativists made it improbable that the Whigs – as Whigs – would be able to seize the initiative. Lincoln himself would play an influential role in the interplay between public opinion and party agenda-setting, and in the stuttering emergence of a new anti-Nebraska, antislavery coalition. The experience left him well placed in 1858 to make a second bid for election to the United States Senate, now as a Republican. His first attempt, three years earlier, had been played out within the precincts of the state legislature, but now he was able, uniquely for the era, to take his candidacy direct to the people. He won the popular vote (though not, given the vagaries of outdated apportionment, the seat) after a campaign in which a speaker at the height of his rhetorical power succeeded in giving ordinary citizens a sense of their extraordinary moral duty to sustain his vision for the future of the American republic.

Lincoln, democratic politics and public opinion

Lincoln's thoughts on democratic politics and on the role of opinion were shaped by his experience of living and working in small western villages and towns, mostly numbering only a few hundred inhabitants; even Springfield, the new state capital, boasted a population of no more than 2,500 in the mid-1840s. These were face-to-face communities where people felt especially close to the institutions of government and to those who represented them. They prided themselves on their democratic faith and practice. Lincoln took the common view that the people were sovereign and that American government rested on public opinion. Even the most capable of public officers, he noted in 1850, 'are wholly inefficient and worthless, unless they are sustained by the confidence and devotion of the people'. Public sentiment might sometimes be wrong but, as he insisted in his Peoria speech, 'A universal feeling, whether well or ill-founded, can not be safely disregarded.' He would later declare, 'In this age, and this country, public sentiment is every thing. *With* it, nothing can fail; *against* it, nothing can succeed. Whoever moulds public sentiment, goes deeper than he who enacts statutes, or pronounces judicial decisions.'[2]

Early in his career Lincoln followed the fashion of promising obedience to the popular will. Standing for re-election to the state legislature in 1836 he told his Sangamon constituents that he would be 'governed by their will, on all subjects upon which I have the means of knowing what their will is; and upon all others, I shall do what my own judgment teaches me will best advance their interests'. But before long he shed this doctrine of 'instruction' and the idea that the politician was mainly a mouthpiece for the views of his constituents. Instead he came to work by the rule that public sentiment was to some degree plastic and that elected representatives had the power to shape it, as well as the moral responsibility to improve it. Opinion-forming was the most potent of all the politician's activities, for it provided the means of changing the government. Just as moral individuals could construct their own character and transform themselves, so public opinion was susceptible to education and re-direction, through the efforts of educators, ministers of religion and elected representatives. In his Lyceum speech of 1838, as elsewhere, he celebrated the power of lucidity, logic and reason to speak to the intelligence, self-respect and moral sense of the people. At the same time, pointing to the lessons of history and alarmed by the mobs that scarred the face of Jacksonian society, he warned against the arrival of some demagogic genius able to enchant a populace that had exchanged 'sober judgement' for 'wild and furious passions'.[3]

Lincoln's preference for swaying opinion by reasoned argument rather than by feeding prejudice remained a constant of his political career. It contributed to his protest over the resolutions of the Illinois General Assembly on slavery in 1837, when he refused to succumb to the visceral anti-abolitionism of most of his colleagues. It separated him from panicking nativists and fellow Whigs during the fever of anti-Catholic rioting and church burning in Philadelphia in 1844, when his Springfield resolutions against the proscription of foreigners earned him the respect of leading Democrats. It informed his opposition to the Mexican War, which he argued had originated in Americans' territorial avarice (reminding him of the western farmer who said, 'I am not greedy about land; I only want what jines mine'), and had been sustained by false patriotism and a wilful blindness to the fact of Polk's aggression. It would become even more self-conscious in his speeches after 1854: while Stephen Douglas played on white Illinoisans' deep racial fears to protect himself from the anti-Nebraska reaction, Lincoln appealed chiefly to their sense of justice and loyalty to the ideals of the Declaration of Independence, and castigated Democrats for striving to 'cultivate and excite hatred and disgust' against the black population. Lincoln was no saint, was careful not to move too far ahead of opinion and did fall into demagoguery at times. But Trumbull was off-target in describing him as 'a follower not a leader in public affairs'. The admiring Carl Schurz – contrasting Lincoln's 'candid truth-telling and grave appeals to conscience' with Douglas's use of the 'arts of the demagogue ... to befog the popular understanding' – was nearer the mark when he judged that Lincoln 'was not a mere follower of other men's minds, not a mere advocate and agitator, but a real leader'.[4]

That Lincoln held to this approach was a measure not only of his sense of duty toward the Founding Fathers but of a well-judged confidence in his ability to connect with the public. Only once in his political career did he lose an election when his name was on the ballot, and that was at his first attempt for office, in 1832. Even then he ran well and in his own precinct of New Salem, where he was best known, he won by an encouraging 227 votes to three. Thereafter he built an ever wider constituency of admirers and never lost his enormous popularity during his years in Illinois politics.

The power of Lincoln's personal appeal can be variously explained, but it clearly owed much to his common touch. Despite his personal flight from the land, he never lost that rapport with country folk that his upbringing in Kentucky and Indiana had fashioned, and which the mix of social backgrounds and classes in New Salem did little to erode. He kept the pronunciation and accent of his native state. As an increasingly successful Springfield lawyer, his tours of the Eighth Judicial Circuit brought him regularly into contact with the ordinary farming folk, artisans, tradesmen and merchants who made up the juries, thronged the court houses and clustered at the hotels. For some lawyers, professional success meant removal to the bustle of Chicago, but Lincoln turned down a partnership there at the end of his term in Congress, according to Judge

David Davis that he might stay close to the people that he knew and loved in the central counties. Of his years in New Salem it was said that his fondness for conversation and visiting had made him known to every man, woman and child for miles around, and it is clear that his later work as a traveling lawyer, allied to his memory for names, gave many central Illinoisans a sense that he recognized them personally. Lincoln was entirely alert to the political benefits of projecting his humble origins, but this did not mean that there was anything contrived about his interest in the common folk. He empathized with those who were, as he had been, struggling self-improvers; he had, in Joseph Gillespie's words, a deep faith 'in the honesty & good sense of the masses'. Lincoln had dignity, considerable reserve, few real intimates and a proper sense of the private: as Nicolay and Hay later remarked, in personal relations with him 'there was a line beyond which no one ever thought of passing'. But he was hardly aloof. He cultivated no airs and graces. In the words of a fellow lawyer, 'in the ordinary walks of life [he] did not appear the "great man," that he really was'.[5]

Lincoln was sharply aware of the figure he cut. His unprepossessing appearance and physical attributes did much to reinforce his appeal as a man close to the sons of the soil. Gangling and ill-proportioned as a boy, the adult Lincoln turned into what Joshua Speed rather brutally described as 'a long, gawky, ugly, shapeless, man'. His angular, leathery face, crowned with wiry hair, usually unkempt, was probably better described as plain, not ugly, and would indeed 'brighten like a lit lantern' with the animation of conversation and infectious laughter. But Lincoln certainly described himself as ugly and used his appearance as a weapon against himself, for humorous effect. It was less his height that merited special comment – though at 6'4" he was exceptionally tall for his time – than the extraordinary proportions of his long legs, large feet and, most remarkable of all, his arms. When he stood straight, with his arms at his sides, and his shoulders in their customary droop, the tips of his fingers reached nearly three inches lower than on the normal adult frame. Whether or not, as one observer claimed, Lincoln's enormous, bony hands resulted from wielding a heavy, cumbersome axe throughout his formative years, there is no doubt that his early regimen helped make him formidably strong. His physical prowess set him apart in New Salem, where a legendary wrestling match with the leader of a group of local rowdies, the Clary's Grove Boys, won him the admiration of all; that same reputation played its part in winning him his militia captaincy in 1832, and later, as a campaigning politician, helped him see off bullies bent on intimidating voters. Lincoln's attire only complemented the picture of an unaffected man of the people. Never the dapper politician, he was essentially inattentive to what he wore. His trousers were invariably too short, sometimes verging on the ludicrous. In his debates with Douglas he usually wore a linen coat but no stylish vest, or waistcoat, over his shirt. His brown hat was as faded as his ever-present green cotton umbrella.[6]

Lincoln used his great gifts in story-telling and humor to reinforce his folksiness, whether amongst the knots of men who gathered informally outside neighborhood stores and on court-house steps, or at set-piece political rallies. He had excelled in telling anecdotes and cracking jokes since boyhood, and the practice became an important part of his professional repertoire. Few could match him for the sheer number and pertinence of the humorous tales with which he illustrated almost any topic. 'The application was always perfect,' Joseph Gillespie recalled, 'and his manner of telling a story was inimitable although there was no *acting* in his manner. . . . [H]ow he could gather up such a boundless supply & have them ever ready at command was the wonder of all his acquaintences.' The stories often operated didactically, as parable, explanation and analogy. Though his early political opponents scolded him for 'a sort of assumed clownishness', his humor really did little if anything to compromise his essential dignity. Generally devoid of malice and sarcasm, and rarely made at anyone's expense, his jokes and anecdotes left no trail of wounded feelings and political bitterness. Many of Lincoln's friends detected in him an underlying sadness and reserve, which set limits to his sociability, but few would have dissented from Mentor Graham's claim that thanks to his lively conversation he was 'one of the most *companiable* persons you will ever see in this world'.[7]

The rapport that Lincoln enjoyed with his public was enhanced by his reputation for honest dealing. The nickname 'honest Abe' was not the fabrication of party publicists but a mark of the universal respect in which he was held as a lawyer of scrupulous honesty. This reputation spilled into the political arena, where he was widely perceived as just and fair-minded in debate, and averse to gaining an advantage by foul means. Turner R. King summarized his political speeches as 'candid – fair – honest – courteous', thus alluding to another source of public admiration, his avoidance of anger and his preference for tolerant debate. 'I never in my life saw him out of humor', recalled the Petersburg lawyer, Nathaniel W. Branson. Hill Lamon knew differently (sometimes, he said, Lincoln 'would burst out'), but he too agreed that Lincoln was in most circumstances good humored.[8]

Many thought Lincoln handicapped in some ways as an orator. His voice was unmusical and high-keyed. Early in a speech, before he warmed up, it was 'shrill-squeaking-piping, unpleasant', according to Herndon, who was not alone in alluding to its shrillness. Carl Schurz, another admirer, found his gestures awkward: 'He swung his long arms some-times in a very ungraceful manner. Now and then he would, to give particular emphasis to a point, bend his knees and body with a sudden downward jerk, and then shoot up again with a vehemence that raised him to his tip-toes and made him look much taller than he really was.' But these were scarcely disabling features. Many judged his gestures 'striking and original', not awkward, while his voice had great carrying power and reached to the extremities of even the largest crowd. Lincoln suffered none of the vocal strain that afflicted Stephen Douglas's rich baritone during their joint debates.[9]

Lincoln's power over his audiences derived far less from his physical attributes than from the clarity and directness with which he appealed to their understanding. Taking pains to provide cogent explanations of complex or obscure subjects had been a hallmark of his youth. Anne C. Gentry remembered how, as 'the learned boy among us unlearned folks', he patiently explained to her the movement of the earth, the moon and the planets. Preparing his addresses, whether to juries or to political rallies, he devoted enormous attention to making himself understood by all, however poorly educated. He spoke extemporaneously, though he prepared notes for the most important of his speeches, and used the clearest, simplest language. It was this concern for clarity that chiefly prompted his anecdotes, not for merriment for its own sake. Observing his developing rhetorical control over a period of three decades, Joseph Gillespie recognized that Lincoln 'confined himself to a dry bold state-ment of his point and then worked away with sledge hammer logic at making out his case'. When the young New Englander Edward L. Pierce encountered Lincoln for the first time, in Chicago in the mid-1850s, he was powerfully struck with the Illinoisan's 'logical and reflective power, and the absence of all attempt throughout his speech to produce a sensa-tional effect'. Pierce considered this an unusual style for the West, but rather failed to notice how far Lincoln had learnt from the 'frontier utilitarianism' of his idol, Henry Clay.[10]

Lincoln especially admired what he called Clay's 'great sincerity and thorough conviction . . . of the justice and importance of his cause'. He was far less enamored of the 'florid and exuberant rhetoric' of a Daniel Webster or the declamatory style of an Edward Everett, both widely esteemed as political orators. As Gillespie said, he 'despised ornament or display'. What made his speeches compelling was a lawyer's mode of analysis allied to a Clay-like earnestness. His oratory fell into the 'forensic' category of Whig rhetoric, typified by historical review, the examination of precedents, close questioning and the call to arms against an identified threat. Having heard him many time before a jury, Judge Thomas Drummond remarked that when thoroughly roused Lincoln 'would come out with an earnestness of conviction, a power of argument, a wealth of illustration, that I have never seen surpassed'. It was an earnestness which could build to impassioned eloquence.[11]

As one of his party's most effective speakers, Lincoln found himself called on regularly to take the stump during state and national canvasses, whether or not he was a candidate for office himself. He first made his mark as a self-composed, assured, often humorous speaker in Sangamon County in the boisterous campaign of 1836. The year of his arrival in the front rank, though, was 1840, when he survived the disfavor into which the Springfield Junto had fallen amongst rank-and-file Whigs. Hurt, like his fellow leaders, by the internal improvements issue, Lincoln feared he would be punished by the county nominating convention, which was dominated by delegates from the country areas. But his value as a talented and entertaining stump speaker overrode other considerations. He not only secured his renomination to the state legislature, but won appointment as a Whig presidential elector. In both the rumbustious Log Cabin campaign of that year and the Clay–Polk canvass four years later, Lincoln spoke far and wide, notably in the southern parts of the state where he could address his fellow Kentuckians in their own accents.[12] It was an enjoyable role, one he performed energetically and well. As well as giving many more people the opportunity to see a rising star, it allowed Lincoln to deepen his knowledge of public opinion in a state where evolving patterns of immigration, settlement and economic development were creating a variety of political subcultures.

Almost 400 miles in length from its northern boundary to its southern tip, Illinois was typical of the then Northwest in its broad patterns of settlement. As in Indiana and Ohio, its northern counties attracted migrants from New England and the wider Northeast, though at the time of Lincoln's arrival, in 1830, that region was still in essence a wilderness. In the southern and central counties, poor white pioneers from Kentucky, Virginia and the border slave states had developed an economy that mixed subsistence, primitive barter and a limited circulating currency; some of them had tried, and just failed, to introduce slavery into the new state. They were, in Governor Thomas Ford's description, 'a very good, honest, kind, hospitable people, unambitious of wealth, and great lovers of ease and social enjoyment'. The arrival of free-state immigrants into the northern prairies and the area around Lake Michigan gave rise to a profound clash of cultures. Southerners treated the northern farmers and merchants – much wealthier, more enterprising – with great suspicion, judging that the 'genuine Yankee was a close, miserly dishonest, selfish getter of money, void of generosity, hospitality, or any of the kindlier feelings of human nature'. Closely related to this was their conviction that all easterners were covert abolitionists, a judgment reinforced by the advance of radical antislavery parties in Chicago and its surrounding counties in the 1840s and 1850s. For their part, northerners regarded the southerner as 'a long, lank, lean, lazy, and ignorant animal, but little in advance of the savage state; one who was content to squat in a log-cabin, with a large family of ill-fed and ill-clothed, idle, ignorant children'. Such stereotypes profoundly affected political stances. Southerners, for instance, opposed the building of a canal from Lake Michigan to the Illinois river 'for fear it would open a way for flooding the State with Yankees'. One Jacksonian bitterly complained that 'the Yankees spread everywhere'. He expected them to overrun Illinois, for they 'could be found in every country on the globe'.[13]

Sectional chauvinism drew extra nourishment from religious antagonism. An important element of conflict during the early years of statehood was the clash between the rough, uneducated gospel pioneers, traveling on foot or by horse, unpaid and ready to suffer chronic physical hardship in the cause of Christ, and a new breed of college-trained, well-dressed, more sophisticated ministers, settled urbanites, who set about establishing Bible, tract and missionary societies, Sunday Schools, and other benevolent and educational operations. The conflict took on a sectional character since these more polished and intellectual preachers, men like John Mason Peck, came largely from the North and East. At issue were religious experience and Yankee cultural imperialism. The preacher 'Daddy' Briggs typified the hard-shell Baptists of southern counties; speaking of the richness of God's grace he declared that 'It tuck in the isles of the sea and the uttermost parts of the "yeth." It embraced the Esquimaux and the Hottentots, and some, my dear brithering, go so fur as to suppose that it takes in these poor benighted Yankees; but *I* don't go that fur.' Where such Yankee-hating reached its most intense people's politics were staunchly Democratic, with Whigs and later the Republicans perceived as the parties most open to New England influence.[14]

Lincoln knew well enough the conflicting outlooks associated with these two cultures, which co-existed in the central counties of the state. A large majority of Springfield's inhabitants in its early days were of Kentucky extraction, but its citizens also included several refined and educated New Englanders, as indeed was true of New Salem: from these

Lincoln learnt something of the flavor of New England well before he first visited that region, campaigning for Zachary Taylor in 1848. Attending Springfield's First Presbyterian Church, he was surrounded by conservatives with the strongest ties to the South, while the antislavery origins of the Second Presbyterian Church proffered first-hand evidence of the more radical outlook of the New England diaspora. We can be sure he grasped the relationship between these attitudes, church loyalties and voting behavior. Amongst the minority of antislavery clergy in Springfield were Albert Hale, pastor of the Second Presbyterian Church, and Lincoln's Baptist neighbor and friend, Noyes W. Miner. Both were college-trained Yankees. Hale, like Lincoln, had taken a stand against the Mexican War. Miner accepted a call from Springfield's Baptist Church in 1854 and, as a determined opponent of slavery, he had an uneasy relationship with the conservatives in his congregation. An old lady with southern connections told him, 'Mr. Miner, . . . your prayers almost kill me.'[15]

Lincoln's campaigning experience kept him alert not just to the importance of these cultural faultlines within public opinion, but to the often pivotal role of the religious affiliations of voters and candidates in shaping electoral outcomes. When, in the summer of 1846, he stood for election to Congress, his opponent was the formidable Methodist circuit-rider, Peter Cartwright. During the final days of the campaign Lincoln discovered that the Democrats were slyly circulating defamatory charges that he was 'an open scoffer at Christianity'. His private disclaimers failing to stop the smears, Lincoln arranged for the publication of a handbill setting out his religious position. 'That I am not a member of any Christian Church,' he wrote, 'is true; but I have never denied the truth of the Scriptures; and I have never spoken with intentional disrespect of religion in general, or of any denomination of Christians in particular.' Following his comfortable victory on 3 August, Lincoln asked the editor of the *Illinois Gazette* to publish the text of the handbill as a means of laying Cartwright's claims firmly and finally to rest.[16]

Cartwright's actions and Lincoln's response indicated a political cosmos profoundly shaped by popular religious culture and especially by its most powerful element, the forces of evangelical Protestantism. The evangelical religion that blossomed during the popular religious insurgency of the early decades of the nineteenth century, the so-called Second Great Awakening, far from being sealed off into its own private world, exerted a potent political influence, encouraging civic responsibility and popular participation in public affairs, shaping party loyalties and agenda, and providing the coin of politics. When Lincoln wrote in the handbill that 'I do not think I could myself, be brought to support a man for office, whom I knew to be an open enemy of, and scoffer at, religion', and that '[no] man has the right thus to insult the feelings, and injure the morals, of the community in which he may live', he recognized both the social grip of religion and the duty of politicians to respect the religious sensibilities of voters. He had expressed similar sentiments three years earlier, in 1843, when privately explaining his failure to secure the Whig nomination for the congressional seat: 'it was every where contended that no christian ought to go for me, because I belonged to no church, [and] was suspected of being a deist'. These influences, he judged, might not have been determinative, but 'they were very strong' and 'levied a tax of a considerable per cent upon my strength throughout the religious community'. He offered no complaint, however. Referring to the successful candidate, Edward D. Baker, a Campbellite, he wrote tellingly: 'As to his own church going for him, I think that was right enough.'[17]

Under the mature second party system both Whigs and Democrats annexed the support of elements within evangelical Protestantism and other Christian traditions, but each party projected itself differently toward that variegated constituency. Democrats offered a home to a variety of 'outsider' religious groups, including those who had suffered at the hands of the recently disestablished churches. In contrast, Whigs made a bid for the support of evangelicals who, while committed to the classic Protestant virtues of self-control and self-discipline, also welcomed an interventionist government that would regulate social behavior and maintain moral standards in public life. The party's publicists presented it as the friend of educational provision, temperance and the humane treatment of those who stood in a dependent relationship to the state, including Indians. They commonly portrayed their opponents as atheists and religious perverts, the allies of Mormons, freethinkers and Roman Catholics. In successive elections in the 1840s Whigs made much of their credentials as 'the Christian party'.

Lincoln's explanation of his failure to win the Whig nomination in 1843 was entirely consistent with this understanding of Whig political culture. He did not blame Christian influence alone for his defeat, but he was certain that Baker had been preferred at least in part because he was known to belong to a socially powerful and numerous Protestant denomination, while he, Lincoln, belonged to no church and was understood to hold unorthodox beliefs. He also judged that his involvement in an absurd duel with James Shields, an episode about which he seems to have felt considerable embarrassment, even shame, had alienated necessary Christian support. It may even be that Lincoln's temperance address to the Washingtonians of Springfield in 1842 had, as William Wolf has suggested, 'rubbed many church members the wrong way' and acted as an additional liability at the Whig convention in 1843.[18] Lincoln's experience did not mean that there was no room in the party for those tainted with religious heterodoxy. After all, Lincoln won the Whig nomination and the subsequent congressional election in 1846. But there were enough Whigs of conventional piety to make an issue of candidates' religious orientation and moral standing.

Lincoln also reflected on the likelihood that, as a member of the Disciples, Baker had with few exceptions 'got all that church'. Moreover, he noted, Mary Todd Lincoln and some of her relatives were Presbyterians, while others were Episcopalians, 'and therefore, whereever it would tell, I was set down as either the one or the other'.[19] Lincoln was uncomfortable with religious sectarianism but he knew that interdenominational conflict was an inseparable part of the experience of central Illinoisans, and that intense religious loyalties and antagonisms, and attitudes toward the proper role of government in sustaining a Christian republic, could determine their choice of party.[20] Though the devout were to be found in all parties, and though local context mattered, certain denominations showed much stronger support for one party over another. Reform-minded, new-school Calvinists were strongly Whig; Democrats' particular strength lay amongst Catholics, antimission Baptists and 'ritualist' Protestants. Many Methodists, Baptists and old-school Calvinists rallied to Whiggery, though vast numbers in these churches, especially the southern-born, remained loyal to a Democratic party rooted in Jeffersonian tolerance of religious pluralism.

Illinois public opinion and the anti-Nebraska fusion movement

Lincoln's sensitivity to popular opinion would prove especially valuable during the period of political revolt and party confusion in the mid-1850s, when his Whig party ceased to exist. Illinois Whigs had stayed within range of their customary share of the vote during the fall elections of 1852, taking 42 percent of the ballots cast, and they even increased their congressional representation in Washington. Yet within four years, by the time of the next presidential contest, most of them had accompanied Lincoln into the Republican camp. Forming the majority in the new party, they helped it to an impressive sweep of state offices. Their votes for the Republicans' first ever presidential candidate, John C. Frémont, came close to adding Illinois to the column of eleven free states which would support him in the electoral college.

During the complex process of party realignment even the most experienced political leaders kept only a tenuous grip on a volatile and unpredictable electorate. Lincoln, both as an observer of that upheaval and one of those most deeply involved in forging the Republican coalition, combined a pragmatic respect for the realities of voters' deeply held attitudes with a conviction that political leaders had the duty to crystallize into a coherent moral case what the public had begun only hesitantly to express. Lincoln's natural political caution combined with his assured reading of Illinois opinion to help fashion a party that would challenge the Democrats far more successfully than the Whigs had ever done.

The two main parties in Illinois owed their stability and continuity after 1840 less to their political structures, which were relatively weak, than to the relevance of their principles to their supporters' lives. Voters looked with suspicion on party organizers. It took time for them to accept that the discipline of party might be consistent with republican values. (Lincoln himself criticized the Democrats' new-fangled convention system early in his career, as *subversive of individual freedom and private judgment*, though in time he grew into a thorough-going party regular.)[21] Even at the height of the Whig–Democrat party system many voters switched parties or split their tickets. Parties lacked permanent, centralized governing councils, and had to depend on conventions, committees, private political clubs, and other short-term campaigning bodies for their institutional energy. In consequence, as the economic issues on which voters' support had been built in the 1830s and 1840s lost their relevance, so party organization proved inadequate to maintain discipline. When two new clusters of public issues asserted themselves in the early 1850s the party coalitions began to look ominously brittle.

By 1850 one in every eight of Illinois's 850,000 inhabitants was foreign-born, and as the population doubled over the next decade the proportion grew to one in five. They included thousands of German and Irish immigrants, mostly Catholic and many employed in railroad construction. It is hard to chart with any precision the hostile nativist response to these arrivals: the secrecy of the local societies formed to pursue a Native American agenda kept them very largely hidden from view. But as well as urging restrictions on citizenship, they included many who wanted to crack down on the newcomers' consumption of lager, whisky and other liquor, from which the civic life of well-regulated Protestant communities was apparently at risk. Their temperance demands threw both major parties into some confusion. Whigs stayed silent from electoral caution, even though their constituency included many prohibitionists; Democrats, historically the refuge of the foreign-born, could scarcely risk supporting a temperance law that reeked of xenophobia and thus limited themselves to a pious declaration against the evils of alcohol. The beneficiaries of both parties' timidity were the Know Nothings.

At the same time, even before the repeal of the Missouri Compromise, both parties were reminded of how much the issues of slavery and race might threaten their cohesion. The Black Law that passed the state legislature in 1853 prevented slaveowners from freeing their slaves in Illinois and prohibited the immigration of free blacks. It enjoyed massive public support, but each party – and especially the Whigs – had a dissenting minority. The next year, when Douglas pushed through the Nebraska bill, he was quite unprepared for the public reaction that followed and the danger it posed to party unity. He noted ruefully that he could have traveled home by the light of his own burning effigies and when he did make the journey back to Illinois from Washington in September he encountered ominous disaffection in Chicago, where flags hung at half mast and bells were tolled for an hour. Lincoln scarcely exaggerated when he declared that Douglas had stunned his fellow citizens, who 'reeled and fell in utter confusion'.[22] The proliferation in the summer of 1854 of cross-party protest meetings, comprising Illinoisans of all classes and conditions, gave both parties warning of the potential wrecking power of popular outrage. In the event, Douglas's network of personal alliances, his formidable control of patronage and his making Nebraska a test of loyalty allowed his party to survive, though not before it suffered losses that would seriously handicap it in electoral battles to come. Whigs, though, would splinter fatally.

Neither party's future course was at all clear, however, when Lincoln and other Illinois leaders looked ahead to the state's fall elections in 1854. Until late August, Lincoln had publicly kept his own counsel, reading and listening to the arguments of others. Only then did he speak out, working energetically to secure the return of his district's Whig congressman, Richard Yates. Lacking cast-iron evidence about Lincoln's personal hopes and strategic view of the campaign, we have to infer them from his speeches, circumstantial indications and second-hand reports. These leave little room to doubt that he saw early on the political opportunities that Douglas's dangerous measure had opened up. If he could harness the popular revolt against Douglas into the service of an enlarged Whig party, conservative and antislavery, he would both serve the cause of freedom and construct the means by which he might return to Washington, this time as a United States senator.

According to William Jayne, the Lincoln family's physician and a staunch free-soiler, Lincoln had reacted with unexplained despair when

Jayne, without prompting, inserted in the Whig *Illinois State Journal* early in September a declaration that Lincoln would himself run for the state legislature. Far from welcoming this announcement, Jayne later recalled, Lincoln 'was then the saddest man I Ever Saw – the gloomiest: he walked up and down ... almost crying'. To Jayne's insistence that he remain a candidate Lincoln replied, 'No – I can't – you don't Know all – I Say you don't begin to Know one half and that's Enough.'[23] Lincoln knew that the state constitution prohibited the election of serving legislators to the United States Senate. To run for the legislature, which was imminently to choose a successor to the incumbent Democratic senator, would rule him out of consideration. But to decline to run would be an act of disloyalty to the party, costing him the very support he needed for his grander objective. Reluctantly Lincoln became an official candidate.

In running as a Whig and campaigning for a fellow Whig, Lincoln stood with those who thought that anti-Nebraska voters would be most effectively mobilized through existing parties. There may have been an element of straightforward political self-interest at work here: any politician looking to be chosen as their US senator by the next legislature could be more confident of influencing familiar colleagues in an old party than in an uncertain new one. At the same time, however, events showed Lincoln's pragmatic wisdom. He recognized that (in contrast to other parts of the Old Northwest, where new 'fusion' parties enjoyed some success) there was as yet little enthusiasm for blending all of Douglas's opponents into a single organization. The minority of more radical Whigs in Chicago and the northern counties, of largely Yankee and English extraction, warmed to the idea of working with radical third-party men – the 'Free Soilers' – in a unified new antislavery force that would replace 'dead and lifeless' organizations, and resist the expansion of slavery.[24] But in central and southern areas Lincoln's fellow Whigs, conservative and largely southern-born, remained unimpressed. Most called simply for the restoration of the Missouri Compromise; a few even sided with Douglas. Lincoln knew that to reconstitute Whiggery in a new Fusion, or 'Republican', party would alienate many more voters than it would bring in.

By his words and deeds during the first week of October 1854, the time of the State Agricultural Fair in Springfield, Lincoln made especially clear his position on the proper relationship between his party and the radical forces. Speaking in the state house, he chided those conservative Whigs who were afraid that an anti-Nebraska stance would expose them to Democratic accusations of abolitionism. 'Will they allow me as an old whig to tell them good humoredly, that I think this is very silly?' Good

Whigs took firm 'national' ground, between the extremes of Douglasite proslavery demagoguery and constitution-defying abolitionism, and should welcome any who wanted to join them on it. 'Stand with anybody that stands RIGHT. Stand with him while he is right and PART with him when he goes wrong. Stand WITH the abolitionist in restoring the Missouri Compromise; and stand AGAINST him when he attempts to repeal the fugitive slave law. In the latter case you stand with the southern disunionist. What of that? you are still right.'[25] Lincoln recognized the importance of drawing antislavery radicals into the Whig coalition, but only on Whig terms. This had been the means of the party's greatest presidential triumph, in 1840, and its absence had been influential in their most galling defeat four years later.

Lincoln's action the day after his Springfield speech made a similar statement, but now to a different constituency. A group of radicals from northern Illinois had come to the state capital to organize 'a party which shall put the Government upon a Republican track'. They were led by Owen Lovejoy and Ichabod Codding, both New Englanders, both Congregational ministers, both with an abolitionist political pedigree. Lovejoy's brother Elijah had been the nation's first abolitionist martyr. They all heard Lincoln in the Hall of Representatives. Mesmerized by the tone and substance of the speech, Lovejoy invited him to join them at their convention the next day. Lincoln was reluctant to get involved. Instead he rode north to keep a court appointment. In his absence, and without permission, the 'Republicans' appointed him to their state central committee. Discovering this by accident some weeks later, he declined the nomination. He told Codding, 'I suppose my opposition to the principle of slavery is as strong as that of any member of the Republican party; but I had also supposed that the *extent* to which I feel authorized to carry that opposition, practically, was not at all satisfactory to that party.' It was one thing to cooperate with the radicals in opposition to the prevailing Nebraska policy, quite another so to steer the Whig ship toward new moorings as to give legitimacy to Democrats' taunts that Lincoln was a covert abolitionist.[26]

Lincoln knew that fusion presented as many difficulties for anti-Nebraska Democrats as it did for the Whigs. Douglas's course had alienated several of his party's ablest men, including Lyman Trumbull, John M. Palmer, Norman B. Judd and John Wentworth. Lincoln saw the political risk they ran in attacking a measure that had been made a test of Democratic party loyalty. Moreover, to resist the Nebraska bill was one thing, to throw in their lot with their historic Whig opponents quite another. Did cross-party agreement over slavery extension provide a basis for longer-term cooperation or unity? What was to stop the minority of able Democrats being swamped and subordinated in a Whig-dominated party? In the event, the elections showed the continuing power of traditional party loyalties, with many anti-Nebraska Democrats staying at home if there were no Democrat candidates to support, but otherwise turning out with enthusiasm.[27]

Political nativism proved a further obstruction to the cause of fusion, and Lincoln needed few lessons in the uneasy fit between Know Nothingism and the anti-Nebraska movement. Many nativists were evangelicals who regarded Catholicism and slavery as equally poisonous to the well-being of a Protestant republic; antislavery Whigs, for instance, commonly populated Know Nothing lodges and temperance societies. But by no means all Illinois nativists were clear-eyed opponents of slavery. Nor were unyielding antislavery men necessarily sympathetic to nativism; those in this category naturally included the foreign-born themselves, especially the Germans, but it embraced native-born Americans, too. Lincoln himself was no friend of Know Nothing principles and was privately contemptuous of nativist intolerance and irrationality. 'How can any one who abhors the oppression of negroes, be in favor of degrading classes of white people?' he asked his friend Speed; Know Nothings wanted to re-write Jefferson's Declaration to read 'all men are created equal, except negroes, *and foreigners, and catholics*'.[28] He was, though, wise enough to recognize nativism's popular force. Many of his close Whig allies became Know Nothings; the order's local leaders wanted to run him for the legislature (an invitation he refused); and his own congressional candidate, the Methodist Richard Yates, was friendly with the same men. When, despite Lincoln's efforts, and following the defection of foreign-born Whigs, Yates became one of the few anti-Nebraska men to lose to a Douglas Democrat, Lincoln had uncomfortable evidence of nativism's destructive potential.

Despite Yates's defeat, the anti-Nebraska forces secured a majority in the General Assembly. This was not exactly a Democratic rout, but it was a chastening defeat for Douglas's men in a state where his party was used to dominance. They relied more than ever on the loyalty of the Irish and those of southern stock, while anti-Nebraskans secured an unprecedented level of political cohesion amongst reform-minded Protestants. Lincoln himself enjoyed a comfortable margin of victory, reflecting his huge personal appeal in Sangamon County, and then embarked explicitly on what he had surely intended all along, a campaign to become the next US senator from Illinois. Amongst other things, this meant refusing his seat in the legislature – the elective body – to make himself an eligible candidate, an action which appeared to put self before cause and did his reputation some harm amongst radical antislavery men.

The new assembly comprised a heterogeneous and fragmented membership of 100, still acutely conscious of the old party labels. Lincoln calculated that 43 were strictly Douglas men: these would seek the return of congressman James Shields, a staunch supporter of the Nebraska bill. The anti-Nebraska majority was constructed from Whigs and Democrats in a ratio of about two to one. Quite a number of these were drawn toward a fusion of all into a new Republican organization. To be elected as senator, Lincoln had to recruit well beyond the Whig core. Amongst radicals of the Fusion-Republican tendency he was compromised by his southern birth and associations, and by reports of his nativism (which, though false, he could not publicly deny without alienating the essential support of Know Nothing members). But thanks to the intervention of the old antislavery war-horse, Joshua Giddings of Ohio, and to the local efforts of his supporters – David Davis, Leonard Swett, Hill Lamon and Herndon, who had personal connections with the radicals – he won over all these Republicans to his cause.[29]

To assure his election Lincoln also needed the anti-Nebraska Democrats who had broken with Douglas. They included Judd and Palmer, who with a handful of others in the balloting stood resolutely by their fellow Democrat, the impeccably antislavery Lyman Trumbull. They felt no kinship with Whigs or Know Nothings and believed that their election as Democrats to a Democrat-dominated Assembly left them no other honorable course. Lincoln led on the first ballot, by 45 votes to Shields's 41. Trumbull secured just five votes, exactly the number Lincoln needed to win outright. But the Trumbull group refused to budge. Thereafter Lincoln's vote gradually slipped. After six inconclusive rounds the regular Democrats dropped Shields for the more electable Joel A. Matteson, the state's popular governor. Anti-Nebraska forces now began to shift toward Trumbull, and by the ninth round Lincoln's total had dropped to 15. Sensing the danger of a victory for Matteson, Lincoln directed the remnant of his followers to help Trumbull, who was narrowly elected on the tenth ballot. Lincoln was deeply disappointed but, unlike his wife, showed no bitterness toward the new senator and his cluster of supporters, with whom he remained on good terms. After all, they owed a debt of gratitude which they would later repay with interest.

The senatorial election delivered a blow to Douglas but it also showed the continued potency of the old party names and the need to rise above them if the full possibilities of the still divided anti-Nebraska movement were to be realized. The Whig label had hurt Lincoln as much as it had helped him. There were lessons to be learnt, but at least he had the time in which to digest them: no election was due in Illinois until late 1856 and his immediate priority was to return to his neglected law practice. Over the next twelve months Lincoln watched as the swirls of public opinion around liquor and nativism prevented a full realignment of antislavery forces. In the summer of 1855 temperance men lost a referendum on prohibition, but only after a stirring campaign in which alliances over drink cut across those over slavery. A similar confusion grew out of the evolving politics of Know Nothingism, which drove a wedge between native-born antislavery voters and a powerful bloc of immigrant antislaveryites, including an estimated 20,000 Germans. The nativist movement continued to grow after the 1854 elections, pulling in well-placed Whigs and prompting the launch of the 'American party' the following summer.

This was an inauspicious setting for Owen Lovejoy's renewed efforts during 1855 to engineer a fusion of all the anti-Nebraska elements. Emphasizing the readiness of the radicals to unite around a moderate platform, he joined Joshua Giddings in trying to persuade Lincoln to lead a new Republican party. Lincoln accepted that a new political combination was needed, but judged the time was not ripe: 'I have no objection to "fuse" with any body,' he wrote to Lovejoy in August, 'provided I can fuse on ground which I think is right', namely opposition to slavery's extension. But the American party's presence made the scheme premature. 'Until we can get the elements of this organization, there is not sufficient materials to successfully combat the Nebraska democracy with. We can not get them so long as they cling to a hope of success under their own organization; and I fear an open push by us now, may offend them, and tend to prevent our ever getting them.' Responding the same month to an inquiry from his old friend Joshua Speed about his political moorings, Lincoln wrote, 'That is a disputed point. I think I am a whig; but others say there are no whigs, and that I am an abolitionist. . . . I now do no more than oppose the *extension* of slavery.'[30] The essentials of the Whig doctrine that had prompted his support for the Wilmot Proviso remained, but the party structures that had accommodated those antislavery views were in flux. As he looked beyond the boundaries of Illinois in the fall of 1855, he saw victories for Republicans, Americans, and, ominously, renascent Democrats – but not Whigs. The year drew to a close with Lincoln and the state's other anti-Nebraska men still lacking the common ground on which to build an inclusive antislavery organization.

Yet forces were at play which would achieve that outcome within a matter of months. First, as Lincoln observed, political nativism proved less robust than its organizers had hoped, and the time would come when antislavery fusionists would be able to take advantage of its grow-ing divisions. The national council of the American party had alienated many of its free-soil northern members by adopting an ambivalent posi-tion on slavery in the territories; a final split between northern and southern wings followed within the year. Moreover, the defeat of the prohibitionist forces in a state-wide referendum gave antislavery fusion-ists firm grounds for rejecting an anti-liquor stance likely to repel voters.

Secondly, and more important still, events outside Illinois during 1855 and the first half of 1856 ensured that even when the initial anger at the Nebraska Act had lost its edge, the disparate elements of the anti-Nebraska coalition continued to hold together. Month after month, presses throughout the free states carried opinion-shaping reports from Kansas territory, cataloging the intimidation suffered by valiant free-soil settlers at the hands of the proslavery forces, especially the 'border ruffians' from Missouri. Newspaper editors lamented illegal voting, mass violence, dra-conian proslavery legal codes and ineffectual territorial administration by the mediocre, timid agents of the remote and pro-southern president, Franklin Pierce. Not all the violence had to do with slavery, nor was it all on one side, but the upshot was white-hot indignation across the North. It stopped anti-Nebraska Democrats from slowly drifting back into the fold of their party. It nourished increased Fusionist-Republican ambition. It led antislavery Whigs to abandon thoughts of reviving their party. Kansas helped keep the steel in Lincoln's soul, if it were needed. His friend Mark Delahay, a free-soil editor there, corresponded regularly with him, and Lincoln's outrage at 'the spirit of violence' and 'foul means' in the territ-ory roused him to give money for the defense of its *bona fide* settlers.[31]

Increasingly sure that the only way forward lay in a new, moderate antislavery party, Lincoln set his compass in 1856, a presidential election year, by attending a state gathering of antislavery editors at Decatur on 22 February. On the same day at Pittsburgh, representatives of Republican parties from across the North met in a national organizing convention. Lincoln, although selected as an Illinois delegate to that meeting, joined the journalists at Decatur instead: Republican fusion had made greater progress elsewhere in the free states than at home, and he knew that the first priority for Illinois was to secure an effective state-wide anti-Nebraska party capable of winning the fall elections. He played a leading role in drafting the declaration of principles and the resolutions. The meeting avoided the name 'Republican', still tainted with abolitionism since the fusion effort in 1854. Taking an essentially moderate line on slavery, it called for the restoration of the Missouri Compromise, upheld the Fugitive Slave Law and accepted non-interference with slavery in the existing slave states, but also affirmed the free-soil principle that slavery was the local exception to the rule of national freedom. To avoid alienating the foreign born, the platform extolled religious toleration and opposed any change in the naturalization laws; at the same time it nodded toward Know Nothings by promising to repel attacks on the common school system – a reference to Catholic attempts to get public funds for their own parochial schools. A state anti-Nebraska convention on 29 May at Bloomington would nominate a state ticket.

Lincoln's role at the February meeting, where he was toasted as 'the next United States Senator', gives the lie to the argument that he was especially diffident in advocating the prospective new party. Still, like Trumbull, Peck and other anti-Nebraska moderates, both Whig and Democrat, he had two understandable reasons for anxiety as he looked ahead to Bloomington. Would Lovejoy and the radicals taint or control the movement? Even if not, would the disparate elements cohere, or prove unstable? As all came to recognize, these were risks that simply had to be run. There was no way back for the anti-Nebraska Democrats, with unforgiving Douglasites in control of the party. There was nowhere else for antislavery Whigs to go. As Herndon told Yates, 'If you do not go, you, Lincoln, and all others will be buried politically forever.'[32]

In the event the Bloomington convention was a brilliant success. Every stripe of antislavery opinion was there: radicals, moderates and conservatives, Whigs and dissident Democrats, Germans and nativists. Yet harmony prevailed amongst the nearly 300 delegates. Moderates set the tone, having controlled the local conventions that had selected many of those present. Lincoln seems to have worked to prevent conservatives fleeing from the unnerving presence of Lovejoy and Codding, but in fact the radicals, alert to the need for pragmatic compromise, caused no trouble. The presence of many volunteers, informal representatives of their communities, did much to give the assembly more the flavor of a mass meeting than a convention, but the party leaders, coordinated by the Whig lawyer Orville Browning, gave shape to the business.

Their task was made all the easier by very recent events in Kansas and Washington. Violence returned to the infant territory after a freezing winter. On 21 May a nasty little incident involving the looting and burning of a free-state press and hotel was promptly labelled 'the sack of Lawrence' by antislavery propagandists. The following day, in the Senate chamber, congressman Preston Brooks of South Carolina beat Charles Sumner, the antislavery senator from Massachusetts, about the head with a gutta percha cane – to avenge what Brooks deemed Sumner's dishonorable verbal assault on his state and his kinsman, Senator Andrew Butler.

'Bleeding Kansas' and 'bleeding Sumner' sharpened the Bloomington delegates' determination to unite. They rallied around a platform framed under Lincoln's eye and which showed the imprint of Decatur in its moderation on slavery, its silence on temperance, and its attack on the proscription of the foreign born. They endorsed a diverse ticket of candidates that gave Democrats the prospect of more than their fair share of the best offices, including the governorship, and rewarded both Germans and former Know Nothings. They appointed delegates to represent them at the imminent Republican national convention, while continuing to avoid using the term 'Republican' in their own proceedings.

Lincoln brought the convention to its climax with a spell-binding, 90-minute speech of unequalled eloquence. Delivered extemporaneously, the address was so inspirational that the reporters present, including Herndon, stopped taking notes. But the brief account of the 'lost speech' points to themes that were foreshadowed in his addresses of 1854, namely the alarming sea-change in southern thought on slavery; the slaveholders' reversal of the policy of the nation's Founders; the need to defend not just the territorial integrity of the Union, but its republican values of freedom and equality; the decadent course of northern Democrats; and the need for all who would oppose the slave power to fuse into a single crusading force. What gave the speech its additional power, according to Herndon, was Lincoln's moving beyond slavery as an issue to be argued 'on grounds of policy', to address 'the question of the radical and the eternal right'. In his Peoria speech Lincoln had asserted that 'the great mass of mankind . . . consider slavery a great moral wrong', and that no statesman could safely disregard that feeling: there is something of the responsible political sociologist in this mode of leadership. At Bloomington, however, it seems Lincoln has become one of the 'mass of mankind' himself, fired by the moral enormities of slavery as well as its policy implications. 'Now he was newly baptized and freshly born,' Herndon recalled, 'he had the fervor of a new convert; the smothered flame broke out; enthusiasm unusual to him blazed up; his eyes were aglow with an inspiration; he felt justice; his heart was alive to the right; his sympathies, remarkably deep for him, burst forth, and he stood before the throne of the eternal Right.' Herndon insisted that his description was not literary hyperbole. Lincoln really had blended logic, pathos and enthusiasm to a degree he had never done before. The speech was 'justice, equity, truth, and right set ablaze by the divine fires of a soul maddened by the wrong'.[33]

What led Lincoln to abandon his customary restraint and appeal so earnestly to the soul of his audience as well as to its head? In part the answer lies in the nature of the assembly and the occasion. Lincoln addressed a gathering broadly agreed on fundamentals. He was not on the stump, faced with coaxing the unpersuaded, the neutral and the openly hostile. Addressing the faithful, Lincoln took on the coloring of his audience; in the company of enthusiasts and converts, even preachers, he saw his task to be one of rallying and inspiring them in preparation for the campaign ahead. But there was probably something deeper at work. Observing the success of the Bloomington convention, the usually self-contained Lincoln must have felt a sense of euphoria and release. The meeting was, if not the culmination, at least a major landmark on the way to establishing the effective political force for which Lincoln had implicitly called in his response to the Nebraska Act. The Peoria speech spoke of 'the liberal party throughout the world': their representatives in America ('lovers of liberty' appalled by a great moral wrong) expected their political leaders to address the ethical concerns that shaped public opinion.[34] Implicit in much of Lincoln's subsequent course was a recognition that the moral constituencies brought into focus by the Nebraska Act needed effective and articulate political leadership. Whether through a continuing Whig party or the subsequent Republican coalition, Lincoln acted from 1854 to 1860 in a way that sought to clarify and publicize the lines dividing what he saw as the two fundamental moral constituencies in the nation, those who saw slavery as wrong, and those who either did not care or praised it as a positive good.

Essential to Lincoln's moral coalition were the huge numbers of reform-minded Protestants, especially the evangelicals. How might they be accommodated? The problem, as he saw only too well, was that their agenda was not just varied, but politically divisive. The nativist and temperance views of so many evangelicals, though compatible ideologically with antislavery, alienated other potential members of the coalition. Lincoln himself was no believer in the legal compulsion of prohibition, nor the friend of Know Nothing proscription. He had neither the appetite nor the language actively to exploit the religious and cultural frictions on which nativism was constructed. But the fracture within national Know Nothingism left the way open to recruit its reforming Protestants into a coalition centered on the moral certainties of antislavery and freedom. A number of these were present in Bloomington and when Lincoln spoke, in celebration of a cemented coalition, he had every reason to speak with the evangelical enthusiasm of the 'newly baptized and freshly born'.

In the fifty or so speeches he made while campaigning for the fall 1856 elections, Lincoln reverted to his more customary rhetorical style, reasoned and unemotional. It better suited his audience of conservative

Whig-Americans in southern and central Illinois, whom he rightly identified as the swing voters. Once James Buchanan, untainted by the Kansas–Nebraska business, had won the Democrats' nomination for president, and the American party had lined up behind an Old Line Whig, ex-President Millard Fillmore, Lincoln hoped the Republican national convention would play equally safe and select John McLean, a Supreme Court Justice and another former Whig. Instead it nominated the dashing western explorer, John C. Frémont. For a while it looked as if Lincoln might secure the vice-presidential place, which would have boosted the party in the Northwest (and reflected his increasing national reputation), but the position went to another ex-Whig, William L. Dayton of New Jersey. Lincoln saw at once the implications of the nominations and set about targeting the likely Fillmore voters, especially in his state's central counties. Ideally, he hoped the Americans would withdraw, or unite with the Frémont men, but since that was unlikely he used his speeches and lithographed letters to show how the American party's campaign would be self-defeating and would promote a Democratic victory. In early August Lincoln estimated that Buchanan would win by 7,000 votes, or four percentage points, if it remained a three-way race.[35] The prediction was impressively accurate: in November, Buchanan's percentage margin was exactly that, his victory (by 9,000 votes, in a high turnout) due to Fillmore's intervention. Conservative Whigs hated the Democrats but they also feared the sectional stance of 'Black' Republicans. Fillmore gave them a way of resisting the overtures of both.

Still, the November results were by no means disheartening. Lincoln could reflect that the Republican party (a name he continued to avoid throughout the campaign) had shown the staying power, the organization, the moderation of program, and the breadth of appeal to win the governorship and the other state offices. He could reflect, too, that he as much as anyone had helped to fashion the new party. He had done so by avoiding impetuous action at a time of profound, uncontrollable shifts in public opinion. By late 1856 the worst upheavals were over. Even so, the process of party construction was not yet complete – and Lincoln's most sustained and celebrated personal engagement with the power of public opinion still lay ahead.

The senatorial campaign of 1858

Voters were due to return to the polls in 1858, to elect a new state legislature. That body in turn would choose a United States senator.

Douglas's term of office was drawing to a close, his re-election far from assured. Lincoln thought the 'Little Giant' could be beaten and knew that many Illinois Republicans considered him the man to do it. These included a network of able and well-placed advisers: members of the new state administration, former political associates in the legislature, and fellow lawyers. Importantly, the leading Trumbull men of 1855, especially Norman B. Judd, acknowledged the force of Lincoln's claim. Amongst the state's main anti-Democrat papers Lincoln had the firm support of the *Chicago Press and Tribune* and the *Illinois State Journal*. No one could doubt that he wanted the senatorship. He had good humoredly said as much to the gathering of editors at Decatur in February 1856. When a keen Republican wrote in the summer of 1857 urging 'that something should be done *now*, to secure the next Legislature', Lincoln did more than generally concur: behaving like a candidate, he gave detailed advice on how to prepare canvass lists – and urged it be done discreetly, to avoid alerting the opposition.[36]

On the national stage, two political developments in the first twelve months or so of Buchanan's presidency would deeply influence how Illinois Republicans made their nomination and then took their campaign to the people. First, in March 1857, the United States Supreme Court, sitting under Chief Justice Roger B. Taney, gave its ruling in the Dred Scott case. Scott was a slave who had been taken by his master, an army surgeon, into Illinois and then Wisconsin Territory, before being brought back to the slave state of Missouri. Since Illinois was a free state and Wisconsin a region from which slavery had been excluded by the Missouri Compromise, Scott sued for his freedom. By a majority decision, the Court rejected the claim. Taney declared that Scott, as a Negro, had no right to sue: the Founders of the republic, considering African Americans inferior, had not meant them to enjoy the rights of citizenship guaranteed by the federal Constitution. Furthermore, in a startling use of the due process clause of the Fifth Amendment, Taney argued that the United States Congress had acted unconstitutionally when it passed the Missouri Compromise and prevented property-holding in slaves in the northern part of the Louisiana Purchase.

The decision of the Democrat-leaning Court, dominated by southerners and southern sympathizers, seemed problematic for Douglas, for if slaveholders had the right to take their chattels into the territories, where did that leave popular sovereignty and local self-determination? Douglas remained unruffled, however, despite the popular outcry in the North. He noted that Taney's ruling related solely to the powers of Congress, not of territorial legislatures, whose 'police regulations' in defense of property were essential to protecting slaveowners' rights: thus, he argued in a speech in Springfield on 12 June, the decision 'sustained' popular sovereignty. At the same time he buttressed his position by exploiting the deep racial prejudices of central Illinoisans, endorsing Taney's view that blacks were not embraced by the Declaration of Independence, and classifying Republicans as 'amalgamationists' bent on a complete social and sexual mixing of the races.

The decision confronted Republicans, too, with a problem. If Congress lacked the power to exclude slavery from the territories, where did that leave the unifying core of the party's program, the use of national power to stop slavery spreading? Lincoln's response, like many of his colleagues', was tempered by his respect for the courts: he saw judicial process, in David Donald's words, as an essential defense against 'the unreasoning populism of the Democrats, who believed that the majority was always right, and the equally unreasonable moral absolutism of reformers like the abolitionists, who appealed to a higher law than even the Constitution'.[37] But, as he explained in his riposte to Douglas on 26 June, he found it impossible to submit to what he considered the 'erroneous' decision of 'a divided court', one based on historical misrepresentation and studied blindness to precedent, and one which could be honestly questioned because it had 'not yet quite established a settled doctrine for the country'. He denied that Republican criticisms amounted to lawless resistance. It was Douglas, the Democrats and their allies on the Court who were engaged in an assault on the constitutional rights of the black race, bound and free. Their exclusionist interpretation of the Declaration of Independence was a corrupting novelty, designed to tighten the grip of slavery: 'if its framers could rise from their graves, they could not at all recognize it.' Confronting Douglas's amalgamationist smears, Lincoln protested 'against that counterfeit logic which concludes that, because I do not want a black woman for a *slave* I must necessarily want her for a *wife*'. The Founders had not meant 'to declare all men equal *in all respects*. They did not mean to say all were equal in color, size, intellect, moral development, or social capacity.' They did, however, consider them 'equal in "certain inalienable rights, among which are life, liberty, and the pursuit of happiness"'.[38]

Lincoln used the Dred Scott decision, and Douglas's defense of it, to contrast the ethical positions of the two parties. Republicans found in the Declaration 'a standard maxim for free society', for which all should labor and which 'even though never perfectly attained' should be 'constantly approximated', so that its deepening influence would increase 'the happiness and value of life to all people of all colors everywhere'. But

Douglas's version, by limiting its meaning by time and place to the struggle of white colonists against the British crown, 'frittered away' the document's value as a universal statement of rights, leaving it a 'mangled ruin'. Starkly put, 'Republicans inculcate, with whatever of ability they can, that the negro is a man; that his bondage is cruelly wrong, and that the field of his oppression ought not to be enlarged.' Democrats, by contrast, 'deny his manhood; deny, or dwarf to insignificance, the wrong of his bondage; so far as possible, crush all sympathy for him, and cultivate and excite hatred and disgust against him; . . . and call the indefinite outspreading of his bondage "a sacred right of self-government" '.[39]

Within a year of the Supreme Court's ruling, political developments in troubled Kansas worked to complicate these simple polarities of party conflict. In the town of Lecompton a constitutional convention met to prepare the way for Kansas statehood. Free-state men, fearing trickery, had boycotted the election of delegates, who set about drawing up a constitution that protected the status of the 200 slaves already in the territory. The convention also stipulated a referendum – not on the entire document, but only on a clause that would allow further slaves into the state. In view of the Lecompton Constitution's proslavery character, 10,000 free-state men abstained, leaving the way clear for the endorsement of the constitution 'with slavery' by a vote of 6,143 to a mere 569. Buchanan would have preferred the whole document to have been submitted to a popular vote, but he could see no illegality in what had been done by a properly constituted body, and was keen to remove a tense if no longer bleeding Kansas from the national political arena. Knowing that his party had the congressional votes to secure its passage, the president gave the Lecompton Constitution his approval.

A defiant Douglas stunned the political world during the early months of 1858 by leading the fight in Washington against its adoption. His energetic revolt against the administration, and unprecedented disloyalty to his party, was a measure of how personally threatening the senator found the president's action. Having badly misjudged popular feeling in the Northwest in 1854 by surrendering on the Missouri Compromise, Douglas could not afford now to abandon his personal gold standard of popular sovereignty out of deference to a southern-dominated administration. Meekly accepting the Lecompton solution, considered even by many northern Democrats as a flouting of the popular will, would be an act of political suicide. Mustering all his considerable skills in debating and infighting, the Little Giant insisted that the slavery clause was not the issue; what concerned him was the paramountcy of local majority sentiment. Under his generalship the disparate forces of opposition,

Republican and Democrat, free-soiler and abolitionist, succeeded in blocking the passage of the constitution through Congress. By virtue of a compromise it was resubmitted to the people of Kansas in August and drew the support of just one voter in seven.

The Lecompton battle won Douglas the everlasting enmity of Buchanan and the extravagant plaudits of long-standing foes. Most outspoken of the band of eastern Republican admirers was Horace Greeley, the editor of the influential *New York Tribune*, which circulated widely throughout the free states and had some 10,000 readers in Illinois. As the congressional struggle reached its climax in the spring, he began to contemplate giving anti-Lecompton Democrats a clear run in the fall elections, perhaps even welcoming them into the party. Lincoln sounded a note of alarm as early as December 1857, complaining to Lyman Trumbull about the *Tribune*'s 'eulogizing, and admiring, and magnifying' of Douglas. 'Does it, in this, speak the sentiments of the republicans at Washington? Have they concluded that the republican cause generally, can be best promoted by sacraficing us here in Illinois?' Mixing exasperation and sarcasm, he added, 'If so we would like to know it soon; it will save us a great deal of labor to surrender at once.' Illinois Republicans overwhelmingly shared Lincoln's indignation at eastern meddling and could not conceive of burying the hatchet with Douglas, their abusive and bitter arch-enemy, in pursuit of 'an unholy alliance'. Party leaders, encouraged by Lincoln, decided to call a state convention in Springfield on 16 June. Its chief purpose would be to announce to the world that Lincoln was the 'first and only choice' of Republicans for the Senate.[40]

In so acting, the Springfield meeting offered a rebuke to eastern brethren and shored up the party against slippage toward Douglas Democracy. Selecting Lincoln also denied regular Democrats the opportunity of fomenting voter confusion and even Republican disunity during the fall campaign: it removed the fear that a newly-elected legislature would send to Washington some other Republican, perhaps the wayward and powerful 'Long John' Wentworth of Chicago, a renegade Democrat. The resolution nominating Lincoln, as he himself intimated, 'was passed more for the object of closing down upon this everlasting croaking about Wentworth' by hostile editors.[41] Pragmatism, then, underlay the action of the Springfield delegates. But what they did, imposing on the state legislature a subordinate role in selecting a US senator by morally removing its freedom to choose, was practically unheard of. The implications for the campaign that followed could scarcely have been more profound. Voters would in effect directly choose their senator. In 1854 Lincoln's campaign for the Senate had *followed* the November polls; the targeted voters were the newly elected General Assemblymen. Now he and Douglas – confirmed as the pre-eminent Democrat at his party's state convention in April – would take their candidacies straight to the people.

The Lincoln–Douglas contest of 1858 brilliantly revealed the extraordinary appetite of the Illinois public for democratic engagement. Later generations have added layers of romantic embellishment to the story, but even after these are peeled away we are still left with a remarkable example of sustained participatory politics. For four months, starting in the heat and dust of summer, the two men stumped their way across the state, covering between them some 10,000 miles by rail, river and road, and delivering around sixty set speeches each, in addition to dozens of shorter, impromptu addresses. It was a punishing schedule demanding great physical endurance, but both candidates drew much psychological strength from contact with tens of thousands of enthusiastic voters, courteous and attentive more often than not. Neither cancelled a speaking engagement, though by the end of the campaign Douglas's voice had largely given out, while Lincoln seemed still to be growing in energy. Regiments of support troops – candidates, speakers, organizers, newspaper editors, musical bands – gave every locality the opportunity to share in what by common consent was a remarkable and unprecedented canvass. 'The prairies are on fire', reported the correspondent of an eastern paper. 'It is astonishing how deep an interest in politics this people take.'[42]

What gave the campaign its particular piquancy were the seven joint debates between the two men. Though only a small part of the total canvass, they drew the largest crowds, attracted a caravan of reporters and stenographers, and stimulated interest nation-wide. Lincoln proposed them, on the advice of Republican leaders, partly because of the early ridicule he attracted for trailing after Douglas and speaking at the same places a day later. Joint debates would let him profit from the bigger numbers that Douglas could draw as a national political figure, and prevent the Little Giant's largely ignoring him. His challenge put Douglas on the spot: Lincoln would be the beneficiary, but to refuse him would imply cowardice. Reluctantly, Douglas accepted the principle of joint discussions, but stipulated only seven debates, not the fifty or so the Republicans wanted. These were to be three-hour meetings, one in each of the state's congressional districts where the men had not yet spoken. Douglas would open and close on four occasions, Lincoln three.

The issue of slavery in the territories dominated the debates. This was not the imposition of politicians upon an unwilling public, but a measure of slavery's perceived relevance amongst politically-alert plain folk. Alluding to slavery's power to stir up men's minds 'in every avenue of society – in politics, in religion, in literature, in morals, in all the manifold relations of life', Lincoln drew a laugh at Alton when he promised his hearers, 'If you will get everybody else to stop talking about it, I assure [you] I will quit before they have half done so.'[43] In some county contests, campaigners addressed local economic concerns, pertinent following the financial panic of 1857, and harnessed popular disputes over the railroads, but neither of the Senate aspirants saw any advantage for himself in these issues. Douglas stuck to the same essential questions in his speeches throughout. Lincoln's had more variety, but his fundamental purpose remained constant from the moment of his first campaign utterance, a 30-minute address in the Hall of Representatives at Springfield on the evening of 16 June, just a few hours after receiving his party's nomination. This, his 'House Divided' speech, provided the strategic anchor for his whole campaign. There was nothing spontaneous about it. He had probably been distilling its ideas for several months. Unusually, he wrote out the whole text, the work of a week or so. Then he committed it to memory, delivering it without notes.

In the first and best-remembered part of that speech, the briefest of its three sections, Lincoln addressed the growing agitation over slavery and declared that the conflict would only cease when 'a crisis shall have been reached, and passed'. Taking a deeply familiar biblical text – 'A house divided against itself cannot stand' – he set out the premise on which he constructed this and all subsequent speeches. Slavery and freedom were incompatible. 'I believe this government cannot endure, permanently half *slave* and half *free*.' But the struggle had to be resolved *within* a continuing Union. 'I do not expect the house to *fall* – but I *do* expect it will cease to be divided. It will become *all* one thing, or *all* the other.' There could be no permanent middle ground between the two conditions. Indefinitely continuing the *status quo* was not possible. Either the Republican policy of arresting the further spread of slavery, while avoiding the direct assault on the institution that the radical abolitionists advocated, would establish a public consensus 'that it is in the course of ultimate extinction'. Or, alternatively, pro-slavery advocates would succeed in making it 'alike lawful in *all* the States, *old* as well as *new* – *North* as well as *South*'.[44]

Lincoln devoted the main part of his speech to showing how events since 1854 provided powerful circumstantial evidence for just such a proslavery conspiracy, one designed to overturn the Founding Fathers' intentions and make the institution national. Through the combined energies of Douglas, Pierce, Taney and Buchanan ('Stephen, Franklin, Roger and James'), the Nebraska doctrine and the Dred Scott decision had forced open all the territories to slavery. All that remained for the completion of their common plan (the filling of a 'nice little niche') was 'another Supreme Court decision, declaring that the Constitution of the United States does not permit a *state* to exclude slavery from its limits'. Lincoln conceded that he did not *know* that there was a preconcerted plan or conspiracy, but he was ready to predict that 'We shall *lie down* pleasantly dreaming that the people of *Missouri* are on the verge of making their State *free*; and we shall *awake* to the *reality*, instead, that the *Supreme Court* has made *Illinois* a *slave* State.'[45] If Lincoln's supposition of a conspiracy stretched the facts, his concern over the 'nationalizing' of slavery was not far-fetched. The right of free states to obstruct the entry of slaveholders and their slaves was already being tested in the courts; it was only a matter of time before Taney and his colleagues could be expected to rule again.

Douglas, on Lincoln's analysis, was a part of the problem, not the solution. Lincoln reportedly told a legal associate during the campaign, 'Douglas will tell a lie to ten thousand people one day, even though he knows he may have to deny it to five thousand the next.'[46] No doubt envy at the senator's greater reputation also played its part, but Lincoln's clear dislike of his rival derived primarily from his distrust of the Little Giant. His main purpose in 1858 was to show that Douglas's doctrine of popular sovereignty was not just practically unreliable as a bulwark of freedom (as Kansas had shown), but that it embodied a dangerous moral neutrality over slavery. The senator's dispute with Buchanan, and his uniting with Republicans in Washington, was only tactical and superficial: it was, Lincoln said, a mere 'squabble', representing no divergence on fundamentals. The truth really lay in Douglas's 'care not' policy, laid out during the Lecompton debates: this worked to create a corrosive climate of moral indifference, ultimately as threatening to freedom as the efforts of the most extreme slaveholder. Douglas, like Fillmore in 1856, inhabited the muddy middle ground of politics and offered a superficially attractive home for conservative free-soilers. Lincoln aimed to show them they were wrong.

Lincoln's attempt to establish Douglas as the ally of proslavery radicalism made strategic sense and drew national attention, but the trenchancy of his language left him open to the charge of extremism himself. Advisers who heard a draft of the House Divided speech urged caution. Asserting the incompatibility of slavery and freedom made him sound like an abolitionist. A Chicago Republican editor feared that Lincoln seemed to pledge the party to a war on southern slavery. Lincoln denied this intention, but later conceded that he might have been engaged in a 'foolish' prediction. By continuing to press the argument, he left himself open to Democrats' counter-attacks. Douglas himself naturally seized on the issue in his first campaign speech, at the Tremont House in Chicago, on 9 July. With Lincoln sitting on the balcony behind him, he castigated his bold advocacy of 'a war of sections, a war of the North against the South'. Using language that he would repeat throughout the campaign, he joined Lincoln to radical abolitionism, a belief in racial equality, the practice of 'amalgamation with inferior races', and 'degeneration, demoralization, and degradation'.[47] These were ideal topics for diverting attention from his own record as senator.

Some charges stuck better than others. Douglas's efforts to associate Lincoln with Lovejoy and the radicals of 1854 rather backfired when Lincoln was able to show that the militant platform which he had allegedly supported was a 'forgery'. Lincoln also had little difficulty in addressing the seven questions which Douglas put to him in the first joint debate, at Ottawa, trying to connect him with the abolitionists of northern Illinois: he firmly reiterated his support for the Fugitive Slave Law, the rights of slaveholders within the states and in the District of Columbia, and for the continuation of the internal slave trade. Douglas might have made more of Lincoln's imprecision about how restricting slavery would effect its extinction: to the limited extent that the senator did address this (by charging that the Republicans would inhumanely starve a growing slave population), Lincoln provided a riposte through his allusions to the colonizing of the black population and to the voluntary aspect of slavery's demise. Far more problematic for Lincoln, however, were Douglas's appeals to the prevailing racial attitudes of his audience.

The taunt of believing the black race the equal of the white dogged Lincoln throughout. It was exactly what his Springfield dialogue with Douglas in June 1857 would have led him to expect and he tackled the issue head on in the first joint debate, at Ottawa, in the north of the state. Facing a politically friendly audience, overwhelmingly Republican, Lincoln denied Douglas's charge that he favored 'perfect social and political equality with the negro', and declared: 'There is a physical difference between the . . . [white and black races], which in my judgment will probably forever forbid their living together upon the footing of perfect equality, and inasmuch as it becomes a necessity that there must be a difference, I, as well as Judge Douglas, am in favor of the race to which I belong, having the superior position.' Then, to loud cheers, he insisted that, even so, 'there is no reason in the world why the negro is not entitled to all the natural rights enumerated in the Declaration of Independence, the right to life, liberty and the pursuit of happiness'. A month later, at Charleston, in east-central Illinois, in front of a more conservative and politically undecided crowd, Lincoln used some of the same language, but now dropped the cautious nod to open-mindedness implicit in the phrase '*probably* forever', made no reference to equal rights or to the Declaration of Independence and elicited considerable laughter by stroking his audience's prejudices over the idea of inter-racial marriage.[48]

These were the remarks of a mainstream Illinois politician seemingly untroubled by the second-class civic status of the black population, so far as he had given it much thought; who was most probably free from many of the common prejudices against black people; who thought those who traded politically on fears of black equality indulged in 'low demagoguism'; and who was acutely sensitive to the particular composition of his audience. His words at Ottawa, in front of Lovejoy and radical abolitionists, are more remarkable for what they asserted for blacks than for what they denied them. At Charleston, by contrast, cautious amongst Old Line Whigs, he avoided the language that had so excited Chicago radicals two months earlier. Then he had declared: 'let us discard all this quibbling about this man and the other man – this race and that race and the other race being inferior, and therefore they must be placed in an inferior position. . . . Let us discard all these things, and unite as one people throughout this land, until we shall once more stand up declaring that all men are created equal.'[49]

Lincoln's remarks on race are best understood in the context of his largely defensive strategy throughout the earlier debates. Douglas appeared to have the initial advantage. Though Lincoln held his own in the first meeting, at Ottawa, his advisers regretted a lost opportunity for lambasting the senator 'as a traitor & conspirator [and] a proslavery bamboozelling demogogue'.[50] On friendly ground, in Freeport, Lincoln in the second debate did take the offensive with a series of questions. Could the people of a territory, he asked, 'in any lawful way . . . exclude slavery from its limits prior to the formation of a State Constitution'? Douglas's reply – the so-called Freeport Doctrine – was not new, but in answering the question in the affirmative he both reasserted the integrity of popular sovereignty and demonstrated his distance from the national administration. Since Douglas's split with Buchanan and the southern Democrats was already beyond repair, Lincoln's main aim was probably to maximize electoral support for the 'Danites', the small band of Buchanan loyalists in Illinois. But the gain, if any, was modest, given that Lincoln's larger purpose was to establish the shared ground between Douglas and the proslavery Democrats. The debate concluded rather lamely and Lincoln's advisers feared that Douglas had kept the advantage.

Over the next two debates, at Jonesboro in the deep south of Illinois, commonly known as 'Egypt', and at Charleston, Lincoln developed no great head of steam. He played safe when confronting the small, southern-born, Democratic and strongly negrophobic audience at Jonesboro, making play of Douglas's Freeport Doctrine; at Charleston he sought mainly to nettle Douglas with the charge, first made by Trumbull, that the senator had secretly worked to deny Kansans a vote on slavery, but the evidence was complex, even tedious, and did little to excite the crowds. Charleston, however, was Lincoln's watershed. In the three final debates, over a period of eight days during the first half of October, Lincoln focused far less on defending himself against Douglas's charges, sidelined the racial issues, concentrated chiefly on the moral issues at stake and reached new heights of eloquence.[51] At Galesburg, a hive of Yankee and Scandinavian abolitionists, a visibly tiring Douglas faced an opponent invigorated by the warmth of the huge crowd in the grounds of Knox College. The following week at Quincy, in the west-center of Illinois, Lincoln ('fresh, vigorous and elastic' according to the *Illinois State Journal*) confidently deployed the same moral case, undeterred by the good numbers of Democratic voters present. Traveling down the Mississippi to Alton for the final debate, Lincoln knew he had to win the river town. Though downstate, it had a sizeable Republican population, including many antislavery Germans who had rallied to Trumbull and to other high-profile Democratic defectors. Lincoln, in what was the last widely broadcast speech of the campaign, here produced his most sustained eloquence, explaining why the advances of slavery had to be stopped and casting the whole conflict with Douglas as a battle between right and wrong.

The poison of slavery and the damage it did 'as a moral, social and political evil' provided Lincoln with his most potent themes at Galesburg, Quincy and Alton. Of all the political issues that had unsettled the republic in its short history, 'this Slavery question has been the only one that has ever endangered our republican institutions – the only one that has ever threatened or menaced a dissolution of the Union – that has ever disturbed us in such a way as to make us fear for the perpetuity of our liberty'. And if political self-interest dictated that slavery be set on a course of ultimate extinction, then the needs of aspiring free white labor similarly demanded it be quarantined. Slavery was the antithesis of economic meritocracy. To the cheers of the Alton crowd, Lincoln explained that 'irrespective of the moral aspect of this question as to whether there is a right or wrong in enslaving a negro, I am still in favor of our new Territories being in such a condition that white men may . . . settle upon new soil and better their condition in life'. This should be the privilege not just of native-born Americans, including emigrants fleeing the economic suffocation of the slave states, but also of 'Hans and Baptiste and Patrick' and *free white people everywhere*, the world over'. Yet where would they be able to go in future, if slaveowners migrated into every territory as Douglas's policy allowed?[52]

Lincoln, though, *did* respect 'the moral aspect', and profoundly so. The ethical elements had been there from the outset of the campaign, in Springfield and Chicago, as they had been since the Peoria speech of 1854, but Lincoln now gave them even greater salience and it was the moral case, not the socio-economic argument, that provided his rhetorical power. He reiterated his fundamental position, that all men, regardless of skin color, possessed the natural rights set down in the Declaration of Independence. 'I hold that . . . [the negro] is as much entitled to these as the white man. . . . [I]n the right to eat the bread without leave of anybody else which his own hand earns, he is my equal and the equal of Judge Douglas, and the equal of every other man.' There was not, in other words, 'a sort of inequality between the white and black races, which justifies us in making them slaves'. Jefferson's document, he repeated, 'meant to set up a standard maxim for free society, which should be familiar to all: constantly looked to, constantly labored for, and even though never perfectly attained, constantly approximated and thereby constantly spreading and deepening its influence, and augmenting the happiness and value of life to all people, of all colors, everywhere'. Lincoln lamented that Douglas and Taney had recently reinterpreted the Declaration's 'sacred principles', in defiance of the intentions of the authors and their immediate successors, including Henry Clay. By asserting that the document did not include black Americans, they had concocted a new doctrine that operated 'to dehumanize the negro – to take away from him the right of ever striving to be a man'.[53]

The Republicans' policy of restricting slavery within its existing boundaries was, as Lincoln represented it, 'nothing more than a return to the policy of the fathers' and to the morality that underpinned it. The republic's Founders had not known how to remove slaveholding, but none of them had expected it to survive for long. They had set their compass by abolishing the Atlantic slave trade and excluding slavery from new territories, placing slavery where 'all sensible men understood, it was in the course of ultimate extinction'. Allusions to it in the Constitution were couched in 'covert language', to avoid marring the 'face of the great charter of liberty'. Republicans, too, would 'so deal with it that in the run of time there may be some promise of an end to it'. They would meet the obligations of the Constitution by leaving it undisturbed in the slave-holding states; they would respect the legitimacy of the Fugitive Slave Law; they would make no move against slavery in the District of Columbia, even though the federal government had the authority to do so. But they would 'oppose it as an evil so far as it seeks to spread itself'.[54]

By contrast, Lincoln cast Douglas as a moral neuter. Painstakingly, he showed that indifference toward the struggle between freedom and slavery was consistent only with seeing no wrong in the peculiar institution: 'no man can logically say he don't care whether a wrong is voted up or voted down. He may say he don't care whether an indifferent thing is voted up or down, but he must logically have a choice between a right thing and a wrong thing. He contends that whatever community wants slaves has a right to have them. So they have if it is not a wrong. But if it is a wrong, he cannot say people have a right to do wrong.'[55] Douglas's 'don't care' position held up only if property in slaves was as morally inoffensive as ownership of horses or other goods.[56] Lincoln drew laughter when he accorded Douglas 'the high distinction . . . of never having said slavery is either right or wrong. Almost everybody else says one or the other, but the Judge never does.'[57]

Douglas's party, Lincoln declared, built its policy around this 'central idea' that slavery was not a wrong. Since by no means all Democrats positively asserted that slavery was right, the party seemed to allow room for antislavery feeling. But this was self-delusion amongst slavery's purported opponents. In practice their party silenced them by asserting the unfitness of time and place, whatever the circumstances. 'You must not say anything about it in the free States, *because it is not here.* You must not say anything about it in the slave States, *because it is there.* You must not say anything about in the pulpit, because that is religion and has nothing to do with it. You must not say anything about it in politics, *because that will disturb the security of "my place."*' Whenever schemes of gradual emancipation surfaced, as in Missouri, Democrats cheered their defeat. At Quincy, perhaps from weariness, Douglas made an uncharacteristic slip, saying the republic could 'exist forever divided into free and slave States', giving Lincoln more ammunition for arguing that the two parties inhabited different moral universes. Indeed, Lincoln insisted, Democrat logic and Douglas's belief that 'upon principles of equality it should be allowed to go everywhere' would make slavery national. He elicited laughter and applause when he remarked, 'Judge Douglas could not let it stand upon the basis upon which our fathers placed it, but removed it and *put it upon the cotton gin basis.*'[58]

Lincoln, then, was determined to show Illinois voters that they faced a clear choice between 'the men who think slavery a wrong and those who do not think it wrong'. Douglas had created an ethical fog, pretending that there existed some sort of middle ground between the forces of slavery and freedom, while simultaneously 'blowing out the moral lights around us'. Douglas denied the moral sincerity of the Republican leadership, claiming that 'the mere ambition of politicians' drove his opponents to attack slavery, but Lincoln scornfully pointed to slavery's independent power to disturb society 'in all the manifold relations of life' well beyond the arena of politics. What had divided the Methodists, and continued to shake the Presbyterians, the Unitarians and the American Tract Society? 'Is it not this same mighty, deep seated power that somehow operates on the minds of men, exciting and stirring them up in every avenue of society – in politics, in religion, in literature, in morals . . . ?' Douglas practiced 'a false statesmanship that undertakes to build up a system of policy upon the basis of caring nothing about *the very thing that every body does care the most about'*. The true statesman confronted the issue, and presented the voters with the clearest of choices. Lincoln set out the options most eloquently at Alton, when he declared that 'the real issue . . . is the eternal struggle between these two principles – right and wrong – throughout the world. They are the two principles that have stood face to face from the beginning of time; and will ever continue to struggle. The one is the common right of humanity and the other the divine right of kings.' The tyrannical principle had taken on different guises in different settings: sometimes the monarch 'who seeks to bestride the people of his own nation and live by the fruit of their labor', sometimes 'one race of men . . . enslaving another race'. In each case the moral choice was transparent.[59]

These October speeches thus assumed the character of political sermons. No admirer of revivalist preaching, Lincoln during the campaign nonetheless adopted the moral earnestness of an evangelical minister, shining a light into the ethical murk generated by Douglas's political initiatives, avoiding anecdotes and jokes, and urging his audiences to decide between good and evil, right and wrong.[60] If he shunned the extremes of evangelical self-righteousness, he still deployed scriptural language and allusion, sometimes for humorous effect (Douglas, he scoffed, warred on Republicans' principles 'as Satan does upon the Bible'), but more usually to offer Christian encouragement for sustaining the principles of his chief text, the Declaration of Independence. 'The Savior, I suppose, did not expect that any human creature could be perfect as the Father in Heaven; but He said, "As your Father in Heaven is perfect, be ye also perfect." He set that up as a standard, and he who did the most towards reaching that standard, attained the highest degree of moral perfection. So I say in relation to the principle that all men are created equal, let it be as nearly reached as we can.' The Declaration's principles were inspired by 'truth, and justice, and mercy, and all the humane and Christian virtues'.[61]

Lincoln's earnest marking out of this moral faultline was driven by a conviction that Douglas genuinely represented an ethical threat to Republicanism.[62] It derived, too, from a belief that the political campaigner should be more than a mere mirror reflecting back the attitudes of his hearers: believing that 'an evil can't stand discussion', Lincoln judged that the campaign's undimmed spotlight on slavery 'taught a great many thousands of people to hate it who had never given it a thought before. What kills the skunk is the publicity it gives itself. What a skunk wants to do is to keep snug under the barn in daytime, when men are around with shotguns.'[63] Lincoln's consciousness-raising approach, however, was anchored in shrewd political pragmatism. He argued a progressive moral case, but did so in the confidence that his words would resonate amongst a huge and growing political constituency predisposed to ask hard questions about the peculiar institution: Protestant churchgoers.

Churches exerted a powerful influence over the lives of antebellum Illinoisans. They offered an opportunity for grass-roots involvement which even political parties, whose local expressions were uneven and often impermanent, did not rival. They also provided crucial channels for the flow of local and national information, which was by no means restricted to narrowly-defined church business. As Linda Evans has noted, Illinois politicians and other opinion-formers regarded the churches as 'a highly desirable prize', since by the late 1850s their ministers, missionaries and meeting houses covered the state.[64] Nearly 800,000 accommodations served the needs of an even larger number of members and 'hearers'; the majority of the adults in the total population of 1,700,000 in 1860 were connected to one church or another.

They embraced all political views, even within the same communion, but antislavery opinions were scattered widely throughout the varieties of Protestantism. The most concentrated expressions of hard-edged abolitionism were found amongst the smaller denominations – the Reformed Presbyterians (or Covenanters), Freewill Baptists, Wesleyan Methodists and, above all, the 10,000 or so Congregationalists. Strongly 'Yankee' in origin and outlook, and mostly located in the northern counties, they articulated an optimistic, postmillennialist creed. The political gulf between these communions and the larger, centrist Protestant denominations, seemingly unbridgeable and widening in the 1840s, narrowed under the pressure of events in the following decade. Even moderates within the three biggest Church families – Methodist, Calvinistic Baptist and Presbyterian – reacted uneasily to the South's role in the growth of sectionalism; alarmed by the Nebraska bill and the subsequent Kansas imbroglio, a variety of conferences, districts, presbyteries and other local denominational gatherings expressed growing anxiety over southern aggression, and passed ever more militant antislavery resolutions. Along with Unitarians, Quakers and 'Christians' (Campbellites), these denominations remained explicitly anti-abolitionist but equally, in the northern and central counties in particular, made no secret of their dislike of slavery, advocating colonization schemes as a step toward emancipation. These sentiments found favor amongst even Episcopalian and Old School Presbyterian conservatives. The Sangamon Presbytery, which embraced the Lincolns' own church, called for 'wise and prudent means' to end slavery – scarcely a radical rallying cry, but an indication that opinion was edging slowly but discernibly toward antislavery politics amongst the tradesmen, merchants, lawyers, doctors and other commercial and professional folk who made up the middle and upper echelons of Springfield's Presbyterian society.[65]

By contrast, the conservatism of the rural and southern-oriented folk that comprised the Disciples, antimission Baptists, and much of the membership of mainstream Methodist and Baptist denominations, made them deeply suspicious of postmillennialist Yankee reformers. The most 'hard-shell' amongst them espoused a 'do-nothing' theology which made them naturally receptive to Douglas's 'don't care' approach to slavery.[66] The state's Catholics, mostly of Irish extraction, were equally alienated by activist Protestants. But the burgeoning immigration from the northeastern states and from Protestant Europe, threw these communities on to the defensive. So, too, did the growing *rapprochement* between abolitionist and anti-abolitionist evangelicals. This process underlay the state's reshaped party alignments of the 1850s, as the abolitionist stream, channeled by Zebina Eastman, Jonathan Blanchard, Owen Lovejoy and other ex-Libertymen and Free Soilers, coalesced with the anti-southern, antislavery flood-tide of Republicanism; it was a process symbolized by the absorption into the *Chicago Tribune* of Eastman's abolitionist *Free West*. Always politically oriented, Illinois abolitionists remained steadfastly resistant to the Garrisonian Christian anarchism that had splintered eastern reform.

From his extended dialogue with the Illinois public, Lincoln knew well enough the mainly Protestant sources of antislavery energy. Though cool toward the moral absolutism of the abolitionists, he still argued his case in terms which he knew would stir up the antislavery moderates of the mainstream churches. His fusion of Jeffersonian and scriptural precepts, set in the context of Whiggish self-improvement, was sweet music to the ears of those antislavery Christians whose church resolutions, circulating in the political as well as the religious press, likewise blended the Enlightenment idealism of the Founding Fathers with New Testament theology. Lincoln rubbed shoulders and talked with people of this kind throughout the campaign, men and women whose names and faces he often knew. Thus, for instance, John Alexander Windsor, a recent refugee from ministry amongst Maryland slaveholders, was introduced to Lincoln at Galesburg by fellow Methodist Henderson Ritchie, who knew them both. Windsor seized the chance to assure Lincoln of his support, shake his hand, and bid him God-speed. Lincoln's religious correspondents also contributed to the small change of the campaign, encouraging him to use 'a little more *positive* language . . . so that everyone, no matter how humble or unintelligent he is, can and must see & feel that you are *right*, & that he [Douglas] is *wrong!*', and to hold on to 'high ground . . . up to the standard of the Christianity of the day'. As one saw it, 'the contest . . . is no less . . . than for the advancement of the kingdom of Heaven or the kingdom of Satan, . . . for an advance or a retrograde in civilization'. Lincoln developed his strategy of moral aggression out of a deep understanding of the audience for whom it was intended.[67]

At its inspired best, Lincoln's rhetoric galvanized Republicans. A Vermilion County Quaker rejoiced that Lincoln was 'fairly mounted on the eternal invulnerable bulwark of *truth*' against an opponent who had 'the devil on his side'. Carl Schurz, who heard Lincoln for the first time at Quincy, was bewitched by the candidate's 'tone of earnest truthfulness, of elevated, noble sentiment, and of kindly sympathy', and his flashes of 'lofty moral inspiration', which the young German contrasted grimly with Douglas's 'unprincipled and reckless' appeals to prejudice. According to the Methodist John Windsor, whereas the inebriate Douglas epitomized 'the astute politician whose supreme concern is to win votes by all means', Lincoln beamed 'with downright honesty, sincerity and goodness', irresistibly creating the impression of a 'conscientious statesman . . . who felt that he had some message of mighty importance imperative upon him to deliver'. At Petersburg, in the final days of the canvass, James Miles shared in an electric thrill as Lincoln mixed words and action in his apostrophe to liberty: 'God gave me these hands . . . to feed this mouth.' Horace White of the *Chicago Press and Tribune*, who accompanied Lincoln for most of the campaign, thought his eloquence unsurpassed 'when his great soul was inspired with the thought of human rights and Divine justice'. And White's colleague, the young stenographer Robert Hitt, judged the Alton speech Lincoln's greatest: its moral clarity captivated this son of a Protestant minister. He was not alone in pointing to the effect on Lincoln's audiences at Alton and elsewhere of his 'melting pathos'.[68]

It was, then, not just the attraction of an entertaining day out that drew snaking processions of vehicles to these vast gatherings, but also the sense of there being huge issues at stake. However, by raising the moral stakes, sharpening the ethical line between himself and Douglas, and saying that those who did not think slavery wrong 'ought to leave us', Lincoln employed a double-edged sword. He could expect the strategy to attract some crucial groups of voters; these included antislavery Democrats, and those Republicans who might otherwise have taken the bait laid by the 'new', re-invented, post-Lecompton Douglas. At the same time, however, it would hardly reassure those Old Line Whigs on whom the 1856 elections had turned in the dozen or so central counties of the state. In these conservative quarters, Lincoln's language seemed only to confirm the earlier anxieties prompted by his House Divided speech. Recognizing this danger, Lincoln used the campaign to emphasize his distance from abolitionists and their schemes of racial equality, and to deny that he represented any threat to the South or to the integrity of the Union. Republicans respected the rights of southerners: anyone so impatient as to disregard the constitutional guarantees protecting slavery 'ought to leave us'. 'There will be no war, no violence', he insisted. To the extent that radical abolitionists had rebuked Lincoln for his caution and for his negative remarks on black equality, swing conservative voters should perhaps have been reassured. But at the same time Lincoln was not without friends, perhaps even admirers, in the radical camp, people sympathetic to his vision of the Republican party as a broad-based, inclusive force bound together by a common perception of slavery as a wrong and by a conviction that its victory alone would bring to an end the nation's chronic sectional agitation.[69]

Lincoln's strategy very nearly worked. He grew increasingly hopeful as election day approached, and when voters trooped to the polls on 2 November, Republican supporters actually outnumbered Douglas Democrats by 4,000 ballots out of the quarter of a million cast.[70] His popular majority showed that Lincoln had managed to consolidate the party's gubernatorial vote of 1856, holding on in particular to substantial numbers of antislavery ex-Democrats whom Douglas had hoped to tempt back into the fold. In this Lincoln owed much to the efforts of his ex-Democrat lieutenants, notably Lyman Trumbull. The Republican senator, weary though he was from the Senate battles with Douglas, set about exploiting his strong personal following and extensive connections with Illinois local leaders, especially in the southern counties. Many of these refugees from the Democracy were foreign-born voters, particularly Germans and Scandinavians, wooed by a Republican party determined to escape the overt nativism of its Whig past. Lincoln and other party leaders understood just how important these immigrant constituencies were. The Republican State Committee called in Carl Schurz from Wisconsin to speak to the Germans of Chicago and the communities near St Louis. An anti-Catholic flavor marked some of the party's campaigning, most evidently in Wentworth's Chicago newspaper, the *Democrat*, which played on the Catholic connections of Douglas's wife, but Lincoln himself avoided crude appeals to specifically anti-papal or more generalized anti-Irish sentiment.

To achieve unequivocal political dominance in Illinois (as across the northern states more generally), however, the Republicans had also to bring about a definitive political shift amongst the Old Line Whigs and in this they failed. The inherent conservatism of those whom Lincoln called 'the old exclusive silk-stocking whiggery' in Sangamon and neighboring counties might have been irredeemable even in the best of circumstances, but Republicans labored under the additional handicap of the stand taken by John J. Crittenden, the elderly and influential Whig senator from Kentucky. In an exchange of private letters, Lincoln learnt that Crittenden, the political legatee of Henry Clay and thus a figure of some standing in Illinois's conservative circles, 'ardently' supported Douglas, believing that he had earned his re-election by his opposition to Lecompton. Lincoln's concern turned to deep chagrin when the Democratic press made the correspondence public in the later stages of the campaign. This certainly contributed to the narrow defeat of the Republican legislative candidates in the five central counties closest to Springfield, every one of which Lincoln might have been expected to win.[71]

Those five defeats mattered. Though Republicans won the popular vote, Democrats enjoyed a combined majority of 54 to 46 in the two houses of the Illinois legislature, which they used to return Douglas to the Senate at joint session in January. An out-of-date apportionment of legislative seats accounted for a modest mismatch between the popular party vote and party representation; this was compounded by a Democrat majority amongst the thirteen state senators not up for re-election. Strictly speaking, then, electoral technicalities caused Lincoln's defeat. But he and other leading Republicans recognized there were profounder lessons. To achieve dominance, the party needed to recruit at least some of those whom Lincoln called 'the nice exclusive sort' of Whigs. As one metaphor-mixing activist explained, unless the party managed to 'secure that conservative part of the old Whig party which the Democrats have been fishing after for the last three years we may as well "hang up de fiddle and de bow"'.[72]

Lincoln, though disappointed, refused to be downcast by his defeat at the hands of his old rival. On the 'dark, rainy & gloomy' evening of election day, aware from the telegraphed returns that the Democrats would control the legislature, he set out for home on a slippery, 'hog-backed' path. He almost lost his footing but, he recalled, 'I recovered myself & lit square: and I said to myself, "*It's a slip and not a fall.*"' It was a theme he pursued in the cascade of consolatory letters he despatched to his supporters. 'The fight must go on. We are right and can not finally fail.' 'The cause of civil liberty must not be surrendered at the end of *one*, or even, one *hundred* defeats.' Even the ingenious Douglas could not indefinitely repeat the conjurer's trick of winning support 'both as the best means to *break down*, and to *uphold* the slave power'; eventually there would be 'another "blow up" in the democracy'. He himself, though, would 'now sink out of view, and . . . be forgotten'. In the next elections, he told Norman Judd, he would 'fight in the ranks'.[73]

Lincoln's doubts were understandable, though we may reasonably wonder if he really believed his political future would be so anonymous or the public so amnesiac. What he could not have doubted, when reviewing the previous four or five years, was that he had been a chief beneficiary of the swirling public opinion which had destabilized the old parties in Illinois and opened the door to political realignment. Through several seasons of public speaking – in the campaigns of 1854, 1856 and 1858 – his steady advocacy of an antislavery argument had done much to color public sentiment, and to effect the displacement of the Whigs by a broader-based Republican party that, far more realistically than its predecessor, could aspire to national power. Seeking to fashion a new institutional order, and alert in particular to the power of evangelical opinion, Lincoln deliberately fused appeals to Protestant millennialism and Enlightenment rationalism. By the time the debates of 1858 reached their climax, Lincoln was earnestly seeking to harness antislavery religious sensibilities not just in Chicago and the Yankee settlements but as widely as possible across the state. His defeat by no means discredited this strategy of moral engagement: just two years later, the power of a crusading party would unlock the gate of the presidency.

Notes

1 Historians of the evolution of American party competition have designated the conflict between Federalists and Jeffersonian Republicans the 'first party system'. Jacksonians and their National Republican/Whig opponents provided the poles of party politics from the late 1820s to the early 1850s. The 'third party system', in which Democrats confronted Republicans, evolved out of the multiple fracturing of parties in the 1850s.

2 *CW*, 2:89, 255–6, 552–3.

3 *CW*, 1:48, 108–15.

4 N&H, 1:233–4, 250, 269–74, 293–4; *CW* 1:337–8, 471–3, 2:409; Olivier Fraysse, *Lincoln, Land, and Labor, 1809–1860*, trans. Sylvia Neely (Urbana, IL: University of Illinois Press, 1994), 84–5, 173; Mark M. Krug, *Lyman Trumbull: Conservative Radical* (New York: A.S. Barnes and Co., 1965), 171; *Reminiscences of Carl Schurz*, 3 vols (New York: The McClure Co., 1907–08), 2:99, 199–200, 205.

5 *HI*, 91, 193, 348, 508, 539; N&H, 1:304–9.

6 *HI*, 588; Waldo W. Braden, *Abraham Lincoln: Public Speaker* (Baton Rouge, LA: Louisiana State University Press, 1988), 108, 201–2, 616, 727; N&H, 1:79–81, 84, 87–95, 172.

7 N&H, 1:69–71,167–9; *HI*, 69, 76, 114, 466, 508.

8 N&H, 1:304–9; *HI*, 76, 91, 465–6, 539.

9 Braden, *Abraham Lincoln: Public Speaker*, 16–17, 97–9, 107; *Reminiscences of Carl Schurz*, 2:93; N&H, 1:304–9.

10 *HI*, 131–2, 508, 683.

11 *CW*, 2:126; N&H, 1:303–9; Braden, *Abraham Lincoln: Public Speaker*, 113, 115; *HI*, 508; Daniel Walker Howe, *The Political Culture of the American Whigs* (Chicago, IL: The University of Chicago Press, 1979), 281–5.

12 N&H, 1:130–1, 173–7, 182–3, 223.

13 Thomas Ford, *A History of Illinois from Its Commencement as a State in 1818 to 1847* (Chicago, 1854), 279–82.

14 Joseph Gillespie, *Recollections of Early Illinois and Her Noted Men* (Chicago, 1880), 6; Ford, *A History of Illinois*, 105.

15 Clinton L. Conkling, 'Historical Data concerning the Second Presbyterian Church of Springfield, Illinois', typescript, 3 vols, Illinois State Historical Society, 1:133–41, 176–9, 3:8–22; Newton Bateman and Paul Selby, eds, *Illinois Historical* (Chicago, 1910), 215; John M. Palmer, *Personal Recollections of John M. Palmer: The Story of an Earnest Life* (Cincinnati, 1901), 48–51; Biographical sketch of N.W. Miner; Mary Hill Miner, 'Recollections', Mary Hill Miner Papers, Illinois State Historical Society.

16 *CW*, 1:382–4.

17 *CW*, 1:319–21; Harry C. Blair and Rebecca Tarshis, *Lincoln's Constant Ally: The Life of Colonel Edward D. Baker* (Portland, OR: Oregon Historical Society, 1960), 8–9.

18 William J. Wolf, *The Almost Chosen People: A Study of the Religion of Abraham Lincoln* (Garden City, NY: Doubleday, 1959), 59–62, 69–70.

19 *CW*, 1:320.

20 John M. Palmer, like Lincoln, was born in Kentucky and moved to central Illinois in the 1830s. His reactions may suggest something of Lincoln's own response: 'religious controversies raged in every neighborhood to an extent that seemed to me to be absolutely unaccountable'. Palmer, *Personal Recollections*, 13.

21 N&H, 1:126.

22 N&H, 1:370–2; *CW*, 2:282.

23 *HI*, 266.

24 William E. Gienapp, *The Origins of the Republican Party, 1852–1856* (New York: Oxford University Press, 1987), 122 (quoting the *Chicago Tribune*).

25 *CW*, 2:273–4.

26 Krug, *Lyman Trumbull*, 86–8; Edward Magdol, *Owen Lovejoy: Abolitionist in Congress* (New Brunswick, NJ: Rutgers University Press, 1967), 109–13; *CW*, 2:288.

27 *CW*, 2:228; Krug, *Lyman Trumbull*, 89–93.

28 *CW*, 2:323.

29 Magdol, *Owen Lovejoy*, 119–20; Willard L. King, *Lincoln's Manager: David Davis* (Cambridge, MA: Harvard University Press, 1960), 107–8.

30 *CW*, 2:316, 322–3.

31 *CW*, 2:321.

32 Stephen L. Hansen, *The Making of the Third Party System: Voters and Parties in Illinois, 1850–1876* (Ann Arbor, MI: UMI Research Press, 1980), 78.

33 *Herndon's Lincoln*, 312–13.

34 *CW*, 2:276, 281–2.

35 *CW*, 2:358, 374.

36 *CW*, 2:412–13.

37 Donald, 200.

38 *CW*, 2:399–407.

39 *CW*, 2:405–9.

40 *CW*, 2:430; *Reminiscences of Carl Schurz*, 2:87–8.

41 Don E. Fehrenbacher, *Chicago Giant: A Biography of Long John Wentworth* (Madison, WI: American History Research Center, 1957), 148–59.

42 Don E. Fehrenbacher, *Prelude to Greatness: Lincoln in the 1850's* (Stanford, CA: Stanford University Press, 1962), 101.

43 *CW*, 3:310–11.

44 *CW*, 2:461–2.

45 *CW*, 2:462–7.

46 *HI*, 731.

47 *CW*, 2:491; Donald, 209–10.

48 *CW*, 3:16, 145–6.

49 *CW*, 2:501, 3:399.

50 J. Medill to AL, 27 Aug. 1858, ALP.

51 According to Governor James Grimes of Iowa, Lincoln mapped out this new debating strategy following their discussions just a few days before the meeting at Quincy. *HI*, 377–8.

52 *CW*, 3:226, 234, 311–13.

53 *CW*, 2:545–7, 3:220–2, 249, 280, 301–4.

54 *CW*, 3:254–5, 276, 307–8.

55 *CW*, 3:315.

56 *CW*, 3:225–6.

57 N&H, 2:123–4; *CW*, 3:225–6, 256, 315.

58 *CW*, 3:233, 256, 276, 314–16; Harold Holzer, ed., *The Lincoln–Douglas Debates: The First Complete Unexpurgated Text* (New York: Harper Collins, 1993), 311.

59 *CW*, 3:234, 254, 310–12, 315–16.

60 Lincoln told Gillespie the campaign 'was too grave & serious' for folksy anecdotes. *HI*, 181.

61 *CW*, 2:501, 546–7.

62 Lincoln continued to emphasize the dangers *after* the election. The issue was for him much more than one of electoral convenience. *CW*, 3:344–5.

63 *RWAL*, 303.

64 Linda Jeanne Evans, 'Abolitionism in the Illinois Churches, 1830–1865' (Northwestern University, PhD thesis, 1981), 111.

65 Evans, 'Abolitionism in the Illinois Churches', 155–6, 175, 329–30.

66 Jasper Douthit, *Jasper Douthit's Story: The Autobiography of a Pioneer* (Boston, MA: American Unitarian Association, 1909), 92–4.

67 *HI*, 259, 654; Phineas L. Windsor, 'A Central Illinois Methodist Minister, 1857–1891', unpublished lecture, March, 1944, Holbrook Library, Pacific School of Religion, Berkeley, 8; *Minutes of the Annual Conferences of the Methodist Episcopal Church, for the year 1858* (New York), 249; A. Smith to AL, 20 July 1858, J.H. Jordan to AL, 25 July 1858, ALP.

68 A. Smith to AL, 20 July 1858, ALP; *Reminiscences of Carl Schurz*, 2:93–6; Windsor, 'A Central Illinois Methodist Minister', 7–8; *HI*, 4–5, 716, 728; Walter B. Stevens, *A Reporter's Lincoln*, ed. Michael Burlingame (Lincoln, NB: University of Nebraska Press, 1998), 89, 229; Douthit, *Autobiography*, 47–8.

69 *CW*, 3:255, 257, 313, 316; *HI*, 574–5, 654; Stevens, *A Reporter's Lincoln*, 86.

70 The Republicans won a total of 125,430 votes state-wide, the Douglas Democrats 121,609, and the Buchanan Democrats 5,071.

71 *CW*, 2:483–4, 3:305, 335–6, 339; N&H, 2:138–43.

72 *CW*, 3:339; David Zarefsky, *Lincoln, Douglas, and Slavery: In the Crucible of Public Debate* (Chicago, IL: The University of Chicago Press, 1990), 206.

73 *DJH*, 244; *CW*, 3:336–7, 339–42.

Chapter Three

The Power of Party: Winning the Presidency, 1858–60

Late in the evening of general election day in 1860, Lincoln and a few friends walked to the Springfield telegraph office to await the returns from the East. Already aware of the Republicans' success in Illinois and other western states, Lincoln was quietly confident of victory. Less than twelve months earlier he had been little more than a leading provincial politician with a mixed record in pursuing national office. Few of those who then thought about such things had given him a serious chance of running for the presidency, let alone entering the White House. Yet hindsight shows a remorseless logic at work in the process by which Lincoln rose from defeat at the hands of Douglas in 1858 to achieve the highest elective office in the land. If his rise was unexpected to most observers, it was certainly not accidental.

In the interplay of the three elements that shaped Lincoln's antebellum career – namely, his own political energies, the shifts of public opinion and the mechanisms of party – it was the third, the operations of party, that did most to bring about his remarkable success in 1860. Winning the presidential nomination demanded the confidence of the Republican organization whose national leadership had several other names from which realistically to choose. Once selected, a presidential nominee was almost completely dependent in reaching office on his party's exertions as a campaigning organization – one disciplined and unified by a sense of shared values and the promise of jobs. Lincoln needed no lessons here: no man, he knew, could get anywhere without party.[1]

Yet parties at a national level were a far cry from the well-oiled machines of the modern era. They lacked permanence, adequate money, and the means of running an integrated, coordinated campaign. The party that Lincoln depended on was in its national form little more than a loose confederation of state organizations, over which national candidates and their advisers exerted only modest leverage. And while some of those constituent state parties were towers of strength, others were snake pits where personal and ideological venom impaired local activity. Still, whatever their organizational shortcomings in 1860, the Republicans suffered none of the self-destructive trauma of their Democratic opponents, stretched on the rack of slavery. Even more important, Republicans enjoyed in popular, local-level enthusiasm what they lacked in institutional polish. The party's philosophical cohesion and crusading fervor, colored by the millennialism of the evangelical Protestants who sustained it, gave their presidential canvass an energy denied to more routine campaigns. As their candidate, Lincoln was the beneficiary of activists inspired by a self-image as 'the Christian party in politics'.

Presidential ambition: Lincoln, his party and the road to the Decatur convention

The moment when Lincoln decided to seek the presidency has to remain a matter of speculation. As a congressman in 1848 he had written about what he would do 'were I president', but these were notes for a campaign speech in support of Zachary Taylor – he, not Lincoln, being the 'I' in question.[2] He would certainly have been gratified by the broad-based support he got when put up for Frémont's running-mate in 1856.[3] It was, however, the debates with Douglas two years later that marked the real watershed in his national recognition. At the outset of that campaign he ruefully contrasted his standing with that of his gilded opponent: 'nobody has ever expected me to be President'. Still, Charles Ray was right to compare Lincoln to Byron, 'who woke up one morning and found himself famous', and within a few months, as David Davis told him, his 'noble canvass' had won friends everywhere and earned him 'a national reputation'. A scattering of newspapers both inside and outside Illinois judged him worthy of an office higher than senator, and Lincoln's conversations at the time hinted at future possibilities. During the campaign he told a young journalist, Henry Villard, 'Mary insists . . . that I am going to be Senator and President of the United States too.' At this, Villard recalled, 'He burst out laughing, shook all over, and exclaimed, "Just think of such a sucker as me as President!"'' When Jesse Fell returned in December 1858 from a tour of the eastern states, including his native Pennsylvania, he told Lincoln that the Illinoisan's growing reputation made him a formidable candidate for the presidency. According to Fell, Lincoln replied that realism and common justice favored Seward, Chase or some other well-established servant of the national party; but he added, 'I admit the force of much that you say, and admit that I am ambitious, and would like to be President . . . but there is no such good luck in store for me as the presidency.'[4]

Lincoln persisted with this etiquette of modesty during 1859. 'I must say I do not think myself fit for the Presidency', he told one admirer. Several Illinois newspapers wanted to float his name as election year approached, but when the editor of the Rock Island *Register* offered to engineer a concerted drive for Lincoln in all the state's Republican papers, he declined. His supporters could not be certain if this marked a genuine lack of ambition or the shrewd calculation of an interested candidate who feared a counter-thrust against a premature boom. Whatever the truth, Lincoln found such presidential gossip helpful, for it confirmed his position as the pre-eminent Republican in the state and did no harm to his chances of a further tilt at a Senate seat. While he reassured Lyman Trumbull that he would be no rival to Trumbull's bid to seek a second term in 1860, he certainly hoped to run himself in 1864.[5]

As presidential election year approached, Lincoln focused his political energy in ways that would do no harm to his chances of the nomination. First, he developed his connections. His debates with Douglas had brought fame, a stream of correspondence and calls to speak from all over the North. For much of 1859 financial exigency kept him hard at work in his law practice, forcing him to decline many of these invitations: 'I shall go to the wall for bread and meat, if I neglect my business this year as well as last,' he explained to a disappointed Iowan.[6] Still, during the later months of the year, with his finances restored, he traveled 4,000 miles to deliver twenty-three speeches. Having made just three out-of-state addresses in the previous five years, he now gave nearly twenty such within just a few months, many of them in Iowa, Kansas and Wisconsin. Most notable, though, was his visit to Ohio in September, to speak at the State House in Columbus and before a mass audience at Cincinnati. Called in by the Republican leaders to counter Douglas's influence in the gubernatorial race, Lincoln prepared two careful speeches that engaged with the Little Giant's most recent reformulation of popular sovereignty. He won new admirers and broadened his base.

Lincoln's second, though not secondary, objective was to sustain his party's philosophical integrity while at the same time making it a broad enough church to win a national election. This was a live issue in the Republican press throughout the later 1850s. Some conservative spokesmen, including the *New York Times*, advocated replacing the policy of non-extension with popular sovereignty, to draw southern Know Nothings into a national 'Opposition' capable of ousting the Buchanan administration in 1860; others suggested an even weaker stance on slavery, simply opposing southern schemes for reopening the Atlantic slave trade. Lincoln, fearing a retreat to lower ground, spent much of his time urging conservatives to resist 'the temptation to lower the Republican Standard in order to gather recruits'. What gave the party its authority was its guaranteed hostility to slavery's spread. Weaken that, to attract southern opponents of 'the rotten democracy', and you 'gain nothing in the South, and lose every thing in the North'.[7]

In pressing this case, Lincoln's chief target remained Douglas and his 'insidious' doctrines. Increasingly estranged from the southern Democrats, Douglas reached out to Republicans, emphasizing his own unyielding hostility to the pet proposals of radical slaveholders, particularly their demand for a federal slave code to protect slavery throughout the territories before their admission to statehood. His representation – in *Harper's Magazine* – of popular sovereignty as the truly national doctrine made a huge impact in September 1859, and was seen as an attempt to fashion a broad coalition of the center, between the extremes of non-extension and a slave code. Lincoln was alarmed but not surprised. Barely had Douglas won the senatorial election in 1858 than Lincoln warned Trumbull that future turmoil amongst Democrats might well spur Douglas to summon all northerners to 'make common cause in electing him President as the best means of breaking down the Slave power'. Lincoln recognized that this would test Republicans' mettle nationally, just as the Illinois party had had to fight for its integrity in 1858. The struggle would be to see 'whether the Republican party can maintain its identity, or be broken up to form the tail of Douglas' new kite'.[8]

Consequently, Lincoln insisted that Douglas had perverted genuine popular sovereignty into nothing 'other than that, if one man chooses to make a slave of another man, neither that other man nor anybody else has a right to object'. No barrier to slavery's spread, the doctrine had caused a 'gradual and steady debauching of public opinion', excluding blacks from the terms of the Declaration of Independence, ranking them with brutes and crocodiles, and acting as 'the miner and sapper' for measures that would bring slavery 'into the very heart of the free North'. If Republicans fell in behind the Little Giant, 'they do not absorb him; he absorbs them'. Douglas sought ideological clones ready to agree 'that the question of negro slavery is simply a question of dollars and cents; that the Almighty has drawn a line across the continent, on one side of which labor . . . must always be performed by slaves'. But Republicans' duty was 'to keep to the faith, to remain steadfast to the right. . . . Stand by your principles, stand by your guns; and victory complete and permanent is sure at the last.'[9]

Lincoln asked his party to show the backbone they had discovered in 1858. Had they then followed Greeley's mistaken advice, 'there would today be no Republican party in this Union'. Antislavery principles were indestructible, of course, and a party that perished through the folly of its confused leaders could eventually be rebuilt around the same truths. 'But in the meantime all the labor that has been done to build up the present Republican party would be entirely lost, and perhaps twenty years of time, before we would again have formed around that principle as solid, extensive, and formidable an organization as we have, standing shoulder to shoulder to-night in harmony and strength around the Republican banner.'[10] There is no clearer statement in all Lincoln's writings on the unique and essential power of party to effect social change, and of its vulnerability to diversion, co-option and the betrayal of principle.

At the same time Lincoln also condemned radical initiatives that endangered party unity. How to deal with the hated Fugitive Slave Law of 1850 proved an especially divisive issue. In most of the free states during the 1850s the radicals sought to repeal or effectively to nullify the measure. Several urged outright disobedience and even armed resistance. In Wisconsin, over the protests of conservative Republicans, radicals adopted an assertive states' rights position, passing a personal liberty law that made the Fugitive Slave Law inoperable. In Ohio some inhabitants of the Western Reserve were imprisoned in 1859 for trying to rescue a fugitive. Emotions ran high. Giddings, Wade and other radicals successfully blocked the renomination of the state supreme court judge who had upheld the constitutionality of the Fugitive Slave Law. The subsequent state election turned on the question of its repeal. A party split was only narrowly avoided by deft footwork over its platform.

Lincoln viewed developments in Ohio with alarm. His own view was clear enough: slaveholders had a constitutional right to the return of their fugitive slaves and, though the federal constitution did not specify the agency of their delivery, Congress was empowered to make all laws necessary and proper for carrying out the responsibilities of government. But what more especially concerned him was the damage done by initiatives of this kind in stirring up bad feeling within the party generally. Their 'tilting' at the law, he told Indiana's Schuyler Colfax, threatened 'utterly [to] overwhelm us in Illinois with the charge of enmity to the constitution itself'. Exchanging letters with Salmon P. Chase, Lincoln insisted that introducing a repeal plank at the Republicans' national gathering in 1860 would 'explode the convention and the party'.[11]

The party's difficulties with the fugitive slave question were, Lincoln thought, symptomatic of a general danger which he raised in his letter to

Colfax: 'the temptation in different localities to *"platform"* for something which will be popular just there, but which, nevertheless, will be a firebrand elsewhere, and especially in a National convention'. Thus, the two-year naturalization law in Massachusetts might serve the interests of the local party, but had Republicans there 'looked beyond their noses' they would have seen that it invited ruin for the party throughout the Northwest. Kansans had embraced popular sovereignty as a means to freedom locally, without seeing its wider dangers. Lincoln urged Colfax, who endorsed the need to harmonize the party's discordant elements, to use his influence in Congress and with state leaders to get them to think nationally and 'at least say *nothing* on points where it is probable we shall disagree'. At the same time Lincoln did what he could in his home patch to reduce the discord between conservative Republicans in central and southern Illinois and the more radical men in the north. He reproved one central state editor for unfairly describing the northerners, essential to the party's electoral success, as 'ultras' and 'nigger-stealers'. 'Why manu-facture slang to be used against us by our enemies?' Republicans should '*help* . . . instead of trying to *hurt* one another'.[12]

On one issue Republicans were broadly agreed: John Brown's astonish-ing, abortive attack on the federal arsenal at Harpers Ferry in October 1859 had the power to damage them at the polls. In the hysteria that followed Brown's botched operation, conservatives damned the party as sponsors of the abolitionist's revolutionary schemes. Lincoln called the charge 'an electioneering dodge', but it was not without foundation.[13] Some Republicans had certainly been involved in financing and planning Old Brown's ventures. Moreover, Republicans' assertion of their constitutional conservatism could not mask some admiration for Brown's brave bearing as captive and martyr. Lincoln's own comments hinted at that ambivalence. Speaking in Kansas, he declared the attack wrong on two counts: 'It was a violation of law and it was, as all such attacks must be, futile as far as any effect it might have on the extinction of a great evil.' The ballot box, not 'violence, bloodshed and treason', was the constitutionally prescribed means of effecting change. But, he also noted, Brown – who 'agreed with us in thinking slavery wrong' – had shown 'great courage, rare unselfish-ness'.[14] At bottom, Lincoln and other moderate Republicans joined with radicals in approving the underlying sentiments that drove Brown on, even as they recognized the justice of his execution. Still, the party leadership's protestations of conservatism, allied with shrewd Democrat-bashing, proved convincing enough to prevent a haemorrhage of support in the free states. The raid, though, ended any hope of engineering an alliance with anti-Buchanan oppositionists in the alarmed border South.

By the close of 1859 several out-of-state papers were floating Lincoln's name in connection with the Republican presidential ticket, stories which he read in the Illinois press. Since Pennsylvania and Illinois were essential to overall victory, some called for a ticket led by the Quaker state's Simon Cameron or John M. Read, with Lincoln as the running-mate. One of Cameron's supporters proposed this to Lincoln, who replied politely but firmly, 'I shall be heartily for it, *after* it shall have been fairly nominated by a Republican national convention; and I can not be committed to it *before*.'[15] Keeping options open was the prudent action of a man who understood that he could do only so much to influence the larger events which would decide the presidential nomination, but that he was by no means powerless. From the closing months of 1859 to the gathering of the Republican convention Lincoln actively worked to make himself better known.

First, he collaborated happily in the publication of his 1858 debates with Douglas. The project was a striking success. A substantial but inexpensive book, which also included his Ohio speeches of 1859, appeared in the spring. Thirty thousand copies had sold by June and a third edition was published to meet the demand. A second project which Lincoln now tolerated, having been unenthusiastic a year earlier, was a short biographical sketch for a Republican paper, the *Chester County Times*, in Pennsylvania. The enterprise was the brainchild of Jesse Fell, who wanted to use his connections in his native state to bring the Illinoisan into sharper political focus. The 'little sketch', as Lincoln called it, was spare, modest and hinted at his characteristic wit. It summarized his ancestry, humble origins and political career in just a few hundred words. 'There is not much of it,' he told Fell, 'for the reason, I suppose, that there is not much of me.' He was anxious that it should not be attributed to his pen. The editor of the *Chester County Times* fleshed out the sketch, which subsequently appeared in many other Republican sheets.[16]

More influential still in projecting Lincoln to a wider audience was the address he prepared after accepting an invitation from Henry Ward Beecher's Plymouth Church in Brooklyn. By the time Lincoln arrived in New York City in late February 1860, he had had a few months in which to research and write his speech, and – with a cultured eastern audience in mind – to buy a new suit. A new organizing committee, including Horace Greeley, William Cullen Bryant and other local party leaders hostile to Seward, turned Lincoln's engagement into one of a series of lectures to be given by prominent out-of-state Republicans and designed to reach beyond the party faithful. They also moved the meetings to the Cooper Institute in Manhattan. Lincoln learnt of the change of venue only on his arrival in the city, and spent his first day adjusting his text for a less formally religious audience. He also sat for the celebrated photographer, Matthew Brady, who managed – by dint of some crafty retouching – to transform a plain man into quite a handsome figure.[17]

The speech proved a stunning success. Although Lincoln's name was well known, most New Yorkers were expecting a rough-edged western stump speaker, but – despite his incongruous appearance and ungainliness – he commanded his audience with a weighty speech which blended historical detail, cogent political analysis and moral intransigence. Drawing on weeks of painstaking research into the views of the Constitution's framers, he argued that none denied the federal government's power over slavery in the territories, which they 'marked . . . as an evil not to be extended'. It was Douglas's Nebraska Act, serving the purposes of southern sectionalists, which marked a radical departure from settled orthodoxy. The so-called 'Black Republicans' were fundamentally conservative nationalists, resisting the novel program of southern extremists. They had neither designed nor encouraged John Brown's 'peculiar' raid, 'an attempt by white men to get up a revolt among slaves, in which the slaves refused to participate'. Southerners who recklessly threatened secession if the Republicans won in 1860 were the real disunionists, adopting the 'cool' logic of the highwayman who blamed his victims for any resulting violence. Republicans' duty was to avoid '*passion and ill temper*', persuade the South that the party intended 'to let them alone', stand up to disunionist threats, and maintain its policy of quarantining slavery. In a sermonic climax that would not have been out of place in Beecher's church, Lincoln declared: 'LET US HAVE FAITH THAT RIGHT MAKES MIGHT, AND IN THAT FAITH, LET US, TO THE END, DARE TO DO OUR DUTY AS WE UNDERSTAND IT.'[18]

The applause, laughter and real warmth of the audience's response prefigured the enthusiastic reviews of the political press. The *New York Times* extolled his ability 'to elucidate and convince . . . to delight and electrify'. Noah Brooks was ecstatic: 'He's the greatest man since St Paul. . . . No man ever before made such an impression on his first appeal to a New York audience.' All four city newspapers printed the speech in full, many others followed, and it soon appeared in pamphlet form. Lincoln's subsequent itinerary of New England became a triumphal tour, during which he was extravagantly introduced as the nation's next president or vice-president. The speech also posed its problems. As he explained to his wife, 'The difficulty was to make nine others, before reading audiences who had already seen all my ideas in print.' He returned to Illinois exhausted but convinced that the presidential nomination was not beyond his grasp; as Herndon put it, his dazzling success 'had stimulated his self-confidence to unwonted proportions'. It had also dramatically increased the sense amongst key Illinois Republicans that Lincoln might be more than just a 'favourite son'.[19]

The state party was essential to Lincoln's hopes, and he had worked energetically but discreetly to achieve two particular objectives in relation to it. First, he had had to ensure that the factionalism which had marked Illinois Republicanism since its birth remained subordinate to a sense of common purpose. Republicans were a philosophical coalition embracing a variety of only partially fused political traditions: pragmatic free-soilers and radical abolitionists, the foreign-born and nativist ex-Know Nothings, conservative Whigs and former Democrats. In such a context, personal feuds, parochial resentments and local conflicts proved difficult to isolate and control. Most damaging of all was the struggle for control of the party in Chicago. Here the feud involved the shrewd state senator, Norman Judd, and his *Tribune* clique on one side, and Mayor John Wentworth, owner of the *Daily Democrat*, and his supporters on the other. Wentworth blamed Judd for Lincoln's defeat in 1858, questioned his financial probity, and attacked him daily in the *Democrat* when Judd declared his candidacy for governor. Retaliating, Judd brought a libel suit against the wealthy mayor. Reconciliation through the two most senior Republicans serving in elective office was out of the question: Governor William H. Bissell was too ill, and Senator Trumbull too closely connected to the ex-Democrat *Tribune* faction.[20]

Both sides appealed to Lincoln, who knew that these local complications threatened the Republicans' ability to carry the state in the national election – with consequences for Lincoln himself. As Wentworth rhetorically asked him, 'How can you expect to be nominated when your chief commercial city wheels out of line, [and] elects a Douglas Mayor[?]' Lincoln could afford to see neither group marginalized. Judd was chairman of the party's central committee; Mayor Wentworth's 'efficient aid & cooperation' was essential to winning the state. Lincoln was ready to act as peacemaker, but knew that in trying to act impartially he ran the risk of alienating the very people on whom he depended. He refused Wentworth's request that he act for him in the libel suit, but suggested a compromise that involved Wentworth's issuing a retraction and Judd dropping the suit. He wrote a letter for public use, declaring his utter confidence in Judd as 'equally true and faithful' to himself and the party, but insistent that this be not deemed an endorsement of any particular candidate for the gubernatorial nomination, since all were his 'good and true' friends. At the stickiest moment of the mayoral race, during his Cooper Union trip, he apparently telegraphed Judd, who then reluctantly agreed to campaign for Wentworth, bringing the *Tribune* with him: Wentworth won the election and the libel suit was not pressed.[21]

Minimizing internal conflict had been the necessary precondition for Lincoln's second goal: to secure his state party's unanimous support at the national nominating convention and to prepare the ground for this without being seen openly to campaign. He knew he could rely on deep personal loyalty amongst the party's otherwise mutually distrustful leaders. Wentworth overstated the case when he told Lincoln that the feuding leaders in Chicago were 'all afraid of you', but the mayor's remark rightly intimated Lincoln's natural authority. Though not a member of the state central committee himself, he had well-placed allies who were. They included not merely the chairman (Judd), but Fell as corresponding secretary. Disliking purely social functions, Lincoln still attended several gatherings that served to keep him mingling with politicians well placed to help him. Though a variety of leading national Republicans had their advocates in Illinois – notably Edward Bates and John McLean, who were valued for their appeal to conservative voters – increasingly Lincoln came to be seen, in the words of one editor, as the man 'sure to consolidate the party vote of this state'. By late 1859 the signs of his interest in the nomination were evident, if still subtle and indirect, as in his telling Judd that 'some of our friends . . . attach more consequence to getting the National convention into our State than I did, or do. Some of them made me promise to say so to you.'[22]

Judd's success in January 1860 in persuading the Republican National Committee to locate the convention in Chicago encouraged the idea that Illinois should rally behind a single name. Soon in Springfield a private meeting of leaders friendly to Lincoln, including Judd and another state committeeman, Jackson Grimshaw, asked him to allow his name to go forward for the presidential nomination. With 'characteristic modesty', Grimshaw recalled, Lincoln said he doubted that he could succeed and asked for time to think. The next day he gave permission, but refused to let his name be used for the vice-presidential slot. This was a canny move to ensure that his aides kept their sights on the highest prize. Lincoln was realist enough not to expect to win at Chicago, but he believed a solid personal vote from his home state would make him unstoppable for the Senate in 1864. As he explained to Judd, early in February, 'I am not in a position where it would hurt much for me to not be nominated on the national ticket; but I am where it would hurt some for me to not get the Illinois delegates.'[23]

Lincoln welcomed the evidence of his growing support in January and February, including the editorial endorsement of Charles Ray and Joseph Medill, the owners of the *Chicago Press and Tribune*. However, it was his visit to the northeastern states that transformed his hopes. According to Herndon, he returned 'as vigilant as he was ambitious'. He sidelined legal work and began 'to trim his political sails'. At times he tied himself in verbal knots as he tried to excuse his ambition, but was frank with Lyman Trumbull: 'The taste *is* in my mouth a little.' As in his pursuit of the Whig nomination in 1846, Lincoln contributed a special mix of untiring energy and discretion. Lacking an oiled political machine or the private funds with which to construct one, he fell back on his usual resources: his pen, employed in producing a stream of confidential and private letters to influential figures inside and outside the state; his feel for the pulse of Illinois politics; his shrewd reading of the broader picture; and his informal network of allies. Hugely important were those members of the state central committee – notably Fell, Judd, Grimshaw and Herndon – who worked zealously to get as many pro-Lincoln delegates as possible elected to the state nominating convention at Decatur on 9 May. Working with the state-wide organization that they had been beefing up since the summer of 1859, and helped by the proliferation of local Republican and Lincoln clubs during early 1860, they looked to the county nominating conventions during March and April to endorse the hero of the Cooper Union. Many did so, but Seward had his supporters in the northern districts, and Bates in the southern. The fact was that the central committee had no iron grip, and many county conventions of what was a decentralized party left it to their delegates to make up their minds at Decatur.[24]

Republicans bustled into the small central Illinois town for the two-day state convention just a week before the national gathering in Chicago. Six hundred delegates and over 2,000 spectators crammed into a specially constructed timber and canvas 'wigwam'. Though Lincoln was known to enjoy broad support for the presidential nomination, as the state's 'favourite son', there was still no certainty that delegates would be formally instructed to support him at Chicago. Then came a piece of transforming political theater. A brilliant initiative of Richard Oglesby, a young Decatur lawyer-politician, turned Lincoln into the apotheosis of the self-made frontiersman, the horny-handed representative of democratic free labor in the struggle against aristocracy and a frozen social order. During a pause in the proceedings, Oglesby teasingly announced the presence of 'a distinguished citizen of Illinois' and moved that he be invited to the stand. Lincoln was unobserved just inside the entrance.

Oglesby named him, to a storm of applause. Then, according to a witness, Lincoln 'was "boosted" up until he found himself, kicking scrambling – crawling – upon the sea of heads between him and the Stand'. As he blushingly took his place on the stage 'Hats were thrown up . . . as if hats were no longer useful.'[25]

Building the drama through dialogue with the audience, Oglesby explained that an 'Old Democrat' of Macon County had something to present. 'Receive it', cried the crowd. Then Lincoln's cousin, John Hanks, made his way to the stand carrying two decorated wooden fence rails, serving as support poles for a banner which read: 'Abraham Lincoln. The Rail Candidate for President in 1860. Two rails from a lot of 3,000 made in 1830 by Thos. Hanks and Abe Lincoln – whose father was the first pioneer in Macon County.' Deafening enthusiasm gave way to calls for a speech. Lincoln, who 'seemed to shake with inward laughter', briefly obliged. He confirmed that he had indeed split rails and built a log cabin near Decatur on first arriving in the state thirty years earlier. Whether or not these were from that site he could not confirm but added, in a happy turn of phrase anticipating the modern sound-bite, that 'he had mauled many and many better ones since he had grown to manhood'.[26]

At a stroke, Lincoln became 'the rail splitter'. It was a powerful image, matching the most potent symbols of previous presidential campaigns. As 'Old Hickory' provided a shorthand for Andrew Jackson's iron will and resolve, and as 'Old Tip' and 'Old Rough and Ready' connected William Henry Harrison and Zachary Taylor with the sturdy nationalism of westward advance and conquest, so the Decatur label made Lincoln the embodiment of the enterprising, socially mobile western laborer. Whether by a stroke of genius or of luck, Oglesby's initiative was brilliantly successful, laying the foundations for a mythic Lincoln that made much more of where he had begun life than where he had ended up. One of those swept along by what appeared to be a spontaneous moment of drama later recognized the calculation behind it. 'I began to think I could smell a very large mouse – and this whole thing was a cunningly devised thing of knowing ones, to make Mr Lincoln President, and that banner was to be the "Battle flag," in the coming contest between "labor free" and "labor slave", between democracy and aristocracy.'[27]

The startling show of enthusiasm for Lincoln led his advisers to discuss their next move. They knew that Seward had considerable support amongst the state's delegates to the national convention; Leonard Swett judged that eight of the twenty-two would 'gladly' have supported the New Yorker. As first business on the second day John M. Palmer proffered a resolution that instructed the Illinois delegation 'to use all honorable means' to secure Lincoln's nomination at Chicago, 'and to vote as a unit for him'. He followed with a speech that neutralized the objections of Sewardites from the northern districts, and the motion passed unanimously. Significantly, the convention offered no second preference for president, to avoid any suggestion that they expected Lincoln to fall at an early hurdle in Chicago. Thanks to his managers and their influence over the party machine, Lincoln had achieved his initial objective: a state party united behind his candidacy.[28]

The Republican presidential nomination

Republicans had a spring in their step as they set out for Chicago. The party had broadened its electoral base since 1856, with something close to an administration rout in the elections of 1858 being followed by further Democratic losses a year later. The Republicans' increased representation in Washington and the state houses reflected both their tighter grip in areas where they were already strong – New England and the upper North – and their advances in the Democratic heartlands further south, including Pennsylvania, where a predominantly Republican coalition, the People's party, had taken control of the legislature. Victory in 1860, the party's leaders well understood, would be theirs if only they could maintain their momentum in Pennsylvania, Indiana, Illinois and New Jersey, the free states beyond Frémont's grasp in 1856. The first two of these would hold their state elections in October; good results there would provide a springboard for the subsequent presidential ballot.

Republicans drew further cheer from more immediate political developments, as the Democrats, meeting in April at their own convention in Charleston, appeared to take a large stride toward self-destruction. The capital of secessionism was not a propitious venue in which to apply balm to the wounds, still raw, inflicted by the Douglas–Buchanan quarrel. Battle lines were drawn over the party's platform, with the southern-rights men demanding federal protection of slavery in the territories, and Douglasites standing by popular sovereignty and the rulings of the Supreme Court. Their version of the platform rejected, William L. Yancey of Alabama and several other delegates from the Deep South withdrew. Unable to agree on a presidential candidate, the convention adjourned on 3 May.

Republican strategists were determined to guard against complacency. Few considered their opponents a spent force, even after Charleston. If, as Edward Pierce believed, '[t]here was a fair chance . . . that the Democrats would rally and unite', then Douglas would be the likely leader.[29] If, on the other hand, the party remained split, Douglas would certainly be a candidate and his divorce from southern radicals would strengthen him with northern voters. Either way, Republicans needed a presidential candidate who would not be politically dwarfed by comparisons with the Little Giant. The party also had to have confidence that its presidential nominee could win in every one of the battleground, or 'doubtful', states. This was a need made all the more pertinent by the banding together in Baltimore, just a week before the Chicago convention, of the residual elements of Old Line Whiggery and the American party. Calling themselves the Constitutional Union party, and standing on a general Unionist platform, they nominated the border-state politician John Bell as president and the urbane Edward Everett of Massachusetts as his running-mate. Their full vote-pulling power remained an imponderable, but their special appeal would undoubtedly lie with those conservative voters in the lower North who had held out against Frémont in 1856.

Lincoln's was just one of a clutch of possible nominees whose names decorated editorial columns on the eve of the convention. A double-page lithograph in *Harper's Weekly* carried Brady's portrait of him, along with representations of ten other hopefuls. Seward took pride of place, as befitted his national standing and status as the party's front-runner. In recent months the senator from New York had worked hard to strengthen his chances by softening his reputation for radicalism. In earlier speeches he had used phrases which (in the case of 'the higher law') seemed to put the promptings of conscience before constitutional obligation and which (when discussing 'the irrepressible conflict') seemed to invite a violent, frontal assault on the South. In fact, Seward was no ideologue; rather, he and his skillful manager, Thurlow Weed, were supremely practical politicians. To reassure the moderate center of the party, he spoke in the Senate at the end of February, disavowing sectionalism, breathing an emollient Unionism and repudiating John Brown. But party strategists remained unclear about Seward's ability to capture the battleground states of the lower North, an uncertainty reinforced by the strength there of former Know Nothings: nativists had not stopped castigating Seward as the traitor to Protestantism, who as governor of New York had supported Roman Catholics' campaign for a share of public funds for their parochial schools. A further question-mark hung over how far Seward would be damaged by his association with Weed's notorious political machine.[30]

Seward's perceived weaknesses gave grounds for hope to his chief rivals, most notably Salmon P. Chase, Edward Bates, John McLean and Simon Cameron. Yet each of these was open to equally powerful objections.

Chase's position on the Fugitive Slave Law made him even more of a radical than Seward, with all that that implied for contesting the battle-ground states. Nor was he helped by his reputation as a free trader and a friend of the foreign-born. Openly too ambitious for his own good, he lacked an organization and overestimated his support, which was not even solid in his own state of Ohio. Bates, a cultured, conservative, former Whig lawyer from the slave state of Missouri, enjoyed the backing of Greeley's *Tribune* and of several tacticians in the lower North, where it was thought he could swing the vote. But he was less benefited by his dependable Unionism than he was weakened by his timidity on slavery: a western leader caustically remarked, 'I go in for electing; but why go in to the bowels of Niggerdom for a candidate?'[31] Bates's open identification with the nativists and his very belated conversion to the Republicans did nothing to build enthusiasm for his cause.

Justice McLean of the United States Supreme Court was a more at-tractive proposition: although a conservative, he had been seriously con-sidered for the Republican presidential nomination in 1856 and had since issued a dissenting judgment in the Dred Scott case. His chances in the 'doubtful' states were good. But as a man of seventy-five, his age became a persisting concern: 'I will not go into the cemetery or catacomb', Fitz Henry Warren declared: 'The candidate must be alive and able to walk at least from the parlor into the dining room.'[32] Cameron's strength derived from his connections as a US senator and a wealthy political boss in a strategically critical state, Pennsylvania. However, his reputation for corruption and lack of scruple, and his doubtful pedigree as a former Democrat and Know Nothing, blighted his appeal and prevented his building significant support outside his home state.[33]

By contrast with these better known aspirants, Lincoln looked far less likely to antagonize the party's critical interest groups. There was enough in his brand of moderate Republicanism to accommodate the aspirations and concerns of a broad range of opinion. Conservative Republicans took heart from his loyalty to the values of Clayite Whiggery, his reverence for the Union, his constitutional respect for the Fugitive Slave Law and southerners' property rights, his disavowal of higher law doctrine, and his avoidance of the moral strictures on southern sinfulness which char-acterized so much abolitionist rhetoric. Yet Lincoln was also well placed to reach out to the more radical elements in his party, several of whom, including Giddings, had confidence in him. His House Divided and later speeches told of resolution in confronting the slave power, ending the spread of slavery and eventually choking it to death. Though not ready to use federal power to attack slavery directly, preferring instead to wait on events, he – as Eric Foner has noted – 'shared the radicals' sublime confidence that they were on the side of history'.[34] He, like them, spoke a language of moral revulsion and, along with other moderates, ensured that in 1860 the party found its center of gravity closer to the radical than the conservative position.

Equally, Lincoln had cleverly positioned himself to be acceptable to both the foreign-born and the nativists. Convinced that principle and pragmatism demanded the party embrace the sizeable immigrant population of the Northwest, especially the German Americans, Lincoln had joined in 1859 with Gustave Koerner, Norman Judd and other leading Illinois Republicans to repudiate the Massachusetts naturalization law. Notably, he wrote to Theodore Canisius, the publisher of the *Illinois Staats-Anzeiger*: 'Understanding the spirit of our institutions to aim at the *elevation* of men, I am opposed to whatever tends to *degrade* them. I have some little notoriety for commiserating the oppressed condition of the negro; and I should be strangely inconsistent if I could favor any project for curtailing the existing rights of *white men*, even though born in different lands, and speaking different languages from myself.' Shortly afterwards, when the *Staats-Anzeiger* was about to fold, Lincoln secretly bought it, leaving Canisius as the contracted editor provided he championed the Republicans.[35] By the eve of the Chicago convention, Lincoln enjoyed the support of a range of German-American leaders, both within and beyond Illinois. Unlike Seward, however, he had not earned the enmity of the nativists. He had taken care, at the height of Know Nothing fervor in the mid-1850s, not to lambast them publicly, keeping his criticisms private.

Lincoln offered the party a useful blend of freshness and proven ability. He had reputation enough to be known as a highly effective opponent of Douglas and popular sovereignty but his relative unfamiliarity on the national stage would allow campaign image-makers to fashion him into a Republican 'type' – a westerner, rail splitter and incorruptible man of the people. His lack of experience in national and executive office counted for less than his record of electoral success. As the various summaries of his life stressed, he had never been 'beaten by the people' since his one and only defeat, as a candidate for the state legislature in 1832; only self-sacrificial magnanimity had thwarted his Senate bid in 1855, as had unequal electoral apportionment in 1858.[36]

Lincoln used the weeks before the national convention quietly to impress members of the out-of-state delegations. In the main he and his advisers negotiated shrewdly. They knew that for Lincoln to be promoted in status from favorite son to the 'stop-Seward' candidate, around whom the battleground states could realistically unite, he had to be able to show real support outside Illinois. Taking encouragement from friendly correspondents in Ohio and Indiana, Lincoln delicately and confidentially set out his strategy. 'My name is new in the field; and I suppose I am not the *first* choice of a very great many,' he conceded in late March. 'Our policy, then, is to give no offence to others – leave them in a mood to come to us, if they shall be compelled to give up their first love.' A month later, he could tell Richard M. Corwine of Ohio: 'Everywhere, except in Illinois, and possibly Indiana, one or another is prefered to me, but there is no positive objection.'[37] Throughout he carefully said nothing to the personal detriment of other candidates, yet was quick to note their respective electoral weaknesses and was far from squeamish in sanctioning early discussions between his advisers and unpledged delegates on arrival in Chicago.

Lincoln itched to be at the convention, but knew it was improper to attend. He was, he said, 'almost too much of a candidate to go, and not quite enough to stay at home'.[38] His fate would be out of his hands, but he could depend on a devoted team of delegates. They were led by the massive and formidable David Davis. Made up of Lincoln's long-standing professional friends and political associates, including Judd, Palmer, Fell, Hatch, Dubois, Swett and Herndon, the group set aside their personal feuds and over five or six days worked themselves to exhaustion. Seward, they judged, could rely firmly on the support of over 150 of the convention's 450 or so voting delegates. Yet they not only stopped the well-placed front-runner but secured the crown for their own man. It was a brilliant and by no means inevitable achievement, the result in part of contingent circumstances but also of the Republican leadership's rational calculation of the party's best electoral interests.

First, the convention's location gave Lincoln a distinct advantage. The national committee had met in the previous December and at Judd's disingenuous prompting had chosen Chicago, deeming it a neutral site which would favor neither Seward nor any of the other prominent contenders. The burgeoning young city, a railroad hub and center of the grain trade, was confidently Republican. Lincoln clubs had been active for weeks, and the *Press and Tribune* (though not Wentworth's *Democrat*) was emphatic for Lincoln. During the week of the convention the city's 100,000 inhabitants played host to tens of thousands of visitors, mainly Lincoln's supporters ferried in at the excursion rate that Judd had negotiated. Lincolnites would pack the specially constructed and gigantic wooden Wigwam on the day of nomination.

Secondly, the tactics adopted by Lincoln's men served him admirably. Davis's team were determined to antagonize no one in their tailored conversations with various state delegations. They extolled their friend's positive attributes: his character and abilities, his romantic progress from humble origins, his potential as a candidate, and his fixed but unthreatening commitment to non-extension. The legend later developed that Davis and his men supplemented this sweet-talking with offers of government positions and even cabinet posts in exchange for pledges. This may have been true in the case of the Pennsylvania delegates after the first ballot: in response to the demand that Cameron be made Secretary of the Treasury, Davis made an offer, but one which was vague enough to be true to the letter of Lincoln's express instruction: '*Make no contracts that will bind me.*'[39] In the main, though, Lincoln's men had no need to resort to bribes. Rather, they appealed to the hard electoral logic which made Lincoln the party's most astute choice.

In baldly asserting that Seward was too dangerous for the battleground states they simply joined a larger chorus which included Greeley, who masked his personal grudge against a former ally by insistent appeals to pragmatism, and Henry S. Lane of Indiana and Andrew Curtin of Pennsylvania, both of them gubernatorial candidates in states where Republicans had yet to occupy the governor's mansion. Former Democrats also worked keenly to block Seward's nomination. The virus of doubt began to affect even delegates from New England, where Seward was assumed to be strong. Their anxieties were encouraged by Gideon Welles of Connecticut and Hannibal Hamlin, who insisted that his Maine cadre at Chicago secure a candidate who could carry the lower North.

If not Seward, then who? Certainly not Chase, whose radicalism made him just as unattractive to the doubtful states. There the likeliest options had for some time seemed to be Bates and McLean, their names more recently joined by Lincoln's. Only three of these four states had favorite sons who would enjoy their delegations' support on the first ballot at least: these were Cameron of Pennsylvania, Dayton of New Jersey and Lincoln of Illinois. Indiana lacked a home candidate: its votes on the first ballot would thus be crucial. Davis and Dubois met some of the Indiana delegates promptly on arrival. They pushed at an open door, helped by the influential Caleb B. Smith, Lincoln's close Indiana friend from their days as Whig congressmen in 1848. Two days before the convention's formal opening, the Indiana delegation declared that it would vote unanimously for Lincoln on the first ballot. Their numbers, when added to Illinois's, would put Lincoln well ahead of Bates and McLean.[40]

Davis's strategy was falling into place. 'Our programme,' Swett later explained, 'was to give Lincoln 100 votes on the first ballot, with a certain increase afterwards, so that in the doubtful Convention our fortunes might seem to be rising, and thus catch the doubtful.' The next step was to secure from the other two battleground states the promise of support on the second ballot. On the eve of voting, Davis, Caleb Smith and a few others met with a similar number from Pennsylvania and New Jersey to agree a candidate. Though factionalism between the Curtin–McClure and the Cameron elements delayed Pennsylvania's final endorsement until the next morning, a clear-headed determination to stop Seward carried the day, helped by a vague pledge about a job for Cameron.[41]

The groundwork laid, the Illinois delegates gathered in the Wigwam on the morning of Friday 18 May. Much has been made of the care with which Judd and others stage-managed the occasion to Lincoln's advantage. Seating the delegations so that the New Yorkers and other Sewardites were sealed off from the 'swing' voters certainly did no harm. Nor did packing the audience with local Lincolnites and engaging the stentorian Dr Ames (whose voice was reputed to carry across Lake Michigan on a clear day) to lead the Lincoln yell. If impulsive action had been needed to overcome doubts about Lincoln's nomination, then the Wigwam's high-decibel solidarity behind their favorite Illinoisan would surely have provided it. But fundamentally it was rational political logic not manufactured excitement that drove Lincoln's cause to its successful climax.

On the first ballot Seward led, as expected, but there were straws in the wind. Instead of sweeping New England, which should have been a bastion of his strength, he yielded New Hampshire to Lincoln, who also took votes in Maine, Massachusetts and Connecticut. Seward also did less well than expected in the slave states of Virginia and Kentucky, where Lincoln won a majority. The New Yorker's $173\frac{1}{2}$ votes, 60 short of what was needed, put him clearly ahead. But in taking the entire Indiana and Illinois vote, and winning more than a scattering elsewhere, Lincoln reached a total of 102, over twice the strength of any one of the other anti-Seward candidates: Cameron ($50\frac{1}{2}$), Chase (49), Bates (48), and McLean (12). A second round of balloting promptly followed. Lincoln continued to advance in New England. When Vermont gave him its entire ten votes, the Sewardites 'started as if an Orsini bomb had exploded'. More dramatic still, Pennsylvania withdrew Cameron's name and gave most of its vote to Lincoln, who also made gains in Ohio and Iowa. By the end of this round, Seward had advanced only modestly, to $184\frac{1}{2}$; Lincoln stood just three and half votes behind; Chase and Bates fell further back.

Lincoln himself had spent the early part of the day playing fives, a favorite ball game, and then moved between the telegraph office, his law office and the office of the *Illinois State Journal*. After the first two ballots he could see the way the tide was running. Eventually news arrived of the third and final ballot. Seward's support had held steady but Lincoln, picking up conservative votes in New Jersey, Pennsylvania, Maryland and Delaware, had passed the threshold of 233 thanks to four votes from Chase's Ohio, and Seward's men had then moved to make the vote unanimous. Lincoln, one of his companions that morning recalled, reacted 'with apparent coolness' but 'a close observer Could detect Strong emotions within'. He jestingly told well-wishers to shake his hand while they had the chance, since 'honors elevate some men'. He set off home, saying: 'Well gentlemen there is a little woman at our house who is probably more interested in this dispatch than I am.'[42]

Lincoln's supporters in Chicago showed rather less self-control. His exhausted managers wept. An Iowan, Charles C. Nourse, shrieked in rapture: 'We have nominated the best man in the country for President and beaten that New York crowd of wire pullers. Why shouldn't we shout? . . . *Whoop!*' Still, high emotion notwithstanding, the delegates' choice of candidate had been driven by rational consideration of electoral need – as, indeed, was their subsequent nomination for the vice-presidency of Hannibal Hamlin, who, as a New Englander and ex-Democrat, would balance a ticket headed by a westerner and former Whig. America's new, mass democratic forms had put a premium on the electable, or 'available', candidate. A sequence of nominations (Harrison, Polk, Taylor, Pierce and Frémont) in every presidential race since 1840 had shown that national political standing and proven executive ability came a poor second to supposed electoral 'availability'. 1860 was not the first time that the actions of a nominating convention prompted surprise bordering on disbelief within Washington's political circles. In Chicago, however, once Republican delegates had concluded that Seward was too risky a choice, there was no such incredulity. Lincoln emerged, as the radical Edward Pierce explained, as 'the only candidate truly reliable who would not, like Seward and Chase, encounter conservative prejudices'.[43]

The 1860 presidential campaign: the power of a righteous party

On the evening of his nomination, Lincoln spoke to a crowd of celebrating Republicans who had paraded to his home after a rally in the state house. He told them 'that he did not suppose the honor of such a visit was intended particularly for himself, as a private citizen, but rather to the representative of a great party'. This was more than simple modesty. Lincoln keenly understood that his election in November would depend, even more than the day's success, on the power of the Republican organization. News of Lincoln's nomination produced a rash of spontaneous local 'ratification meetings' across the North, marked by cannon salutes, bonfires, fireworks, drums, processions, banners and the pealing of church bells. In Chicago one observer thought 'Babel had come again, and the Democratic Jericho shook at the shouts and blowing of trumpets and holding of torches in the left hands of the Republican Gideons'. Promising as these immediate signals seemed, a more sustained effort would be needed to put Lincoln in the White House.[44]

First, after the frictions of the convention, the party had to be seen to unify behind a candidate not universally approved. One irate New Englander complained: 'You fellows at Chicago . . . knew that above everything else these times demanded a statesman, and you have gone and given us a *rail splitter*.' None of the high-ranking deputation that carried the convention's decision to Springfield, few of whose members knew Lincoln personally, was so scornful, but as they gathered awkwardly in the Lincolns' provincial parlor, noting his ungainliness and modesty, some entertained private misgivings about his ability to cope with the ordeal ahead. Yet Lincoln's intelligence and human qualities made their mark during a brief, informal discussion. As they left, one of them remarked to Carl Schurz: 'Well, we might have done a more brilliant thing, but we could hardly have done a better thing.'[45]

The grief of the defeated aspirants at Chicago stopped short of rancor. Bates, following a visit from Browning, published a letter of unequivocal support for Lincoln ('a sound, safe, national man'), though he declined to take the stump. Cameron publicly endorsed the Republican ticket within days. In Ohio, the McLean brigade pledged their support and Chase, though he felt deeply betrayed, did not blame Lincoln, in whom he declared complete confidence. Crucial amongst the Sewardites was Thurlow Weed. Davis persuaded the maestro of New York politics to visit Springfield within a week of the convention. Lincoln reported that his visitor 'asked nothing of me at all. He merely seemed to desire a chance of looking at me, keeping up a show of talk while he was at it.' After five hours of discussions, Weed departed, deeply impressed by Lincoln's political sagacity and 'intuitive knowledge of human nature'. Meanwhile, Seward himself spoke publicly of his confidence in Lincoln and urged his friends to set aside their disappointment. Lincoln reciprocated by allaying fears that he would freeze out his opponent's supporters when he distributed presidential patronage. Davis, speaking for Lincoln, assured one of Seward's chief lieutenants that, as candidate and president, the Illinoisan would use every available talent and 'deal fairly with all'.[46]

Achieving a broad unity was an essential prerequisite of victory. The Republicans' second task was to run a more cohesive campaign than that of the loose-knit party of 1856. Unlike the Whigs, who had never entirely shed their suspicion of institutional discipline and professional managers, the Republicans acknowledged the benefits of an effective machine. By 1860 Weed and Seward had done much 'to inspire and crystallize' the party's organization, particularly at state level.[47] During the forthcoming campaign the chief burden would fall on these battle-hardened state committees. In five cases – Iowa, Minnesota, Wisconsin, Ohio, and New Jersey – Republicans had won control of their state in the previous year's elections; in the far west and border South were six states where the party, though organized, had no prospect of victory. But in eleven other states Republicans faced spring or fall campaigns. Lincoln's fate would depend on the success or failure of a roster of hopeful gubernatorial candidates that included Curtin of Pennsylvania, Yates of Illinois, Lane of Indiana, and the radicals John A. Andrew of Massachusetts and Austin Blair of Michigan. By comparison with these energetic state machines, a congressional committee under Preston King and a national committee, headed by Governor Edwin D. Morgan of New York, proved relatively weak and under-resourced, their task being to help coordinate the operations of an essentially confederated, decentralized party. Morgan would chair the seven-member 'sub-national committee' responsible for running the campaign, but he was preoccupied with his own re-election and most of its day-to-day work fell on the shoulders of a keen strategist, George C. Fogg of New Hampshire, with Weed providing a sense of direction.

Organizationally, the party lacked many of the advantages of their opponents, for the Democrats controlled the postmasterships and other federal offices that commonly energized partisan effort. However, the Republicans' hopes of victory helped motivate many office-seeking activists, while their comparatively modest treasury did little to cramp a campaign that benefited from public enthusiasm and extemporized events. Just as important, the Democrats suffered an institutional nightmare, as the June conventions of a split party sent Douglas into presidential combat against his former allies in the 'southern' Democracy. In his own heartlands, Douglas kept control of the party machinery, leaving the administration Democrats, led by John C. Breckinridge, with the task of constructing new local agencies. In the South the problem was reversed, and Douglas's men found themselves sucked into a legal and administrative quagmire.

Lincoln followed custom for the duration of the campaign, by avoiding any suggestion of direct personal involvement. He made no speeches, gave no public interviews, issued no letters or statements of public policy. Attending an open-air meeting in the capitol grounds at Springfield, he declined to sit on the platform, and when called on to speak he simply shook his head. Whether the memory of Clay's self-defeating verbosity in 1844 influenced him is not clear. His discretion was certainly what the Republican managers wanted and they squeaked their disquiet at the slightest public hint of an initiative. When, in his formal acceptance of the nomination, Lincoln simply declared his approval of the Chicago platform, which he would take care 'not to violate, or disregard . . . in any part', Indiana's Richard Thompson promptly urged: 'For God's sake don't write another letter for the papers.'[48]

In practice, of course, Lincoln was far more deeply engaged than it appeared. An instinctive electoral strategist, as well as a salient campaigner in every presidential contest since 1840, he had no intention of placing his future exclusively in the hands of others. He handed over his legal cases to Herndon, took on a secretary and established an open-door office in the state house. There he did more than exchange conversational pleasantries with a stream of old acquaintances, portrait painters, photographers and other visitors. He digested campaign reports from journalists and political correspondents. He read newspapers. He despatched hundreds of private letters, some written for him, some sent in his own hand, all urging confidentiality; only occasionally did he lapse into damaging indiscretion, as when he flippantly suggested that visiting Kentucky would invite a lynching. He signaled party unity by greeting Seward at the Springfield railroad station, when the New Yorker paused *en route* to Chicago. His chief concern throughout was party management: smoothing out factionalism and ensuring the Republicans' machine was as efficient and well targeted as possible. Thus, determined to win in Springfield itself and in Sangamon County, where Douglas held majorities in 1858, Lincoln personally went to examine the battle plan. When he learnt that campaigners 'would probably wait until a few days before the election before any systematic effort would be made in the city', he became 'very energetic in his actions and Language' and more or less imposed his own plan for luring doubtful voters.[49]

Sangamon was important because of its significance as a redoubt of Old Line Whigs whose wider influence throughout the lower North would shape the election as a whole. Lincoln's sources consistently told him that Bell and the Constitutional Union party, not Douglas, were the real enemy. Working vicariously through his 'flying squadron' of Davis, Swett, Judd and other personal friends, and using his secretary, John Nicolay, to deliver his letters and so avoid the scrutiny of Democratic postmasters,

Lincoln made concerted efforts to discourage these conservatives from setting up a separate Bell ticket or, failing that, to keep them weak.[50] Davis was especially energetic in this regard, not least in Indiana, where a Republican success in October would mean – in Lincoln's words – that 'failure is scarcely possible' in November.[51] Davis met Caleb Smith and other Indiana leaders, and extracted money from the national committee to bring in a galaxy of speakers.

There is no better instance of Lincoln's discreet, behind-the-scenes involvement in campaign organization than his intervention in the equally crucial October state of Pennsylvania. There the chronic factional feuding between the Curtin–McClure forces and Cameron's men threatened to disable the campaign. Cameron's allies tried to supplant McClure's state committee with their own auxiliary, but were outwitted. Both camps peppered Lincoln with letters, which included charges of financial mismanagement. Lincoln was determined not to take sides, but to get both groups to 'look to the present and the future only'. He sent Davis and Swett to investigate, on the pretext of conducting a general review of progress. Over the course of two days McClure let them scrutinize every aspect of his operations. Much impressed the efficiency of the party's machine, which had set up 2,000 local committees state-wide, they confessed to the misplaced doubts that had led them to come. McClure learnt the lesson that Lincoln 'took nothing for granted', and the two men's subsequent correspondence aired campaign issues in a spirit of mutual confidence and esteem.[52]

'I do what I can in my position, for organization,' Lincoln remarked to Henry Wilson of Massachusetts, 'but it does not amount to so much as it should.' He knew, naturally, that victory would depend not on his own efforts, but on a regiment of energetic Republican committees developing an irresistible appeal on the back of the usual sequence of ratification meetings. Lincoln feared that the party might neglect the 'irksome labor' of organization-building, but the concern was largely ill-founded. The spontaneous local responses in May gave way over the summer to county and then state-wide meetings to ratify the electoral ticket, with tens of thousands swarming to these and their attendant processions, parades, brass bands and barbecues. During September and October almost daily rallies in some locality or another brought business to a halt and the campaign to its climax. Behind all this activity stood a burgeoning network of Republican clubs, extending into previously uncolonized areas of the lower North and border South. The strongest raised funds not just for themselves but for needier Republicans in the most pivotal contests. All supported semi-military marching companies of enthusiasts known as 'Wide Awakes', uniquely clad in oilcloth capes and caps, to protect them from the dripping kerosene of their torches. Lincoln had encountered their prototype earlier in the year, in Hartford, Connecticut, where they had originated during the gubernatorial election. By November they would become a ubiquitous feature of the Republican campaign and would add far more than mere decoration and color: they brought a real sense of power, momentum and even invincibility to the party's activities. Rattled Democrats founded their own companies – which in Brooklyn took the name of 'the Chloroformers', designed to 'put the Wide Awakes to sleep'.[53]

Republican organizers whetted the public appetite with a feast of political oratory. In halls, squares, river landing places and the replica 'wigwams' that sprouted in many of the larger cities, a stream of Republican orators took their message to the people. Speakers found themselves pressed into service at impromptu meetings beyond their planned itineraries. They included the biggest names in the party, directed by the national or state committees to the areas where their particular appeal could do most good. Seward's radicalism made him a prize attraction in the farther Northwest and New England. Tom Corwin, Frank Blair, Caleb Smith and other conservatives worked Indiana. Chase addressed free-soil Democrats in Michigan. Henry Wilson's attributes as a former shoemaker's apprentice and ex-Know Nothing made him a natural choice for audiences of working men or nativists. Schurz spoke to German Americans, Justin Morrill to protectionists.

Republican authors and editors enriched this diet with a glut of printed material. In a nation boasting more newspaper titles than any other country in the world, hundreds were Republican sheets: the party had over 120 in Ohio alone. Many offered low subscription rates for the campaign's duration. Tracts and speeches, which had poured from the Republican Association of Washington and various regional presses since the previous presidential contest, saturated the country. Campaigners matched propaganda to the audience. 'I believe the most effective Document for all the region North of Rock River will be [the radical] Lovejoy's last speech – then for the whole state prepare a Document composed of choice selections from Lincoln's,' one Illinois activist told Richard Yates, adding mischievously: 'I think Jeff Davis' last speeches would be good to distribute down in Egypt – vs Douglas Democracy.'[54] As this implied, Lincoln's speeches of 1858 and 1859 were extensively circulated as campaign texts, and the candidate himself prepared his Cooper Union speech for publication, which the Young Men's Republican Union issued in an annotated edition.

No antebellum presidential contest was complete without its campaign biographies: within weeks of his nomination the party had made available four separate accounts of Lincoln's life, and eighteen appeared in all. The most dependable was John L. Scripps's 32-page version, based on a personal interview. Both men's scrupulousness and conscientiousness, when combined with Lincoln's modesty, made the exercise as enjoyable as drawing teeth. Scripps found his interviewee 'painfully impressed with the extreme poverty of his early surroundings – the utter absence of all romantic and heroic elements'. Lincoln told him: 'It is a great piece of folly to attempt to make anything out of my early life. It can all be condensed into a single sentence, and that sentence you will find in Gray's Elegy: "The short and simple annals of the poor." That's my life, and that's all you or any one else can make of it.'[55] Even so, the party machine found it more than adequate. After its simultaneous publication in Scripps's *Chicago Press and Tribune* and Greeley's *New York Tribune*, the biography appeared as a cheap pamphlet that sold over a million copies before election day.[56]

Republican organization gave structure and focus to the Republican campaign, but its impressive energy had its source elsewhere, in a cluster of potent ideas. In essence, Republicans plaited three strands of popular thought into the core policy of the Chicago platform, the non-extension of slavery. In declaring its hostility to an aggressive slave power, the party wore the mantle of conservative constitutionalists, defending the threatened ideals and intentions of the republic's Founders. At the same time, by seeking to quarantine slavery, Republicans posed as the champions of economic enterprise, the dignity of work and democratic capitalism. Finally, and perhaps most potent of all, the policy gave the party its purchase on the constituency of antislavery Protestants, for whom containment provided a plausible means of eventually extirpating a moral wrong. The record of Lincoln's words and experience provided Republican campaigners with rich material for each of these themes.

The Chicago platform's policy on slavery was essentially radical. Denouncing popular sovereignty, it asserted the federal government's constitutional duty to enforce what the due process clause demanded: a legal ban on slavery in the territories. The more inflammatory language of the 1856 platform was excised but, following Giddings's intervention, delegates agreed to set out in full the egalitarian principles of the Declaration of Independence. Radicals like Schurz left Chicago proud of their achievement. Yet, at the same time, the platform gave Republicans the chance to campaign as conservatives and traditionalists who cherished the values and policies of the Founding Fathers. Their declared intent was not innovation but restoration: they offered a 'primitivist' return to the nation's republican roots, prising the levers of power from the hands of sectional 'slaveocrats' bent on expanding slavery westwards, reopening the Atlantic slave trade and founding a new empire in the Caribbean. In deference to southerners' constitutional rights, the platform implicitly disowned John Brown's raid: the party would 'maintain inviolate' the rights of each state 'to order and control its own domestic institutions'. But, they insisted, banning the spread of slavery was no less respectful of the republic's ancient landmarks. The real radicals were those demanding federal slave codes and the sanctification of slavery. Republicans' rhetorical strategy was to show, in the words of Governor Morgan and the national committee, that they alone had the backbone to resist the 'persistently insolent and aggressive' demands of a pernicious slave power.[57]

These earnest claims to moderation and conservatism were designed to counter the charges of the Bell–Everett and Douglas men that their opponents' 'House Divided' radicalism would shiver the Union into fragments. Republicans treated the disunionist threats of southern radicals with skepticism, remaining insouciant in the face of incendiary, lurid propaganda that predicted bloody convulsions should the emancipationist Lincoln win. But Union-loving conservatives in the lower North mattered electorally, as Breckinridge hotheads did not, and the party moved to meet the challenge of wooing voters who disliked slavery but hated abolitionism. Presenting themselves and their candidate as the heirs of Henry Clay, Republican speakers insisted that the Chicago platform embodied old, 'national' Whiggery and lauded Lincoln as 'a sound conservative man'.[58] Lincoln himself, despite calls to quieten public alarm, said nothing, confident that those who were genuinely open-minded would find reassurance in his published speeches. For the past decade he had been at pains to show how southerners and Democrats were themselves the constitutional iconoclasts, reinterpreting the Declaration of Independence to exclude black Americans, and willing to 'reject, and scout, and spit upon' the policies of the nation's Founders. The House Divided speech had warned against the new extremism that threatened to make slavery national. More recently, the theme of Republican 'conservatism' formed the core of his widely distributed Cooper Union address.[59]

Promising to embargo slave labor outside its existing state boundaries served, secondly, to crystallize the Republicans' appeal as economic modernizers. The platform set out a stall of policies designed to establish the party's progressive credentials. The promise of river and harbor improvements, and of a railroad link to the Pacific, addressed the inter-ests of northwestern farmers and grain exporters aggrieved by Buchanan's pocket veto of a friendly measure early in 1860. A 'free homestead' plank sought to give Republicans a credibility amongst working men that their Whig predecessors, with their evident lack of enthusiasm for westward movement, had not enjoyed. In some western areas, the issue of free farms overshadowed all other issues, for in the aftermath of the panic of 1857 thousands of farmers were faced with foreclosure or selling the land they were struggling to buy under the Pre-emption Law. When President Buchanan vetoed an already weakened homestead bill in June 1860 he cut western Democrats off at the knees. 'Does anybody suppose that Abraham Lincoln would ever veto such a bill?' asked a jubilant Greeley, perhaps recalling that when they were fellow congressmen Lincoln had shown an unWhiggish sympathy for the homestead cause.[60]

There was no greater euphoria at Chicago than amongst the Penn-sylvania delegates when the committee on resolutions reported the tariff plank. Protection was a politically explosive issue. As Lincoln himself knew, the old Whig policy of high duties to safeguard domestic manu-facturing might well inspire the iron interests of the Keystone State, without which the election would probably be lost, but many western Republicans and even some easterners remained at best unenthusiastic at the prospect of higher charges for imported raw materials and manu-factures. In the event, the platform was short on specifics but pregnant with possibility. It did enough to underscore the main difference be-tween the party's economic program and the Democrats', and to enthuse those protectionist voters who mattered, not only in Pennsylvania but also in parts of the Northwest. Republican campaigners celebrated Lincoln's pedigree as a 'Clay tariff man' and revelled in the Democrats' maladroit blocking of Justin Morrill's tariff bill in the Senate. Penn-sylvania Democrats were aghast at their party's self-inflicted wound, and complained to Douglas that in the state's manufacturing districts the Republicans 'say nothing of the nigger question, but all is made to turn on the Tariff'.[61]

Improvements, homesteads and tariffs helped Republicans reach out beyond the Whigs' natural middle-class constituency to embrace working men eager to share in America's burgeoning capitalist economy. But more important than any of these in signaling the party's devotion to economic progress, social opportunity and meritocracy was the promise to seal the boundaries of slavery – the badge of an archaic, frozen social order, inimical to technological, scientific and intellectual advance. Seward's 'irrepressible conflict' invoked the class, not racial, antagonism between North and South: the incompatibility of slaveowners who selfishly eyed the western territories, and free laborers who patriotically aimed to stop them: 'There is no negro question about it at all. It is an eternal question . . . between aristocracy and democracy.' Innumerable other speeches, including Schurz's appeals to German working men, similarly located the two labor systems in a set of irreconcilable values.[62]

Lincoln's own words harmonized sweetly with the broader chorus. During the 1858 debates he had not paid much attention to the economic effects of slavery on white labor, but several of his addresses in 1859 and 1860 showed signs of giving it careful thought. In his widely distributed Cincinnati speech, he had drawn on his understanding of the labor theory of value to explain the relationship of labor and capital. Labor was the prior engine of human activity. Through their industry, sobriety and honesty men accumulated wealth. With that capital, laborers enjoyed the freedom to hire those who lacked land or their own workshops. Such hired hands were not consigned to permanent dependence and formed only a small proportion of the country's laborers (one in eight, he estimated). Rather, they understood, just as he had in his youth, the meaning of hope, opportunity and self-improvement. Slaves, however, knew only the lash and unremitting hopelessness. This was why 'the mass of white men are really injured by the effect of slave labor in the vicinity of the fields of their own labor'.[63] Some months later, while in the East, a shoemakers' strike gave him a pertinent setting for reasserting these differences: *"I am glad to see that a system of labor prevails in New England under which laborers CAN strike* when they want to. . . . I *like* the system which lets a man quit when he wants to, and wish it might prevail everywhere.' And, with more color-blindness than was the case in many of his western speeches (where the economic aspirations of white men often seemed the whole story), he added: 'I want every man to have the chance – and I believe a black man is entitled to it – in which he *can* better his condition – when he may look forward and hope to be a hired laborer this year and the next, work for himself afterward, and finally to hire men to work for him! That is the true system.'[64]

Symbols proved even more potent than words in establishing Lincoln as the purest exponent of free labor ideology. Splintered fence rails decorated the campaign as obtrusively as cider barrels had refreshed the canvassers of 1840. The Decatur originals made their appearance in Lincoln's Chicago headquarters, 'lighted up by tapers, and trimmed with flowers by enthusiastic ladies', a bizarre altar to meritocracy and self-help. The party's dedicated campaign newspaper in the Northwest took the name of *The Rail Splitter*, while Lincoln's eldest son, Robert, was punningly re-christened the 'Prince of Rails'. The crude symbols of axe and log cabin obscured the more complex reality: of a candidate supported by some of the wealthiest farmers and land speculators in Illinois; of a lawyer who had fled with relief from a life on the land, to become the agent of the biggest corporate interests in the Northwest, the railroads. But if the symbols conjured an unsubtle image, it was by no means a false one. Lincoln fused a personal history of extraordinary social mobility with a continuing warmth toward the ordinary folk amongst whom he had lived, worked and had his being. David Davis was innocent of simple sentimentalizing when he reflected that his friend 'loved the struggling masses – all uprising toward a higher Civilization had his assent & his prayer'.[65]

Republican campaigners' promise to bar the door against southern expansionists worked, thirdly, on an ethical level. Strenuously determined not to be tarred with the brush of abolitionism, leaders from both the radical and moderate sections of the party nonetheless couched their anti-extensionism in the earnest language of conscience and moral purpose. Their campaign became a crusade. Some passengers on the Republican vessel might be there for reasons of political habit or material calculation, but the crew spoke in language designed to harness the potent forces of millennialist Protestants. Addressing evangelicals' worries about the 'steady and tireless march' of aggressive slaveholders, as incanted in sermons, church resolutions and far-flung newspaper editorials, party spokesmen set the antislavery battle in a gospel context, appealing for Christian soldiers to take up arms in what George Washington Julian described as 'a fight . . . between God and the Devil – between heaven and hell!' According to William Burleigh, the belief in an irrepressible conflict between free and slave labor was 'Christ's doctrine of righteousness conflicting with evil'. Joshua Giddings's principled stand at Chicago – the prophetic appeal of a Presbyterian stalwart – served as a metaphor for the wider canvass.[66]

Lincoln's own rhetorical and political strategy since 1854 entirely legitimized this crusading element of the Republican campaign. He had more and more clearly sought to draw an indelible line of political cleavage between those who thought slavery right and those convinced it was wrong, and so to build a single anti-Democrat coalition. His Ohio speeches of 1859 retained the sharp moral perspective of the final three joint debates with Douglas. At Cincinnati he had told an audience that included Kentucky slaveholders: 'I think Slavery is wrong, morally, and politically. I desire that it should be no further spread in these United States, and I should not object if it should gradually terminate in the whole Union.' There must, he continued, be 'a national policy in regard to the institution of slavery, that acknowledges and deals with that institution as being wrong. . . . I do not mean to say that this general government is charged with the duty of redressing or preventing all the wrongs in the world; but I do think it is charged with the duty of preventing and redressing all wrongs which are wrongs to itself.' He urged 'all the elements of the Opposition' to unite on the principled anti-extensionist ground that Republicans could never vacate. To applause he said, 'The good old maxims of the Bible are applicable, and truly applicable to human affairs, and in this as in other things, we may say here that he who is not for us is against us; he who gathereth not with us scattereth.' Six months later Lincoln's riveting Cooper Union speech marked the rhetorical climax of this strategy, celebrating the party's role as the home for those dedicated to the 'faith that right makes might'. Republicans should not be misled by 'sophistical contrivances . . . such as groping for some middle ground between the right and the wrong, vain as the search for a man who should be neither a living man nor a dead man[;] . . . such as Union appeals beseeching true Union men to yield to Disunionists, reversing the divine rule, and calling, not the sinners, but the righteous to repentance'.[67]

Parading in the robes of righteousness and godliness, Republicans in 1860 brandished their Whiggish pedigree. Just as Whigs had striven to present themselves as the guardians of Christian respectability, so Lincoln's party aimed to marshal the energies of the religiously devout behind a standard-bearer seen to be, in the words of the *Chicago Press and Tribune*, 'worthy of the holy cause'.[68] In doing so they buttressed Lincoln's sound antislavery credentials by claiming two related qualities for him: firm Christian piety and incorruptible honesty. Each of these connected to the larger theme of Republicans' devotion to the Protestant faith and its values.

Lincoln the candidate took on the hue of sound Protestant othodoxy. As Scripps's biography explained: 'He is a regular attendant upon religious worship, and though not a communicant, is a pew-holder and liberal supporter of the Presbyterian church in Springfield, to which Mrs. Lincoln belongs.' Lincoln was extolled in the press as one who had 'always held up the doctrines of the Bible, and the truths and examples of the Christian religion, as the foundation of all good'. He enjoyed the confidence of the religious community and was a staunch believer in Sabbath schools; the *Albany Evening Journal* exulted that an opinion poll of Sunday school excursionists from Ogdensburgh, New York, overwhelmingly supported him. Party publicists also celebrated Lincoln as a man of blameless behavior. He never used profane language. He did not gamble. He avoided all intoxicating liquor, even wine.[69] In this portrait there was enough truth to absolve Republican editors of outright perjury. Lincoln had indeed attended the First Presbyterian Church since 1850; he was known amongst his neighbors, including the Baptist minister Noyes W. Miner, as 'a temperance man' who was 'never known to profane the name of God'. But, as we have seen, Lincoln was no pious evangelical Protestant.[70]

The reality of Lincoln's private beliefs, however, mattered less than that his promoters kept him clear of the taint of 'infidelity', so electorally troublesome for him in the 1840s, and projected him as the rescuer of the nation 'from the rule of a Godless . . . Administration'. Republicans, as had the Whigs before them, commonly castigated Democrats for a moral laxness which they ascribed to religious heterodoxy, and especially to the ethical ravages wrought by Catholic influence. Lincoln himself never sought directly to exploit religious sectarianism for electoral gain, but amongst the Republican editors who upheld his Christian integrity were those who eagerly branded Stephen Douglas with the mark of the Beast. They cast the Little Giant as a renegade: born in Vermont, he emigrated 'early enough to avoid contracting many of the Puritan virtues which add luster to the character of that people'. A moral leper and a drunkard (one report told of his being helped, inebriated, out of his railroad car), Douglas 'trifle[d] with the law of Sinai as freely as a hoary-headed gambler would . . . throw dice on a New Orleans sugar barrel for "pig tail" tobacco!' Having abandoned his family's Calvinism in favor of close ties with the Catholic hierarchy, he had visited Rome and allegedly submitted to the Pope, receiving absolution and 'the right hand of fellow-ship'. His marriage to a Catholic wife and the support of Romanist voters in 1858 pointed to his 'secret understanding' with Church leaders, 'whereby he is to have their votes . . . for a consideration'. The 'troop of wild Irish' would surely support Douglas again in 1860 and, with their man in the White House, make Archbishop John Hughes 'the keeper of the con-science of the King'. But vote for Lincoln, insisted the *Rail Splitter*, 'and this Government [would] still remain in Protestant control'.[71]

Republicans' anti-Catholicism played upon a number of related but distinct fears: the theological-ecclesiastical anxieties of staunch Protest-ants who regarded Rome as the Antichrist and the murderer of religious liberties; the social phobia of nativists who equated Catholicism with Irish immigrants and a dram-shop culture of 'blackguardism, . . . riot and soul-sickening blasphemy'; and the political antipathy of antislavery reformers who believed the Roman Church to be minted from the same metal as a slave power equally hostile to republican freedoms. The Republican platform stood silent on the Catholic question. But the party's anti-Catholic posture had been well established through the later 1850s, and many of its speakers and candidates in 1860 were known nativists and anti-Romanists. 'Catholicism and Republicanism are as plainly incompatible as oil and water', declared Charles Ray's *Chicago Press and Tribune* early in the campaign, recognizing that Republican success depended on attracting the 'Protestant' American party voters of 1856, not least in Lincoln's own backyard of Sangamon County. When a possible fusion of Bell's Constitutional Union men and Douglas Democrats threatened to weaken Lincoln's prospects in New York and elsewhere, Republicans sneered at the unnatural yoking of 'the Puritan and the Black-leg', of 'rowdyism and conservatism', and of 'seditionists and law-abiders'.[72] In the event the 'Protestant' Lincoln benefited from an anti-Catholic animus which he had done nothing to inflame and of whose political exploitation he almost certainly disapproved. Curiously, the Democrats generally failed to exploit the ambiguities of Lincoln's 'infidel' past, by which they might have compromised his value as a Protestant champion of orthodoxy, an omission which appears even odder in the light of their creativity in 1856, when they had regaled voters with imaginative tales of John Frémont's 'Catholicism'.[73]

If winning nativist support was essential to Republican victory, so too was garnering a decent proportion of foreign-born voters. The party's leaders knew that immigrants comprised a critical 20 percent of the electorate in the Northwest. The Irish were mostly barnacled to the Democratic party, but the large German population provided a more plausible target for Republican propaganda. At Chicago Schurz had helped design the homestead plank and repudiate the Massachusetts naturalization law with the specific aim of appeasing the Germans. He and Koerner left the convention confident that they could loosen the Democrats' hold over their fellow-countrymen. From New York to Wisconsin they energized a cadre of German-language speakers and newspaper editors, each appealing to free-soil consciences, and rebuking audiences of Democrat-inclined farmers, tradesmen and laborers for tamely submitting to 'party-serfdom'. They faced an uphill but not impossible struggle. Democrats tried to connect Lincoln with his party's nativist elements, by alleging that he had been a member of a Know Nothing lodge in Quincy at the height of the 'dark lantern' excitement. Lincoln resisted a public denial, which might have cost him valuable nativist votes, trusting that his 'Canisius letter' of the previous year and the influence of the *Illinois Staats-Anzeiger* would be enough to stymie Democratic maneuvers.[74] Stunningly –

thanks to the volubility of Schurz and other loyal Germans, and to Lincoln's silence – Republicans managed to mix anti-Catholic oil and pro-immigrant water.

Closely related to the Republicans' use of anti-Romanist sentiment was their stress on corruption in the national administration and their relish for a language of purification that Whigs had so adroitly used before them – most notably in 1840, when they turned Harrison into a crusader against Jacksonian filth. Twenty years on, after forming three of the last four national administrations, Democrats once more faced the charge of steering the nation toward moral crisis. Republicans' promise to encourage 'a revival of *moral honesty and integrity*, in all departments of life' took on even greater urgency after June 1860, when the report of the congressional Covode Committee exposed the Buchanan administration's dishonesty in Kansas affairs and government contracts. An abridged edition became a mainstay of the Republican campaign.[75] The Democrats, claimed Republican editors, in language blending genuine outrage and political calculation, formed 'the rendezvous of thieves, the home of parasites and bloodsuckers, the enemy of God and man, the stereotyped fraud, the sham, the hypocrite, the merciless marauder, and the outlawed renegade and malefactor'. The administration had 'sunk the nation into a gulf of corruption and misrule', putting at stake 'the very existence of the Republic'. The times demanded 'moral independence in politics' and a new Luther.[76]

Lincoln met that need. What Democrats treated with scorn – his lack of executive experience – became a source of campaigning strength, a promise of simple government. Across the North, Republican speakers and writers seized on his reputation for Calvinist integrity. Joshua Giddings told a ratification meeting at Oberlin that 'every beat of "honest Abe's" heart was a throb of sincerity and truth'. The *Chicago Press and Tribune* insisted that he was 'above all, religiously honest'. His legal career, explained the *Ohio State Journal*, showed 'no crooked turns, no evasion, no duplicity in his past life, official or private. All is plain, manly, straightforward and consistent.' A Connecticut paper maintained that he 'always conducts his argument on high moral ground. Is this right or wrong, is the first, last, and only question he asks.' Pertinently, the *Rail Splitter*'s masthead comprised a likeness of Lincoln's 'homely but honest face' above the legend, 'An Honest Man's the Noblest Work of God'. Democrats' efforts to counter these Republican thrusts invoked the testimony of Charles Hanks that his cousin was an ambitious, unprincipled partyswitcher who, having been a Democrat when he first arrived in Illinois, had jumped ship because he lived in a Whig district, and subsequently joined the Republicans through the lure of office. Douglas's paper in Springfield lamented the 'vulgarity' and 'impurity' of his jokes ('His qualifications for side-splitting are quite as good as for rail-splitting ... but neither vocation is supposed to be carried out extensively in the white house') and drily added that, politically, it could be assumed that 'Mr. Lincoln's honesty is about on a par with the scheming office-hunters generally of his class and party'. But his opponents found it hard seriously to shift the widespread perception of Lincoln as 'the very soul of integrity'.[77]

By these means Republicans became the godly party crusading for righteousness. As in 1856, they flavored their conventions with prayer and encouraged clergy to take a salient role in the political campaign. Although some of the most radical antislavery evangelicals demanded still higher ground, many influential religious editors and prominent ministers like Henry Ward Beecher and Josiah Bushnell Grinnell became active supporters. In contrast to 1856, however, when Frémont's alleged Catholicism proved a damaging diversion, the party now had a presidential candidate well fitted for each of the critical issues: slavery, Catholicism and corruption. In consequence, Republicans fought the campaign with supreme ideological confidence. 'We stand upon a rock, and the gates of hell shall not prevail against it,' Caleb Smith told the Chicago delegates. Editors believed their platform embodied 'the *moral instincts and feelings of the nineteenth century*'. 'Democratic Jacobins' were in a battle against 'civilization and Christianity', the 'moral sentiment of the nation', 'the pulpit, the church, the academy'. Schurz could recall no other campaign 'in which the best impulses of human nature were so forceful and effective and aroused the masses to so high a pitch of almost religious fervor'. When Republicans gathered for the great Springfield meeting in August, it seemed to one observer that their hearts were filled with the prayer: 'May God speed the right.'[78]

A few Democrats responded in kind by pointing to ministerial celebrities who had endorsed their own party: Jedediah Burchard, the Presbyterian revivalist; the Methodist, Henry Clay Dean, who was on the Democrats' slate of presidential electors in Iowa; and Peter Cartwright.[79] But in general, Democrats and Constitutional Unionists jeered at the Republicans for claiming to be 'the *decency, moral* and *Christian party*'. Thus when Springfield's joyful Lincoln men pealed church bells on news of his nomination in May, the town's Douglasite paper protested: 'black republicanism has ever recognized pulpits and church bells as party adjuncts, but yesterday's performance run the thing a little beyond the line of decency'. In nearby Pana, Douglasites told of Republicans marking the

Chicago convention by singing 'Old Hundred', 'Pisgah', and calling for prayer – in the shade of 'the sainted [John] Brown'. Democrats derided Republicans as 'a religious Sect' with a 'holy zeal for its one idea', the natural allies of 'blue light puritans' and 'fanatical Sabbatarians', who were working to unite church and state, and universalize New England morality: if the party 'had not slavery for a hobby, it would be vexing us about some other questions of morals or of social arrangement'. This was the party of 'ultra and fanatical' ministers who aimed to turn Lincoln into one of God's 'instrumentalities' in the great battle against slavery; of Owen Lovejoy, 'the old nigger stealer', 'great negroite', and abolitionist, whose 'sacred drippings' (stump speeches) aimed to secure the election of his like-minded friend. Responding with ridicule to what it considered Republican sanctimony, the *Campaign Plain Dealer* of Cleveland, Ohio, proffered 'A Political Sermon. By the Rev. Hardshell Pike', a satirical riposte to the jeremiads of Lincolnite ministers. Taking as his 'tex' the reading *'He split some rails in Illinoy and bossed a roarin' flat-boat'*, the Douglasite preacher developed his theme:

The pizin crew who oppose us tell us to come to ABRAHAM's buzzum, when the fact is he hain't got no more buzzum than a chest of jiner's tools has. . . . Maybe he's a good man. I'm not here to maline him, my Brethering. No doubt he kin split a fair rail. Probly he's a kind man in his family & pays his grocer's bill promptly, but my Brethering, he can't keep a hotel. He's too small a man – too weak a sister – to be President.[80]

The October state elections triumphantly vindicated the Republicans' campaign strategy of targeting the swing voters in the pivotal states. Ohio gave the party ticket a majority of 12,000. More encouraging still, Lane in Indiana and Curtin in Pennsylvania swept to their governor's mansions by stunning margins of 10,000 and 32,000 respectively. The two men who had done most to block Seward at Chicago now appeared to remove the final obstacles to a Lincoln presidency, by drawing into the coalition enough nativists, Old Line Whigs and immigrants to ensure that in November the Constitutional Union ticket would enjoy little credibility amongst conservative anti-Democrats. Lincoln told Seward that the results exceeded his highest hopes: 'It now really looks as if the Government is about to fall into our hands.'[81] Douglas grimly concurred and abandoned the stump in the western states. 'Mr. Lincoln is the next President. We must try to save the Union. I will go South.'[82]

Not even attempts at cooperation amongst his opponents would deny him. The leaders of the Douglas, Breckinridge and Bell forces in Pennsylvania, New Jersey and New York, fearing that a Republican victory would provoke the secession of southern states and so strike a commercial body blow at New York, Philadelphia and their hinterlands, tried to agree 'fusion' tickets, but with only limited success. Continuing recriminations between the 'treacherous' Douglasites and 'secessionist' Breckinridge men did little to restore a pragmatic unity to the fragmented Democratic party. At the same time, the Irish and other foreign-born Democrats could not easily forget the nativist antecedents of the Constitutional Union party (and, in case they were inclined to do so, Republican editors were only too ready to issue helpful reminders). Fusion of a limited kind was engineered in New Jersey and Pennsylvania; in New York, despite more effective cooperation, Lincoln still ran comfortably ahead.

As this suggests, Lincoln's victory on 6 November was not in any simple way the consequence of a divided opposition, though that is what the tally of presidential ballots might seem to indicate, for Lincoln won with less than 40 percent of the popular vote nationally: 1,866,452, to Douglas's 1,376,957, Breckinridge's 849,781 and Bell's 588,879. This, however, offers a misleading measure of Lincoln's relative strength. More telling was his comfortable victory in the electoral college, by 180 votes to Breckinridge's 72, Bell's 39 and Douglas's 12. This he achieved by securing a clear majority of the vote in almost every free state in which he ran. In New York, Pennsylvania, Ohio, Massachusetts and other populous states with the largest number of presidential electors, support for Lincoln exceeded the combined popular vote for his opponents. Only in California, Oregon and New Jersey did his ticket win electoral votes with fewer than 50 percent of ballots cast, and these electors (14 in all) were not crucial to the outcome. Thus, even if we combine all the opposition ballots behind a single candidate, state by state, Lincoln still retains his ascendancy in the electoral college, by 169 to 134.

Hypothesizing a united opposition vote, however, is entirely unhistorical. For Republicans to have faced a united Democratic opposition, as they had done in 1856, either the Douglas or the Buchanan forces would have had to concede their position. This was implausible in the circumstances of 1860, given the split over Lecompton, Douglas's political realism and the tightening grip of proslavery extremism in the southern party. Had – against all likelihood – a Democratic compromise been patched together, the party would have lost the support of free-soil elements in the North, or southern rights men in the South, or both. Douglas undoubtedly retained the votes of some northern antislavery Democrats precisely because he was seen to be untainted by connection with the 'doughface' administration. In other words, the divided opposition – given how things had come to stand by 1860 – may have maximized the anti-Lincoln vote, rather than making the Republicans' victory more likely. (Where the divisions *may* have helped Lincoln, however, was in the October state elections, especially in Indiana, where personal antipathies ran so deep that many Breckinridge men actually sustained the Republicans against the forces of the hated Douglas.)

More significant than the Democrats' schism in paving the way for Lincoln's victory was his party's success in squeezing the conservative American vote of 1856. Compared with Fillmore, Bell performed miserably in the free states. In the crucial southern regions of Indiana he held on to just one vote in five, in southern Illinois to just one in eight. Here Lincoln doubled – at least – Frémont's share of the vote. As early as June a hopeful Herndon had sensed that in the western states 'the "old line Whigs" are fast coming out for us – are going almost unanimously and wildly for Lincoln'.[83] In the end a combination of a relatively moderate platform and the candidate's lawyerly Whig constitutionalism and southern roots helped to assuage conservatives' fears of Republican radicalism. Symbolically, the party won in Springfield itself, reversing the Democrats' victory of 1858, and in Sangamon County Douglas's majority was now reduced to just a few votes.[84]

The Republican heartlands remained, as they had been for Frémont, not the conservative lower North, but the countryside and the small towns in regions most saturated with New England influences. With only a few exceptions – Chicago was one – Lincoln ran poorly in the largest cities: leading businessmen, including those with southern trading connections, were commonly hostile, as were unskilled and poorer foreign-born workers. It was amongst skilled working men and market-oriented farmers that Republicans did best. The Massachusetts *Springfield Republican* located the party's strength in 'the great middling-interest class', men 'who work with their own hands, who live and act independently, who hold the stakes of home and family, of farm and workshop, of education and freedom'. The party of 'free soil, free labor and free men' struck a powerful chord with certain economic interests in the free states.[85] Yet the Republican appeal related less to voters' immediate material interests than to their attachment to ideas of self-improvement, achievement through self-discipline, and economic independence.

These ideas commonly derived their moral aspect from religious authority. It is clear that Republican voting patterns related quite strongly to religious and church affiliations and to the ethnic identities with which they were interwoven. Veteran reformers as well as youthful idealists rallied to the party and to Lincoln as incorruptible representatives of a particular variety of ramrod-backed, reforming Protestantism. There is little doubt they enjoyed the support of the smaller, earnestly anti-slavery denominations, including Quakers, Freewill Baptists, Wesleyan Methodists and Free Presbyterians. But how successful were Republicans in living up to their self-image as the 'Christian party' by securing the votes of the bulk of the free states' evangelical churchgoers?

Lincoln's own analysis provides a proper caution against the notion of Protestant political uniformity. During the campaign, in a conversation with Newton Bateman – the Superintendent of Public Instruction for Illinois, whose room in the state capitol adjoined his own campaign headquarters – he produced the results of a recent canvass of Springfield voters. These included the names of the city's clergymen. Bateman recalled Lincoln's frustration that self-proclaimed God-fearing men could so have misread their Bibles as not to care whether slavery was voted up or down: 'Here are twenty-three ministers of different denominations, and all of them are against me but three; and here are a great many prominent members of the churches, a very large majority of whom are against me.'[86] As we have seen, Lincoln had a strong grasp of the religious features of his state's electoral geography and political cultures, and of Springfield's standing at the cross-roads between Yankee reformism and southern-oriented conservatism. Against the predominant Democrat and Constitutional Union clergy stood a minority of New Englanders, including two Connecticut-born pastors: Albert Hale, of the antislavery Second Presbyterian Church, and Noyes W. Miner, Lincoln's Baptist neighbor, who would spend election day in 1860 at the polls, doing 'the hardest day's work he ever did challenging votes and trying to keep things straight'.[87]

Lincoln's words did not mean that he considered Republicanism uniformly weak within Illinois evangelical Protestant churches. The party was particularly well supported by New School (though not Old School) Presbyterianism as well as by most of the state's 200 Congregational churches.[88] Equally significant was the considerable loyalty to Lincoln, especially in the northern counties, amongst the state's largest denomination, the Methodists. The editor of the Northwest's most influential Methodist newspaper, Thomas M. Eddy, was a staunch Republican. When, during the course of the campaign, Anthony Bewley, a northern Methodist preacher, was lynched by a Texas mob, Eddy took up the case as the most recent instance of the slave power's flagrant violation of Americans' constitutional rights. In an open letter to President Buchanan, he pointedly noted that this southern 'reign of terror' drove Methodists to ask: 'Can an administration be found which will protect the rights of conscience and the freedom of worship?' Though previously divided in their voting habits, Methodists would cast their 'united suffrage' for the man able to uphold their rights. Eddy's threat caused no small stir. His thinly-veiled endorsement of Lincoln was reprinted in the columns of the *Chicago Press and Tribune* (where the Methodist Scripps proved a bridge to his denomination) and other Republican papers throughout the free states.[89]

Even in central Illinois, where they were relatively weak, Methodist Republicans made up in enthusiasm what they lacked in numbers. Leonard F. Smith, for instance, a young, Canada-born, itinerant preacher, experienced on 8 August one of the most memorable days in his life: rising at 3.00 a.m., he and a fellow Methodist had traveled from beyond Jacksonville by horse-drawn wagon and railroad to attend the great Lincoln ratification meeting in Springfield; stunned by the numbers, he marveled at the color and pageantry, especially the torchlight procession of 2,000 Wide-Awakes, and eventually arrived back home after five the following morning fortified in his political creed. Though his senior fellow ministers included Peter Cartwright, 'old Father Gillham' and other southern-born Democrats, Smith resolutely attended Republican rallies, barbecues, and pole-raisings, firm in his conviction that to work for Lincoln's victory over a party 'characterized by a noisy dirty ignorant rabble' was a proper expression of his religious faith.[90]

Across Illinois and the wider North Republicans significantly extended their influence within Protestant churches. Unlike Frémont in 1856, Lincoln ran impressively amongst German Reformed and other German Protestant voters. Even more telling were the evangelical accessions from the American party. Lincoln also made converts amongst long-standing evangelical Democrats, though these were probably less instrumental in his victory than the accession of first-time voters into what William Seward described as 'a party chiefly of young men'. Leonard Smith, at twenty-two, was voting in his first presidential election. So, too, was John Wanamaker, secretary of the Philadelphia YMCA and a Lincoln enthusiast after the joint debates with Douglas in 1858.[91]

Although Lincoln's Republican party did not fashion a monolithic evangelical vote, its achievement was extraordinary: regimenting the moral energies of evangelical churches more effectively than ever before in the cause of political antislavery and civic purification. It was, after all, the Republican party which most successfully focused the moral energy of postmillennialist Protestants and exploited the public discourse they had elaborated over three decades. In part theirs was a negative discourse of anxiety and paranoia, which played on fears of Freemasons and Catholics as conspirators against the Christian republic, and which contributed to

Free Soilers' and Republicans' elaboration of a hated slave power. But evangelical perceptions also brought into politics a more positive stress on conscience, Calvinistic duty and social responsibility – a creed which reached its apogee in the early Republican party. For some this meant securing the slaves' liberty above all else; but many others linked this to emancipating white freemen from the despotism of the slave power. These pious Republicans went further than previous American evangelicals in identifying the arrival of God's kingdom with the success of a particular political party. Ministers who in the campaigns of 1856 and 1860 took part alternately in revival meetings and Republican rallies gave notice that religion and politics had fused more completely than ever before in the American republic.

Of course, Lincoln's Republican party was not simply or even principally an instrument of the reforming, optimistic evangelicalism unleashed by the Second Great Awakening. Economic interest and bitter antisouthern feeling were important elements of the Republican mix. But Carl Schurz was not alone in insisting that selfish materialism had taken second place to 'the purely moral motive' in the hearts of mainstream Republicans.[92] And Lincoln's candidacy, far from being in tension with the party's Protestant morality, served its purposes well. The party was both more and less than 'the Christian party in politics', but in the eyes of northern antislavery moralists it deserved that name more than any other political force they had known. In Lincoln, with his mix of lawyerly, constitutional conservatism and unyielding, earnest moralism, they had a standard-bearer admirably suited to their combined needs as pragmatic coalition-builders and high-minded crusaders.

Notes

1 *CW*, 3:460–2.

2 *CW*, 1:454.

3 Illinois put Lincoln's name forward; he won support in 11 states, from Maine to California.

4 *CW*, 2:506; N&H, 2:176–83; William E. Baringer, *Lincoln's Rise to Power* (Boston, MA: Little, Brown, 1937), 42–3; *RWAL*, 154.

5 *CW*, 3:355–6, 377, 395; *HI*, 365.

6 *CW*, 3:399–400.

7 *CW*, 3:378–9, 387–8.

8 *CW*, 3:345, 405.

9 *CW*, 3:365–70, 405, 423–5.

10 *CW*, 3:365–70.

11 *CW*, 3:384, 386, 390–1, 394.

12 *CW*, 3:389–91.

13 *CW*, 3:503.

14 *CW*, 3:496, 502.

15 *CW*, 3:491; Baringer, *Lincoln's Rise to Power*, 117–21.

16 *CW*, 3:341, 510–12; N&H, 2:183–5; Baringer, *Lincoln's Rise to Power*, 127–8.

17 N&H, 2:216–25.

18 *CW*, 3:522–50.

19 N&H, 2:216–25; Baringer, *Lincoln's Rise to Power*, 153–64; *CW*, 3:555; *Herndon's Lincoln*, 369.

20 Don E. Fehrenbacher, *Chicago Giant: A Biography of Long John Wentworth* (Madison, WI: American History Research Center, 1957), 148–9, 162–70; Mark M. Krug, *Lyman Trumbull: Conservative Radical* (New York: A.S. Barnes and Co., 1965), 100, 157.

21 Willard L. King, *Lincoln's Manager: David Davis* (Cambridge, MA: Harvard University Press, 1960), 132; *CW*, 3:507–8.

22 King, *David Davis*, 133; Donald, 242; *Central Illinois Gazette* (i.e. William O. Stoddard), 7 Dec. 1859, in Baringer, *Lincoln's Rise to Power*, 130–1; *CW*, 3:509.

23 *HI*, 247; *CW*, 3:517.

24 Baringer, *Lincoln's Rise to Power*, 145, 149; *Herndon's Lincoln*, 369–70; *CW*, 4:33, 43, 45.

25 *HI*, 462–3; Baringer, *Lincoln's Rise to Power*, 180–5.

26 *HI*, 463; *CW*, 4:48. The banner-writer was in error: it was John, not Thomas, Hanks who split the rails.

27 *HI*, 463.

28 A.K. McClure, *Abraham Lincoln and Men of War Times* (Philadelphia, PA: Times Publishing Co., 1892), 23; Baringer, *Lincoln's Rise to Power*, 186–7.

29 *HI*, 683.

30 Baringer, *Lincoln's Rise to Power*, 192, 322–3; *Reminiscences of Carl Schurz*, 3 vols (New York: The McClure Co., 1907–08), 2:176–9, 184.

31 *Reminiscences of Carl Schurz*, 2:169–72, 184–7; Robert Cook, *Baptism of Fire: The Republican Party in Iowa, 1838–1878* (Ames, IA: Iowa State University Press, 1994), 124.

32 Baringer, *Lincoln's Rise to Power*, 172. Lincoln played on the issue of McLean's age and noted the possible complications following from his resignation from the US Supreme Court either before or after an election campaign. *CW*, 4:46.

33 *Reminiscences of Carl Schurz*, 2:175.

34 Eric Foner, *Free Soil, Free Labor, Free Men: The Ideology of the Republican Party before the Civil War* (New York: Oxford University Press, 1970), 208.

35 *CW*, 3:380, 383.

36 *CW*, 3:512.

37 *CW*, 4:34, 47–8.

38 Donald, 246.

39 King, *David Davis*, 136–8; McClure, *Lincoln and Men of War Times*, 78–9; *HI*, 677.

40 *HI*, 683–4; King, *David Davis*, 136–8.

41 Baringer, *Lincoln's Rise to Power*, 219; N&H, 2:262–9; King, *David Davis*, 139–41.

42 *HI*, 490–2.

43 Baringer, *Lincoln's Rise to Power*, 288; N&H, 2:277–8; *HI*, 677.

44 *CW*, 4:50; Baringer, *Lincoln's Rise to Power*, 303.

45 Baringer, *Lincoln's Rise to Power*, 313; *Reminiscences of Carl Schurz*, 2:188.

46 Howard K. Beale, *The Diary of Edward Bates* ['Volume IV of the Annual Report of the American Historical Association for the Year 1930'] (Washington, DC: US Government Printing Office, 1933), 132, 136; Marvin R. Cain, *Lincoln's Attorney General: Edward Bates of Missouri* (Columbia, MO: University of Missouri Press, 1965), 116; William B. Hesseltine, *Lincoln and the War Governors* (New York: Alfred A. Knopf, 1955), 65; King, *David Davis*, 144–5.

47 The words were McClure's, who knew about these things. McClure, *Lincoln and Men of War Times*, 22.

48 *CW*, 4:52; N&H, 2:286–7; King, *David Davis*, 148; *Reminiscences of Carl Schurz*, 2:196–7; Baringer, *Lincoln's Rise to Power*, 326.

49 *CW*, 4:69–70, 97, 99; *HI*, 486.

50 Hesseltine, *Lincoln and the War Governors*, 65–6. Lincoln's overtures to James O. Putnam of New York, who deserted Fillmore, and Richard W. Thomson of Indiana, who tried to prevent a Bell ticket, were especially significant. *CW*, 4:79, 82–4, 89.

51 *CW*, 4:87–8.

52 *CW*, 4:103–4; McClure, *Lincoln and Men of War Times*, 39–41.

53 *CW*, 4:109; N&H, 2:284–6; Reinhard H. Luthin, *The First Lincoln Campaign* (Cambridge, MA: Harvard University Press, 1944), 174.

54 Luthin, *The First Lincoln Campaign*, 183.

55 *HI*, 57.

56 Judd, fearing a composition by committee, had championed Scripps as the best qualified biographer. N.B. Judd to W. Butler, 26(?) May 1860, Butler Collection, Illinois State Historical Society.

57 Republican circular of spring 1859, quoted in Michael F. Holt, *The Political Crisis of the 1850s* (New York: John Wiley and Sons, 1978), 209.

58 Foner, *Free Soil, Free Labor, Free Men*, 217 (quoting Tom Ewing of Ohio).

59 *CW*, 3:430, 537; 4:130, 132–5, 444.

60 Luthin, *The First Lincoln Campaign*, 177.

61 Luthin, *The First Lincoln Campaign*, 208.

62 Luthin, *The First Lincoln Campaign*, 188; *Reminiscences of Carl Schurz*, 200–1.

63 *CW*, 3:446, 449, 462–3. Lincoln explored the moral antipathies between 'free labor' and 'mudsill' societies in his address to the Wisconsin State Agricultural Society, Milwaukee, 30 Sept. 1859. *CW*, 3:477–80.

64 *CW*, 4:24–5.

65 N&H, 2:283–4; HI, 348.

66 Albany Argus, 26 Sept. 1860; New York Tribune, 12 June 1860; Albany Evening Journal, 22 Sept. 1860; Ohio State Journal, 25 June 1860.

67 CW, 3:440–3, 453, 460–2, 547–50.

68 Chicago Press and Tribune, 15, 16 May 1860.

69 John Locke Scripps, Life of Abraham Lincoln, ed. Roy P. Basler and Lloyd A. Dunlap (Bloomington, IN: Indiana University Press, 1961), 165; Chicago Press and Tribune, 21, 23 May 1860.

70 William E. Barton, The Soul of Abraham Lincoln (New York, 1920), 76–7; Noyes W. Miner, 'Personal Recollections of Abraham Lincoln', 14–20, 37, Illinois State Historical Society. Miner lived across the street from the Lincolns, on the corner of 8th and Jackson. Springfield Democrats responded by hinting that Lincoln had kept a dram shop in his New Salem days, and by insisting that he deserved no more credit for eschewing the sale of 'ardent moisture' than solid Democratic citizens 'who never drew liquor for a profit'. Illinois State Register, 4 June 1860.

71 New York Tribune, 15 June 1860; Rail Splitter (Cincinnati; facsimile edition, Chicago, 1950), 1 Aug. (quoting Steubenville Herald), 15 Aug. 1860; Illinois State Register, 4 June (quoting the Quincy Whig), 22 Oct. 1860; Chicago Daily Times and Herald, 27 Oct. 1860.

72 William E. Baringer, 'Campaign Technique in Illinois – 1860', Transactions of the Illinois State Historical Society for the Year 1932, 267; Jay Monaghan, The Man Who Elected Lincoln (Indianapolis, IN: Bobbs-Merrill Company, 1956), 185–6; W. Jayne to J.M. Palmer, 11 July 1856, J.M. Palmer Papers, Illinois State Historical Society; Rail Splitter, 12 Sept., 3 Oct. 1860.

73 One Republican loyalist told Lincoln early in the campaign that in Philadelphia 'your enemies . . . are circulating the report that "in religious opinions you are an open & avowed Infidel"', but this was not a persistent theme. T.C. Henry to AL, 26 May 1860, ALP. Lincoln's duel with Shields also prompted questions in some quarters but generated no animated debate. J.W. Sullivan to AL, 26 May 1860, ALP.

74 CW, 4: 85–6; F.E. Leseure to AL, 26 July 1860, ALP.

75 At one point 40,000 copies a day streamed from Republican presses. Luthin, The First Lincoln Campaign, 175–6.

76 Cincinnati Gazette, 26 March 1858; New York Tribune, 16 May, 25 June 1860; Reminiscences of Carl Schurz, 2:101–4.

77 Chicago Press and Tribune, 19, 23 May, 13 July (for Ohio State Journal) 1860; The Hartford Press, quoted in New York Tribune, 21 May 1860; Campaign Plain Dealer, Cleveland, 28 July 1860; Illinois State Register, 5 June, 14 July 1860.

78 Baringer, Lincoln's Rise to Power, 298; Rail Splitter, 29 Aug. 1860; Reminiscences of Carl Schurz, 191–3; Quincy Whig and Republican, 18 Aug. 1860.

79 Campaign Plain Dealer, 28 July 1860; Rail Splitter, 29 Aug. 1860; Daily Chicago Times, 22 July 1860. Republicans were contemptuous of these double standards: 'It makes a

great difference whether your bull gores my ox, or my bull gores your ox.' *Quincy Whig and Republican*, 18 Aug. 1860.

80 *Illinois State Register*, 19 May, 28 May (quoting the *Pana Democrat*), 14 June (quoting the *Joliet Signal*), 25 June, 14 July, 4, 14 Aug., 13, 16, 24 Oct. 1860; *Campaign Plain Dealer*, 11 Aug. 1860.

81 *CW*, 4:126–7.

82 Robert W. Johannsen, *Stephen A. Douglas* (New York: Oxford University Press, 1973), 797–8.

83 Luthin, *The First Lincoln Campaign*, 184.

84 In Sangamon, Lincoln polled 3,556 votes to Douglas's 3,598: a switch of just 22 votes would have given him the county. King, *David Davis*, 157.

85 William E. Gienapp, 'Who Voted for Lincoln?', in John L. Thomas, ed., *Abraham Lincoln and the American Political Tradition* (Amherst, MA: University of Massachusetts Press, 1986), 68–72; Cook, *Baptism of Fire*, 126–7.

86 Though the substance of this conversation would become a matter of notorious dispute between Josiah Holland and William H. Herndon, both men agreed that Lincoln had noted bitterly that all but three of the Springfield clergy opposed his election. Barton, *The Soul of Abraham Lincoln*, 114–27. *Williams' Springfield Directory: City Guide and Business Mirror, for 1860–61*, comp. C.S. Williams (Springfield, 1860) lists 28 ministers in the town in 1860. Harry E. Pratt's analysis of the polling data indicates that 11 of the 28 did not vote: these included both Catholic priests, the Universalist minister, three Methodists (including Fred Myers, a free black, ineligible to vote), a Baptist, a Christian, and a Lutheran. File, Illinois State Historical Society.

87 Miner, 'Recollections', 6.

88 In 1860 there were over 13,000 members in 206 Congregational churches in Illinois; the 168 New School Presbyterian churches embraced 9,021 members. *Northwestern Christian Advocate*, 3 Oct. 1860. The pastor of the First Congregational Church in Chicago, William W. Patton, opened the second day's proceedings at the Republican national convention in 1860. *Chicago Press and Tribune*, 21 May 1860.

89 *Northwestern Christian Advocate*, 12 Sept. 1860.

90 Leonard F. Smith, 'Diary', 8, 29 Aug., 3, 10 Sept., 9, 15, 18 Oct. 1860, Illinois State Historical Society; also, James Shaw, *Twelve Years in America: Being the Observations on the Country, the People, Institutions and Religion; with notices of Slavery and the Late War* (London, 1867), 114–15, 286.

91 Gienapp, 'Who Voted for Lincoln?', 66–7, 74–6; Herbert A. Gibbons, *John Wanamaker*, 2 vols (New York: Harper & Brothers, 1926), 1:30–9.

92 *Reminiscences of Carl Schurz*, 2:191–3.

❖

Chapter Four

Confronting the Limits of Power: From President-elect to War President, 1860–61

Lincoln slept fitfully on the night of 6 November 1860. His election victory, the climax of a career in democratic politics, brought only modest personal satisfaction and left him feeling, 'as I never had before, the responsibility that was upon me'. His indeterminate forebodings would soon give way to hard decision-making, as threats of secession and predictions of civil war proved to be more than tactical scaremongering. Indeed, within little more than a year of his electoral triumph the president had succumbed to a mood of dark despair. Restoring harmony to a Union that faced a well-armed and hostile Confederacy of eleven states, nine million inhabitants, several hundred thousand square miles and substantial economic resources – a preposterous ambition, as it seemed to many foreign observers – was daunting enough. It was barely credible at a time when the Union's finances lay in tatters, its massive volunteer army remained characteristically stalled and its stubbornly cautious general-in-chief lay seriously ill with typhoid fever. Small wonder that since taking office Lincoln had discernibly aged, his face lined and his hair now flecked with grey. In the early days of January 1862 he lamented to the quartermaster-general: 'The bottom is out of the tub. What shall I do?'[1]

Lincoln's feelings of near-impotence were understandable in the circumstances and marked only an intensifying of the strong sense he had had since his election of being swept along by events whose momentum and direction he could barely control. The turbulence of these fourteen months would have tested the mettle of even the most seasoned statesman. It seems hardly surprising that Lincoln, an absentee from Washington politics for over a decade and lacking first-hand experience of executive power, should have evinced signs of uncertainty and anxiety, and made mistakes.

Yet, whatever Lincoln's personal limitations and the circumstantial constraints on his power during this period, what is striking is the clarity and even boldness with which he provided answers to the chief strategic questions that he faced. In each of the three phases into which this period can be divided Lincoln identified and responded to the most urgent challenges with notable single-mindedness. First, during the four months of Buchanan's lame-duck presidency, as the states of the Deep South moved from threatening secession to realizing it, Lincoln resisted all calls for compromise over the heart of the Chicago platform on which he had been elected. The president-in-waiting was prepared to run the risk of a *de facto* break-up of the Union rather than relinquish the Republicans' high ground of non-extension: to yield on that would be to invite the disintegration of his party, the only political force capable of implementing the egalitarian principles of the Declaration of Independence.

During the second phase, the weeks of uneasy peace between the eve of Lincoln's inauguration and the outbreak of hostilities at Fort Sumter, the new president's political focus shifted from the rightness or wrongness of slavery to the constitutional integrity of the Union. He set himself the goal of preventing any further erosion of the Union by defending the remaining federally-held forts in the seceded states, while at the same time sticking to his inaugural pledge not to be the first to shed blood – so ensuring that, if and when hostilities broke out, the North would remain united in cross-party patriotism. Throughout the third phase, the early months of what Lincoln came to see would be a long and grim struggle, the president showed his unbending determination conservatively to restore the Union 'as it was', to ensure that the April coalition of support, including loyalists within the upper tier of slave states, was sustained and maximized. Equally, he remained resolute in representing the conflict as an internal rebellion to be resolved without the intervention of foreign powers.

In sum, Lincoln during these uncertain months would not seek to provoke war but he would resist the course of 'peace at any price' and do more than any other single individual to shape the circumstances of the war's immediate outbreak. Most significant of all, he would lay the only strategic foundations on which the Union could hope eventually to succeed. Throughout it all he maintained an attentive but not subservient engagement with public sentiment which would provide the essential basis both of his power as president and commander-in-chief, and of Union victory.

In the antechamber to power: holding the party line

For four months after the November election formal power remained in the hands of Buchanan's outgoing administration, and for most of that time Lincoln, the private citizen, stayed in Springfield. It was the hapless Buchanan who had the responsibility of dealing with the erupting secession movement in the lower South, earning derision for his feeble argument that it was wrong but beyond his power to stop. South Carolina and six other states took their initial steps toward separation believing, mistakenly, that Lincoln was diabolic abolitionism personified, but rightly seeing his election as an historical watershed, the moment when a political party with no ideological kinship or organizational ties with the South would take the levers of federal power for the first time. National attention anxiously turned to the outgoing Congress, controlled by the Republicans, and to the party's new leader, the president-elect.

A lack of formal authority did not mean an absence of responsibility or of informal influence. Hordes of politicians, journalists, artists and friends descended on the state house in Springfield, where Lincoln received them in the governor's office. Some were supplicants for office, some well-wishers. All were eager to know how the new leader would respond to the mounting crisis. Hungry for information, he himself assiduously read the newspapers and the daunting torrent of mail that poured in, much of it proffering conflicting advice. 'He reads letters constantly – at home – in the street – among his friends. I believe he is sorely tempted in church', reported the youthful John Hay, whom Lincoln had appointed to assist John Nicolay, his private secretary. The besieged leader's sense of standing at a watershed in his own and the country's life took symbolic shape in his choosing to grow a beard. The psychological significance of this is unclear. It was not affectation (or, as punsters suggested, 'putting on 'airs'). It may have reflected a degree of insecurity. His secretaries later insisted that 'he easily and naturally assumed the leadership of his party' in these months, evincing confidence and geniality in his personal interviews.[2] But he would not have been human had he not felt real anxiety over what lay ahead.

Before his election Lincoln had faced calls to signal to the alarmed South the essential moderation of his own position. These now grew ever louder. From southern Unionists came requests that he pay a reassuring visit to a slave state, or publish a selection of his speeches to trumpet his constitutional conservatism on fugitive slaves and other litmus issues. Northerners of various political stripes, including conservative members of his own party, like Henry Raymond of the *New York Times*, urged the value of a speech or public letter to correct southern misconceptions and restore confidence to business and financial markets. Lincoln, however, in tune with most Republican leaders, and those radical correspondents who urged him to ignore 'the tremors of conservatives or the howlings of traitors', was disinclined to add to what was already in the public domain. Reassured by some correspondents that most southerners were reconciled to his administration and that 'the madmen' were in a minority, Lincoln made no accredited and substantive public statement for three months after his election. He stayed silent, he told unsympathetic border-state editors, not 'merely on *punctilio*' – to speak out as a mere private citizen would be a breach of etiquette – but because he feared it would do positive harm, laying himself open to further distortion of his position and to the accusation of timidity, even cowardice. 'For the good men of the South ... I have no objection to repeat seventy and seven times. But I have *bad* men also to deal with, both North and South – men who are eager for something new upon which to base new misrepresentations'; 'The secessionists, *per se* believing they had alarmed me, would clamor all the louder.' As for those '*respectable scoundrels*', who had encouraged the unjust fears underlying the commercial uncertainty, they should 'repair the mischief of their own making; and then perhaps they will be less greedy to do the like again'.[3]

Lincoln judged his course vindicated when, two weeks after his election, he used a rally at Springfield to speak by proxy. Providing a short passage to be incorporated into Lyman Trumbull's speech, Lincoln sat alongside the senator as he sought to reassure southerners of the Republicans' conservative intentions. The outcome was no more than Lincoln had expected, despite Trumbull's making Lincoln's text more emollient still. The president-elect took no comfort in telling Henry Raymond that hostile southerners considered the speech 'an open declaration of war against them', at the same time that some Republicans thought it intimated the abandonment of their party's principles. 'This is just ... what would happen with any declaration I could make. These political fiends are not half sick enough yet. "Party malice" and not "public good" possesses them entirely. "They seek a sign, and no sign shall be given them." ' He had earlier told a clamant Tennessean, for whom he had an equally pertinent scriptural text, 'If they hear not Moses and the prophets, neither will they be persuaded though one rose from the dead.'[4]

In private, however, Lincoln was readier to signal his likely course and to offer reassurances. When Alexander Stephens, a congressional colleague in the late 1840s, delivered a stunning anti-secession speech in the Georgia legislature Lincoln opened a hopeful correspondence. If southerners really did fear that his administration would '*directly*, or *indirectly*, interfere with their slaves, or with them, about their slaves' then Lincoln sought to reassure him 'as once a friend, and still, I hope, not an enemy' that the fears were groundless: 'The South would be in no more danger in this respect, than it was in the days of Washington.' In response, Stephens called on Lincoln to speak out 'to save our common country. A word fitly spoken by you now would be like "apples of gold in pictures of silver."'[5] The request was unavailing and there the correspondence closed.

At the same time Lincoln entertained the idea put to him by David Davis and other party leaders that he appoint a loyal and able, but non-Republican, southerner to his cabinet as a signal of friendship to the South. Lincoln was not optimistic: who were these 'white crows', he asked Weed. Still, he made an approach to an elderly Kentucky Democrat and Unionist, James Guthrie, who declined on account of infirmity, and then to John A. Gilmer, a Whig Unionist of North Carolina, who eventually declined, too. Lincoln was not especially disturbed: he feared the effect of such an appointment both on cabinet unity and on 'the confidence of our own friends'. Besides, well before Gilmer's refusal, it had been made public that Lincoln's attorney-general would be the conservative Edward Bates. As a resident of a slave state (Missouri) and 'a representative man', he would, Lincoln believed, reassure southerners. He was sadly mistaken. A man who had been a serious candidate for the Republican nomination would hardly dispel slaveholders' apprehensions.[6]

This was but one instance of Lincoln's larger misreading of the southern surge toward secession. Throughout the winter he, along with the Republican leadership more generally, remained at least one step behind the organizers of southern withdrawal. Talk of secession they treated at first as little more than the hot-air threats of unrepresentative fire-eaters, whose proposed secession ordinances would surely fail. When South Carolina finally declared its exit from the Union on 20 December it seemed the act of an unrepresentative and foolish community ('too small for a republic, too large for a lunatic asylum', in the acerbic judgment of one of its residents).[7] When six other states of the lower South followed in short order, it appeared that they were assuming no more than a temporary bargaining position. Lincoln consistently – and perhaps understandably – misjudged the meaning of much southern Unionism and overestimated its tenacity. As a Kentuckian with many continuing border-state connections, he well understood the depth of commitment to the Union in the upper South, particularly amongst its Clayite Whigs, but he mistakenly projected its loyalism on to the slaveholding states as a whole. His overtures to Alexander Stephens falsely supposed that the Georgian's arguments were a repudiation of the principle of secession, rather than a prudential calculation of how his state could best protect slavery.

Lincoln may also have misjudged things in not doing more to reassure anxious southerners that he would not use his patronage powers to place hard-line Republicans in federal appointments in the slave states. Here was an issue about which his views were not on record. Fears ran deep amongst slaveholders that once in power he would nominate antislavery men for postmasterships and other offices, through which they could establish a 'Black Republican' fifth column across the South, and target slaves and non-slaveholding whites with abolitionist propaganda. When Gilmer raised the issue, Lincoln responded at once. 'As to the use of patronage in the slave states', he wrote reassuringly, 'where there are few or no Republicans, I do not expect to inquire for the politics of the appointee, or whether he does or not own slaves. I intend in that matter to accommodate the people in the several localities. . . . In one word, I never have been, am not now, and probably never shall be, in a mood of harassing the people, either North or South.'[8] But Lincoln resisted Gilmer's request that he make a public statement on the matter.

Even so, Lincoln's general policy of silence was not unwise. The episode of the Trumbull speech showed clearly enough the dangers of speaking out. Moreover, silence was appropriate to his constitutional position, which would remain uncertain until the counting of the electoral college votes on 13 February ('the most dangerous point for us').[9] Most important of all, given his larger purposes, public pronouncements would have run the danger of sucking him into a debate at the very time that he was coming under pressure from many quarters to make concessions. Disunion underway, the seceded states seized most of the federal forts and arsenals within their boundaries. The ineffectual Buchanan entertained thoughts of a national convention. A variety of compromise proposals bubbled up in Congress in December, including a hopeful scheme from Senator Crittenden of Kentucky which, as befitted the political heir of Henry Clay, attracted most attention. Lincoln's support would be essential to winning Republicans' approval.

As a plan of pacification, Crittenden's proposal was extremely well conceived: a series of constitutional amendments would remove slavery from the reach of the federal government for all time. Its key provisions were an amendment that would reinstate the Missouri Compromise line of 36° 30' in US territories, 'now held, or hereafter acquired', with a guarantee of slavery's permanence south of that line, and free labor's to its north; a further amendment would bind future generations not to amend any of the provisions of the Constitution that related to slavery. Amongst a nervous population, especially the commercial interests in the lower North and the eastern cities, the plan enjoyed considerable support.

A swelling chorus of approving voices alarmed hard-line Republicans, not least because it included conservative elements of their own party. 'I know there are a few timid men amongst us', wrote one of Lincoln's correspondents, urging him to beware the dangerous influence of New York, Philadelphia and Boston within the party, and reminding him that 'the great mass of the Republican voters are imbued with an intense hostility to slavery. The moral sentiment of the people is aroused. It's the fulcrum of the movement.'[10]

Lincoln needed no persuading. No sooner did he learn that several congressional Republicans were warming to the idea of concessions than he wrote in unequivocal terms to his friends in Washington, notably the Illinoisans Lyman Trumbull in the Senate, and Elihu B. Washburne and William Kellogg in the House. 'Let there be no compromise on the question of *extending* slavery', he instructed them, warning against the delusion of popular sovereignty or the Missouri line. Shortly afterwards he sent a similar message to Weed, to be communicated to a gathering of Republican governors, and used the *New York Tribune* for what was the most public expression of his position.[11] For a lawyer whose inclination was, in David Davis's words, to 'compromise a lawsuit whenever practicable', Lincoln's approach in this instance was remarkably steely and unyielding. As Herndon told Wendell Phillips, Lincoln's response to the compromisers was: 'Away – off – begone! If the nation wants to back down, let it – not I.' Rather than yield, he told a Missouri Republican, 'he would sooner go out into his back yard and hang himself'.[12] Why was Lincoln so determined? The answer lies in a threefold compound of constitutionalism, concern for his party, and moral certainty.

First, Lincoln was adamant that to renege on the fundamentals of the party's Chicago platform even before he had taken the oath of office would be to sabotage the nation's constitutional, democratic processes, and yield up republican government to blackmailers and bullies. True, the Republican party had swept to power on a largely northern vote, but the development, though unprecedented, had been entirely constitutional. Making concessions would be to admit that a fairly defeated minority could properly overrule the decision of the majority. 'We have just carried an election on principles fairly stated to the people', Lincoln told a wavering Republican congressman from the lower North. 'Now we are told in advance, the government shall be broken up, unless we surrender to those we have beaten, before we take the offices. In this they are either attempting to play upon us, or they are in dead earnest. Either way, if we surrender, it is the end of us, and of the government. They will repeat the experiment upon us *ad libitum.*'[13]

Secondly, Lincoln knew that to yield on the issue of containing slavery would sunder his party. This was the glue that held together what was an otherwise fragile amalgam of interests. Although a minority of congressional Republicans showed some enthusiasm for the emergency conciliatory measures under consideration in House and Senate committees, and were ready to yield the high ground of the party platform, for Lincoln passively to have allowed that element to grow would have been to accept – in Henry Adams's words – 'a complete disorganization of our party'. Lincoln's decisive intervention to prevent the advance of a conciliatory policy within the congressional party prevented the split that many Republicans knew would result from pursuing compromise. As he saw on the eve of his election, endorsing concession would alienate essential support. 'Even if I were personally willing to barter away the moral principle involved in this contest', he told a visitor to Springfield, 'I would go to Washington without the countenance of the men who supported me and were my friends before the election; I would be as powerless as a block of buckeye wood.' His power-base was his party. Its loss would be suicidal.[14]

The fact is, however, that Lincoln was *not* ready 'to barter away' his principles: his stubbornness in defense of what he believed was right provides, above all, the key to his political behavior during these months. Both in word and action he revealed his deep sense that the nation faced an historic moment of moral crisis, from which it must not be diverted by trickery and rhetorical nightmares of ruin and bankruptcy.[15] His major speeches since 1854 had cast the nation's predicament as a struggle between the rightness of an economic and social order based on the promises of the Declaration of Independence and, on the other side, the moral evil of slavery. Lincoln set out the conflict very simply in his correspondence with Alexander Stephens and John Gilmer: 'You think slavery is *right* and ought to be extended; while we think it is *wrong* and ought to be restricted. That I suppose is the rub.' It was, he added, 'the only substantial difference between us', but for Lincoln the logic of that fact was a moral compulsion to act, constitutionally and without anger, against slavery as soon as opportunity arose. That day had dawned. Concessions could only postpone, not prevent, an inevitable crisis; they would have a (literally) 'demoralizing' effect. 'If there be [any compromise], all our labor is lost', Lincoln told his Washington lieutenants, 'and, ere long, must be done again. . . . The tug has to come, & better now, than any time hereafter.' Albert Hale, Presbyterian minister in Springfield, reported Lincoln's repeated warning that 'compromise has no end. Slavery is the evil out of which all our other national evils and dangers have come. It has deceived and led us to the brink of ruin, and it must be stopped. It must be kept where it is now.'[16]

Lincoln's determination to prevent his party becoming 'a mere sucked egg, all shell and no principle in it',[17] ensured the party stood more or less united against any weakening of Republican territorial policy. As Congress continued to consider a variety of measures during January and February, Lincoln used his secretary-of-state-in-waiting, William Seward, as his Washington agent, hauling him back from his apparent dalliance with the Crittenden proposals.[18] He was, he told Seward, prepared to entertain guarantees relating to the hard realities of slavery's presence in the United States: fugitive slaves, slavery in the District of Columbia, the domestic slave trade. In these instances, 'I care but little, so that what is done be comely, and not altogether outrageous.' He conceded the value of a constitutional amendment guaranteeing slavery's security within the southern states. He was even grudgingly ready to go along with Charles Francis Adams's plan to admit New Mexico as a slave state.[19] But over the broader spread of slavery he remained 'inflexible', not least because of slaveholders' imperialist ambitions toward Cuba and the wider Caribbean: there was, he told James T. Hale, 'but one compromise which would really settle the slavery question, and that would be a prohibition against acquiring any more territory'. Thus for most of the congressional session Republicans prevented the most feasible proposals, Crittenden's, from coming to a vote; at the last gasp were the measures presented, only to be formally rejected. Similar proposals emanated at the end of February from the ineffectual Washington Peace Conference, called by Virginia and other anxious border states, and destined, in James Russell Lowell's cruel words, 'to convince thoughtful persons that men do not grow wiser as they grow older'. This ill-assorted band of secessionist sympathizers, suspicious Republicans, upper South Unionists and northern conservatives sent a Crittenden-cloned constitutional amendment to Congress during its dying days, where it enjoyed only minimal support.[20]

Lincoln watched events from Springfield until mid-February, despite Seward's suggestion that he come early to Washington. Quite why he stayed put is not clear. It certainly kept him away from the fever and paranoia that Buchanan's equivocation and the presence of leading secessionists bred in the capital. It avoided any accusation of panic. Above all, perhaps, it kept him at a remove from the legions of compromise. By the time he prepared to leave home he could reflect with some satisfaction that there had been no weakening in the moral spine of Republicanism. And that meant that he had secured his primary aim through these winter months: not to take office as a broken president of a broken party.

But he also knew now that the price of that achievement was to inherit a broken Union. Refusal to conciliate would do nothing to check the separationist gallop of the lower South, whose seven states had all passed ordinances of secession by 1 February. Representatives of six of those states met at Montgomery, Alabama, on 4 February and over the next five weeks laid the basis of the southern Confederacy.

As he considered the dangerous direction of events early in 1861, Lincoln set down on paper his thoughts about the relationship between the nation's core values and the constitutional framework. America's great prosperity derived from its Constitution and Union, but its 'primary cause' was the Declaration's ideal of universal liberty: 'the principle that clears the *path* for all – gives *hope* to all – and, by consequence, *enterprize*, and *industry* to all.' Taking his metaphor from Proverbs, perhaps prompted by his recent exchange with Stephens, Lincoln held that the Declaration was an 'apple of gold', framed by the Union, 'the *picture* of *silver*'. Crucially, the Union 'was made, not to *conceal*, or *destroy* the apple; but to *adorn*, and *preserve* it. The *picture* was made *for* the apple – *not* the apple for the picture. So let us act, that neither *picture*, or *apple* shall ever be blurred, or bruised or broken.'[21] Lincoln's actions during the crisis winter had prevented the breaking or bruising of the apple, the nation's chief glory. His task as his inauguration approached was to begin the repair of the damaged but indispensable picture, the Union.

From Springfield to Sumter: building a united front

Lincoln was in sombre mood as he prepared to leave Springfield. He made an emotional visit to his stepmother, held a reception for friends and said goodbye to his law partner, Herndon, promising that, if he lived, 'I'm coming back sometime, and then we'll go right on practicing law as if nothing had ever happened.' Over a thousand gathered at the railroad depot to listen, moist-eyed, to his touching farewell speech on the morning of 11 February. Sadness soon gave way to better spirits, exhilaration and then exhaustion during a two-week journey that took the presidential party by a roundabout route to Washington, *via* Indianapolis, Cincinnati, Columbus, Pittsburgh, Cleveland, Buffalo, Albany, New York City, Trenton, Philadelphia and Harrisburg. Lincoln's family, secretaries, bodyguard (Hill Lamon) and a few political associates, including Davis and Judd, met an almost non-stop display of enthusiasm from boisterous crowds, official receptions, parades and impromptu gatherings, accompanied by flag-waving, ovations, bonfires and salvos of artillery.[22]

The journey, though, was much more than a noisy carnival. Lincoln had a serious, two-fold purpose, hinted at in his private farewell to Herndon: 'I am decided; my course is fixed; my path is blazed. The Union and the Constitution shall be preserved and the laws enforced at every and at all hazards. I expect the people to sustain me. They have never yet forsaken any true man.' First, breaking his public silence, he aimed to rally a loyal people behind broad-based appeals to a common patriotism, pushing slavery to the margins and avoiding specific statements of policy toward the seceded states. Lincoln's reception committees were studiedly non-partisan; the crowds themselves comprised men and women of all political and religious persuasions. Being welcomed by the conservative Millard Fillmore at Buffalo was more important than speaking in the radical Joshua Giddings's Ashtabula district ('more intensely republican than the most republican of republicans in other localities'), an invitation he declined. The embodiment of a victorious party had to become the constitutionally elected representative of all the people.[23]

Lincoln set the tone in his first remarks of substance, at Lafayette, Indiana, to a sea of unfamiliar faces: 'While some of us may differ in political opinion', he reflected, the common bonds of 'christianity, civilization and patriotism' ensured that 'we are all united in one feeling for the Union'. The Revolutionary struggle, the example of 'those noble fathers – Washington, Jefferson and Madison', the ideas of liberty and equality of opportunity for all, as incorporated into the Declaration and Constitution, giving 'hope to the world for all future time': these would be Lincoln's continuing themes, the reasons why the Union was worth saving. If it could not be saved upon these principles, then 'I would rather be assassinated on this spot than to surrender it'. At the same time he sought to harness the common religious sensibilities of his audience by pointedly stressing his dependence upon (sequentially) 'Divine Providence', 'God', 'the Providence of God', 'that God who has never forsaken this people', 'the Divine Power, without whose aid we can do nothing', 'that Supreme Being who has never forsaken this favored land', 'the Maker of the Universe', 'the Almighty', and 'Almighty God'. These themes converged with particular clarity in his address to the New Jersey Senate, at Trenton, near to the site of Washington's celebrated crossing of the Delaware: 'I am exceedingly anxious that this Union, the Constitution, and the liberties of the people shall be perpetuated in accordance with the original idea for which that struggle was made, and I shall be most happy indeed if I shall be an humble instrument in the hands of the Almighty, and of this, his almost chosen people, for perpetuating the object of that great struggle.'[24]

Lincoln provided a personal focus for diffuse loyalism. Speaking with considerable skill, both in formal addresses to state legislatures and in impromptu but careful remarks at receptions and temporary railroad halts, he established a personal rapport with the curious tens of thousands who turned out to meet their next president. At Dunkirk, in upstate New York, where some 12,000 or so had gathered around a specially constructed Union arch over the track, Lincoln stepped from his car, expressed his regret at having no time to speak, placed his hand on the staff bearing the stars and stripes, and simply said, to a tumult of applause from a hat-swinging and handkerchief-waving crowd, 'I stand by the flag of the Union, and all I ask of you is that you stand by me as long as I stand by it.' Nicolay described 'a current of electrical communion' that commonly ran from speaker to audience, as crowds encountered an unpretentious, sympathetic, kindly but resolute man who 'was of them as well as for them'; and less partial sources reported Lincoln's obvious success in patriotic outreach to his fellow citizens.[25]

Lincoln's second purpose was to test and read the public mood. He had already composed his inaugural address, whose themes had been building in his mind since his election, and perhaps before, and now he had the opportunity to try out elements of his larger argument as he moved east. (The document itself traveled in his carpet bag, initially in the custody of his son Robert, who earned a rare taste of his father's temper when he let it out of his sight on the very first day.) Early on Lincoln presented ideas quite tentatively, as questions, but the encouraging warmth of response reassured him just how broad-based northern Unionism was. At Indianapolis, in a speech whose substance he had carefully pondered before leaving home, he stressed that his remarks were suggestions only and, instead of stating bluntly that secession was illegal and revolutionary, pursued an interrogatory approach. 'By what principle of original right is it that one-fiftieth or one ninetieth of a great nation, by calling themselves a State, have the right to break up and ruin that nation as a matter of original principle? Now, I ask the question – I am not deciding anything', said Lincoln to sympathetic and continuing laughter, 'where is the mysterious ... right ... for a certain district of country with inhabitants ... to play tyrant over all its own citizens, and deny the authority of everything greater than itself.' Lincoln got the answer he wanted to hear: state secession was a constitutional nonsense.[26]

A similar 'fury of enthusiasm', as it seemed to the traveling party, accompanied Lincoln's more resolute remarks about the restoration of *de facto* national authority over the new Confederacy. He spoke of his peaceful intent ('The man does not live who is more devoted to peace than I am'), the need for patience, the artificiality of the crisis, his view that there should be no armed 'invasion' of southern states, and his determination that 'there will be no blood shed unless it be forced upon the Government'. But at the same time he hinted at the limits of federal tolerance and at his scorn for secessionists' using the term 'coercion' to describe the federal administation's defense of its routine authority. To cheers he asked, 'if the Government, for instance, but simply insists upon holding its own forts, or retaking those forts which belong to it, or the enforcement of the laws of the United States in the collection of duties upon foreign importations, or even the withdrawal of the mails from those portions of the country where the mails themselves are habitually violated; would any or all of these things be coercion?' In the New Jersey General Assembly, he made his steeliest comment of all. After declaring his devotion to seeking a peaceful settlement, he said very deliberately, 'But it may be necessary to put the foot down firmly', lifting his own foot lightly before pressing it quickly down on the floor. This, reported the *New York Tribune*, provoked 'cheers so loud and long that for some moments it was impossible to hear Mr. L.s voice'. Andrew Jackson, iron-willed defender of the Union against South Carolinian 'nullifiers' and secessionists thirty years earlier, was the admired presidential model, not strait-jacketed, enervated James Buchanan.[27]

Lincoln also used the journey to stress his dependence on his people's support during the crisis ahead. This was not simple flattery, nor the routine expression of truisms, but a means of testing the opinion of those of all parties without whom he knew that he – 'an accidental instrument' and temporary servant – would fail. 'When the people rise in masses in behalf of the Union and the liberties of their country, truly it may be said, "The gates of hell shall not prevail against them"', he told a cheering crowd in Indianapolis. 'In all the trying positions in which I shall be placed . . . my reliance will be placed upon you and the people of the United States – and I wish you to remember now and forever, that it is your business, and not mine . . . to rise up and preserve the Union and liberty, for yourselves, and not for me.' At Trenton he asked his audience directly, 'if I do my duty, and do right, you will sustain me, will you not?' and elicited gratifying and reassuring cries of 'Yes', 'Yes', 'We will'.[28]

By the end of his journey's twelfth and final day, on George Washington's birthday, Lincoln could reflect on a trip during which he had spoken directly to more people outside Illinois than he had ever done before. As president, events would prevent his repeating this sustained face-to-face exercise, but for now the rousing cries of 'Lincoln and Union forever' assured him of broad-based support within the free states for a determined policy of maintaining federal authority over the southern separatists. Night-time events on 22 February momentarily threatened to dent both Lincoln's confidence and the public's faith in his firmness, as he yielded to the urgings of close advisers and Pinkerton detectives to travel surreptitiously over the last short leg of his journey to Washington, to avoid violence and perhaps death at the hands of Baltimore plotters. The upshot was ridicule in much of the press, which exercised its fertile imagination at Lincoln's expense. But the episode in practice changed little and did nothing to alter Lincoln's judgment that the policy embodied in his inaugural address would enjoy broad public support.

Ten days later, watched by thousands, Lincoln stood in Washington before a capitol building still under construction, preparing to take his oath of office and protected from a distance by companies of riflemen, batteries of flying artillery and a cavalry guard. These were symbols of a fractured Union in crisis, but the opening passages of Lincoln's address sought to reassure the country 'that the property, peace and security of no section are to be in anywise endangered by the now incoming Administration'. He would ensure the enforcement of the Fugitive Slave Law and other constitutional provisions designed to protect slaveholders. He would accept a constitutional amendment formally guarding 'the domestic institutions of the States' against federal interference. He took the oath 'with no mental reservations'. The Union was no threat to the South.[29]

That Union, however, was perpetual and indivisible. So dictated the principles of universal law: 'no government proper, ever had a provision in its organic law for its own termination'; 'if the United States be . . . but an association of States in the nature of contract merely, can it, as a contract, be peaceably unmade, by less than all the parties who made it?' This, too, was the transparent verdict of the nation's own history: the Union predated the Constitution and had been formed for perpetuity. State ordinances of secession, then, were legally void; violence against the authority of the United States was an act of revolution or insurrection. Following his 'simple duty' as directed by the Constitution, Lincoln would ensure that the laws were 'faithfully executed'.

But what would this mean in practice? Secession had been accompanied by the separatists' widespread seizure of federal forts, arsenals and other installations, but a few remained under Union control. Lincoln would use his power 'to hold, occupy, and possess the property, and places belonging to the government, and to collect the duties and imposts'. But there would be 'no invasion – no using of force against, or among the people anywhere'; no 'obnoxious strangers' would be pressed into federal offices unfilled locally; and the mails would not be delivered against the wishes of the community.

Lincoln realized that his promises would effect no change of heart amongst rebels who sought 'to destroy the Union at all events'. But, convinced that the wreckers did not comprise a southern, and certainly not a national, majority, he spent most of the remainder of his address offering reasons why his 'countrymen, one and all', both the 'dissatisfied' and the contented, should share his faith in popular government, in the rule of a majority constrained by a Constitution which worked to protect the rights of minorities. Only when a majority trampled on those rights was revolutionary dismemberment of the polity morally justified. But the points of current controversy – above all the powers and responsibilities of Congress toward slavery in the territories – were not explicitly covered by the Constitution. In such cases the minority must acquiesce in the government of a majority 'held in restraint by constitutional checks, and limitations, and always changing easily, with deliberate changes of popular opinions and sentiments'. A legally-guided, virtuous and vigilant majority was 'the only true sovereign of a free people. Whoever rejects it, does, of necessity, fly to anarchy or to despotism.' Lincoln, as president, was its authorized agent, impotent to negotiate the destruction of the Union. No great harm could be done in the four short years of any one administration, responsible as it was to the 'great tribunal' of the American people.

Lincoln appealed for patience to allow for the workings of 'intelligence, patriotism, Christianity, and a firm reliance on Him, who has never yet forsaken this favored land', and drew to a close by affirming the nation's bonds of affection: 'The mystic chords of memory, stre[t]ching from every battle-field, and patriot grave, to every living heart and hearthstone, all over this broad land, will yet swell the chorus of the Union, when again touched, as surely they will be, by the better angels of our nature.' But the new president's eloquence would cut little ice with those who were ostensibly its main target: the people of the lower South who could either revoke the secession ordinances or, by challenging federal authority where it continued to function within the separatist states, intensify what Lincoln defined as their aggression against the Union. When he addressed them as 'fellow citizens' and spoke of disunion as 'formidably attempted' – but by implication not achieved, or achievable – he used language destined, if not intended, to widen still further the chasm between Washington and them.

Lincoln, though, had in mind a wider audience: the citizens of the loyal states who had not voted for him in November, but whose support he needed if he were successfully to face down the secessionists. Not least he had to scotch the fears of critics who believed that he desired 'to add civil war to disunion'.[30] His target included the citizens of the eight states of the upper South, where secession had been resisted and successfully voted down in February, and through some of which Lincoln had proposed to travel *en route* to Washington until concerns for his security supervened.[31] It was with these people in mind that he declared that the government would not 'assail' the seceded states and that 'the momentous issue of civil war' lay not in his hands, but with the separatists, who could, he insisted, 'have no conflict, without being . . . [themselves] the aggressors'. And it was with special regard for the sensibilities of southern loyalists that he heeded the advice proffered by Seward and Orville Browning to tone down some of the steelier and more menacing phrases of the speech's first draft, which had declared an intent to 'reclaim' fallen federal forts.

Party triumphalism, too, was conspicuously absent from a speech designed to bind conservative Democrats and Bell–Everett men, along with their recent Republican opponents, into a broad pro-Union alliance. In consequence, the antislavery Republican conscience made but a fleeting appearance. Lincoln's one reference – brief, though powerful – to a moral confrontation came when he adopted the formula he had used in his recent letters to Gilmer and Stephens: 'One section of our country believes slavery is *right*, and ought to be extended, while the other believes it is *wrong*, and ought not to be extended. This is the only substantial dispute.' Lincoln's first draft of the address had quoted directly from the Republican platform of 1856 and its celebration of the principles of freedom in the Declaration. But shortly before 4 March he removed this passage, together with all specific mention of the Republican party and the Chicago platform of 1860. This was Seward's hand at work. Republicans, he told Lincoln, 'will be loyal, whatever is said'. The new president should do what Jefferson had done in the crisis of 1800 and sink 'the partisan in the patriot'; 'you cannot lose the Republican party by practicing in your advent to office the magnanimity of a victor'.[32]

Lincoln achieved his aim, garnering support from well beyond his party's boundaries. It helped that at the inauguration ceremony Stephen Douglas, true to his private pledge of solidarity, stood close at hand, holding Lincoln's hat and reportedly offering a *sotto voce* running commentary of approval ('Good'; 'That is the right doctrine'; 'That is no coercion').[33] The speech won plaudits from much of the opposition press. Lincoln had said 'all that he should have said', one Douglasite editor thought; another found in its 'deep spirit of fraternal kindness' an irresistible invitation to join in the 'holy work' of rescuing the Union. But critics remained and mixed reflex abuse with substantive concerns. Many Breckinridge and even some Douglas papers discerned a declaration of war on the lower South. Brokers anticipated a feverish stockmarket. The inaugural had 'too much fight in it', Lincoln learnt. For all its clarity, ambiguities remained. His conciliatory words sat uneasily with the menacing potential of his policy toward fallen federal forts and revenue collecting.[34] Still, in winning over some opponents Lincoln had taken a significant step toward becoming the president of a people, not the leader of a party. 'I think the honest portion of the American people are with you', a New York correspondent told the new president after taking cross-party soundings, 'and will hold themselves subject to your direction'.[35]

Republicans, naturally, provided a chorus of approving voices. Editors praised a 'strong, straightforward and manly' address whose 'wire-woven sentences' proffered a blend of firm, unhurried purpose and conciliatory calm. This declaration of war 'against treason' would surely rally bipartisan support. New York's Governor Morgan complimented Lincoln on words that were 'kind in spirit, firm in purpose, national in the highest degree'. If some detected a whiff of over-leniency, few feared any compromise on fundamentals. 'Republicans are delighted that there is no abandonment of Republican principle', exulted one of Lincoln's Springfield circle. The inaugural promised firm adherence to the Chicago platform, including the confining and choking of slavery. Lincoln's declaration that 'vital questions' should not be 'irrevocably fixed' by Supreme Court judges, regardless of the views of the sovereign people, elicited warm applause. There would be no repeat of the Dred Scott *dicta*.[36]

The party's antislavery radicals took additional encouragement from the slate of cabinet nominees which Lincoln sent to the Senate on the day after his inauguration. For the Treasury Department he had chosen the formidable Salmon P. Chase, who for two decades had done more than most to shape and energize the forces of political antislavery. Chase's name was not a surprise but nor was it assured until late in the day. His nomination guaranteed that the 'ultras' or 'straight-outs', as radicals were known, would have a forceful and intellectually impressive spokesman at the highest level.

The framework of his cabinet had begun to take shape in Lincoln's mind even before his election, and during the sleepless night following his victory he had jotted down the names of seven advisers. His thinking was characteristically hard-headed. He wanted a balanced cabinet that would reflect the breadth and diversity of Republicanism. He also recognized his own inexperience and the political qualities of those he had defeated for the Republican nomination: Seward, Chase and Bates. It says much for Lincoln's self-assurance that he was so ready to surround himself by some of the largest and self-regarding talents in the party. But pursuing this project proved a disjointed, frustrating and occasionally unhappy affair. Lincoln was cautious, and conducting discussions at a distance did not help. Vice-president-elect Hamlin, Bates, Weed (on behalf of Seward), Chase and Cameron all made separate visits to Illinois. Seward took umbrage at the slowness with which Lincoln invited him to take the State Department. Chase was non-committal in the face of what amounted merely to a provisional offer. In Cameron's case a firm offer was made and accepted, but then retracted. Only two appointments had been agreed before Lincoln left for Washington. After his arrival there, at Willard's Hotel, he faced the determined lobbying of rival factions and felt the hard truth of what John W. Forney had told him: 'You cannot select anybody who will not give dissatisfaction in certain quarters.'[37]

Achieving a balanced cabinet was no easy task, given the many different elements to be counterpoised. The party was an amalgam of ex-Whigs and ex-Democrats; quasi-abolitionist radicals, moderates and negrophobic conservatives; free traders and protectionists; nativists and friends of the foreign-born. Lincoln had also to take account of political geography, state interests, understandings (if not outright promises) entered into at the Chicago nominating convention, personal rivalries and antipathies, and the *amour propre* of some sizeable egos. His final list of seven advisers, which varied in only two instances from his draft of November, included four ex-Democrats: Chase at the Treasury, Gideon Welles as secretary of the navy, Montgomery Blair as postmaster general, and Cameron at the War Department. The three original Whigs comprised Seward, as secretary of state, Bates as attorney-general, and Caleb Smith as secretary of the interior. To those who worried about the apparent numerical imbalance, Lincoln commonly replied that 'he was himself an old-line Whig, and he should be there to make the parties even'.[38]

Lincoln successfully struck other balances. Welles of Connecticut provided representation for New England, Smith of Indiana and Chase of Ohio for the Northwest, Blair and Bates for the border slave states of Maryland and Missouri, and Seward for New York. Cameron, though hated by many in his state party and tainted with the odor of corruption, was there to reassure the high tariff men of Pennsylvania, anxious about the influence of the ardent free-trader, Chase. Lincoln's most delicate task was to bind to his administration the mutually hostile Chase and Seward. The New Yorker had accepted Lincoln's offer in late December and subsequently did his best to prevent the appointment of his rival. Thinking of himself as the real power of the incoming administration and confidently pursuing a conciliatory, bridge-building policy toward the South, Seward was appalled when Lincoln, who had invited the Republican senators to express their views over the Treasury appointment, offered it to Chase, who was taking a hard-line approach to the secessionists. Seward wrote to Lincoln for permission to withdraw his consent to serve – a bluff, intended to result in Chase's exclusion. But Lincoln was determined to keep both men, telling Nicolay 'I can't afford to let Seward take the first trick'.[39] He followed with his own bluff, letting Seward learn indirectly that he would keep Chase, while Seward would be exiled as minister to England. Seward withdrew his letter.

Despite its messy process of construction and the clear signals that it would lack real harmony, the new cabinet immediately served two useful purposes. Lincoln both reassured his party hardliners that there would be no backsliding from true Republicanism, and at the same time sought to signal to non-Republicans in the North and the anxious border South that his would be a broad-based administration, attentive to conservative sentiment. It did not satisfy those who thought the crisis demanded an all-inclusive, cross-party cabinet, but – through Blair's appointment in particular – reached out a hand to anxious Democratic Unionists and the border South, and notably to teetering Maryland.[40]

On the same day that Lincoln concluded his cabinet-building he got news which threatened to shatter the very consensus he sought to develop. His inaugural had been designed to provide a breathing space, to give the loyal elements in the rebel states a chance to assert themselves. Instead, he learnt from the commander of the federal garrison at Fort Sumter, Major Robert Anderson, that without further supplies the Union force could survive only another six weeks before surrendering to the Confederate authorities in Charleston. Lincoln now faced the most testing introduction to executive office of any president. He later reflected 'that all the troubles and anxieties of his life' had no equal to those that bore down on him over the next five and a half weeks.[41] As the emergency built to its climax in a bombardment of the fort, he strained to devise and maintain a course of action.

In this he had to contend with a variety of handicaps, some of them personal and self-inflicted. Executive business was sometimes delayed because he made mistakes over procedures (he felt, he said, 'like the Justice of the Peace, who would often speak of the first case he had ever tried, and called it, his "great first case least understood" '). More seriously, he consumed far too much time dealing personally with the hordes of job-seekers who day and night clogged up the White House. He was 'so badgered', he told an old friend, that sometimes he thought 'the only way that he could escape from them would be to take a rope and hang himself' from a tree on the south lawn. 'Why don't you disperse the selfish, mercenary crowd?' demanded Orville Browning, alarmed by his friend's fatigue.[42] But Lincoln valued personal oversight of patronage appointments too highly to relinquish the business. Perhaps, too, he found in this multitude of finite and manageable tasks an emotional refuge from the larger, more dangerous issues that loomed.

His ensuing exhaustion would have mattered less had he been confident of sound advice and solid information. But the voices of his military and political advisers sang an uncertain and disharmonious tune, and sound intelligence was hard to come by. General Winfield Scott offered a dispiriting response to Lincoln's inquiries. Anderson's surrender was inevitable: the troop numbers and naval force required to relieve him could not be raised in time. But Gustavus Vasa Fox, an ex-naval officer to whom Lincoln warmed, took a more positive view. When Lincoln on 15 March asked his cabinet members for their written views, the only advocates of reinforcement were Chase and Blair, Fox's brother-in-law. Seward, still hopeful of a successful negotiation and confident that he was the man to pursue it, stood resolutely against any action that might erupt into civil war. To get a better sense of opinion in the lower South, Lincoln sent his friends Stephen A. Hurlbut and Hill Lamon to Charleston and learnt the bleak news that Union sentiment was dead in South Carolina: 'There is positively nothing to appeal to', Hurlbut reported: 'The Sentiment of National Patriotism . . . has been Extinguished.' The next day, 28 March, General Scott stunned Lincoln with new advice: not only Sumter, but Fort Pickens, off the Florida coast, should be evacuated too. His argument was political not military: giving up this securely held Union fort would 'soothe' the eight states of the upper South and ensure their continued loyalty. Blair plausibly suspected that Scott was acting as Seward's mouthpiece, though when on 29 March Lincoln asked cabinet members for their views on the relief of each of the two forts, the secretary of state joined in a unanimous vote for sustaining Pickens. Seward continued to oppose the relief of Sumter, but now the cabinet balance had swung and only Smith stood by him.[43]

The events of these two days marked a crisis that left Lincoln fraught and migrainous, but finally resolved to act. He told Welles and Cameron on 29 March to prepare an expedition for Sumter that might leave as early as 6 April. He also ordered a separate relief expedition to Pickens to proceed. But even now Lincoln's plans were hampered by interdepartmental secrecy, a lack of liaison, and outright rivalry between the navy and army, respectively responsible for the separate Sumter and Pickens operations. Through an oversight of his own, and the scheming of Seward, who continued to hope for the failure of the Sumter enterprise and who had indirectly pledged to Confederate commissioners in Washington that the fort would be evacuated, the best ship was denied to Fox's fleet, which set out for South Carolina from New York on 9 April. By then Lincoln had told Anderson that supplies were on their way and that the fort would be reinforced if the Confederates resisted. He had also, at Seward's encouragement, notified the governor of South Carolina that he should 'expect an attempt to supply Fort-Sumpter with provisions only; and that, if such attempt be not resisted, no effort to throw in men, arms, or amunition, will be made, without further notice'. The message left the Confederate authorities at Montgomery unmoved. When Fox's fleet arrived, on 12 April, Charleston's guns fired the first shots of the civil war.[44]

For all the uncertainty that characterized these weeks, there was still continuity and coherence in what Lincoln did. He navigated a course between the two express commitments he had entered into in his inaugural. First, he would not preside over the erosion of the Union. Whatever ambiguity existed over whether he was going to *retake* lost forts, he had been entirely clear about holding those still under Union control. He continued to stand by what he had told Scott and others throughout the winter. These garrisons, and especially Sumter, situated as it was in the crucible of secessionism, were potent symbols of national authority. For the administration voluntarily to abandon them would be to confirm to the watching public the nation's own suicide. Despite insistent voices demanding a 'hands off' policy to reassure southern Unionism and defuse the crisis, Lincoln showed little sign of yielding.[45]

One version of events in early April suggests that Lincoln did at the last moment entertain the idea of evacuating Sumter, as an exchange for a pledge of undying Unionism from Virginia. There anti-secessionists dominated the sitting state convention. Seward, still working for a change of policy toward Sumter, raised Lincoln's hopes of the swap. 'A state for a fort is no bad business', the president allegedly remarked. John B. Baldwin, a convention member, came to the White House for a furtive conversation on 4 April. By his own account he received no hard offer. Perhaps Lincoln did make one. If so, he did it so indirectly that it left Baldwin mystified. Either way, the evidence remains inconclusive.[46] It is more than likely that Lincoln had far less faith in Baldwin's ability to deliver than had Seward and that, having made a crossing of the psychological Rubicon by his orders of 29 March, there was no going back.

The second of Lincoln's inaugural commitments was his promise not to coerce or assail the South. This effectively ruled out repossessing lost installations, or pre-emptive strikes against the Confederates to ensure the security of forts still held. The logic of standing by his two promises was to wait for Confederates to react, perhaps forcibly, to the non-violent upholding of federal authority. In debating Lincoln's intentions within this framework for action, historians have spilt gallons more ink than the blood shed at the time of Sumter's fall, when but one life was lost. The interpretations run the gamut from those who see him recognizing at an early date the inevitability of war, and deliberately maneuvering the Confederates into shooting first and attracting the blame for hostilities, to the more sympathetic judgment that Lincoln did all he could to maintain peace in a context where the other side had already, through secession, engaged in political violence and revolution, and where there was just a chance that the Confederates might avoid using force against unarmed relief efforts. In the absence of cast-iron evidence about the workings of Lincoln's mind, the debate cannot be unanswerably resolved. But some things are beyond reasonable doubt.

Lincoln himself quite soon after the Sumter crisis told his brother-in-law 'how intensely anxious he had been to arrange the national troubles without war – how deep his sympathies were with both sections of the country – and how hard he had struggled to avoid bloodshed'. The president's stress-induced sickness in the last days of March provides a measure of this particular anxiety. But it showed, too, that Lincoln knew he was running a high risk of war by ordering a relief expedition to Sumter. Not only had the Confederates fired on the merchant steamer, the *Star of the West*, when Buchanan had tried to send supplies in January, but Hurlbut had just reported that any attempted reprovisioning would provoke Charlestonians' resistance. Before Fox's fleet departed, Lincoln met several northern state governors at the White House to discuss the preparedness of state militias and the availability of troops for the defense of Washington. Two months earlier he had shared with Browning the view that 'far less evil & bloodshed would result from an effort to maintain the Union and the Constitution, than from disruption and the formation of two confederacies'. It was a position that the crisis forced him to review but not, when it came to the crunch, to change. Whether he would have done so had he known the scale of the human suffering that would follow is as much an imponderable for the historian as the moral rightness or wrongness of the decision that he took.[47]

Lincoln's executive leadership during these weeks drew criticism from Union loyalists at the time and has not won universal approval from historians since. He has been charged with groping his way, being slow to take initiatives and to secure information, and too ready to wait on events. Edwin M. Stanton, a robust Unionist, accused Lincoln and his colleagues of being gripped by mounting panic as they addressed the Sumter problem. Carl Schurz and other activists told him that demoralized Republicans blamed the party's recent losses in local elections on the administration's vacillation and apparent readiness to back down. The secretary of state implicitly charged the president with drift, in a notorious memorandum to Lincoln, dated 1 April: 'We are at the end of a month's administration and yet without a policy either domestic or foreign.' Editorial columns warmed to the theme. The government's approach, lamented the *New York Times*, was nothing 'beyond that of listless waiting to see what may "turn up"'.[48]

But Lincoln had inherited a nightmare that left him with few realistic options. The route of peaceful separation was anathema to him and rejected by a majority of northerners. That of coercing the seceding states back into the Union was closed, since he lacked the means: neither the outgoing president nor Congress had made any provision for augmenting the entirely inadequate forces of the regular army and the ramshackle state militias. Given his relative helplessness, what is remarkable is Lincoln's decision to resist calling Congress into special session, and his appetite for taking responsibility himself. When Seward brazenly suggested that he himself take on the 'energetic prosecution' of a new policy, turning attention from domestic to foreign affairs, Lincoln remarked 'that if this must be done, *I* must do it', drily adding that in addressing the evolution of policy 'I wish, and suppose I am entitled to have the advice of all the cabinet'.[49] Whatever the stresses of executive office, Lincoln would not dodge them or load them on to others.

In one essential, in particular, Lincoln proved more than adept. He followed a course shrewdly designed to maximize support for the administration if and when hostilities broke out. He remained sensitive to public views in the loyal states at a time when the swirls and shifts of opinion made it no easy matter to define and keep abreast of the popular mood. Party labels during these weeks provided no assured guide to attitudes to what was, after all, an unprecedented crisis. Republicans themselves responded variously to the rumors stoked in mid-March by Seward's intimations to the Confederate commissioners that the president would peacefully relinquish Sumter. Some party loyalists reassured Lincoln, whose policy they assumed it was, that this was the only realistic military option, and no dishonor. A few anxiously hoped that evacuation would be part of a drive to secure reunion through conciliation. One New

England editor even jettisoned the Chicago platform, to call for a compromise on territorial slavery. Mostly, though, Republicans were determined not to let the growing 'vigor, intelligence, and success' of the *de facto* Confederate government be used as an argument for appeasement. During late March and early April, with the Union apparently enervated, a more militant note widely entered the Republican press and was echoed by Lincoln's correspondents. Those who had advocated delay, to allow time for national healing and the revival of southern Unionism, were now far readier to reconsider military action. The pulse quickened further during the first week of April, when it became clearer that the administration was going to act to defend its property. A Milwaukee editor aired the common thought that 'there are worse evils than war'.[50]

Amongst non-Republican opinion, too, the patterns of response proved far from predictable. Douglas's patriotic praise for Lincoln's inaugural marked a sensational and significant break with the Democrats' assault on Republican fanaticism, though its effect was rather to complicate opposition politics, not halt them. The Little Giant himself was involved in a mid-March Senate stand-off with Republicans over how to interpret Lincoln's speech. For Douglas it meant peace, and he wanted Republicans to shore up that policy with constitutional guarantees. They, however, read it to mean merely that Lincoln would not make war on anyone; it did not commit him to conciliation or appeasement. In some desperation, and afraid that any clash over the forts would alienate the upper South, Douglas began to develop a scheme of peaceful separation within the framework of a customs union. Many northern Democrats followed Douglas's lead as they moved into these uncharted political waters, mixing some partisan criticism of the administration with evident anxiety over the future of the Union. Some Democratic nationalists, however, proved even harsher critics of Lincoln's 'weakness' than those of his own party: several Breckinridge men of the previous November now abandoned their southern-rights champion, and urged Lincoln not to cringe before 'southern dictation' and 'the phantom prowess of the boasting traitors'. And old-style Unionist Whigs, faced with either enforcing the Constitution and law or protecting the nation from the danger of war, fractured into those who criticized Lincoln's 'supineness, cowardice, imbecility' in confronting traitors, and others for whom enforcement 'would be the greatest folly in this age of follies'.[51]

But for all of the eddies and swirls of opinion, the wider current flowed in only one direction: there was an underlying and near-universal assumption that by one means or another the 'holy cause' of Union must be sustained.[52] Even those who urged peaceful separation mostly did so in the belief that the 'Cotton Confederacy' would be ready to return within a few years. Lincoln's task, then, was to shape his actions to present the Union as itself the victim of assault in any confrontation, not as the aggressor, and so harness the power of a deep popular patriotism. His likely final policy toward the forts was predicted by a perceptive Douglas Democrat several weeks in advance: acting defensively, the administration would 'compel the seceded States to perform such acts of aggression or offense as should be resisted. Thus would the cause of war be cast upon the seceders.'[53] And this, of course, was how the endgame at Sumter unfolded. Lincoln chose not to reinforce Anderson secretly, turned Fox's expedition into an unarmed relief effort and ensured that the world would see his pacific intent by notifying the governor of South Carolina of what he intended.

The guns at Sumter provided Unionists with a catharsis of action after weeks of suspense and anxiety. What Browning described as a 'tempest of patriotic indignation' found expression in mass gatherings, religious meetings, state legislative chambers and furious editorializing. Lincoln's secretaries labored under a mountain of heartening mail. The bombardment of the fort had operated, declared an old Whig acquaintance of the president, 'like an electric shock upon the Northern mind'. Local Republican leaders pledged the administration all resources necessary to 'crush the head of the rattle snake'. 'The North West', Joseph Medill promised Lincoln, 'will back you with their last man, dollar and bushel of corn.' 'Men and money at this crisis, will be forthcoming to any amount', insisted another. The administration could rely on an army of three, four, five hundred thousand men – perhaps three quarters of a million, if needed.[54]

Conscience and counting-house appeared to rally as one in defense of the national government. A variety of individual Christians and church gatherings – Indiana and New York Methodists, Philadelphia Presbyterians, Welsh Congregationalists, New England clergy – rushed to tell the president of their resolve. Lincoln should understand, a New Hampshire correspondent told him, that 'the friends of the Pilgrims are your friends'. At the same time, the caution of conservative financiers, merchants and manufacturers vaporized in the intense heat of patriotism, leaving John Hay to rejoice that, while cotton had for too long shut northern ears 'to every sound but the jingling of dollars', the storm of outrage proved 'that the voice of a Puritan conscience is louder than the hum of a thousand looms'.[55]

Everywhere, it seemed, common anger at the South's perfidy welded together previous political antagonists. Chicago Republicans and Democrats were 'a unit', Isaac Arnold telegraphed Lincoln. In Wisconsin they stood 'shoulder to shoulder'. Pennsylvania knew 'no division of parties'. Democratic stalwarts and previous anti-coercionists in New York now 'desire to know no party but the union party until the question is settled whether we have a Government or not': 'I did not vote for Lincoln', said one, 'but I would vote for him now, just as I would for Washington, Jefferson, Jackson.' Even the southern rights Democrats of lower Illinois, Trumbull reported, had had to succumb to the strength of public sentiment. Fearing an attack on the offices of his southern-leaning *New York Herald* and stunned by the evidence of northern single-mindedness, James Gordon Bennett enjoyed a Pauline conversion and declared, 'There will now be but one party, one question, one issue, one purpose in the Northern States – that of sustaining the government.'[56]

Whatever apprehension he might feel about the struggle ahead, Lincoln could at least savor this consolidation of opinion. He would later reflect to Orville Browning, who in February had advised Lincoln to keep 'the traitors . . . constantly and palpably in the wrong' and make them the aggressors, that this was the very approach he had followed in dealing with the South Carolinians. 'The plan succeeded', he purred. 'They attacked Sumter – it fell, and thus, did more service than it otherwise could.' Similarly, he told Gustavus Fox that the attempt to relieve Sumter, though unsuccessful, had still advanced 'the cause of the country'. Friend and foe endorsed his verdict. 'The loss of Sumter', the Bostonian Oliver Ellsworth told Lincoln, 'was the greatest victory the people ever realized; it has done its work effectually.' In New York, where the *Times* and *Tribune* saw in the circumstances of surrender 'a most brilliant success' that had tarred the Confederates with 'the entire responsibility of commencing the war', the southern-rights *Evening Day-Book* gloomily identified 'a cunningly devised scheme' to achieve northern political unity. 'And some Democrats', it lamented, 'have been just such dunderheads as to fall into this pit dug for their reception. Blind, deluded people!'[57]

Strategies for 'a people's war'

When, on Sunday 14 April, all Washington learnt that Anderson had capitulated at Sumter, Lincoln's immediate actions gave notice that he would himself take executive control of the war and devise its overall strategy. That afternoon he asked his cabinet to consider a proclamation in which he called on the states to raise 75,000 militiamen to put down 'combinations too powerful to be suppressed by the ordinary course of judicial proceeding', and to repossess the forts and other federal property then beyond Union control. Published in the next day's press, the proclamation also summoned Congress into special session on 4 July. The delay would allow the militia's term of service to be extended to three months (by law it could serve for no more than thirty days after the opening of a congressional session), but just as important was the opportunity it gave Lincoln to establish his control unhindered. Before Independence Day he took further executive action, establishing a blockade of the ports of the rebel states, increasing the size of the regular army and navy, calling up over 40,000 three-year volunteers, and entrusting $2 million of Treasury funds to private individuals to buy arms. Most controversially, on 27 April he suspended the privilege of the writ of habeas corpus along the corridor between Washington and Philadelphia, to allow the summary military arrest, without trial, of those who threatened the passage of troops to the nation's capital. In all this he enjoyed public and informal congressional support, and consulted political figures who mattered most, but left no doubt about who was in command.

The steps that Lincoln took during the early stages of the war showed an impressive and instinctive grasp of strategic essentials. He had three main objectives. He must nourish and sustain northern political support beyond the narrow confines of the Republican party. He must do all in his power to strengthen the Unionist elements in the upper tier of slave states. And, while tightening a noose around the Confederacy, he had to prevent the war becoming an international conflict. Policies or actions which undermined these goals would disable the Union cause and threaten defeat.

*

Lincoln knew that no one would be more important to advancing the goal of cross-party, inclusive Unionism, and building on its tentative appearance in March, than the Titan of the northern Democrats, Stephen Douglas. On the evening of 14 April, Lincoln spent two hours at the White House alone with his old rival. Douglas pledged his unstinting support in bringing about the restoration of the Union, now possible only through the bloodshed that he had worked himself to near-exhaustion to prevent. In the next day's papers Douglas delivered to an attentive country an account of this cordial meeting, and in effect instructed Democrats in their patriotic duty. The two men, he reported, had spoken 'of the present & future, without reference to the past'. While remaining 'unalterably opposed to the administration on all its political issues', he would 'sustain the President in the exercise of all his constitutional functions to preserve the Union, and maintain the government, and defend the Federal Capital'.[58]

Douglas proved true to his word, heading back to Illinois by train and along the way delivering urgent speeches designed to stiffen the backbones of waverers. At the capitol in Springfield he delivered an electrifying address, bitter toward those southern leaders he felt had conspired to destroy the Union, and explained why party must now give way to country. In what would be the final speech of his life, a week later in Chicago, he hammered the same message to a huge and admiring cross-party audience: 'There can be no neutrals in this war, *only patriots – or traitors.*' As Republicans lionized Douglas, he met the deep skepticism of the Democrats' peace wing, whose suspicions he tried to calm with a public letter. Denying that he was in Lincoln's pocket, he insisted that Democratic ascendancy would come only by remembering 'that a man cannot be a true Democrat unless he is a loyal patriot'.[59]

Acting as the voluntary agent of the administration at a time when many people were ready for political guidance, Douglas exerted real influence. In consulting him so promptly, Lincoln had seemed to promise an informal Democratic influence over administration policy. Douglas would shackle 'Black Republicanism' and guarantee 'the integrity of the Union', judged a friend from Maryland, confident that for this reason the state would not secede. In Illinois, Douglas played a part in the complex of forces that converted dissident-waverers to committed Unionism, including congressmen John A. Logan and William Richardson, and the editor of the *Chicago Times*, Cyrus McCormick. Across the North leading Democrats who looked to Douglas took a prominent part in Union rallies throughout April and May. When Douglas, physically spent, met his premature death in early June it deprived his weakened and disunited party of their only figure of genuinely national authority. But the likely effect on the Union seemed just as damaging. Lincoln's White House and Seward's State Department were draped in mourning. Government offices closed. 'The loss at this crisis', wrote the most influential Republican editor, 'must be regarded as a national tragedy.'[60]

Douglas, however, was by no means alone in urging that his party 'drop politics'. The Lincoln administration could rely on several other well-placed, non-partisan 'War Democrats' to deliver the same message over the coming months. They included the New Yorkers John A. Dix, John Cochrane and, most notably, Daniel Dickinson, who proved tireless at Union rallies; the westerners John McClernand and David Tod; and, from the border, Andrew Johnson. Several of these staunch advocates of war had been Breckinridge men in November, as too had Benjamin F. Butler of Massachusetts, Daniel E. Sickles of New York and a clutch of western editors. Their bitterness took on a sharper edge when Breckinridge himself chose to 'go South'.

Even in the first flush of patriotic anger, however, many Democrats remained unpersuaded by Douglas's strategy. The most hostile were Peace Democrats in the southern counties of the Old Northwest, in the border South, and in and around the city of New York. When Douglas reached Springfield at the end of April he reported to Lincoln that he had 'found the state of feeling here and in some parts of our State much less satisfactory than I could have desired or expected': he had particularly in mind the 'Egyptians' of southern Illinois. Such party leaders as James A. Bayard of Delaware and Clement L. Vallandigham of Ohio were oppositionists from the start, and could rely on editors like Samuel Medary of the Columbus *Crisis* and Benjamin Wood of the *New York Daily News* to be trenchant in the cause of peace. Vallandigham promptly countered Douglas's press release of 15 April with a polemic against Lincoln's coercive war: 'sober second thought', he predicted, would calm the 'surging sea of madness' and prevent 'thirty millions . . . butchering each other'.[61]

Even Democrats who saw the need for war, and blamed the South for its onset, were not easily persuaded to drop party politics for the duration of hostilities. A generation's political competition between Democrats and their Whig/Republican opponents had left a legacy of deep ideological and emotional antipathy, and an inability to see politics in any other terms. One aspect of this 'partisan imperative', as Joel Silbey has termed it, was the culturally programed hostility of Democrats to the party of Lincoln. Many continued to dismiss Republicans as Yankee-Puritan fanatics, bigots, zealots, meddlers and ideological imperialists. Without them there would have been no political breakdown of the Union and thus no war. What guarantee was there that the 'violent and revolutionary' abolitionists in the Republican party would not crush its 'conservative and patriotic' wing?[62] How would Democrats keep their independence on issues beyond the common pursuit of reunion, if they lined up behind the administration? James Bayard feared that through the folly of non-partisanship Democrats would be 'swallowed up by the Republicans'. Douglas, of course, had no intention of winding up his party, but Bayard's anxiety was realistic enough. Republican strategists did indeed see the advantages to Lincoln and the administration of 'no-partyism', as they called it. To 'sink the partisan in the patriot' did little or no harm to Republicans, for it meant the terms 'nation' and 'administration party' became more or less synonymous; but at the same time the strategy threatened to paralyze and neuter the Democrats.

With the opposition party in some disarray, Lincoln maintained the pressure for cooperation by keeping or placing prominent Democrats in military command. During his first weeks in office he had followed convention, dismissing over a thousand of Buchanan's political appointees and replacing them from the hordes of Republican loyalists hungry for a share of the patronage. Meanwhile cabinet secretaries and legislators were responsible for filling thousands of other federal government jobs. Sweeping away 'corrupt' Democrats was no more than the party had promised when campaigning for the return of 'honest Abe'. But it was also in keeping with the custom of rewarding party activists, keeping them disciplined and loyal to the administration: this would take on particular significance as the 1864 election approached. More immediately, however, it did nothing to win the goodwill of Democrats: Irish-Americans felt hard done by and Douglas himself thought Lincoln had 'dealt hardly with me, in removing some of my friends from office'.[63] But Lincoln had more freedom for cross-party bridge-building when it came to accepting regiments from Democratic strongholds, often largely Irish, and appointing generals, whose commissioning lay in the president's hands.[64] Democrats had been well-represented amongst the officers of the regular army on the eve of secession, but during the subsequent crisis most of these went South. Their replacements came from the ranks of West Point professionals and from civilian life, and Lincoln acted to ensure an across-the-board political (as well as geographical and ethnic) representation. Many Democrats secured high-profile positions of command as a result, including Ben Butler, John A. Dix, John ('Black Jack') Logan, John A. McClernand, Dan Sickles, and Lew Wallace: they in turn could open the door to fellow Democrats. The administration also signaled that the Democratic allegiances of those already in service would be no bar to advancement. Don Carlos Buell, Irvin McDowell, and Montgomery C. Meigs of the War Department staff, for example, all won promotion for preparing Washington against an expected attack.

Lincoln was keen to judge the strength of Democratic Unionism and the quality of its leadership when the special session of the Congress convened. Republicans comprised two out of every three senators and enjoyed a comfortable majority in the House, but the minority of Democrats and border-state Unionists were his special concern. Lincoln had already begun thinking hard about his message by early May, when he tested out some ideas on his secretaries. He knew he had to provide a compelling rationale for the war and to show that the administration's purposes were essentially conservative. He began with a summary of the events that produced the Sumter crisis, to show his own forbearance and to underscore the unwarranted aggression of the rebels. Their assault on the Union raised profound issues – of universal import – relating to the integrity of popular government and to the rights of man. The question, explained Lincoln, in phrases that he would polish at Gettysburg in 1863, was 'whether a constitutional republic, or a democracy – a government of the people, by the same people – can, or cannot, maintain its territorial integrity, against its own domestic foes'. Were all republics inherently and fatally flawed? 'Must a government, of necessity, be too *strong* for the liberties of its own people, or too *weak* to maintain its own existence?'[65]

The rebels had chosen to abandon a government based on the popular will and had adopted a constitution which, 'unlike our good old one', omitted the phrase, 'We, the People'. Their declaration of independence had excised Jefferson's words, 'all men are created equal'. They had, then, in 'pressing out of view, the rights of men, and the authority of the people' provoked 'a People's contest' on behalf of a Union committed to 'maintaining in the world, that form, and substance of government, whose leading object is, to elevate the condition of men – to lift artificial weights from all shoulders – to clear the paths of laudable pursuit for all – to afford all, an unfettered start, and a fair chance, in the race of life'.[66]

The war's purpose was thus protective and conservative: to defend the values and political philosophy of Washington and the Founders in the face of national disintegration. For revolution, look south: secession was an illegal, insurrectionary act by rebellious individuals against a perpetual Union. And since that Union remained unbroken, there should be no 'uneasiness in the minds of candid men, as to what is to be the course of the government, towards the Southern States, *after* the rebellion shall have been suppressed'. As president, he reassured conservatives, he would continue to be guided by constitutional law, and when peace returned 'probably will have no different understanding of the powers, and duties of the Federal government, relatively to the rights of the States, and the people' than he had had on assuming office. That 'probably' was a mark of Lincoln's caution and intellectual honesty in the face of the imponderables of war, and perhaps a warning too, but the essential message was clear: individuals might be punished for their rebellion, but the Constitution would continue to protect southern slaveholders in their property rights. The federal authorities would not instigate social revolution in the South.[67]

As a further nod toward the concerns of conservatives, Lincoln sought to show that that he had fully complied with his constitutional duty both before and after the fall of Sumter. In what was a high-wire act of persuasion he said nothing that would compromise his determination as chief executive and commander-in-chief to keep control of the war's prosecution, but at the same time he looked to Congress to endorse what he had done since 15 April. Pressing the argument that he had made his various proclamations, 'whether strictly legal or not', in response to 'a popular demand, and a public necessity', he asked that Congress ratify them, and added the extraordinary statement, 'It is believed that nothing has been done beyond the constitutional competency of Congress.' More delicate still was the issue of Lincoln's limited suspension of habeas corpus, which by now had come under the hostile scrutiny of Roger Taney. Given the Constitution's silence on where the power of suspension lay – with the president or with Congress? – Lincoln volleyed the argument back to the Chief Justice: the president had indeed, as Taney had noted, taken an oath to 'take care that the laws be faithfully executed', but 'are all the laws, *but one*, to go unexecuted, and the government itself go to pieces, lest that one be violated?'[68]

Lincoln gave notice that as president he would mix Jacksonian executive energy with a Whiggish understanding of the law-making authority of the legislature. This was a recipe for rallying broad cross-party support, both within Congress and beyond. With the exception of the suspension of the writ, which would remain a chronic source of division, legislators overwhelmingly approved Lincoln's emergency measures. And they more than met his request for men and money, by authorizing the raising of up to half a million troops, and providing an appropriation of $500 million through bond issues, increased protective duties, and direct taxation, including an income tax. The same broad-based Unionism found expression, too, in the welcome proffered to the resolutions which the slave-state Democrats, John J. Crittenden and Andrew Johnson, introduced on the eve of the war's first large-scale military engagement. After the numbing, humiliating Union defeat at Bull Run, the two chambers of Congress, echoing the president's message, resolved almost unanimously 'that this war is not waged, on our part, in any spirit of oppression, nor for any purpose of conquest or subjugation, nor purpose of overthrowing or interfering with the rights or established institutions' of the states.

The fusion of Lincoln's declared conservative purposes and popular patriotism worked to contain and weaken the Democrats as an electoral force during the first year of the war. They fought the fall state elections hesitant and confused. In several instances, responding to the 'no-party' initiative, the party's local and state conventions stopped meeting. When they did convene, nominations for office did not inevitably follow. Many

'War Democrats' believed they should run no candidates during the crisis, and effectively left the party, to be subsumed within Republicanism. Others did run, but on separate tickets against party regulars, and split the vote; by 1862 these troublesome separate tickets had given way in some areas to 'Union party' organizations, by which Republicans sought to fight the opposition. War Democrats were an elite, not a mass movement, and left the core vote of the party undisturbed, but for Lincoln they represented a propaganda coup, valuable exemplars of a large-hearted Unionism. And although the Democratic party retained its organization, its dominating group of regulars comprised red-hot patriots who shared the stated priorities of the administration. Many of these flocked to the ranks in the spring and summer of 1861, often urged on by state-level Democratic office-holders, most notably Governor William Sprague of Rhode Island. For the time being, at least, Vallandigham and the Peace Democrats seemed to the White House only a minor irritant, not a significant threat.[69]

*

Despite Lincoln's best efforts to present the secessionists as the aggressors, he was unable to prevent the departure of four more slave states after Sumter fell. He called up far fewer militiamen than he actually required, well short of the Confederate forces then in arms, but across the upper South state governors interpreted Lincoln's call for troops as an aggressive preliminary to 'invasion'. Virginia's state convention passed an ordinance of secession on 17 April, endorsed by a popular referendum five weeks later. Like-minded political leaders took similar energetic action in North Carolina, Tennessee, and Arkansas. There were substantial Unionist minorities in southern Appalachia, but by early June the Confederacy had formally embraced all of these states. They brought with them a combined population of over three and a half million people, and huge resources, mainly agricultural and mineral, but also the largest iron works in the South. Soon afterwards the Confederates seized the federal naval base at Norfolk and the arsenal at Harpers Ferry.

On the course of the northernmost tier of slave states would almost certainly hang the outcome of the war, and Lincoln recognized this. 'These all against us, and the job on our hands is too large for us. We would as well consent to separation at once.'[70] By absorbing Delaware, Maryland, Kentucky and Missouri, the Confederacy would not only gain some three million people and further material resources, but Washington's days as the Union's capital would be numbered, the Ohio river would provide the South with a natural defense, the Union would be faced with recovering a land mass of intimidating dimensions, and the domain of slavery would stand undivided and energized in its life-and-death struggle with freedom. It seemed inconceivable that a Union reduced to nineteen million people would be able to subdue twelve million Confederates – even had Unionism run as strongly amongst the ordinary people of the South as Lincoln initially and over-optimistically believed. But which way would these states jump? Delaware, with its tiny slave population, was certain for the Union, but the same could not be said of the others. Their economic interests tugged them northwards, yet they shared an interest with the South in the social arrangements of slavery. And to both sections they were tied by blood.

Lincoln's immediate preoccupation after 15 April was to secure the safety of Washington. If he overestimated the capacity of the Confederates to launch an immediate assault, his anxiety over the unpreparedness of the capital was entirely understandable. To protect the city it was essential to control Maryland and its railroad routes to the north, but Baltimore was a hothouse of secessionism, as was the eastern shore. On 19 April, as the first Washington-bound northern regiment made its way from one Baltimore station to another, pro-Confederate rioters shot dead several soldiers and wounded others. The depleted regiment made it to Washington, but for the next six days the capital was cut off from the north by rail and telegraph, and, in Hay's words, prey to 'feverish rumors'. Lincoln's nervous tension did not affect his judgment in one crucial respect, however: he prudently resisted calls from cabinet members for retaliation and the use of force to bring further troops through the city. But he was equally determined not to yield to the Baltimore crypto-secessionists who sought a promise that he would send no more troops across the state. There was, he told them frostily, no other way of defending the capital. 'Our men are not moles, and can't dig under the earth; they are not birds, and can't fly through the air.'[71]

But they could sail. When Ben Butler cleverly avoided Baltimore by bringing a regiment by boat down the Chesapeake Bay to Annapolis, and from there on 25 April by rail to Washington, Lincoln 'smiled all over'. The balance now swung. As troops poured in and strengthened his grip on the capital, Lincoln was able to play a more confident game of cat and mouse with the Maryland secessionists. Rather than arrest the disunionists before the state legislature convened – as Butler and Scott wanted – Lincoln ordered them to hold off. A show of Union force on Baltimore's Federal Hill and the limited suspension of habeas corpus on the military line between Philadelphia and Washington emboldened the state's

Unionists and gave Lincoln 'to think that if quiet was kept in Baltimore a little longer Maryland might be considered the first of the redeemed'. It proved a realistic hope. Union candidates swept the board in the June congressional elections. That fall, with General John A. Dix's troops firmly in control, a Unionist won the governorship, thanks to the strength of loyalist sentiment in the western and central counties, and to the arrest of some editors and disunionist members of the state legislature.[72]

Concern for the safety of Washington, together with Lincoln's determination to encourage slave-state Unionism wherever it revealed itself, also shaped the president's course in western Virginia. Loyalism was strong there, as it was in other parts of the Allegheny–Appalachian range, including eastern Tennessee and western North Carolina, and was nourished by a long-standing anti-aristocratic animus against the wealthier and politically dominant slaveholding areas of the Tidewater and Piedmont. When Virginia acted to secede, leading men from the western counties wrote to Lincoln asking for the administration's help in resisting this 'coercion' and establishing a loyal state government in their part of the state. Lincoln directed Nicolay to reply cautiously, while 'leaving the door open'. Shortly afterwards he promised them active military assistance. Control here would increase the capital's security, provide a shield for the contiguous parts of Ohio and Pennsylvania, support federal forces in the Shenandoah Valley and offer protection to eastern Kentucky, a base from which the Union could pursue a project dear to Lincoln's heart – the liberation of the loyalists of eastern Tennessee.[73]

In June, following George B. McClellan's rout of the Confederate forces at Philippi, a Unionist convention at Wheeling moved to implement one of the two schemes before it. Members set up a 'restored' state government as a rival to the secessionist government in Richmond, and elected as governor Francis H. Pierpont, a Wheeling coal dealer and lawyer. He in turn organized a legislature, which sent two senators and three representatives to Washington, where Congress admitted them. Lincoln duly endorsed this Wheeling administration, despite its resting on a modest vote in only one part of the state. 'Those loyal citizens', he told Congress, 'this government is bound to recognize, and protect, as being Virginia.'[74]

The second proposal was even more controversial. It called for the loyal counties to be formed into a separate jurisdiction, the state of 'Kanawha' (later West Virginia). After a protracted process of conventions and elections through the fall and winter, a constitution for West Virginia won popular approval in April 1862. In May, the 'restored' legislature of Virginia agreed to the formation of the new state and so technically met the Constitution's stipulation that the division of any state should only occur with that state's consent. But given the very small numbers of voters who participated and the exclusion from the exercise of all areas under the sway of the Richmond authorities, the whole process was at best constitutionally dubious and extralegal. Congress, however, passed the bill to admit West Virginia, leaving Lincoln with a hard decision. He consulted a divided cabinet in which the attorney-general and two others protested that the measure breached the Constitution. Alert to the argument that this was no better than secession, 'and tolerated only because it is our secession', Lincoln nonetheless chose what he admitted was the 'expedient' course. Since the act tended 'the more strongly to the restoration of the national authority throughout the Union', he signed it, on the last day of the year.[75]

The mixture of firmness, clear vision and delicacy of judgment that served Lincoln well in his handling of affairs in Maryland and West Virginia rather deserted him when he confronted the remote western border state of Missouri. He surely understood its strategic importance: the state was a tongue of slavery surrounded on three sides by a free population and a salient that commanded the river system of the Northwest. But he was handicapped by his ignorance of its complex and fractious politics. In his cabinet he heard two discordant Missouri voices: the moderate Edward Bates, spokesman for the state's conservative Unionists; and, through Montgomery Blair, the arguments of the postmaster general's influential brother Frank, tied to the radical camp.

The hard question for Lincoln was how roughly to handle the state's disunionists, who were clustered in the Missouri river counties and around St Louis. The incautious Nathaniel Lyon, commanding the pro-Union forces in St Louis, had successfully removed the city's federal arsenal across the river to loyal Illinois on 25 April. He then forced the surrender of the pro-southern militia at Camp Jackson, just outside the city, on 10 May. Riots followed and lives were lost. Conservative Unionists counseled a policy of moderation, to chloroform the secessionists, and found an ally in General William Harney, commander of the Department of the West. Radical Unionists, led by Blair and Lyon, and working through Montgomery Blair in Washington, successfully persuaded Lincoln that the conservatives underestimated the depth of the rebel threat.[76] Both Bates and Winfield Scott backed Harney, but Lincoln reluctantly gave Frank Blair discretion to remove the general in an emergency. In short order Blair replaced Harney with Lyon and sabotaged the truce that Harney had arranged with the pro-secession forces. By mid-June Lincoln's miscalculation in giving discretionary power to Blair was clear enough: Missouri was in open warfare.

Historians have generally been less persuaded than have the president's secretaries that Lincoln acted wisely in his dealings with Missouri. Nicolay and Hay thought that Harney and the conservatives had been 'blinded and lulled' by the smooth words of traitors: the reality of embryonic rebel companies and a threatened invasion from Arkansas compelled Lincoln and Blair to act.[77] Most historians, however, conscious of the chronic terror, guerrilla raids and feuding in wartime Missouri, have been more impressed by the thought that Harney's caution would have served the Union better at this cross-roads in the war and given time for the loyalism of the state's majority to assert itself.[78] This is a plausible criticism. Lincoln's perception would certainly have been sharper had he been able to rely on a disinterested, locally-based adviser. His judgment may also have been skewed by his reading of the presidential election result in Missouri, where Union sentiment looked stronger than in any other slave state. Douglas and Bell had taken the lion's share of the presidential ballots, while the southern rights candidate, Breckinridge, had secured a very much smaller percentage of the vote than elsewhere in the South. On this reading, if the decisive use of force were to work pre-emptively anywhere against secessionism, then Missouri was the obvious place to employ it. However, we may reasonably ask – given the violence and frontier lawlessness of antebellum Missouri, its reputation as a political snake-pit and the opportunities presented by civil war for the settling of old scores – whether another policy in 1861, even Harney's, would have secured the permanent pacification of the state for the Union.

Historians, by contrast, have given Lincoln high marks for his approach to the border state which he knew he dared not lose, Kentucky, where he adopted the patient waiting game he had chosen not to pursue in Missouri. The tenacity with which Lincoln chased the prize of Kentucky's loyalty had less to do with emotional concern for his native state or his calculation of the state's substantial resources in livestock, agricultural produce and manufactures, important though these were, than with an acute awareness of its strategic significance for the whole border region. 'I think to lose Kentucky is nearly the same as to lose the whole game. Kentucky gone,' he argued, 'we can not hold Missouri, nor, as I think, Maryland.'[79] Kentucky *held*, by contrast, meant command of the south bank of the Ohio river, vital as a commercial artery, a defensive military line and a bridge between the eastern and western theaters of war.

Lincoln, however, knew better than to force the pace of Kentucky Unionism, in which he had some reason to be confident. He had a far better feel for opinion there than in Missouri, thanks in part to the Todd family – divided in its loyalties – and especially to his old friend Joshua Speed, now of Louisville, and his brother James. He also arranged to receive the Lexington newspapers, the loyal *Observer* and the disunionist *Statesman*. When the pro-southern governor, Beriah Magoffin, indignantly refused Union calls for troops and warned both sides to keep out, Lincoln kept calm. He had 'an unquestioned right at all times' to move federal troops across a state's territory, he told a leading Kentucky Unionist, but 'if Kentucky made no demonstration of force against the United States he would not molest her'. So, for the time being, he strengthened 'the Ohio line' by attending to the other side of the river. Within days of the outbreak of war, the administration ordered the despatch of federal troops to Cairo, Illinois, at the strategic junction with the Mississippi; but, respecting the Kentucky legislature's proclamation of 'neutrality', Lincoln resisted pressure from the governors of Ohio, Indiana, and Illinois to send Union forces into the state. The occupation of Cairo was too much for some Blue Grass neutralists. One state senator wrote a truculent protest against 'an unwarrantable usurpation', to which Hay composed a sarcastic response in Lincoln's name. The president 'would certainly never have ordered the movement of troops, complained of, had he known that Cairo was in your Senatorial district'.[80]

Lincoln's waiting game – what Lowell called 'the little Bopeep policy' – seemed cowardly and humiliating to many in the North. Tolerating neutrality meant tolerating only qualified loyalty, allowing merchants to trade with the Confederacy as well as the Union and watching the secession-minded Magoffin charting a disunionist course. But it also meant giving the Whig Unionists of the Clay–Crittenden tradition time to organize against full-blown separatism and to secure a convincing victory in the June congressional elections. It meant using Sumter's hero, Robert Anderson, a native Kentuckian, now located across the river in Cincinnati, to recruit Kentucky volunteers for the Union army; and it involved sending another native, the young navy lieutenant, William Nelson, surreptitiously to help organize and arm the loyalist Home Guard in the state. By August the tide had so turned that Unionists easily dominated the legislature and Nelson now began openly assembling four Union regiments on Kentucky soil. In response to Magoffin's plaintive call for its removal, Lincoln declined to act against a force which, he noted, was made up exclusively of Kentucky volunteers and enjoyed popular support.[81]

'[N]eutrality *wont* continue long', Hay wrote in his diary on 22 August: 'we want to go through the state – and the North will not permit the disarming of the Unionists.'[82] He was prescient in his prediction, even if he could not foresee the particular two-fold events that would shortly end Kentucky's uneasy non-alignment and lock most of the state into Lincoln's waiting arms. One of these was the rash move into Kentucky of Confederate forces, at Columbus on the Mississippi river, on 2 September. General Gideon Pillow – proving as impetuous a liability to Jefferson Davis as Nathaniel Lyon had to Lincoln in Missouri – viewed Ulysses S. Grant's occupation of Belmont, Missouri, as a Union springboard for seizing Columbus and controlling the river traffic. Pillow persuaded his commanding officer, Leonidas Polk, to authorize a pre-emptive move, which Jefferson Davis endorsed, but which stirred the Kentucky authorities into anguished protest. The trap now sprung, Grant moved Union forces across the Ohio into Paducah. Neutrality was at an end, so engineered that Lincoln could not be tarred with the brush of aggression. The legislature declared for the Union. As further troops from both sides pushed in, the North secured the balance of control, with Confederates strung out and vulnerable across the counties south of the Green river region.

Simultaneously, however, parallel events in neighboring Missouri threatened to undo all of Lincoln's tactful good work in Kentucky. At St Louis on 30 August, John C. Frémont, commander of the Department of the West, issued a stunning proclamation. Desperate to quell guerrilla savagery and reduce Confederate support, particularly in the slaveholding counties, Frémont acted by putting Missouri under martial law, threatening to court-martial and execute civilians in arms, to confiscate the property of citizens who aided the enemy, and to free the slaves of rebels. It was the measure of a general increasingly out of his depth, alienated from his initial patron, Frank Blair, and now under the radical influences of Owen Lovejoy, John A. Gurley, and his wife, Jessie Frémont. Frémont later recalled that Lincoln had told him, as he left to take up his western command in July, 'I have given you carte blanche; you must use your own judgment and do the best you can.' In this spirit, he now chose not to warn the president about a development which threatened to destabilize Unionism in Kentucky and constituted Lincoln's greatest political challenge of the wartime months of 1861.

Lincoln responded promptly, sending a special messenger with a confidential letter to Frémont. Afraid of Confederate retaliation, he ordered the general to secure his prior approval before shooting anyone under the terms of the proclamation. Then, alert to the 'great danger' that confiscation and freeing of slaves 'will alarm our Southern Union friends, and turn them against us – perhaps ruin our rather fair prospect for Kentucky', Lincoln asked Frémont to bring the proclamation into line with the terms of the Confiscation Act that Congress had passed in early August.[83] That enactment allowed the Union, through judicial proceedings, to confiscate and free those slaves assisting Confederate forces.

Reports from trusted Unionists soon confirmed Lincoln's fears that the proclamation could torpedo his border-state strategy, at the very moment that events at Columbus promised a successful denouement. The Speed brothers sent urgent and distressed warnings that Kentuckians, loyalist and disunionist alike, would resist an edict which threatened to free perhaps 20,000 of their slaves. Joshua, sleepless with anxiety, predicted that Frémont's folly would 'crush out every vestage of a union party in the state' if not annulled: 'you had as well attack the freedom of worship in the north or the right of a parent to teach his child to read – as to wage war in a slave state on such a principle'. Others insisted that without Lincoln's immediate disavowal of emancipation, 'Kentucky is gone over the mill dam'. From Anderson the president learnt that, on hearing that Frémont had 'actually issued deeds of manumission, a whole company of our Volunteers threw down their arms and disbanded'.[84]

Frémont, however, remained blind to Lincoln's larger strategy. Angered by what he saw as a rebuke, he refused to do what the president had privately requested and instead asked, in a letter that his wife took personally to the White House, that he be publicly ordered to retreat. Although a far more formidable politician than her husband, Jessie Frémont met her match in Lincoln and failed to shift the humorlessly smiling president during an uncomfortable interview. 'The General should never have dragged the Negro into the war,' she recalled Lincoln telling her. 'It is a war for a great national object, and the Negro has nothing to do with it.' Responding in a public letter to Frémont's demand that he be openly countermanded, Lincoln 'very cheerfully' modified the original proclamation to make it conform to the terms of the Confiscation Act. He knew that deleting the most objectionable parts of the document was essential for the continued loyalty of Kentucky. Conservatives rushed to pay tribute to a president whose 'consistent, prudent, & just' intervention had shored up Unionism. 'There is a good deal of old Whig left in me yet', he acknowledged.[85]

As horror yielded to celebration in Kentucky, popular sentiment in the wider Union moved in the other direction. Frémont's proclamation had dazzled the country, earning plaudits well beyond the confines of radical antislavery for recognizing the logic of the war. From the outset, Lincoln's correspondents had peppered him with entreaties to turn the weapons of war on slavery itself. Carl Schurz told Hay early on that even many Democrats judged that 'now is the time to remove the cause of all our woes', namely slavery. Ben Butler's military expedient of treating the runaway slaves of rebel slaveholders as 'contraband' of war drew applause, as part of 'the logic of events'. The argument generated even more force amongst political leaders after the shock of the Bull Run defeat. At the same time as the conservative Johnson–Crittenden resolutions were securing broad-based support at Washington, the military imperative of an assault on rebel slaveholding found favor, too. The Confiscation Act, passed after fierce debate and against the remonstrations of Kentucky's Crittenden, sprang from this widespread desire to punish treason and weaken 'the commissariat of the rebel army'.[86]

In countermanding the edict, Lincoln stirred up a storm of indignation. An 'old fogy' president had effectively sawn his dynamic general off at the knees. Moncure Conway told Greeley that Lincoln's name now prompted public groans, not cheers. Protests inundated the White House, particularly from the Northwest. 'No disaster – not even the fearful one at Bull Run – has so dispirited and paralysed the friends of the Union', lamented an Illinoisan. There were fears for the effect on recruitment. While some anti-abolition nationalists, commonly Democrats, tendered Lincoln their support, far more striking was the cross-party chorus of criticism from conservatives who lauded a decisive act of war. The *National Intelligencer*, the *St Louis Republican*, the *Chicago Times*, and even Bennett's *New York Herald* had all hailed Frémont's action. None of the anguished noises of the conservative press surprised Lincoln any more than the letter of regret from his old associate and fellow Kentuckian, Orville Browning, who wanted the president to understand 'the unqualified approval' which 'every true friend of the Government' afforded the edict. True, Browning acknowledged, 'there is no express, written law authorizing it; but war is never carried on, and can never be, in strict accordance with previously adjusted constitutional and legal provisions'. Traitors who warred upon the Constitution and the laws had no right to invoke their protection. The government had the power to dispose of a traitor's life. 'Is a traitor's negro', he asked, 'more sacred than his life?'[87]

Lincoln professed astonishment that his friend's customary legal caution should have deserted him. His response began by showing Browning how the proclamation failed rudimentary legal and constitutional tests. Confiscating property in perpetuity and liberating slaves was '*purely political*, and not within the range of *military* law, or necessity'; it trespassed on the domain of lawmakers and was 'simply "dictatorship"'. Then, in the core of the letter, he set out with crystal clarity the essence of his strategic thinking, as formulated and applied in 1861. He knew that he could win easy popularity by endorsing Frémont's action. 'No doubt the thing was popular in some quarters', he reflected, 'and would have been more so if it had been a general declaration of emancipation.' But he would do nothing that would hazard the loss of Kentucky and, with it, 'lose the whole game'. A 'restlessness for new positions' must not destabilize the broad coalition. Rather, he urged Browning, 'back me manfully on the grounds upon which you and other kind friends gave me the election, and have approved in my public documents, [and] we shall go through triumphantly'.[88]

Whatever its shortcomings, Lincoln's border policy proved remarkably effective. By the time Lincoln sent his message to Congress in December the non-Confederate South had been very largely secured. He pointed with legitimate satisfaction to the constancy of 'noble little Delaware', to Marylanders' endorsement of the Union at the ballot box, to Kentucky's being 'decidedly, and, I think, unchangeably, ranged on the side of the Union'; to the comparative pacification of Missouri; and to western Virginia's loyalists being 'masters of their own country'. Having initially refused to supply a single soldier, Maryland, Kentucky and Missouri had now put over 40,000 troops into the Union army, three times those they sent to the Confederacy. Further, he urged the military construction of a railroad to connect Unionists in eastern Tennessee and western North Carolina with Kentucky and the other loyal areas.[89] As it happened, Lincoln was far too sanguine about Missouri, and would be chronically disappointed by efforts to liberate important pockets of Appalachian Unionism. But in the main he was right to believe that events had vindicated his course. The upper South would continue to play its part in the evolution of his thinking during and after 1862, while gradually losing its overall strategic importance.

*

Cementing non-Republican northerners and border-state loyalists into the Union coalition would make little difference to the balance sheet of advantage if one or more of the great European powers should throw its resources behind the South. Lincoln had no first-hand knowledge of foreign affairs, but he knew enough to understand that civil wars left nations prey to outside interference. 'A nation which endures factious domestic division, is exposed to disrespect abroad', he told Congress, 'and one party, if not both, is sure, sooner or later, to invoke foreign intervention.'[90] Lincoln had no intention of involving himself in the day-to-day business of foreign policy: this would be left to his accomplished secretary of state. But he was equally ready to intervene whenever events threatened his larger strategic objective. Ideally, foreign powers should recognize that the Union was involved in putting down an internal insurrection, accept that the Confederate 'government' was illegitimate, offer the rebels no material or moral support, and respect the blockade of southern ports. But the bottom line was avoidance of war.

The Union's key relationship, the administration knew, was with Great Britain, the world's greatest naval power. France, too, was a significant force, but it was unlikely to take any action independent of Britain. It was, then, alarming that within weeks of the fall of Sumter, on 14 May, Lord Palmerston's government issued a proclamation of neutrality, recognizing the Confederates as belligerents. Other European powers followed suit. Seward, raging 'like a caged tiger' and swearing as only he could, saw this as overt encouragement of the rebels.[91] For the Europeans, however, it was little more than a conventional response in time of war, falling well short of diplomatic recognition and flowing logically from Lincoln's blockade of the southern ports, a measure they were ready to recognize. A blockade had status in international law: it was the action of one sovereign power against another and, when effective, it demanded the respect of neutrals. In imposing it, Lincoln undercut his claim that the Union was simply putting down a domestic uprising. A nation could not, after all, blockade itself. After consulting Charles Sumner, who chaired the Senate Foreign Relations Committee, Lincoln set about tempering the militant dispatch which Seward – in warmongering mode – had composed for Charles Francis Adams, the United States minister in London. The president's revisions revealed a sharp eye for diplomatic nuance, without yielding the substance of the American position. Lincoln also ordered the urbane Adams to communicate only the substance of the document, and not to read or show it to the British Foreign Secretary.

Simmering resentment continued to mark relations between the two countries for the next six months, boiling over into a diplomatic crisis in December over the celebrated *Trent* affair. The Union navy's seizure from a British mail packet of two Confederate commissioners bound for diplomatic service in Europe became the occasion of wild, patriotic rejoicing at home and white-hot indignation in Britain. Generally regarded as an ocean bully, long disdainful of neutral rights, Britain now found itself in the unaccustomed role of victim. The technicalities of Captain Charles Wilkes's action in removing James M. Mason and John Slidell from the *Trent* were far from clear-cut, though the balance of legal advantage lay with the British: by removing the commissioners in a search-and-seize operation, without taking the vessel to a prize court for adjudication, the

Americans seemed to be in breach of international law. But it was the affront to the Union Jack and injured pride, as much as points of law, that moved Palmerston and Earl Russell to rattle their sabres.

Only slowly, while Britain ordered naval and military reinforcements to Canada and the western Atlantic, did Lincoln come to appreciate the depth of the crisis. Once more he benefited from regular discussions with Sumner, whose friendship with the English Liberal reformers, John Bright and Richard Cobden, made the senator a barometer of British opinion. There was real risk, Sumner knew, that the hysteria of the 'Rule Britannia' political class might force Palmerston to act in defense of British honor. Seward's *alter ego* and government agent, Thurlow Weed, was also in Britain taking the political temperature, and urged forbearance on Lincoln. The president's preferred escape route, one which would have had the merit of cooling passions on both sides and making the prisoners' release more palatable to American public opinion, was arbitration by an international third party. He composed a draft dispatch which proposed settling the immediate affair by these means, on the understanding that whatever the arbiters determined should settle 'the law for all future analogous cases, between Great Brittain and the United States': in other words, by yielding now America would at least protect her own neutral rights in the years ahead. He was evidently still serious about an initiative along these lines when he privately read his draft to an approving Orville Browning on 21 December; both men 'agreed that the question was susceptible of a peaceful solution if England was at all disposed to act justly with us'.[92]

Lincoln's intended approach was put in question two days later, however, when the British minister to Washington, Lord Lyons, presented the British government's formal demand for an apology and for the release of the envoys within a week. In the sobering knowledge that France would side with Britain, the president called his cabinet together on Christmas Day. Seward – 'loaded to the muzzle' with international law – took the lead in arguing the case for releasing the Confederate envoys, on the technical grounds that Wilkes had had every right to detain and search the *Trent*, but that he should have taken the vessel to a prize court. Sumner, present at Lincoln's invitation, read out letters from Cobden and Bright to a similar purpose. Chase, too, tasting wormwood and gall as he did so, conceded the justice of the secretary of state's argument. Bates, though unimpressed by the legal arguments (he had initially judged the seizure of the diplomats wholly lawful), did see the force of necessity: 'We cannot hope for success in a super added war with England, backed by the assent and countenance of France.'[93]

There was, however, no immediate agreement. After four hours the cabinet adjourned. According to the attorney-general, Lincoln, along with some others, showed a 'great reluctance' to acknowledge that 'to go to war with England now, is to abandon all hope of suppressing the rebellion'. It is certainly true that as the meeting broke up Lincoln told Seward that he would put together a case for not releasing the envoys, and asked the secretary of state to press ahead with a concessive answer for Lord Lyons: the reconvened cabinet could then compare the cases the next day. But this did not mean that Lincoln was prepared to risk war, or that he had failed to understand the undoubtedly ruinous consequences of a conflict with Britain. Rather, he seems to have been using debate, as he did with big issues at other times, to test the very ground on which he intended to stand. In the event, he offered no counter-argument to Seward's, telling him that he had found it impossible to construct one. That evening he assured Browning that there would be no conflict, just as he had told Sumner two days earlier: 'There will be no war unless England is bent on having one.'[94] Lincoln's chief anxiety had for some time ceased to be whether to release the envoys; rather, as his arbitration proposal suggested, it had become how to do so with least damage to national dignity. Seward gave his colleagues a way out by producing a legal rationale for backing down. On 26 December the reconvened cabinet swallowed the bitter pill and agreed to surrender the Confederate prisoners. The next day Seward informed Lyons that the United States – delighted that Britain now embraced the freedom of the seas and respect for the rights of neutrals – would free the captives and make reparation for Wilkes's illegal act, but would offer no apology for a deed not authorized by the administration. Honor had been maintained, at least in part.

Hindsight suggests that the rhetorical smoke and thunder of the *Trent* affair obscured a cold, sharp calculation of national advantage in both the Union and British governments. It was in the strategic interests of neither to be swept into war. But rational action follows only from rational thought, and for that the decision-makers on both sides can take credit. Of these, none was more responsible than Lincoln for the preservation of a wary peace. Throughout he was a restraining influence, dampening rather than stoking the fires of chauvinism. Sensibly, he avoided all reference to the brewing crisis in his annual message to Congress. He readily listened and deferred to those from whom he could learn, notably Sumner and a now statesmanlike Seward, who well knew when and when not to be bellicose, and who enjoyed good personal relations with Lord Lyons. However attached Lincoln might have been to his own arbitration proposal, he chose not to press it when circumstances moved on. By these means he charted a course through stormy seas to calmer but still choppy waters beyond. Other perils lay ahead in the Union's international relations, especially relating to the blockade, to the construction of Confederate raiders in European shipyards, and to British and French efforts at mediation. But Lincoln had navigated past the greatest point of danger, determined that he would not have 'two wars on his hands at a time'.[95]

'What shall I do? The people are impatient . . .'

Throughout these tumultuous months from his election to the end of 1861 Lincoln was constantly engaged in what came naturally to him: judging public sentiment. The habits and democratic sensitivities of Lincoln the peacetime politician would become essential elements of his wartime leadership. Never the prisoner of opinion, he nonetheless took his major decisions with at least one eye on popular feeling. Thus Lincoln's public silence after his election was a calculated response to his reading of southern opinion and the needs of the Republican majority. Convinced that determined Unionism ran broad and strong, he took an unyielding stand over the forts in March and April. He was ready to defy the broad-based support for Frémont's proclamation, not out of disdain for public sentiment, but because he attached greater strategic importance to local opinion in the pivotal border regions. During the *Trent* affair he was as concerned to resolve the crisis as to avoid, in Bates's words, 'the displeasure of our own people – lest they should accuse us of timidly truckling to the power of England'.[96]

In the event, the *Trent* crisis inflicted only limited popular damage but, given the broader picture, Lincoln's anxiety was well justified. By the end of 1861 the Union public had had little to cheer. Apart from some successful incursions at the margins of the Confederacy – notably Hatteras Inlet and Port Royal Sound – Union forces had as yet made little discernible progress by land or sea. July's traumatic rout at Bull Run had prompted what Greeley described to Lincoln as 'sullen, scowling, black despair' and a sober realization that this was to be no easy or short-lived conflict. It brought changes in the high command, a flood of new recruits, the spur to an anti-war party, and a gradual revival of hope as the new leader of the Army of the Potomac, George B. McClellan, brought his remarkable energy and managerial skills to constructing a disciplined, powerful force from the three-year volunteers. Yet, six months later the few martial landmarks in the public memory were moments of disappointment, such as Grant's inconclusive engagement at Belmont, or occasions of sickening ineptness, notably at Ball's Bluff.[97]

But inglorious defeat at least intimated some sort of energy. What was more troubling to the Union's loyal citizenry was the sense that, for all the signs of preparation for war, their political and military leaders lacked either the appetite or the capacity for purposeful action. Under Simon Cameron, the War Department appeared to be proficient in venality but little else. As the tiny War Department of early 1861 ballooned to face the demands of equipping and organizing an army of half a million men, instances of unbusinesslike contracts and profiteering multiplied. If the secretary was not himself guilty of corruption – the weight of opinion is in his favor – he was widely perceived as such. He was certainly, as the president came to recognize, ignorant, lax and incompetent. Lincoln faced earnest demands for his removal and suggestions that Joseph Holt, a staunch pro-war Democrat, replace him.[98] Of course, the enormous challenge Cameron faced was in part structural: it was no easy matter to bring centralized, federal order to an operation in which proud states kept control over raising troops and commissioning regimental officers, where the administration lacked systematic, comprehensive information, and where private recruiters further complicated matters. But a secretary of war with the same vision, system and grasp of detail that Welles brought to the Navy Department could have shored up public confidence and would not have swollen Lincoln's mailbag with demands that he be replaced. Lincoln, however, continued uneasily to tolerate Cameron's incompetence. Only in mid-January 1862 did he replace him, though not with Holt but with another backboned Democrat, the formidable Edwin M. Stanton.

Dishonest contracting, fraud and ineptness also characterized military administration in the West. Frémont, as commander of that Department, could fairly accuse Washington of a myopic preoccupation with the eastern arena and of starving him of the equipment and funds he needed to subdue Missouri and move down the Mississippi. But he was also the author of many of his own difficulties, for he lacked both administrative method and the political shrewdness needed for the chess-board of western intrigue. He lost the confidence of many officers and foolishly fell out with his patrons, the Blairs, who badgered Lincoln for his removal. By mid-October the president was in possession of a clutch of adverse first-hand reports on the western commander from the secretary of war and a pack of watchdog generals. One of them, Samuel R. Curtis, advised Lincoln that the only real question was the timing and manner of Frémont's departure, to be judged with special regard to public opinion, 'an element of war which must not be neglected'.[99]

From this lesson in the obvious Lincoln might have drawn the opposite conclusion, namely that he should leave Frémont in place. As rumors spread of the commander's likely removal, he was deluged with the fiercest torrent of mail of his first year in office. 'I do Beg of you for Gods Sake for Humanitys Sake for our Western Countrys Sake Keep John C. Frémont in his present Position', pleaded a fellow Illinoisan. Writer after writer represented the West, excepting only extreme negrophobes and 'rabid democrats', as united in its faith in Frémont as the man destined to 'sweep rebellion from the Valley of the Mississippi'. His removal would be 'a catastrophe', 'bad business', and 'a suicidal policy': it would, Lincoln learnt, paralyze the army, alienate the German and Irish population, from whom a high proportion of his troops were drawn, freeze voluntary enlistments, and prompt desertion or even mutiny. If the more extreme predictions of 'a fire in the rear', a political coup, and making Frémont a military dictator cut little ice in Washington, Lincoln could be in little doubt of the damage that his dismissal would do to popular morale and to the standing of the administration. As John Hay noted, it was not easy to act when it was widely believed, east and west, that all opposition to Frémont arose from his emancipation proclamation and 'thus assumes the form of a persecution for righteousness sake'. Frémont himself, by re-issuing his proclamation and working successfully to cultivate the western press, hoped – so Frank Blair believed – to 'make public opinion . . . overawe the President and his Administration'.[100]

In the event, Lincoln followed the advice of Blair, Curtis and others who insisted that retaining Frémont would prove militarily disastrous and invite losing Missouri, but who also advised delay. 'The time may come when it would be safe to . . . [act]', one wrote in early October: 'It may be in a few weeks. But it is not now!' A little over three weeks later, on 2 November, Lincoln grasped the nettle and removed his western commander. Wails of public outrage followed – from St Louis, to which Frémont returned as a hero and antislavery martyr, to New England. According to the *Cincinnati Gazette*, sober loyalists 'of all political parties' could be seen 'pulling from their walls and trampling underfoot the portrait of the President'.[101]

In part this anger derived from a sense that the administration had moved against the wrong commander. East of the mountains, the summer's tributes to McClellan for creating a well-drilled army and fortifying the capital gave way as autumn advanced to mounting public impatience over battlefield inactivity; once he had engineered the removal of the ailing Scott and, on 1 November, been appointed general-in-chief, he became personally more exposed to criticism. Incredulous editors and congressmen were perplexed to see an army of some 200,000 men standing immobile during the fine weather of late fall. Hearing the rumblings of public disquiet and prodded by those radicals whom Hay called 'the Jacobin club', the new session of Congress established a Joint Committee on the Conduct of the War to ginger up military operations. In view of McClellan's studied deafness to popular clamor and his deeply-rooted caution, it is bizarre and ironic that some blamed Lincoln and cabinet conservatives for holding him back.[102]

Had the public been privy to McClellan's near contempt for his commander-in-chief, they would have been even more deeply concerned. He came to an early view that Lincoln was 'an idiot', a restrained judgment compared with his later scathing allusions to the president as 'a well meaning baboon' and 'the *original gorilla*'. He found the president's efforts to master strategy and the technicalities of war to be as ridiculous as they were exasperating; and as a natural Democrat he had little respect for 'the imbeciles' who comprised the rest of the administration. Only Blair, who shared McClellan's negrophobia and conservative view of war aims, earned his good opinion. Driven by a mix of self-esteem and a Calvinistic conviction of his preordained role as the nation's deliverer, he had no qualms about snubbing the president and on at least one occasion treated him with such insolence that John Hay accurately read it as 'a portent of evil to come'.[103]

Characteristically, Lincoln resisted the temptation to stand on his dignity, and continued for longer than was prudent to reassure the cautious McClellan that he would shield him from impetuous critics: 'You shall', he said in mid-October, 'have your own way in the matter.' The Bull Run episode, with its bloody retreat to Washington, had left Lincoln emotionally raw and declaring that, after that, 'hell . . . has no terror for me'; he took on his own shoulders the blame for what Winfield Scott judged a premature fight, brought on by the urgent demands of press and public to move 'forward to Richmond'. This experience went some way toward explaining Lincoln's tolerant response to McClellan's planning and operations, yet he also knew it was unwise to lose sight of public morale. McClellan complained when Benjamin F. Wade, soon to become the first chairman of the Committee on the Conduct of the War, opined that defeat was no worse than delay and 'could easily be repaired, by the swarming recruits'. But Lincoln's response was revealingly ambivalent. He 'deprecated this new manifestation of popular impatience but . . . said it was a reality and should be taken into the account. At the same time

General you must not fight till you are ready.' Eventually, in early 1862, he began to exert his authority in an attempt to prod McClellan into action.[104]

The shortcomings in military operations cast doubt on Lincoln's own leadership. A chorus of Unionist voices, moderate as well as radical, questioned the competence of the president and his administration's resolve. The loyalist press sadly identified drift, inefficiency, and ignorance. 'They are blundering, cowardly, and inefficient', Wade complained. 'You could not inspire Old Abe, Seward, Chase, or Bates with courage, decision, and enterprise with a galvanic battery.' Lincoln's first annual message to Congress on 3 December disappointed those who looked for a forceful expression of government purpose to lift the country's mood. As a calm synthesis of administrative reports, it won two cheers for showing the 'business-as-usual' strength of the Union, but only its closing discussion of the merits of free labor and republican government went any way toward stirring a public increasingly desperate for a signal of governmental energy. When Lincoln acted to demand that Cameron withdraw his well publicized proposal to arm the slaves, it only confirmed that the president was an 'old fogy'. 'Old Abe is now unmasked, and we are sold out', grieved the editor of the *Chicago Tribune*. Doubts marked the cabinet itself. Chase had no great faith in the president, and Bates ended the year confiding that Lincoln, though 'an excellent man', lacked '*will* and *purpose*, and . . . the *power to command*'.[105]

Lincoln felt understandably desperate as 1862 dawned. With McClellan bed-ridden, military operations were frozen. No one, not even the president, knew his plans. The western forces under Henry W. Halleck and Don C. Buell stood paralyzed. The costs of raising and maintaining 700,000 Union men in arms were bleeding the Treasury dry. Banks suspended specie payments. The president spoke of 'borrowing' McClellan's army and even taking the field himself. On 10 January, the day that he would hold the first of four meetings of an *ad hoc* war council, he starkly summed up his predicament in conversation with Montgomery C. Meigs: 'General, what shall I do? The people are impatient; Chase has no money and he tells me he can raise no more; the General of the Army has typhoid fever. The bottom is out of the tub.'[106]

The people were indeed impatient, but they were scarcely defeatist. Whatever their disappointment and frustrations, Union loyalists felt no irremediable sense of alienation. Lincoln could draw on reservoirs of goodwill and on feelings of patriotic obligation directed less at himself personally than at his office and the associated institutions of government. Republican editors counseled patience. The New York *Independent* defended Lincoln against the charge of promise-breaking: 'He has simply found out how much faster one can speak than act – how much easier it is to criticize administrations, than to administer.' A prominent spokesman for northwestern antislavery, Thomas M. Eddy, coupled expressions of concern over the Union's confused policy toward rebels' slaves, with 24-carat loyalty to the administration: 'We will sustain the government with the last dollar, and to the last extremity; we will not doubt the honest intent of its officers.'[107]

Here, within this ethically-driven patriotism, lay the most potent long-term resource of the Union, in what was now becoming a protracted war. If Lincoln were to prevent a permanent division of the nation – and he began to contemplate such a sundering during these stressful days[108] – his task was to nurture and exploit these sources of patriotism. The war to date, during 1861, had demanded a strategy that maximized Union support. Lincoln's keen insight into the overriding importance of the border had determined his policy since April. But the conservatism that suited the men and women of the border would provide inadequate inspiration in the longer term for the Union as a whole. Over the course of the conflict Lincoln would have to reshape and rearticulate the war's stated purposes, and thereby seek to inspire the devotion of the mass of instinctive Unionists in the face of setbacks, suffering and loss. He came to see that his power ultimately depended on harnessing the freely offered energies of loyal citizens who were driven more by 'Yankee' religious imperatives than by the pragmatic conservatism of the lower North.

Notes

In the notes for this chapter all newspaper and manuscript citations are for 1861, unless otherwise indicated.

1 *Diary of Gideon Welles: Secretary of the Navy under Lincoln and Johnson*, 3 vols (Boston, MA: Houghton Mifflin, 1911), 1:82; *Lincoln's Journalist*, 165; *RWAL*, 328.

2 *Lincoln's Journalist*, 17–18; N&H, 3:257. Thurlow Weed, no mean judge, was enormously impressed by Lincoln's assurance when he visited him in December. Glyndon G. Van Deusen, *Thurlow Weed: Wizard of the Lobby* (Boston, MA: Little, Brown, 1947), 261.

3 S. Haycraft to AL, 13 Nov. 1860, H. Raymond to AL, 14 Nov. 1860, 'True Patriot' to AL, 12 Nov. 1860, J.B. McKeehan to AL, 13 Nov. 1860, ALP; *CW*, 4:134–5, 138–40 (the scriptural allusion is to Matthew xviii 22).

4 *CW*, 4:130 (Luke xvi 31), 141–2, 145–6 (Matthew xii 39, xvi 1–4).

5 *CW*, 4:146, 160–1.

6 D. Davis to AL, 16 Nov. 1860, ALP; David M. Potter, *Lincoln and His Party in the Secession Crisis* (New Haven, CT: Yale University Press, 1942), 148, 154; *CW*, 4:173.

7 N&H, 2:374.

8 *CW*, 4:152.

9 *CW*, 4:170.

10 J.B. McKeehan to AL, 13 Nov. 1860, ALP.

11 *CW*, 4:149–51, 154; Potter, *Lincoln and His Party*, 159–60. Whether or not directly prompted by Lincoln himself, the Springfield *Illinois State Journal* (17 Dec. 1860) wholly endorsed his stance: 'Let there be no wavering, no faltering now – no treacherous counsel – no base surrender of principle.'

12 N&H, 1:301–3; *RWAL*, 253, 436.

13 *CW*, 4:172; *Lincoln's Journalist*, 22.

14 Potter, *Lincoln and His Party*, 131; N&H, 3:280.

15 When a visiting New England manufacturer invoked the commercial harm and unemployment caused by the political uncertainty, Lincoln said bluntly that he was unwilling 'to barter away the moral principle involved in this contest, for the commercial gain of a new submission to the South'. N&H, 3:279–82.

16 *CW*, 4:149–52, 160; *RWAL*, 193.

17 *RWAL*, 436.

18 Seward's intentions remain opaque, but many believed he was leaning towards conciliation, to the puzzlement and alarm of his erstwhile radical supporters. *Reminiscences of Carl Schurz*, 3 vols (New York: The McClure Co., 1907–08), 2:211–12.

19 The plan's chief purpose was to woo the loyal border states. Were the worst to happen and the measure were to pass, few thought slavery would thrive in New Mexico. David M. Potter, *The Impending Crisis 1848–1861* (New York: Harper and Row, 1976), 533–4.

20 *CW*, 4:172; Potter, *Lincoln and His Party*, 302; James Russell Lowell, *Political Essays* (London: Macmillan, 1888), 76; N&H, 3:227–33.

21 *CW*, 4:168–9.

22 *RWAL*, 254; *Lincoln's Journalist*, 24; N&H, 3:289–93; Nicolay, *Oral History*, 107–20.

23 *RWAL*, 254; *Lincoln's Journalist*, 32.

24 *CW*, 4:192, 199, 236, 240.

25 *CW*, 4:219–20; *Lincoln's Journalist*, 33; Nicolay, *Oral History*, 110.

26 *CW*, 4:196.

27 *Lincoln's Journalist*, 27, 40; *CW*, 4:195, 236–7, 240–1.

28 *CW*, 4:193–4, 236–7.

29 *CW*, 4:262–71.

30 Philadelphia's *Morning Pennsylvanian*, 18 Feb., in Howard Cecil Perkins, ed., *Northern Editorials on Secession*, 2 vols (1942; repr. Gloucester, MA: Peter Smith, 1964), 2:609.

31 Between 4 and 28 February secession was successively voted down in Virginia, Tennessee, Arkansas and Missouri, and North Carolina. Unionists kept control in Maryland, Delaware and Kentucky.

32 N&H, 3:319–23.

33 *Western Christian Advocate* [Cincinnati], 13 March; Robert W. Johannsen, *Stephen A. Douglas* (New York: Oxford University Press, 1973), 844–6.

34 See, for example, *Albany Atlas and Argus* (Douglasite), *New York Journal of Commerce* (Breckinridge), and the especially shrewd editorial of the *Providence Daily Post* (Douglas), in Perkins, ed., *Northern Editorials*, 2:628–9, 631–3, 645–7.

35 H.D. Faulkner to AL, 5 March, ALP.

36 E.D. Morgan to AL, 5 March, ALP; Perkins, ed., *Northern Editorials*, 2:618–24, 629–31, 638–42.

37 J.W. Forney to AL, 22 Nov. 1860, ALP; *Lincoln's Journalist*, 45–6, 50.

38 N&H, 3:368–9.

39 N&H, 3:370–2.

40 'One who loves his Country' to AL, 5 March, ALP.

41 *The Diary of Orville H. Browning*, ed. Theodore Calvin Pease and James G. Randall, 2 vols (Springfield, IL: Illinois State Historical Library, 1925), 1:476.

42 *HI*, 207; O.H. Browning, 26 March, ALP.

43 S.A. Hurlbut to AL, 27 March, W.H. Seward, Cabinet Memorandum, 29 March, ALP.

44 *CW*, 4:301, 321–4.

45 *CW*, 4:159, 164–5; J.A. Gilmer to AL, 9 March, N. Green to AL, 14 March, ALP.

46 *HI*, 400–1; *RWAL*, 20, 207, 335; *DJH*, 28, 285; Daniel W. Crofts, *Reluctant Confederates: Upper South Unionists in the Secession Crisis* (Chapel Hill, NC: University of North Carolina Press, 1989), 301–7.

47 Nicolay, *Oral History*, 17–18; S.A. Hurlbut to AL, 27 March, ALP; *Diary of Browning*, 1:453. Cf. O.H. Browning to AL, 26 March, ALP.

48 C. Schurz to AL, 5 April; J.H. Jordan to AL, 4, 5 April; 'A Republican' to AL, 3 April, ALP; *CW*, 4:317; *New York Times*, 3 April, in Perkins, ed., *Northern Editorials*, 2:660–1.

49 *CW*, 4:317–18. Lincoln's remarks, in a letter to Seward, were probably never sent.

50 *Newburyport Herald*, 25 March, *New York Times*, 3 April, *Milwaukee Daily Wisconsin*, 3 April, in Perkins, ed., *Northern Editorials*, 2:654–8, 661, 666–8; J.L. Hill to AL, 14 March, O.H. Browning to AL, 26 March, C. Schurz to AL, 5 April, J.H. Jordan to AL, 4 April, 5 April, Anonymous to AL, 10 April, ALP.

51 *Columbus Daily Capital City*, 22 March, *Troy Daily Whig*, 4 April; *Cincinnati Daily Times*, 3 April, in Perkins, ed., *Northern Editorials*, 2:652–3, 664–6, 668–71.

52 *Columbus Daily Capital City*, 22 March, in Perkins, ed., *Northern Editorials*, 2:653.

53 *Dubuque Herald*, 16 March, in Perkins, ed., *Northern Editorials*, 2:701.

54 O.H. Browning to AL, 18 April, E.B. Holmes to AL, 20 April, H.P. Tappan to AL, 19 April, J. Medill to AL, 15 April, J.M. Read to AL, 20 April, J. Allison to AL, April [n.d.], O. Ellsworth to AL, 19 April, ALP.

55 New York City Welsh Congregational Church to AL, 16 April; Philadelphia Presbyterian Church to AL, 16 April, L.A. Miller to AL, 16 April, A.J. Sessions to AL, 16 April, G.W. Woodruff to AL, 18 April, T.B. Gary to AL, 18 April, R. Dickerson to AL, 15 April, ALP; *Lincoln's Journalist*, 56–7.

56 I.N. Arnold to AL, 13 April, J. Medill to AL, 15 April, J.R. Doolittle to AL, 18 April, Philadelphia Citizens to AL, 15 April, T.B. Rodgers to AL, 18 April, E.B. Holmes to AL, 20 April, J. Hesser to AL, 15 April, R.M. Blatchford and M.H. Grinnell to AL, 15 April, L. Trumbull to AL, 21 April, ALP; *Lincoln's Journalist*, 355; Douglas Fermer, *James Gordon Bennett and the New York Herald: A Study of Editorial Opinion in the Civil War Era* (New York: St Martin's Press, 1986), 187–91.

57 O. Ellsworth to AL, 18 April, ALP; *New York Times*, 15 April, *Buffalo Daily Courier*, 16 April, *New York Evening Day-Book* [Breckinridge], 17 April, in Perkins, ed., *Northern Editorials*, 2:715–18.

58 Johannsen, *Douglas*, 859–60.

59 Johannsen, *Douglas*, 868–69.

60 Christopher Dell, *Lincoln and the War Democrats: The Grand Erosion of Conservative Tradition* (Rutherford, NJ: Fairleigh Dickinson University Press, 1975), 59, 68–70; James A. Rawley, *The Politics of Union: Northern Politics during the Civil War* (1974; repr. Lincoln, NB: University of Nebraska Press, 1980), 34.

61 Robert W. Johannsen, ed., *Letters of Stephen A. Douglas* (Urbana, IL: University of Illinois Press, 1961), 511; L. Trumbull to AL, 21 April, ALP; Frank L. Klement, *The Limits of Dissent: Clement L. Vallandigham & the Civil War* (Lexington, KY: University Press of Kentucky, 1970), 62–3.

62 Joel H. Silbey, *A Respectable Minority: The Democratic Party in the Civil War Era, 1860–1869* (New York: W.W. Norton, 1977), 46, 49. The phrases are those of the New York Democrat Horatio Seymour.

63 Johannsen, *Douglas*, 859; T. Fitnam to AL, 28 Aug., ALP.

64 G. Koerner to AL, 17 May, C.H. Ray to AL, 20 May, ALP.

65 *DJH*, 20; *CW*, 4:426.

66 *CW*, 4:438–9.

67 *CW*, 4:433–9.

68 *CW*, 4:428–31.

69 J.W. Forney to AL, 4 Oct., R.W. Thompson to AL, 6 Oct., ALP; *Lincoln's Journalist*, 74–5.

70 AL to O. Browning, 22 Sept.; *CW*, 4:532.

71 *DJH*, 4, 11; J. Henderson to AL, 13, 16 April, ALP.

72 Allan Nevins, *The War for the Union*: vol. 1: *The Improvised War* (New York: Charles Scribner's Sons, 1959), 86 [*New York Tribune*]; *DJH*, 16; J.A. Dix to S. Cameron, 13 Sept., J.A. Dix to AL, 9 Oct., R. Johnson to AL, 7 Nov., ALP.

73 *DJH*, 15; G.W. Caldwell to AL, 25 April, J.G. Nicolay to G.W. Caldwell, 1 May, ALP; *N&H* 4:329–31; *HI*, 628.

74 *CW*, 4:427–8.

75 *CW*, 6:27–8.

76 Lincoln may also have been influenced by St Louis correspondents who cast Harney as the dupe of secessionists. T. Woodruff to AL, 1 May, S.T. Glover to AL, 24 May, ALP.

77 N&H, 4:215–22.

78 For a recent dissenting analysis, see Louis S. Gerteis, *Civil War St. Louis* (Lawrence, KS: University Press of Kansas, 2001).

79 *CW*, 4:532.

80 Lowell H. Harrison, *Lincoln of Kentucky* (Lexington, KY: University Press of Kentucky, 2000), 133–4; J.M. Johnson to AL, 26 April, ALP; *DJH*, 19.

81 Lowell, *Political Essays*, 88–9; R. Anderson to AL, 19 May, A.A. Burton to W.H. Seward, 24 May, J.F. Speed to AL, 27, 29 May, G.B. McClellan to AL, 30 May, B.W. Ballard to AL, 7 June, L. Combs to AL, 14 Aug., B. Magoffin to AL, 19 Aug., ALP; *CW*, 4:497.

82 *DJH*, 24.

83 *CW*, 4:506.

84 J.F. Speed to AL, 1, 3 Sept., G. Adams and J. Speed to AL, 2 Sept., L. Combs to AL, 6 Sept., J. Holt to AL, 12 Sept., J.F. Bullitt et al. to J.F. Speed, 13 Sept., R. Anderson to AL, 13 Sept., ALP; *CW*, 4:532.

85 J.C. Frémont to AL, 8 Sept., W.R. Prince to AL, 20 Sept., ALP; *RWAL*, 164, 506; *CW*, 4:518.

86 *DJH*, 12–13, 19, 22; *Northwestern Christian Advocate*, 12 June, 4 Sept..

87 Nevins, *War for the Union*, 1:340; J.G. Roberts to AL, 17 Sept., J. Allen to AL, 21 Sept., H. Jones to AL, 24 Sept., O.H. Browning to AL, 17 Sept., ALP.

88 *CW*, 4:531–3.

89 *CW*, 5:37, 50; T.S. Bell to AL, 6 Dec., ALP.

90 *CW*, 5:36.

91 The description is Sumner's. D.P. Crook, *The North, the South, and the Powers 1861–1865* (New York: John Wiley & Sons, 1974), 84.

92 T. Weed to AL, 7 Dec., T. Weed to W.H. Seward, 4, 11 Dec., ALP; *CW*, 5:62–4; *Diary of Browning*, 1:516–17.

93 *RWAL*, 570; John Niven, ed., *The Salmon P. Chase Papers*: vol. 1: *Journals, 1829–1872* (Kent, OH: Kent State University Press, 1993), 318–20; Howard K. Beale, *The Diary of Edward Bates 1859–1866* (Washington, DC: Government Printing Office, 1933), 201–2, 215. Ex-president Fillmore also advised Lincoln to avoid the 'double calamities' of two wars. M. Fillmore to AL, 16 Dec., ALP.

94 Beale, *Diary of Bates*, 216; *RWAL*, 399, 433; *Diary of Browning*, 1:518.

95 J.G. Randall [and Richard N. Current], *Lincoln the President*, 4 vols (New York: Dodd, Mead, 1945–54), 2:41.

96 Beale, *Diary of Bates*, 216.

97 A.W.H. Clapp to M. Blair, 31 Dec., R.W. Thompson to unknown, 1 Jan., 1862, H. Greeley to AL, 29 July, A. Shuman to W.H. Seward, 9 Aug., J.W. Forney to AL, 16 Aug., ALP.

98 J. Miller to W.H. Seward, 1 Aug., G. Davis to AL, 4 Aug., J.A. Hamilton to AL, 11 Aug., ALP.

99 L. Trumbull to AL, 1 Oct., F.P. Blair, Jr, to M. Blair, 1 Sept., 1 Oct., S.T. Glover to M. Blair, 2 Sept., M. Blair to AL, 3, 4 Sept., 7 Oct., S.T. Glover to AL, 20 Sept., ALP. See also, T. Ewing to AL, 17 Sept., C. Beasley to AL, 27 Sept., R.K. Brown to AL, 29 Sept., S.R. Curtis to AL, 12 Oct., ALP.

100 J.C. Patterson to AL, 21 Sept., J.M. Biscound to AL, 12 Sept., T.A. Miller to AL, 20 Sept., J. Knox to AL, 3 Oct., 'A True Friend' to AL, 5 Oct., J.R. Conner to AL, 17 Sept., E.C. Hurst to AL, 19 Sept., J. Butt to AL, 19 Sept., Anon to AL, 19 Sept., G.P. Koerner to AL, 8 Oct., E.S. Fife to AL, 18 Sept., J.D. Willers to AL, 21 Sept., J. Knox to AL, 3 Oct., S.T. Glover to AL, 20 Sept., F.P. Blair, Jr, to M. Blair, 1 Oct., ALP; *Lincoln's Journalist*, 120.

101 J.H. Jordan to AL, 9 Oct., ALP; Allan Nevins, *The War for the Union*: vol. 2: *War Becomes Revolution* (New York: Charles Scribner's Sons, 1960), 383–4.

102 *Lincoln's Journalist*, 129.

103 Stephen W. Sears, ed., *The Civil War Papers of George B. McClellan: Selected Correspondence 1860–1865* (New York: Ticknor & Fields, 1989), 106–17, 113–14; *DJH*, 32, 286.

104 *DJH*, 25, 28–9; *RWAL*, 136.

105 Nevins, *War for the Union*, 2:385, 402; *Lincoln's Journalist*, 158–9; *Independent*, 5 Dec.; Beale, *Diary of Bates*, 220.

106 *Diary of Browning*, 1:523; *RWAL* 328.

107 *Independent*, 2 Jan. 1862; *Northwestern Christian Advocate*, 8 Jan. 1862.

108 Earl Schenck Miers, ed., *Lincoln Day by Day: A Chronology 1809–1865*, 3 vols (Washington, DC: Lincoln Sesquicentennial Commission, 1960), 3:87.

Chapter Five

❁

The Purposes of Power: Evolving Objectives, 1861–65

The president who five months into the war told Jessie Benton Frémont that the African American had 'nothing to do with' the conflict and should not be 'dragged' into it would eventually, of course, enter the American pantheon as the Great Emancipator. A year after rescinding his western commander's proclamation of freedom, the president issued his own ultimatum to rebel slaveholders. The landmark Emancipation Proclamation that followed was succeeded by state-level political action against slavery in various parts of the loyal and reconquered South. Urged on by the president, Congress eventually approved an antislavery amendment to the federal Constitution. A war that had begun as an effort to save the Union evolved under Lincoln's leadership into an agency of the slaves' freedom.

Thirty months after his crisp words to Mrs Frémont, Lincoln reflected in a letter to a Kentucky editor, Albert G. Hodges, that unexpected and unplanned 'events', not he, had controlled his policy toward emancipation.[1] In tandem, these two sets of remarks seem to invite the conclusion that the 'Great Emancipator' was no more than the accidental beneficiary of haphazard wartime developments. Indeed, in the judgment of the most polemical of modern critics, Lincoln was a foot-dragging liberator, 'forced into glory' against his conservative, white-supremacist, instincts.[2] A more substantial and subtle assault on the mythic Lincoln derives from the argument that it was above all through the African Americans' own actions that the slaves won their freedom. The tens of thousands of blacks who streamed into Union camps from both loyal and rebel regions of the South forced an issue on federal authorities that they could not duck. Well before Lincoln acted, colluding military officers and congressmen moved to treat these runaways as confiscated property, or contraband, to be sheltered and employed in the northern armies. At the same time, well away from the military arena, a change took place in the balance of racial authority within southern farms and plantations, weakening slavery from within, as enlisted white overseers and owners left increasingly assertive slaves under the control of women and old men.

To argue, as some have done, that the slaves freed themselves and that Lincoln's role was hesitantly to catch up with events is, however, to oversimplify a complex historical process. Final, irreversible freedom required the defeat of the Confederates and a new constitutional settlement. Slaves certainly played a role in weakening the Confederacy from within, while from without the 200,000 African Americans who served as federal soldiers, sailors, servants, teamsters and laborers may well have tipped the advantage toward the Union. But there was more to northern victory than that. Of paramount importance was the leadership of a president and commander-in-chief who understood that there could be no certain freedom without a restored Union and that prematurely making emancipation the formal goal of war would shatter the broad-based coalition on which that very restoration depended.

In reality, Lincoln was not a passive figure buffeted by forces beyond his control. His administration is the story of a president who kept his focus on strategic essentials, who chose not to pursue diversions, however worthy (as with reform of the corrupt Indian service), who was capable of pulling surprises and who was quite prepared when the time came 'of laying strong hand upon the colored element'.[3] Though ready to leave important tracts of the policy domain – notably foreign affairs and the national finances – largely to the direction of trusted ministers, Lincoln resolutely kept in his own hands all decisions bearing upon slavery, emancipation and race. He achieved a mastery over his cabinet, occasionally soliciting opinions but mostly informing his ministers of decisions already reached. Jealous of the constitutional powers of the executive, as he understood them, he resisted legislative encroachment and took advantage of the long intervals between congressional sessions to keep the initiative. John W. Forney watched in admiration as Lincoln grew in political office to become 'that great, wonderful mysterious inexplicable man: who holds in his single hands the reins of the republic: who keeps his own counsels: who does his own purpose in his own way no matter what temporizing minister in his cabinet sets himself up in opposition to the progress of the age.'[4]

The story of Lincoln's presidential leadership is at heart the story of how he used the power at his disposal to redefine the Union's explicit purposes to embrace liberty, and even equality, for all. But, as Lincoln explained, he had to exercise that power under constraint. Constitutional duty, the obstinate realities of the battlefield and opinion on the home front severely hemmed in his freedom of action. These, however, were evolving, not static, constraints. Constitutional duty might seem to demand protection for slavery, but not at the expense of national integrity; indeed, duty to the spirit of the founding document might even require amendment of the Constitution itself. At the same time, the events of war churned public opinion, bringing many former anti-abolitionists to embrace military emancipation and the arming of the blacks. The challenge for any Union president in these circumstances was to identify the moment when the country would accept an advance to new ground. Lincoln's great – possibly greatest – achievement was to take a stethoscope to Union opinion and read it with such skill that he timed to perfection his redefinition of national purpose. This unerring sense of timing was for political insiders the key to the president's greatness. 'Lincoln is the most truly progressive man of the age,' claimed Forney, 'because he always moves in conjunction with propitious circumstances, not waiting to be dragged by the force of events or wasting strength in premature struggles with them.'[5]

The story of the evolving purposes of the Union's war is also the story of Lincoln's personal development. Those who withstood unmoved the buffeting of war were rare indeed. Inevitably, Lincoln's private understanding of his moral obligations, and of the meaning of the conflict itself, evolved under the grueling burden of leadership, the wider suffering of wartime, and personal grief. Unfathomable as the private Lincoln has to remain, there is every sign that his understanding of providential intervention both shaped the thinking by which he reached the most profound of his decisions, for emancipation, and – even more powerfully – steeled his nerve to stand by the implications of that decision once made.

Reading the public

Lincoln openly acknowledged that the steps by which he redefined the war for the Union as a war against slavery were guided by his reading of public opinion, and that he feared too early an embrace of emancipation would shatter the Union consensus. Not pushing mainstream sentiment toward emancipation faster than it wanted to go meant turning a deaf ear to the urgent appeals of antislavery radicals, while simultaneously nudging border-state conservatives toward greater realism. But the question arises: how could he be sure what that mainstream opinion was? As a state politician, the Illinois circuit lawyer and aspirant for elective office had enjoyed a face-to-face relationship with his constituents, but the nation's president and commander-in-chief was mostly restricted to the executive mansion. Political friends saw the danger, warning him against the 'disingenuous and selfish clamor at the Capitol'. But remote from his roots, increasingly exhausted by the unremitting burden of office, bombarded by conflicting advice, rarely straying from the vicinity of Washington, and prevented by convention from gauging the popular mood through stump speaking, how could he know and track the turbulent thoughts of ordinary Americans and avoid, as an Indiana loyalist feared, 'the possibility of loosing the public confidence'.[6]

Election returns offered a series of snapshots of political opinion. On average a significant congressional or state election occurred in the North every other month during the four years of war. Lincoln, whose grasp of electoral topography and arithmetic was second to none, spent many an hour in the telegraph office at the War Department, awaiting and analyzing outcomes. Broadly speaking, election results allowed the administration to chart its standing in public esteem throughout the war. Republicans' success in New England in the spring of 1861 appeared to endorse the policy of coercion of the Confederacy. Later that year, the party's winning several state contests outside New England with the support of War Democrats seemed to vindicate the conciliatory approach toward border-state conservatives. The satisfactory returns in the fall of 1863 could also be taken as a broad endorsement of the administration's course and became the signal for a further call for volunteers. On the other hand, the state and congressional contests in the fall of 1862, the most serious electoral test of the war to date, provided the administration with an alarming popular rebuff. Significantly, however, there was no unanimity about what particular aspect of policy had chiefly caused the alienation. Using voting figures as a commentary on matters of national policy was little better than reading braille with a gloved hand.

Dealings with political leaders at national and state level held out for Lincoln opportunities for more nuanced analyses of popular mood. From his deliberately broad-based and inclusive cabinet he heard often dissonant voices advancing a range of views which ran the gamut of Unionist opinion – disharmony, in this case at least, acting as a source of presidential strength not weakness. More sensitive still to public feeling were those in elective office, notably state governors and United States congressmen, whom Lincoln considered his eyes and ears in each constituency. From Andrew G. Curtin of Pennsylvania, Richard Yates of Illinois, Oliver P. Morton of Indiana, John A. Andrew of Massachusetts, William A. Buckingham of Connecticut and other loyal governors, the president received commentaries on the general management of the war, on electoral prospects and on the public's view of particular administration policies across a range of salient issues: confiscation, colonization, emancipation, black troops, the draft, reconstruction. But, as Lincoln discovered to his cost, though they were closer than he to the grass-roots, their judgments were not infallible. Thus, taking William Dennison's advice in the spring of 1861 to heed popular will and convert the 90-day militia men into three-year volunteers, Lincoln was forced into retracting his approval in the face of the men's anger and threat of mutiny.[7] Governors and other state politicians had their own axes to grind, of course, and Lincoln had always to remain on the lookout for self-interested pleading disguised as objective testimony. His grasp on the slippery confusion of events in Missouri, for instance, was undoubtedly weakened by the ambiguities and defectiveness of his information. Unsurprisingly, he sent his own White House secretaries, John G. Nicolay and John Hay, on a variety of missions to establish the state of local political feeling, just as he had used Lamon and Hurlbut to sound out opinion in South Carolina early in 1861.

Newspapers, the lifeblood of the American political system, provided Lincoln with another means of keeping his finger on the pulse of opinion. In his days as an aspiring Illinois politician he had been an insatiable reader of the party political press, but the rigors of office gave the harassed president far less time to indulge this appetite. Francis Carpenter, the portrait painter who observed his daily routine over a six-month period in 1864, recalled only one instance when he saw Lincoln casually browsing through a newspaper. Actually, papers abounded in the White House. In addition to the three Washington dailies (the *Morning Chronicle*, *National Republican* and *Star*) which were laid out on Lincoln's study table, a variety of the Union's leading papers provided his secretaries with the materials from which they could mine the interesting editorial matter and items of political importance they judged they should bring to the president's attention. When for a brief interlude early in the war events conspired to interrupt the daily flow of papers, a sense of isolation and even desperation seized the occupants of the executive mansion. Lincoln had a healthily skeptical attitude to press criticism, which rarely moved him to anger and which he commonly dismissed as 'noise' and 'gas' generated by ignorance and editorial self-importance. On the biggest of issues, emancipation, he said 'he had studied the matter so long that he knew more about it than they [the editors] did'.[8]

Still, Lincoln could not afford to ignore the journalistic corps altogether. Indeed, some became friends and invaluable channels of information. Such was Noah Brooks, an acquaintance from Illinois days, who became a near-daily visitor at the White House after his posting to Washington by the *Sacramento Daily Union*. Like Simon P. Hanscom, the antislavery Bostonian who edited Lincoln's favorite paper, the *Washington National Republican*, and also became a frequent caller, Brooks acted as a sounding-board and source of political gossip.[9] Others, like Henry Raymond of the *New York Times*, were less personally close to the president, but enjoyed his respect (despite Raymond's having called for Lincoln's deposition during his first months in office). When in the dark days of the summer of 1864, the New Yorker brought him reports of opinion hardening against the administration, he came as close as he ever did to abandoning the high ground of antislavery Unionism.

Loyal editors also bombarded the president with unsolicited advice in hundreds of private letters. These, however, represented only a small fraction of the mail that at times threatened to submerge the White House secretariat. Nicolay handled Lincoln's huge correspondence before his inauguration; subsequently the responsibility fell on Hay's young shoulders. As the volume rose, to reach a peak of two mailbags (some 500 letters) daily during the mid-point of Lincoln's re-election year, an additional secretary was required. Much of the correspondence comprised requests for civil jobs and military commissions. There were diatribes and hate mail, too, from which Lincoln was generally shielded. But many letters came from those whom one secretary described as the 'good and true', often unlettered and humble, pouring out their 'deepest heart sorrows' and offering their advice on the conduct of affairs. Of course, Lincoln had time to handle only a fraction of what arrived, perhaps a dozen or so letters a day; according to Hay, the president personally read no more than one letter in fifty. But those he did review, together with the summaries and annotations provided by his secretaries, gave him a chance literally to read public opinion. Each phase of the conflict prompted earnest suggestions about the best policies and strategy for victory.[10]

Lincoln's mail also brought tides of formal representations and recommendations, a few from constitutional bodies, including state legislatures and city councils, but mostly from the regular meetings of voluntary organizations, and a variety of *ad hoc* gatherings convened to press a particular cause. Resolutions from chambers of commerce, Union Defense Committees, Republican–Union party meetings and college alumni streamed into the White House. But it was the religious-humanitarian organizations, dominated by the mainstream evangelical church families and their radical offspring, which on occasions turned the stream into a torrent. It is unlikely that Lincoln read, marked, learnt and inwardly digested every one of the resolutions that actually reached his desk (themselves only a sample of a daunting total), but he undoubtedly noted their general tenor and the pulses of public concern that they represented.

Many correspondents wrote as an alternative to paying the personal call on the president that the constraints of geography, time and expense prevented. Yet the most remarkable feature of Lincoln's tenure of office were the throngs of ordinary citizens who came to the capital to pour through the White House doors, intent on a private interview on one of the president's regular public days. Lincoln never lost his determination to remain accessible – to be 'the attorney of the people, not their ruler'. William Seward remarked that 'there never was a man so accessible to all sorts of proper and improper persons'; the president himself described his office hours as 'the Beggars' Opera'. He never lost his keen sense of his own ordinariness and his kinship with common folk. He cherished republican simplicity, shunned the imperial style and protested strongly when Henry W. Halleck detailed a cavalry detachment, clattering along with sabres and spurs, to guard the presidential carriage.[11]

In consequence of what Henry J. Raymond called Lincoln's 'utter unconsciousness of his position', ordinary men and women regarded him more as a neighbor to be dropped in upon than as a remote head of state. 'Mr Lincoln is *always* approachable and this is greatly in his favor', explained the Washington correspondent of the New York *Independent*. 'The people can get at him and impress upon him their views without difficulty.' Though his visitors included, in the words of one observer, 'loiterers, contract-hunters, garrulous parents on paltry errands, toadies without measure, and talkers without conscience', Lincoln was adamantly opposed to restricting access. 'I feel – though the tax on my time is heavy – that no hours of my day are better employed than those which bring me again within the direct contact and atmosphere of the average of our whole people.' Each meeting, he maintained, served 'to renew in me a clearer and more vivid image of that great popular assemblage out of which I sprung . . . I call these receptions my "*public-opinion baths*;" for I have but little time to read the papers and gather public opinion that way.' Sometimes he felt himself bombarded and besieged but, even so, these encounters with ordinary folk worked to invigorate his 'perceptions of responsibility and duty' and undoubtedly gave him more pleasure than the wearying formal White House receptions and 'levees' which custom demanded. Probably more than any other single agency, they provided the oxygen lacking in the rarefied political air of wartime Washington, and seemed if anything to strengthen Lincoln's faith in the wisdom of the common people, rather than undermine it. John Hay discerned a mark of genius in the president's 'intuitive knowledge of the feeling and wish of the people'.[12] But that intuition depended as much on perspiration as inspiration, and on a careful, even laborious, reading of the confusing multiplicity of signals of the public mood.

'Every indispensable means': toward the Emancipation Proclamation

Lincoln, at various times, before different audiences, repeated that his oath of office obliged him to use 'every indispensable means' to preserve the Union. Means that under normal conditions would be deemed unnecessary, even extra-constitutional, might *in extremis* become 'an indispensable necessity' to achieve a lawful end. He used the phrase first in July 1861, when – even as he sought to reassure conservatives – he left the door open for a changing power relationship between the federal government and the rebel states.[13] The current of events during the first half of 1862 led Lincoln to decide to override the peacetime guarantees of slave property and declare Confederate slaves the subjects of military emancipation.

Well before 1861 was out, millions of Unionists had already concluded that crushing slavery had become 'indispensable' to victory. Lincoln was not one of them, but their urgent voices left him in little doubt that abolition had ceased to be the preserve of moral zealots alone. Many anti-southern pragmatists, Democrat as well as Republican, joined the radicals in declaring their enthusiasm for Frémont's proclamation and even Cameron's plan for arming blacks. And when the conservative Henry W. Halleck, replacing Frémont, issued his General Order No. 3 excluding runaway slaves from Union lines, on the implausible grounds that they acted as spies for the Confederacy, the western commander faced broad-based censure.

Across the Union, including the conservative lower North and the border, even those who wanted 'nothing to do with "abolition" in the common sense of that term' bombarded Lincoln with calls for bold and decisive measures against 'the monster' slavery, 'the real cause of this war', 'the Groundwork of the Rebellion', and the Confederates' 'weak point'. To protect the human property of treasonous slaveocrats, whose resistance consumed the blood and dollars of loyal citizens, defied wisdom as well as morality. A Delaware loyalist complained about the schizophrenia of 'fighting Slavery with one hand and sustaining it with the other'. To the same end, a Virginia-born Unionist told the president: 'I myself . . . have no prejudices against Slavry, as a local institution but when the question, is narrowd down to the existance of the Govement or Slavry, who will hesitate to make a choice?' Slavery's days were numbered. 'You will be forced before long to proclaim universal liberty – the people are ripe for it and the politicians are coming to it.'[14]

Lincoln was properly unpersuaded when loyalists variously reported that Frémont's bold stroke enjoyed the acclaim of 'every Republican and nine tenths of the Democrats', of '99 out of every 100'. But he still had no reason to doubt what one Wisconsin correspondent told him, that 'in the midst of this war . . . I am only one of thousands who have changed views very much'. Lincoln knew that the times were out of joint, that the conservative Cameron, through his report, had become the unlikely hero of Thaddeus Stevens and the 'brimstone radicals', and that his own cautious leadership now placed him to the right of those who had once criticized him as a backwoods abolitionist. Before the war, moderates had ridiculed the idea of an 'irrepressible conflict', denied that slavery and freedom were incompatible, and rebuked Lincoln for the radicalism of his statement that the government could not endure 'half slave and half free'. Now the roles were reversed. Rooting out slavery, the Democrat George Bancroft told Lincoln, was 'the universal expectation and hope of men of all parties'. John Hay watched in wry wonderment: 'It is a most instructive sight to see the Illinois emancipationist converted into an earnest conservative, and resolutely resisting the solicitations to abolition persistently urged by those who so bitterly denounced his radicalism a few years ago.'[15]

Lincoln's annual message to Congress in December 1861 thus trod cautiously and played to conservative sentiment in briefly discussing colonization as a means of expatriating freedmen 'at some place, or places, in a climate congenial to them'. Yet it was not the document of a man insensitive to emancipationists' promptings. He drew attention to his endorsement of the Confiscation Act of July 1861, by which some slaves had already been freed; he intimated that individual states might choose to adopt its principles; and he promised to consider any further emancipatory law that Congress might pass. Then he declared, in what would become a familiar formulation, that 'all indispensable means must be employed' to secure the Union. True, he gave a reassurance that he would do all he could to prevent the conflict degenerating 'into a violent and remorseless revolutionary struggle', and insisted that 'we should not be in haste to determine that radical and extreme measures, which may reach the loyal as well as the disloyal, are indispensable'. But the implication was clear: if the Union's survival depended on emancipation as a last resort, he would not rule it out. Significantly, Lincoln accompanied these remarks with the pregnant aside that he must keep 'all questions

. . . of vital military importance' in his own hands. Some months would elapse before Lincoln thoroughly sifted the arguments relating to the war powers of the president, but already there was a hint that military considerations might allow the commander-in-chief constitutionally to pursue emancipation.[16]

Even so, the overall tone of the president's address did nothing to shake the confidence of Democrats and conservative Republicans that there was an old Whig under Lincoln's skin and that, in McClellan's words, 'the Presdt is perfectly honest & is really sound on the nigger question'. For the same reason, it did nothing to inspire the congressional group of Republican radicals slowly cohering around Wade, Trumbull and Zachariah Chandler – Hay's 'Jacobins' – who thought Lincoln unequal to the nation's crisis, denounced his cautious pragmatism as unprincipled drift and despaired of his refusal to attack the rebels' most vital of interests. In a meeting between Lincoln and his Committee on the Conduct of the War on the last day of 1861 Wade told him: 'Mr President, you are murdering your country by inches in consequence of the inactivity of the military and the want of a distinct policy in regard to slavery.'[17]

Lincoln's oft-quoted remark that his policy was to have no policy might seem only to confirm Wade's stern judgment, but the president's words were as misleading as they were jocular. During the winter months of 1861–62 he continued his 'southern strategy': recognizing slavery's constitutional protections, reassuring the border loyalists and keeping the South divided. The radicals' demands he judged an invitation to catastrophe and their strategic ineptness could at times provoke even this most equable of presidents into bad temper. He shocked Edward Pierce, the young idealist responsible for the freedmen of the Sea Islands, with his irritable scorn for the 'great itching to get negroes within our lines'. But, as his annual message implied, he needed to keep his options open. Radical demands for emancipation might be a dangerous irrelevance; but they might turn out to be simply premature. When, early in 1862, George Templeton Strong raised the issue of radical pressures, the president told the conservative lawyer a tale of itinerant Methodists in frontier Illinois who, as they journeyed, quarreled about how to get over an 'ugly' river. Lincoln warmed to the 'old brother' who said, 'Brethren, this here talk ain't no use. I never cross a river until I come to it.'[18]

The story was apposite. No crossing over from the old Union to radical new terrain would be required if, as seemed increasingly plausible, the armies' spring offensive brought a prompt collapse of the rebellion. Lincoln's despair and frustration at the military inaction of early January had slowly lifted. McClellan returned to vigor. Stanton brought his own distinctive energy to the War Department. The president himself, earnestly digesting manuals of military strategy, ordered a general advance of all forces on 22 February. By then, indeed, western armies under George H. Thomas (at the battle of Mill Springs) and Grant (taking Forts Henry and Donelson) had swept Confederate forces from Kentucky and much of Tennessee. It seemed reasonable to hope that the imminent operations of the Army of the Potomac, whether by Lincoln's preferred option, a frontal assault on the rebel army at Manassas, or by McClellan's alternative, an advance on Richmond from the east, would snuff the life out of the Confederacy and restore the Union as it was.

Within the constitutional arrangements of the old Union, however, Lincoln saw a way of both reinforcing his 'southern strategy' and yet also putting slavery into retreat. He urged with increasing vigor the merits of compensated emancipation, voluntarily entered into by the states, but funded by the federal government. He had suggested a prototype scheme to Delaware loyalists late in 1861; his preference was for a 31-year process of gradual manumission, at a cost to the nation of $23,200 per annum.[19] As the state with the smallest slave population, Delaware seemed the most favorable place to start, but to Lincoln's great disappointment his allies in the state legislature failed to win over a majority of the deeply suspicious representatives, and no bill was introduced. Undeterred, and perhaps influenced by reports of a weakening of proslavery and disunionist sentiment in the borderlands, he took a more dramatic, high-profile and unprecedented initiative.

On 6 March 1862 he sent a special message to Congress, recommending that the Senate and House adopt a joint resolution promising congressional financial support to 'any state which may adopt gradual abolishment of slavery'. Lincoln presented compensated emancipation as a means of shortening the war, not as an act of humanity to the slaves. If the loyal slave states would simply begin such a program, he argued, it would shatter the Confederacy's hopes of the upper South's defection – and this 'substantially ends the rebellion'.[20] There were financial considerations, too: the cost to the nation of compensating slaveholders would be modest compared with the spiraling expenditure on the war. Congress, he acknowledged, had no constitutional power to impose a compensatory scheme, but a commitment to practical assistance would help persuade the relevant state legislatures of the *bona fides* of the federal authorities.

No president had previously attached his name to an emancipationist proposal. Partly to reassure the states in question, but partly to cajole them into action, Lincoln addressed representatives of Delaware, Maryland,

West Virginia, Kentucky and Missouri at the White House, on 10 March. They had already read in his special message that they would have a 'perfectly free choice', but they could not have missed an implicit threat, too. Lincoln had rehearsed the need to use 'all indispensable means' to secure the Union, noting that war itself was one such means, 'and it is impossible to foresee all the incidents, which may attend and all the ruin which may follow it. Such as may seem indispensable, or may obviously promise great efficiency towards ending the struggle, must and will come.' Confronted now by sharp and anxious questioners, Lincoln offered an emollient response, telling the border men 'he had no designs beyond the action of the States on this particular subject. He should lament their refusal to accept . . . [the proposal], but he had no designs beyond their refusal to accept it.' The *status quo*, he implied, was barely sustainable. The presence of the Union army worked to destabilize and erode slavery, as slaves of loyal masters fled into the camps, and became the source of 'continual irritation' between the military and civilian authorities, plaguing him with 'conflicting and antagonistic complaints'. It was quite possible 'in the present aspect of affairs' that, financially at least, slaveholders had more to lose from holding on to their slaves than by accepting compensation.[21]

Congress moved to pass the joint resolution by large majorities and on 10 April Lincoln gratefully approved it. Six days later he signed into law an act providing for immediate emancipation of the 3,000 slaves in the District of Columbia, where he had no doubt about the constitutional power of Congress to act. If it was not the bill he would himself have drafted, it met two of his principles: the compensation of slaveowners and federal appropriations in support of voluntary colonization. But it disappointed him that the first move toward 'abolishment' in the border had been taken not by individual slave states, but by the federal government. He continued during the spring to appeal eloquently to border loyalists, invoking 'the signs of the times', their own self-interest and their historic opportunity to do good. But despite his skillful avoidance of partisanship, moral reproach or an argumentative tone, and his emphasis on the opportunity for securing change that would come 'gently as the dews of heaven, not rending or wrecking anything', his appeal went unanswered.[22] The racial antipathies of poor white laborers and deep conservatism of most border slaveowners outweighed the support of the more realistic planters, moderate yeomanry and mountain folk, and the pockets of real antislaveryites.

If most border loyalists were fearful or unmoved by Lincoln's initiatives, the response of mainstream northern opinion ranged from approving to jubilant. Though Stevens and an abolitionist minority lambasted the president's lack of ambition, it was more significant that Sumner, Chase and other radicals, together with progressive religious groups, lauded what they correctly identified as an historic watershed. Equally important was the praise emanating from the political center of conservative Republicans and even moderate Democrats. Raymond's *New York Times*, after initial doubts over the costs of Lincoln's plan, lauded him for striking 'the happy mean'. The warm response to emancipation in the District confirmed for Lincoln the continuing shifts in the tectonic plates of public opinion.[23]

But the limits to what moderate Unionists would accept were clearly exposed by General David Hunter's actions in the Department of the South, which encompassed the South Carolina, Georgia and Florida coast. Confronted by thousands of abandoned slaves, Hunter saw their military possibilities. In two successive orders he liberated those in Union hands and, on 9 May, freed all slaves in the department, implausibly stating that slavery and martial law were incompatible. By declaring every slave free and encouraging the formation of a black regiment, Hunter exceeded Frémont's actions in Missouri and opened himself up to an onslaught of conservative and moderate voices, including the *New York Times*. Reverdy Johnson and others found the legal reasoning absurd, but they worried even more about the order's implicit invitation to slave insurrections and its likely effect on border Unionism. 'This act has done us more harm than a loss of two battles', one New Yorker told Lincoln, 'and has made Kentucky & Maryland almost against us if not wholly.' Radicals were far more sanguine. Chase urged the president to let the order stand, and Schurz, though agreeing that it was rather premature and too 'ostensibly proclaimed', cautioned Lincoln against a response that would tie his hands at a time when attitudes were rapidly changing.[24]

Lincoln, on friendly terms with Hunter, declared the order 'altogether void', but not before he had squared his intentions with his cabinet and leading congressmen. Though many radicals rebuked his hesitation and timidity, Lincoln revealingly avoided the torrent of outrage that had accompanied his previous year's treatment of Frémont. In part, this was because of Hunter's less tenable position in law and because of the signals Lincoln had emitted by his message of 6 March. But it was also because a careful reading of Lincoln's words, as Schurz explained, indicated another step in the evolution of the president's thinking about his constitutional powers and opened the prospect of future radical action. The government had given no military commander the authority to make slaves free, Lincoln declared. But, significantly, he added that 'whether it be competent for me, as Commander-in-Chief . . . , to declare the Slaves of any state or states, free, and whether at any time, in any case, it shall have become a necessity indispensable to the maintenance of the government, to exercise such supposed power' were 'questions which, under my responsibility, I reserve to myself'.[25] He did not categorically answer those questions, but by invoking, yet again, the notion of indispensable necessity he gave a clear signal of the way his mind was moving.

Precisely when Lincoln accepted the legitimacy and need for a presidential emancipation proclamation is impossible to say. The best evidence suggests that he was tussling with the issues from late May and had come close a final decision by the end of June. By then his scheme of compensated emancipation was stalled: the Confederacy was not to be mortally wounded by the self-sacrifice of loyal border slaveholders. Some more profound weapon was needed to reverse the trend of a war which, since the victories of early 1862, had brought the Union only meager returns. Apart from Grant's bloody western success in the equal slaughter at Shiloh (which consolidated the Union's position and opened up the prospect of splintering the Confederacy down the line of the Mississippi) and Farragut's seizure of New Orleans, there was little to cheer. Rather, the chief story was one of Lincoln's strained, even distrustful, relations with a hesitant McClellan, whose Peninsula strategy revealed itself to be a sluggish progress toward Richmond during May and June, and – after the ugly, hard engagements in the Seven Days' Battles – an unforced retreat in early July back down the Peninsula to Harrison's Landing on the James river. Many had doubted the general's fidelity to the cause; Lincoln had questioned only his energy and temperament for battlefield engagement. Either way, the outcome was galling military failure.

That failure brought grief but no great surprise to Lincoln, now physically racked by the burden of worry and responsibility. He had never felt real confidence in the Peninsula strategy and even before its humiliating anticlimax he expected that new measures of warfare would be needed. Building on the broad reading of federal war powers earlier proffered by John Quincy Adams and embracing the argument recently developed by William Whiting, a solicitor in the War Department, Lincoln had concluded (as he had not when revoking Frémont's proclamation nine months earlier) that, as commander-in-chief, he had the right to free the enemy's slaves for military purposes. Equally, he had reached the view that the measure was politic, that the time had arrived to treat emancipation as one of those 'indispensable necessities' for national salvation to which he had so regularly referred. When he visited McClellan at Harrison's Landing, the commander handed him a confidential letter setting out his 'general views' on the rebellion and urging that Union policy should not be to 'war upon population; but against armed forces and political organizations'; there should be no confiscation of property or 'forcible abolition of slavery'. It was the approach to war that for fourteen months had failed to deliver victory. Indeed, final victory now appeared depressingly remote. Lincoln pointedly refrained from any response, save cool silence, and so gave eloquent indication of what he had in mind.[26]

The failure of the Peninsula campaign sent shock waves through the northern public, on whose response Lincoln would hang the timing of any emancipation initiative. Events in Virginia had rammed home with grievous ferocity what the grim battles of the early spring had already taught the more discerning: that this could no longer be treated as a short war. In prospect were enormous financial sacrifices, new danger of European intervention to restore cotton supplies, further demands for volunteers, and the possibility of conscription. From editors and political leaders Lincoln learnt that military events had achieved what the clamor of radical Republicans had signally failed to do: secure unusual political convergence around a policy of military emancipation, since slavery was now increasingly regarded as 'the lever power of the rebellion'. It was time to take the kid gloves off and target the home front that nourished the Confederates' battlefield prowess. Border loyalists joined New England radicals and Protestant reformers in insisting that a proclamation of freedom would infuse the Union cause with 'new life and vigor'. 'Do not believe half traitors who will tell you that others will rebel in these Border States in consequence of such an act', one West Virginian officeholder told Lincoln: 'On the contrary men all beg for this policy! . . . The useful, producing, industrious virtuous classes will Stand-by you in all this. Only be true to them.'[27]

Increasingly confident that Union public opinion had shifted into a new alignment and that border-state hostility to military emancipation could be contained, Lincoln prepared to act. He needed to keep the initiative, for Congress was itself discussing confiscation with the confidence that came from sensing a new public mood. This was but the latest in a sequence of congressional antislavery measures introduced through the spring and early summer. An article of war prohibiting the military from returning fugitives to their masters, a law prohibiting slavery in the territories, the ratification of a treaty with Britain to strengthen measures against the slave trade: these were the legislative expressions of the convergence of moderate and even conservative Republicans around the free-soil program of the radical New Englanders who ran most of the committees. Almost all Republicans now rallied behind a proposed Second

Confiscation Act which would free the slaves of all rebels, not just those who took up arms against the Union, and gave the president power to admit them into military service. Lincoln took an acute interest in these debates, concerned to ensure that vindictiveness did not crush out constitutional process. His interventions – and threatened veto – angered some of the radicals, but he secured important changes. On 17 July he signed the bill, ignoring the warnings of some conservatives and border loyalists against approving a measure which signaled a war of subjugation and threatened to fragment the Union coalitions. He still had residual doubts, chiefly over the stipulation that the slaves of traitors should be 'forever free': did not forfeiture that extended 'beyond the lives of guilty parties' fall foul of the Constitution? But he withheld his veto, on the understanding that Congress would address his concerns.[28]

That Lincoln had crossed a watershed emerged subtly but clearly in his meeting with border-state representatives at the White House on 12 July. He again pressed the arguments he had used in March, urging them to think again about gradual, compensated emancipation. 'Unprecedentedly stern facts' made the position of loyal slaveholders highly precarious – by implication, far more precarious than four months earlier, when the spring offensive had appeared to promise a speedy restoration of the old Union, leaving slavery undisturbed. He stressed two practical considerations. The first related to the tens of thousands of fugitives crossing into Union camps, including slaves from the loyal border. By the congressional article of war of 13 March, the threat of court-martial hung over the heads of officers returning any slaves, even those of owners who claimed to be Unionists. Lincoln knew from his own postbag the outrage of loyalist masters who had suffered loss at the hands of scrupulous military emancipators.[29] This is what informed his warning: 'If the war continue long, as it must, if the object be not sooner attained, the institution in your states will be extinguished by mere friction and abrasion – by the mere incidents of the war. It will be gone, and you will have nothing valuable in lieu of it. Much of its value is gone already.'

Secondly, Lincoln noted his obligation to maintain broad unity amongst loyalists – 'none too strong' even when united – at a time of a revolution in public mood. He had, he noted, repudiated Hunter's proclamation and believed he had done right, but in so doing he had given 'dissatisfaction, if not offence, to many whose support the country can not afford to lose'.[30] Equally significant, antislavery pressure continued to grow, and – he implied – he would have to heed it. Lincoln could not have made it much clearer that, in sustaining a new public consensus which yoked moral abolitionism and utilitarian emancipation, he would abandon the border-state strategy that had shaped his policy during the first year of the war.

Whichever course these border men had chosen to pursue – and the majority stubbornly declined to act – Lincoln would undoubtedly have continued with his new plan of action. Before the congressmen had time to reply, he had told two of the more conservative members of his cabinet, Seward and Welles, of his evolving ideas. Welles recorded how, as they shared a carriage on Sunday 13 July, Lincoln had 'earnestly' discussed the matter, saying that he 'had about come to the conclusion that it was a military necessity absolutely essential for the salvation of the Union, that we must free the slaves or be ourselves subdued'. As field-hands and military laborers, slaves gave the Confederates formidable strength. 'Extraordinary measures' – emancipation by proclamation – had become the *indispensable means* 'to preserve the national existence'.[31]

Lincoln told his full cabinet of his intentions nine days later, on 22 July. He had not assembled them 'to ask their advice, but to lay the subject-matter of a proclamation before them'. He read out a draft, most of which offered no surprises: it gave formal warning of the intended seizure of rebels' property under the Second Confiscation Act, and it repeated his support for compensated, gradual emancipation when voluntarily adopted by any state. It was the final sentence that contained the bombshell. As commander-in-chief, he ordered – 'as a fit and necessary military measure' for restoring the Union – that on 1 January 1863 'all persons held as slaves within any state or states, wherein the constitutional authority of the United States shall not then be practically recognized, . . . shall then, thenceforward, and forever, be free'.[32]

Lincoln caught most of his ministers off-balance. Their responses served only to underline the cabinet's essential lack of harmony. Uncharacteristically, the conservative Bates concurred, while the radical Chase said he would prefer to see emancipation pursued untrumpeted, by local commanders empowered 'to organize and arm the slaves'. Less surprisingly, Stanton was warmly in favor, while Blair – fearing the electoral consequences – was opposed. Only Seward, who knew what was coming and had had time to reflect, made Lincoln pause for thought by urging that he postpone the proclamation until after a military victory. Following 'our repeated reverses', he feared that immediate action might be viewed not as a great act of humanity to 'Ethiopia' but 'as the last measure of an exhausted government, . . . our last *shriek*, on the retreat'.[33]

Lincoln hesitated and adjourned the meeting. He was sure that Union opinion was ready for a proclamation of freedom, but saw too that immediate action might only intensify public depression. He put his draft away, expecting only a short delay. But instead of the necessary battle-field victory, the summer produced only nervousness followed by further humiliating defeat. After the collapse of the Peninsula campaign, and to McClellan's fury, Lincoln had given Halleck overall command of the army and placed all the Union forces in northern Virginia under the self-confident John Pope. A staunchly antislavery Republican, Pope pleased the president with his plans for an aggressive war and direct advance on Richmond, but confidence turned to renewed anguish with the second battle of Bull Run in the final days of August. Pope's miscalculations, McClellan's jealous reluctance to help, and even hints of treachery amongst some of the officers of the Army of the Potomac, together engineered a shattering Union retreat on 30 August. Lincoln, though shocked by McClellan's conduct and aware that many were angrily calling for the general's head, stunned his disbelieving cabinet and the public by remov-ing Pope and consolidating the Virginia forces under McClellan, whom he judged best able to reorganize defenses. When John Hay told him about the strength of public hostility toward the general, Lincoln replied, 'He has acted badly in this matter, but we must use what tools we have.'[34] And when Lee invaded Maryland in early September, the president reluct-antly followed Halleck's advice and returned McClellan to permanent command.

Conditions during the two months after the cabinet discussion of 22 July were, then, scarcely propitious for issuing a proclamation. Indeed, one suggested reading is that they propelled Lincoln into reconsidering his emancipation policy, with the real prospect that he would back away from a war on slavery.[35] The evidence is inconclusive. Certainly he dis-cussed the pros and cons of a proclamation with visitors and friends, giving the appearance of keeping an open mind. But Nicolay and Hay, better placed than most to judge, plausibly attributed his growing irrit-ability and 'overstrung nerves' at this time to his having to be less frank than he wanted about a decision taken and from which he had no inten-tion of retreating.

In a celebrated response to a querulous Horace Greeley, Lincoln showed his capacity for a brilliant layering of meaning. On 19 August, the New York editor had accused him in the *Tribune*'s columns of disdain for twenty million freedom-loving Unionists and of pampering the border states. Conceivably, Greeley had guessed at the president's intentions and was trying to smoke him out. If so, Lincoln managed an even more skillful response. In a public letter, pointedly placed in Forney's loyal *Washington Chronicle*, not the *Tribune*, the president declared, 'My para-mount object in this struggle *is* to save the Union, and is *not* either to save or to destroy slavery.' Here was a repudiation of abolition as the war's purpose. But then, in a balancing statement, he reassured emancipationists that he had the power to engage in its destruction and would not hesitate to do so if need demanded: 'If I could save the Union without freeing *any* slave I would do it, and if I could save it by freeing *all* the slaves I would do it.' His closing remarks also gave a signal: 'I have here stated my purpose according to my view of *official* duty; and I intend no modification of my oft-expressed *personal* wish that all men every where could be free.'[36]

Cleverly, Lincoln had managed to reassure radicals that he was preparing for a dramatic step and conservatives that he had no such intention. Sydney H. Gay of the *Tribune* happily reported a general impression that 'you mean presently to announce that the destruction of Slavery is the price of our salvation'. Yet Thurlow Weed was sure the 'ultras' had taken a knock: 'They were getting the Administration into a false position. But it is all right now.' And Orville Browning, now withdrawn into his conservative shell, told the president that he had 'reassured the country'.[37]

Lincoln produced a similarly layered response to the interdenominational delegation of Chicago churchmen who put the emancipationist case to him on 13 September. There was more than a hint of irritation and of devil's advocacy in his inquiry: 'What *good* would a proclamation of emancipation from me do . . . ? I do not want to issue a document that the whole world will see must necessarily be inoperative, like the Pope's bull against the comet! Would *my word* free the slaves, when I cannot even enforce the Constitution in the rebel States?' But, he reassured them, he had no constitutional objections, 'for, as commander-in-chief . . . , in time of war, I suppose I have a right to take any measure which may best subdue the enemy'. He had raised his objections to indicate the difficulties which he felt – with evident impatience – that they had failed to appreciate. Still, closing the hour-long interview, he reassured them that he had 'not decided against a proclamation of liberty to the slaves, but [held] the matter under advisement'. The subject was 'on my mind, by day and night, more than any other. Whatever shall appear to be God's will, I will do.'[38]

Greeley and the Chicago Christians were just part of a much larger bombardment. Throughout high and late summer letters and memorials poured into the White House, beseeching Lincoln to enforce the Confiscation Acts, issue a proclamation of general emancipation, set up recruiting offices for blacks in every camp, and conduct the war 'in earnest and with the utmost vigor'. A Unionist congressman rushed back from Kentucky to Washington to demand that, since 'public opinion was undergoing such a change in regard to the rebellion', Lincoln should 'seize all the able bodied negro men belonging to the rebels'.[39] A torrent of church resolutions repeated the call for immediate and universal emancipation. 'Property in man, always morally unjust, has become nationally dangerous', warned Robert Dale Owen.[40]

There is no good reason to believe that Lincoln seriously intended backing away from what he had decided on 22 July. The arguments used then grew stronger with the passing weeks: crushing the Confederacy seemed even more remote; with the flow of recruits drying up only new inspiration would fill the quotas; the foreign powers appeared closer to recognizing southern independence; and Lincoln could see support for a proclamation burgeoning, even in the border. He may have placed his final decision in the hands of God, as he told the Chicago deputation, but he looked for that Providential sign on the battlefield, not from private revelation. A military success remained the key to action. As McClellan chased Lee, the president later told his advisers, 'he had made a vow, a covenant, that if God gave us the victory in the approaching battle, he would consider it an indication of the Divine will, and that it was his duty to move forward in the cause of emancipation'.[41]

The battle of Antietam on 17 September was no great Union triumph, but it was enough of a success to drive Lee out of Maryland and let Lincoln act. On Monday 22 September, he convened a special cabinet meeting. In excellent humor, he declared that 'his mind was fixed, his decision made' and that he needed no advice 'about the main matter – for that I have determined for myself'. He would keep 'the promise to myself, and' – Chase spotted a hesitation here – 'to my Maker'. After reading out a revised version of his proclamation, he invited suggestions over drafting and minor matters. Discussion, Welles noted, proved 'long, earnest, and, on the general principle involved, harmonious'. Only Blair had serious reservations, worrying about the impact on border Unionists and the army, and about the re-energizing of the Democrats. But Lincoln, though nervous over how the public would respond, judged that inaction was an even greater danger.[42]

Lincoln was capable of jewelled oratory but the preliminary Emancipation Proclamation, as published in the morning newspapers of 23 September, shared the dry, legalistic prose of his July draft, as well as its constitutional reasoning. He declared that all people held as slaves in those parts of the Union still in rebellion on 1 January 1863 'shall be then, thenceforward, and forever free', but he took no rhetorical advantage of the coincidence that the period of grace was exactly one hundred days. This was no declaration of universal freedom – which, of course, he believed he lacked the power to proclaim – and no statement of natural rights. He would, however, ask Congress to offer financial aid to all slave states which adopted schemes of emancipation and were not in rebellion on New Year's Day. And, in an addition to his July draft, he said he would continue to support a favored enterprise, the voluntary colonization of African Americans abroad.[43]

Just twelve days earlier Lincoln had authorized the signing of a contract between the federal government and the Chiriqui Improvement Company, a group of speculators who had convinced him that mining the coal deposits in this province of Panama would comfortably sustain a colony of African Americans. And within a few weeks Lincoln would show equal interest in the proposal of a deceitful adventurer, Bernard Kock, to establish a settlement of 5,000 blacks on a Haitian island, Ile-à-Vache. At the same time Lincoln tried to sell the idea to African Americans. In August he called a small group of blacks, mainly ex-slaves, to the White House to set out the merits of voluntary emigration to Central America: blacks would escape white prejudice and enjoy the prospect of an equality that eluded them in the United States.[44] But the larger audience of blacks for whom the message was intended remained generally unconvinced and hostile, and each project was flawed, to be eventually abandoned. Lincoln's enthusiasm for colonization was real enough – it clouded his judgment when dealing with slippery promoters – but there was a large element of stage management in all his public dealings and statements related to black emigration. He had an eye on white opinion, as well as black. Colonization was the sugar around the pill of emancipation.

The immediate public reaction to his proclamation encouraged Lincoln to think that he had got the timing more or less right. He probably allowed himself a wry smile at the rapturous praise of Theodore Tilton, James Miller McKim, Gerrit Smith and a host of other abolitionists who had previously been more sparing in their favors: 'God bless you for the word you have spoken! All good men upon the earth will glorify you, and all the angels in Heaven will hold jubilee.' Protestant churches congratulated an act of righteousness. Much centrist opinion was equally encouraging. Republican gatherings, some state legislatures and seventeen governors meeting at Altoona, Pennsylvania, warmly endorsed 'a great & imperative War measure essential to the salvation of the Union'. The conservative Republican senator Ira Harris reported, 'I was startled when I first saw it. But it did not take me long to get reconciled to it. And now I find, every day, that men vastly more conservative than I have ever been are giving in their adhesion to the doctrine of the proclamation. . . . It is one upon which we can all stand and fight and win and save the Country.'[45]

It was not all sweetness and light. Governors of the four loyal slave states, as well as New Jersey, withheld their endorsement. Unionists in the upper Confederacy saw an act of treachery. Browning and several other leading conservative Republicans were unconvinced. European opinion proved at best mixed, with progressives regretting a less-than-universal freedom and conservatives appalled at an apparent incitement to servile insurrection. In many cases, abolitionists' initial rapture gave way to a chafing at the proclamation's perceived moral compromises, including the possibility of slavery's survival in areas which the advance of Union armies would otherwise have made free. Most significant of all, a battalion of Democratic editors launched a tirade against a doubly perfidious administration, dangerous both in its despotic recasting of the objects of war and in its invitation to racial revolution: Lincoln, shedding the pretence of moderation, had emerged in his true colors as the fanatical Puritan meddler.

Lincoln later said that he had not expected the proclamation to achieve very much at first, but he was surely not prepared for the political rapids that threatened to capsize the administration over the next three months.[46] If the events themselves, including a serious electoral setback and a dramatic cabinet crisis, were not primarily or directly caused by the measure itself, the larger issue that they raised – Lincoln's objectives – was intimately connected to it. The unsettled political landscape led to fears (and hopes) that the president would renege on his commitment to freedom, withdraw his proclamation and revert to a strategy for a more limited war. How close did he come to a reversal of policy?

Opposition Democrats had high hopes of the fall elections. McClellan, who when the proclamation was issued had considered a public protest against it, or even resigning, chose to issue his own address to the Army of the Potomac. He cautioned against hot-headed discussion of the new policy, but added that 'the remedy for political errors, if any are committed, is to be found . . . in the actions of the people at the polls'. Republicans braced themselves. The Democrats had been preparing since the summer to capitalize on the 'imbecility' of the administration. In July William D. Kelley had told Lincoln that locally, in Philadelphia, the Democrats were 'more perfectly organized than I have ever known'. None of their men were enlisting. 'If they can retain their own people while 30,000 or more of ours go to the field they achieve a grand political result.' Now, as McClellan implied, the Emancipation Proclamation handed Democrats an additional weapon. They were experts at playing the race card and stirring white fears about the 'Africanizing' of the North. In Illinois especially, where Stanton had ordered the settlement of 'contrabands' in farms across the central belt, David Davis predicted serious electoral damage. Then, on 24 September, Lincoln suspended the writ of habeas corpus nation-wide, placing under martial law 'all persons discouraging volunteer enlistments, resisting militia drafts, or guilty of any disloyal practice, affording aid and comfort to Rebels'. This, and the hundreds of arbitrary arrests which had followed Stanton's enforcement of the recent Militia Act, laid Lincoln open to charge of 'dictatorship'. 'We shall now be assailed front, flank and rear by our enemies', John W. Forney sighed, as he contemplated the two proclamations.[47]

In the event, the Democrats made impressive gains. They took control of the states across the lower North, from Illinois, through Indiana, Ohio and Pennsylvania, to New Jersey and New York, where Horatio Seymour seized a stunning victory against a badly-divided Republican state party. Even across the Republicans' more natural terrain, in the upper Northwest around the Great Lakes, they advanced. In all, the Democrats won thirty-five Republican-held congressional seats and secured a bridgehead from which they could hope to advance to a presidential victory in 1864. The Republicans still comfortably controlled Congress but, dazed by their political mauling, they feared the effect on Union morale. Sumner told Lincoln that the New York outcome was 'worse for our country than the bloodiest disaster on any field of battle'. Writing from Illinois, Jesse Dubois took fright over results that 'bode no good to the country', warning Lincoln: 'the rebels in Tennessee are as exultant over them as the Chicago Times and say openly that if they can sustain themselves this winter the Northern people will compel this Administration to abandon the contest'.[48]

The post-mortem cast an exhausted president into a deeper well of depression. Conservatives blamed government by proclamation. Since slavery's death depended on military advance, insisted one western Republican, the only effect of an unnecessary emancipation order had been to resuscitate the Democrats 'to active life'. Others lamented the order sanctioning arbitrary arrests, resulting in the harassment of loyal citizens by 'a horde of irresponsible and contemptible detectives'. By contrast, radicals explained the election defeat not on overzealousness or proclamations, but on Lincoln's retaining in military command and appointive office the complacent, the inert and the outright hostile. 'Our armies must be pressed forward, & the proclamation must be pressed forward', Sumner insisted, '& the country must be made to feel that there will be no relaxation of any kind.' Schurz declared McClellan, Buell and Halleck out of sympathy with the true goals of the administration, and grumbled about the undue influence of foot-dragging Democrats. Lincoln demurred, reminding Schurz that only a broad-based, cross-party effort could suppress the rebellion. Instead, he argued, the Republicans' vote had been depressed by the higher level of enlistments amongst their own supporters than the Democrats and had not been helped by the disparagement of the administration by the Republican press. He did, though, accept that 'the ill-success of the war' underlay the defeat and implicitly accepted the need for more vigor.[49]

There was a degree of self-deception in Lincoln's analysis: the proclamations had been more damaging than he conceded. But he was right to see the stalled progress of the Union armies as the public's chief concern, and he now geared for action. He removed the politically out-of-touch Buell as commander of the Army of the Ohio on 24 October, but sensibly waited for all voting to be over before moving to dismiss McClellan, after further weeks of exasperation. Prominent Republicans and War Democrats rejoiced at this intimation of 'energy' at last. 'I have been forced to the conclusion', Daniel Dickinson told Lincoln, that McClellan 'is better suited to be superintendent of a cemetery where dead men require digging, than for the commander of an army of the living where movement is necessary to success.'[50] There were obvious perils in removing a commander still very popular with his men, but Lincoln's choice of Ambrose E. Burnside as his successor – widely, if mistakenly, regarded as close to McClellan – helped neutralize the danger.

Lincoln's reaction to election defeat, then, was not to question the wisdom of his Emancipation Proclamation, and his changes in military command reinforced the view of conservatives that he had moved irrevocably on to radical terrain. Radicals themselves, however, took more persuading of an administration transfigured, and read into the events of the final weeks of 1862 evidence of its disastrous incompetence and hesitation over strategy, as well as intimations of backsliding from the antislavery high ground so recently scaled. They waited apprehensively for the president's annual message of 1 December and found little reassurance in what they heard.

Lincoln had worked hard at his text. Its most animated, earnest and eloquent passages – over half the message – dealt with slavery and its future, but he barely mentioned the Emancipation Proclamation. Rather, having reiterated the sentiments of his inaugural address, that the 'only great element of national discord amongst us' were the transitory differences rooted in the rightness or wrongness of slavery, he set out a scheme by which that strife might be 'hushed forever with the passing of one generation'. He proposed three constitutional amendments, providing for compensation in federal bonds to states that opted for a gradual emancipation by 1900; making 'forever free' all slaves who 'enjoyed actual freedom by the chances of war', and compensating loyal owners; and authorizing federal funding 'for colonizing free colored persons, with their own consent, at any place or places without the United States'. It was a scheme prefigured in his words of March and June to Congress and the border representatives.[51]

Radicals gave a mainly chill response to proposals they condemned as backward-looking. Was Lincoln, as his Democratic opponents charged, more or less conceding the unconstitutionality of his Emancipation Proclamation? The proposals were impracticable, too, for ratification would depend on the support of at least some of the rebel slave states. Henry Winter Davis summed up a disquiet shared even by conservative Republicans when he described the plan as 'illusory to the loyal states and ridiculous in relation to the disloyal states'; Chase told Lincoln it would 'weaken rather than strengthen your administration'.[52]

In deeming it a conservative message, the president's critics had a case. Lincoln's instinctive moderation and respect for constitutional process permeated proposals through which, however unlikely it was that they would be fully embraced, he wanted to be seen to be doing his presidential duty. A nation in revolutionary flux was on the brink of a war of subjugation, but until that moment arrived he had a responsibility to strive for the peaceful, graduated, compensated, conservative plan of emancipation that he had always favored – hence his emphasis on leaving the initiative with the states, on avoiding 'vagrant destitution' and 'the evils of sudden derangement', on the justice of the whole nation paying the costs and on the benefits of the voluntary deportation of blacks.

Lincoln's proposals served two immediate political purposes. First, they were designed to encourage Unionists in rebel states to respond positively to the threat of the Emancipation Proclamation before it was too late. In particular Lincoln hoped to accelerate the moves toward the restoration of loyal governments that had accompanied the advance of Union forces. In Arkansas, Tennessee, Virginia and especially Louisiana he had given instruction to his generals to build political support for the fall elections. The annual message gave him a further opportunity for pressure: wherever rebellion yielded to restoration and reconstruction, there September's order would be stayed and a conservative course of reform substituted. Lincoln's proposed amendments, then, have to be seen, as he saw them, as a peace measure. He may, as David Donald has suggested, even have believed that the combination of martial stick and reformist carrot would shortly secure a near-complete collapse of the rebel states by chain reaction. But whatever Lincoln's expectations – and they are hard to read – he understood that wherever the proclamation was stayed an alternative plan of emancipation was required.[53]

The gradualist scheme had a further purpose. The Republicans' severe loss of support in the fall elections had flashed a warning signal. Although Lincoln had refused to be stampeded into revoking the Emancipation Proclamation, or maintaining McClellan in command against his better judgment, he needed in some way to re-colonize the center ground that he seemed to have vacated. The annual message gave him a chance to re-establish his credentials for moderation.

In the final analysis, however, the annual message was scarcely a conservative document. Lincoln looked forward as well as back. 'As our case is new, so must we think anew, and act anew.... The dogmas of the quiet past, are inadequate to the stormy present.' Not only did he stand by his September proclamation, by implication the most revolutionary of the war measures to date, but he had begun to think about how permanent constitutional law could secure the changes that the proclamation, a mere war measure, would effect. Equally, his proposals sought to energize emancipationists in the loyal border states and destroy slavery in places well beyond the proclamation's remit. And – in a lengthy passage which confronted economic racism even more powerfully than it advocated voluntary deportation, and made a start in educating whites to tolerate a free black population in their midst – Lincoln challenged, as he had never before, the 'largely imaginary, if not sometimes malicious' argument that emancipation would depress the wages of white labor, and that freedmen would 'swarm forth, and cover the whole land'.[54]

Most striking of all, Lincoln not only presented emancipation as a *necessary means* 'for restoring and preserving the national authority throughout the Union', but now, however indirectly, he signaled the slaves' freedom as one of the *purposes* of war. In a memorable climax, prefiguring his theme at Gettysburg, Lincoln acknowledged that there might be other ways of saving the Union, but believed his own plan offered the best hope. 'In *giving* freedom to the *slave*, we *assure* freedom to the *free* – honorable alike in what we give, and what we preserve.' Emancipation, initially only a weapon for securing a Union devoted to freedom, would, through the nobility of the action and the liberty it secured for those in bondage, itself become an essential element of that larger freedom of all Americans. 'We shall nobly save, or meanly lose, the last best, hope of earth.'[55]

Whatever modest reassurance the radicals might have drawn, in Chase's words, from the 'noble sentiments' of Lincoln's peroration, it did not survive the Union catastrophe at Fredericksburg on 13 December.[56] Burnside's battlefield misjudgment was scarcely Lincoln's fault – indeed, he had sought to warn against the very course that brought disaster – but the loss of over 12,000 men in the worst defeat to date plunged northern opinion into the darkest desperation and even defeatism. It also prompted the most profound government crisis Lincoln had faced. Popular anger against Halleck, Stanton and even the president himself prompted a special caucus of thirty-two Republican senators. Focusing on the administration's weakness, the cabinet's chronic disharmony and Lincoln's seeming lack of system, they turned their most determined fire on Seward. From Chase in particular – in personality and policy the chalk to Seward's cheese – they had learnt of the secretary of state's 'back-stairs influence' over Lincoln and of the conservatism and half-heartedness which were widely deemed to have blocked an energetic prosecution of the war. Resolved to secure a reconstructed cabinet, they agreed to send a deputation to the White House. Anticipating their action, and unready to see the president put into a false position, Seward sent Lincoln his resignation.

Stunned, but determined not to lose control of his administration, Lincoln rallied and skillfully played out the crisis with a calmness and urbanity that obscured his inner anxiety. If he let Seward go, he would be making a public statement that the radicals were in control, that the administration was no longer broad-based and that the Union party consensus had fragmented into the polarized partisanship of a resurgent Democracy and hard-line Republicanism. He surprised the deputation of senators by inviting the whole cabinet (without Seward) to the second of their two meetings with him, and then secured from a wrong-footed and deeply embarrassed Chase the admission that really there had been no disunity in the cabinet. Conscious that he was tarred with the charge of double-dealing, Chase spent an uneasy night before hesitantly producing a letter of resignation in the president's office. Lincoln seized it, aware that it was the weapon to resolve the crisis: he would persuade both secretaries to withdraw their resignations, reassert his mastery, and above all – with 'a pumpkin in each end of my bag' – maintain the administration's balance. After two days of 'hell', he could smile a little.[57]

The radicals' attempt to take control of the administration had failed. If Lincoln needed confirmation of the meaning of his triumph it came by way of a reported remark made by Jefferson Davis during the crisis 'that there would soon be a rupture in the Cabinet of Lincoln's, and that the appointment of men who favored the emancipation scheme' – thus alienating Kentucky – 'together with the late Democratic victories, would ensure the ultimate triumph of Southern Arms'. In fact, the radicals' defeat did not, despite the fervent hopes of opposition Democrats and stolid border Unionists, mean Lincoln's abandonment of the promises of September, though the memorials that bombarded him during the final days of the year, including a barrage of letters from the Republican presidential electors of 1860, indicated that antislavery loyalists too were anxious about a last-minute presidential stumble. On New Year's Day, 1863, steadying his arm after a morning of vigorous handshaking, Lincoln signed the final proclamation of emancipation.[58]

Far from retreating from the radicalism of his September order, Lincoln advanced a step further. As well as declaring free all slaves in states and parts of states still in rebellion, he authorized the enlistment of blacks, admitting them into the Union armed service 'to garrison forts, positions, stations, and other places, and to man vessels of all sorts'. Even before the onset of hostilities, free blacks had expressed their readiness to risk their lives for the Union, and their repeated demands that they – and the multiplying contrabands – be allowed to enlist were taken up by white radicals, including Schurz, Tilton and Beecher. By July 1862 Lincoln had begun to acknowledge the case for allowing commanders to arm freedmen in specific locations and signed the Confiscation Act that gave him discretion to receive blacks into service. Some generals took path-breaking initiatives: Hunter and Saxton with contrabands in the Department of the South; Butler with the free black citizens of New Orleans. But, fearing the effect on public opinion, Lincoln was not prepared to move to a general arming of African Americans. In August, Browning, acting as the president's ears in Illinois, endorsed Lincoln's stance. 'The time may come for arming the negroes. It is not yet.' Men repeatedly said, 'If [Lincoln] . . . will accept one black Regiment he will lose twenty white Regiments by it.' When, that same month, Indiana offered to raise two black regiments, the president refused them, just as he did the 6th colored regiment earnestly proffered by Rhode Island's Governor Sprague in September.[59] The Emancipation Proclamation was quite enough to ask conservative Unionists to digest for the moment; with elections in the offing in the fall of 1862, he would not ask them to swallow black enlistments too.

Still, arming blacks was a logical consequence of a proclamation justified as a military measure. Arguments that had begun to weigh in July, tipped the scales by the close of the year, fusing opportunism and idealism. The Union army needed men. Heavy enlistments and drafts deprived the home front of its manpower. Putting freedmen in uniform would keep them off the northern labor market. It would also prepare them for the responsibilities of freedom and help remove 'reasonless and unchristian prejudice against the African race'.[60] If Lincoln shared the common anxiety that blacks were unequal to the task, it was assuaged by his reading George Livermore's recent pamphlet, a gift from Sumner, on their substantial role as soldiers during the Revolution. Addressing the fear that arming blacks might trigger slave insurrections, Lincoln enjoined on those freed by the proclamation 'to abstain from all violence, unless in necessary self-defence'.[61]

Lincoln's low-key declaration prompted no immediate transformation of policy toward black enlistments, but it was the critical turning point. Conservatives like Edward Bates may have been uneasy, at best, and border Unionists alarmed, but it met with delight amongst African-American spokesmen and radical Republicans. One intimation of the new direction in policy was the dog that did not bark: colonization, brandished as a policy in September, received no mention. Lincoln had not lost all interest in voluntary deportation – the Ile-à-Vache scheme was still afloat – and his commissioner of emigration, James Mitchell, believed that the arming of 'a few thousand negroes' would not stand in the way of their being 'subsequently removed'.[62] But Lincoln's present silence eloquently intimated that he saw the internal contradiction in asking blacks to leave the country on whose behalf he was inviting them to risk their lives.

Over sixteen months, by increments, Lincoln had moved. From firmly repudiating emancipation as a weapon of war, he had moved to declare the advancing Union forces the liberators of millions in bondage. From tolerating the return of fugitive slaves to rebel masters, he had moved to invite freedmen to take up arms against those who had shackled them. From defining the war's purpose as the re-establishment of a Union committed to no more than a gradual melting away of the peculiar institution, he had moved to champion a nation energized by the prospect of slavery's imminent and permanent removal. Whatever Lincoln would later say to Albert Hodges, this fundamental reformulating of objectives occurred not because the president was passively bobbing about on the tidal surges of events, powerful though these were, but because he took initiatives, bringing to bear a strong political will, a radar system acutely sensitive to public opinion and a gift for timing. Not least, he thought so long and hard before taking a new position that, as Charles Sumner told Harriet Beecher Stowe, 'it is hard to move him . . . once he has taken it'. This ratchet meant that the decision for emancipation, once presented to the cabinet on 22 July would not easily be retracted; it also explains why in November, two months after issuing the preliminary order, he said privately that 'he would rather die than take back a word'.[63] The ratchet was an expression both of Lincoln's temperament and his intellectual character. As such, it was also related to Lincoln's understanding of his place within the workings of Providence, to which we must now turn.

Faith and purposes

When Lincoln extended the means of war to embrace emancipation, he explained his actions – to his cabinet, to the Chicago clergy – in terms which intimated that he was listening to God's will. We will never get to the bottom of Lincoln's private religious thought, or definitively weigh the competing claims about his personal piety. But there are unmistakable signs that, from the time of his election, he attended to religion with growing seriousness, that his ideas about God's role in the universe sustained a marked change, and that these notions informed how he thought about his administration's purposes.

The presidency transformed Lincoln's life, and there need be no surprise that the changes he underwent made him more reflective about the claims of faith. Decades of campaigning for political power had been an inspiring joy: he thrived during his debates with Douglas, even putting on weight. He had relished the prospect of office and in conventional times he would probably have relished the reality of executive power. But the demands of a cruel presidency threatened to crush even one who was more physically tough, mentally focused and emotionally self-sufficient than most. Bearing the responsibility and guilt for a war of unexpected savagery was burden enough. 'Do you ever realize that the desolation, sorrow, grief, that pervades this country is owing to you?' a disconsolate Republican unnecessarily inquired. But beyond that Lincoln had to face the trials of personal loss. Friends and close colleagues – Elmer Ellsworth, Edward Baker and others – spilt their blood. Then there was the death of his beloved eleven-year-old child, Willie, from typhoid fever in February 1862, leaving him broken-hearted, taking his wife to the brink of a nervous breakdown and sending them both into months of deep mourning. Mary herself provided Lincoln with but modest emotional support. If historians have tended to overstate the degree of their domestic disharmony – one has judged the marriage a 'fountain of misery' – it is still clear that the problem of Mary's extravagance, insecurity and social misjudgments gave Lincoln off-duty as much pain as balm.

Occasionally his White House secretaries would help him relax. John Hay became something of an adopted son, to whom Lincoln would recite Scripture and dramatic poetry to help calm his mind. The theater brought him some escape, as did occasional exeats from Washington to visit the troops. But the physical drudgery and emotional rigors of the presidency were essentially unrelieved and inescapable. Less than two years into the war, Noah Brooks discovered that the 'happy-faced lawyer' he had seen stumping for Frémont in 1856 was now a grizzled, stooped figure, with 'a sunken deathly look about the large, cavernous eyes'. A little while later Lincoln 'said quaintly that nothing could touch the tired spot within, which was all tired'. Racked by weariness 'beyond description' (though suffering only rare bouts of illness), Lincoln entered his second term in 1865 old before his time.[64]

A cocktail of exhaustion, responsibility and guilt need not of itself prompt an interest in religion, but it probably does help explain why in Washington Lincoln became a more habitual churchgoer than ever before. Attendance was expected of the president, of course. Lincoln, with a choice of churches, found congenial the familiar old school doctrine of the New York Avenue Presbyterian Church, helpfully untainted by secession and southern Democracy. According to John DeFrees, the president had several conversations with its pastor, Phineas D. Gurley, 'on the subject of religion, about the time of the death of his son Willie'. Equally, Lincoln's Bible-reading became a greater source of comfort than ever. Friends noticed it. Joshua Speed thought that 'he sought . . . to make the Bible a preceptor to his faith and a guide for his conduct' as president. Browning recalled their spending a Sunday afternoon in the White House library together, when 'he was reading the bible a good deal'. Mary Lincoln implied that he studied the Scriptures more intently as the war proceeded. His habit attracted attention. On a steamboat trip down to Norfolk, he was observed in an out-of-the-way corner 'reading a dog eared *pocket* copy of the New Testament all by himself'. It was not an affectation.[65]

Attention to religion is not the same as a profession of faith, though there were those, like Speed, who judged that the pre-war skeptic now 'sought to become a believer', and others who saw in the wartime Lincoln such a deepening of devotion that they thought he had realized the ambition. Noah Brooks stated that Lincoln had spoken to him of 'a process of crystallization' in his mind during the crisis after his election, and that he constantly prayed. In the main, though, those who felt they got close to Lincoln during the war saw no change of heart, or an evangelical-style conversion: rather, they thought his trials had released a latent interest in religion. Browning recalled a 'naturally . . . very religious man' and Leonard Swett considered him so 'full of natural religion' that, as he confronted 'great responsibility and great doubt, a feeling of religious reverence, and belief in God – his justice and overruling power – increased upon him'. Mary Lincoln told Herndon, 'he was a religious man always, as I think', beginning to address the subject seriously when Willie died, and 'felt religious More than Ever about the time he went to Gettysburg'. But 'he was not a technical Christian' – indeed, Christ himself is notably absent from his authenticated words. Lincoln was not being falsely modest when he told Gurley and a group of Presbyterian visitors, 'I have often wished that I was a more devout man than I am.'[66]

Lincoln's sense of his devotional inadequacy was only sharpened by the persistent efforts of the Christian community to guide him. Never before in his life had he been made so forcefully and inescapably aware of the religious imperatives driving the populous groups who made up northern Protestantism. Mainstream Protestants represented a formidable constituency, and their combined expressions of opinion, especially when underscored by sympathizers amongst the president's political colleagues, presented an insistent drumbeat that Lincoln could not so easily ignore.

Collectively, three broad themes emerged. First, the Union amounted to more than a glorious experiment in liberty and republicanism, the rebellion to more than simple treason: the struggle for national destiny resonated beyond the earth-bound political sphere. Illinois Congregationalists told Lincoln that the rebels, by launching 'a revolt against the Divine scheme for the world's advance in civilization and religion', had embarked on 'impious defiance of Divine Providence'. From cranks as well as political friends, Lincoln heard a common message: 'One God! One Union! One People! . . . all the powers of hell are just now against us.' Orville Browning held that 'God is entering into judgment' with the cotton states, and continued to remind Lincoln that the Union cause was 'as holy . . . as ever engaged men's feelings'. James Doolittle knew that 'God the Almighty must be with us', and in the dark days of late 1862 Edwin Stanton found hope in the knowledge that 'our national destiny is as immediately in the hands of the Most High as ever was that of the Children of Israel'.[67]

Secondly, Lincoln learnt that in this sanctified, manichean struggle between darkness and light he was God's chosen instrument. 'It is your high mission under God to save us', Elias Nason told him at start of hostilities, and repeatedly he heard the sentiment that 'God has raised [you] up for such a time as this'. Lincoln's campaign biographer, the

Methodist John Locke Scripps, reminded him that he had 'voluntarily accepted the highest responsibilities which any one not endowed with the Godhead could assume' and that from God alone would come the strength, will and wisdom he needed. As the agent of divine providence, he would enjoy the prayers of all faithful people. From every quarter Lincoln received the reassurance that, in the words of one correspondent, 'Heaven give you & your Advisors the Wisdom for Our emergency is the daily prayer of Millions.'[68]

God, however, would listen only if Lincoln followed His teachings. For the vast majority of religious petitioners – Protestant, largely evangelical and strongly leavened with New England and new school Calvinism – those lessons were clear. As the Chicago Congregationalist, William W. Patton, explained, the war was 'a just rebuke from God, of the tolerance of slavery by our fathers after the revolution, & of the numerous concessions made to it from that period to the present'. The conflict of arms, once underway, could only be stayed by ending the whole nation's complicity in an 'unchristian & barbarous' system, 'the abomination that maketh desolate'. Emancipation alone would free the Union from the sin of covenant-breaking, of reneging on the pledge of freedom in the Declaration of Independence.[69]

Lincoln avoided complete immersion in these evangelical waters swirling around him, but under the pressure of wartime events he was without doubt swept along to a new religious understanding, one much closer to the historic Calvinism that had profoundly shaped most of northern Protestantism. At the heart of evangelicals' dialogue with Lincoln stood a bundle of notions about God, humankind and the workings of providence: that the Almighty was an all-seeing, active force in history, ready to dispense retributive justice on a naturally sinful people and delinquent nation, but also ready to intervene to help human efforts when directed at a righteous end. Belief in the operations of providence, as several historians have emphasized, played a large part in Lincoln's thinking throughout his life. Before the war, he regarded providence as a superintending but remote and mechanistic force, which operated not by capriciously suspending the rules of the universe, but by working predictably within them. As war president, however, he discovered new meaning in the Calvinism with which he had been acquainted over a lifetime. Lincoln's 'providence' now became an active and more personal God, an intrusively judgmental figure, more mysterious and less predictable than the ruling force it superseded.

Precisely when this shift in conception occurred is hard to pin down. The consensus is that Lincoln's invocations of providence during the first year of the war, and his increasing public calls for God's assistance, precede the change and can be slotted into his antebellum framework of understanding.[70] Even so, Lincoln himself later remarked that 'from the beginning' he had seen that 'the issues of our great struggle depended on the Divine interposition and favor. If we had that all would be well.' A clear sign of the change came with Lincoln's proclamation for a national day of fasting and prayer, after the defeat at Bull Run, in which he confessed private and national sins, acknowledged a justly vengeful God and prayed for His intervention in support of Union arms. If the Calvinist language here may have reflected not conviction, but formulaic convention, the same cannot be said of Lincoln's words to Browning at about the same time. When his friend urged that only by striking against slavery would the Union open the door to divine assistance, Lincoln replied, 'Browning, suppose God is against us in our view on the subject of slavery in this country, and our method of dealing with it?' Browning later admitted he had been deeply impressed by this reply, 'which indicated to me for the first time that he was thinking deeply of what a higher power than man sought to bring about by the great events then transpiring'.[71]

The idea of an unfathomable God, operating actively but mysteriously to shape events, surfaced again in Lincoln's remarks during the summer of 1862. A visiting delegation of Quakers urged him to proclaim freedom to the slaves. 'Perhaps', he replied, 'God's way of accomplishing the end which the memorialists have in view may be different from theirs.' That this was an authentic expression of his innermost views is evident from an arresting personal memorandum, probably composed in September, after the disaster at Second Bull Run. 'In great contests each party claims to act in accordance with the will of God', Lincoln wrote. 'Both *may* be, and one *must* be wrong. God can not be *for*, and *against* the same thing at the same time.' There followed, however, not a statement of Unionist certainty, but a startling hypothesis: 'In the present civil war it is quite possible that God's purpose is something different from the purpose of either party. . . . I am almost ready to say this is probably true – that God wills this contest, and wills that it shall not end yet.' God *chose* to let the contest begin. 'And having begun He could give the final victory to either side any day. Yet the contest proceeds.'[72]

These were the words of a man whose changing ideas on divine intervention indicated some movement toward the evangelical mainstream, but whose hesitancy over equating the Union cause with God's will, or with Christian holiness, set him apart from it. This was just one aspect of his ambivalence in the face of orthodoxy. Lincoln shared most Protestants' understanding of his dependence on, and responsibilities to, a higher power. 'It has pleased Almighty God to put me in my present position', he told his old Springfield neighbor, the Baptist minister Noyes Miner, in the spring of 1862, 'and looking up to him for divine guidance, I must work out my destiny as best I can.' Impressed, Miner concluded that 'if Mr. Lincoln was not a christian he was acting like one'. At other times, too, Lincoln spoke in orthodox language – of his 'firm reliance upon the Divine arm', of seeking 'light from above', and of being 'a humble instrument in the hands of our Heavenly Father'. Even more significant, he began to use the possessive pronoun – 'responsibility to my God', 'promise to my Maker' – in ways that suggested a belief in a more personal God. Yet at the same time, as he tried to discern God's wishes in the 'signs of the times', he showed much more humility than did most Protestant preachers. As he said rather testily to the delegation from the Chicago churches, religious men who were 'equally certain that they represent the Divine will' had badgered him with opposite demands. 'I hope it will not be irreverent for me to say that if it is probable that God would reveal his will to others, on a point so connected with my duty, it might be supposed he would reveal it directly to me; for . . . it is my earnest desire to know the will of Providence in this matter. *And if I can learn what it is I will do it!*' But since he could expect no miracles or direct revelation, he had to use the limited means available to him: observation and rational analysis. 'I must study the plain physical facts of the case, ascertain what is possible and learn what appears to be wise and right.'[73]

Lincoln's new religious position, expressed in his search to discover God's purposes, was inextricably entwined with his developing emancipation policy during the spring and summer of 1862. It culminated in his remarks at the landmark cabinet meeting on 22 September when, according to Welles, Lincoln explained how he had vowed ahead of Antietam that he would interpret victory as 'an indication of Divine will, and that it was his duty to move forward in the cause of emancipation': not he, but 'God had decided this question in favor of the slaves'. This does not mean Lincoln's religious transformation 'caused' the change in war policy, to which he was being beckoned by military need, political pressure and the slaves' own pursuit of freedom. Rather it represented Lincoln's need for new sources of philosophical support at a time when the old ones were losing their power. Unlike the majority of evangelical Protestants, who could easily shelter emancipation within ready-made millennial doctrine, Lincoln had to seek out a new theological framework of his own, albeit one with familiar elements of Calvinism. In earlier times and in other moods, he would – as we have noted – 'ridicule the Puritans'. But by New Year's Day 1863, the president and the earnest Protestants who entreated him had come to stand on much the same ground of practical policy, even if they had got there by different intellectual routes.[74]

Faithfulness of purpose: emancipation, reconstruction and black citizenship

'I can only trust in God I have made no mistakes', Lincoln told a crowd of well-wishers who had gathered to congratulate him on his preliminary proclamation. The remark was that of a president who would continue for the remainder of the war to address issues from the standpoint of both religious conviction and hard-nosed pragmatism. Those two elements reinforced each other, ensuring that Lincoln would hold to his new policy of emancipation as steadfastly as he had to his 'fundamental idea', the restoration of constitutional government. The president who could emotionally say at the time of the Peninsula debacle, 'I expect to maintain this contest until successful, or till I die, or am conquered, or my term expires, or Congress or the country forsakes me', would bring the same steely resolution to the cause of black liberty.[75]

Lincoln expected no dramatic change to follow from his final proclamation. Indeed, events suggested he was right about its likeness to an ineffectual papal bull, for the Union cause suffered further buffeting through the winter and spring of 1863. The proclamation, by signaling that the war had become an antislavery crusade, stirred disaffection within sections of the army and further energized political dissent, both amongst opposition Democrats and within the most conservative elements of the Union coalition. Pro-Confederate forces, particularly in the Midwest, grew bolder. The border remained unsettled. When the planned spring offensive eventually got underway in April, high hopes quickly fizzled. Samuel du Pont's ambitious naval expedition against Charleston flattered to deceive. On the Mississippi, despite Grant's maneuvers, the enemy continued to control the seemingly impregnable batteries at Vicksburg, the last strong link between the eastern and western sections of the Confederacy. In eastern Tennessee, Rosecrans remained immobilized by the narrowness of his own strategic vision. Then, in early May, events in the eastern theater once more turned disappointment into the profoundest despair as the Army of the Potomac, now under Joe Hooker's command, succumbed to a further crushing defeat at Chancellorsville. During the first six months of 1863, with his administration berated as indecisive and incompetent, Lincoln had little to show for his emancipation policy.

The mood changed radically in the early days of July, with dramatic news from both eastern and western fronts. On Independence Day Lincoln's face, now ravaged by exhaustion and strain, lit up with rare joy at the news of George Meade's triumph in Pennsylvania, a bloody three-days' encounter at Gettysburg which had forced Lee to turn tail; within days he learnt of Grant's even more stunning and tactically brilliant success in securing the decisive fall of Vicksburg. Though expectations of imminent final victory would soon be cruelly dashed, early July marked a military and psychological sea-change in the Union. Lincoln would increasingly describe his Emancipation Proclamation as an irreversible order, making explicit what previously he had merely implied: black freedom had become an objective of the war. 'I think I shall not retract or repudiate' the Emancipation Proclamation, he told Stephen Hurlbut in late July. 'Those who shall have tasted actual freedom I believe can never be slaves, or quasi slaves again.' Nathaniel Banks received a similar message in August. 'For my own part', Lincoln wrote, 'I think I shall not, . . . as executive, ever return to slavery any person who is free by the terms of that proclamation, or by any of the acts of Congress.' Later that month, in a statement calculated for its public impact, he announced that 'the promise [of freedom] being made must be kept'. And in September, delighted by military advances in Tennessee, he told Governor Andrew Johnson to get emancipation written into a new state constitution.[76]

Lincoln's determination took memorable form in his address at the dedication of the new national cemetery at Gettysburg in November. In declaring 'a new birth of freedom' to be the goal of war he chose not to allude specifically to slavery and the black race. But, lest there were any doubt, he told Congress plainly a few weeks later, 'while I remain in my present position I shall not attempt to retract or modify the emancipation proclamation; nor shall I return to slavery any person who is free by the terms of that proclamation, or by any of the acts of Congress'. He took pains to reassert those precise words in his following year's message, in December 1864, and pointedly added, 'If the people should, by whatever mode or means, make it an Executive duty to re-enslave such persons, another, and not I, must be their instrument to perform it.'[77]

During 1864 and the final months of his presidency, Lincoln consistently acted in this spirit. When, in the summer, he came under pressure to respond to what some deemed peace overtures, he classified 'the integrity of the whole Union, and the abandonment of slavery' as nonnegotiable. (Only once, in the darkest days of late August 1864, believing his electoral defeat inescapable, did he contemplate an offer of peace without emancipation.) Earlier, he had insisted on writing into his party's election platform a pledge of support for an emancipation amendment to the Constitution. Fearing that his proclamation, by deriving its authority from military need, might lack legal force after the war and be overturned by a hostile judiciary or Congress, he saw in a thirteenth amendment the only means of guaranteeing that African Americans be 'forever free'. Once re-elected, he used patronage and every legitimate lever to secure its passage through the lame-duck Congress that had previously failed to endorse it. As the process of state ratification began, he took pride in the lead his own state of Illinois had taken in approving a measure which freed all slaves, not just those in the rebellious areas covered by his proclamation. On this 'King's cure for all the evils', he told an impromptu gathering of supporters, 'he could not but congratulate all present, himself, the country and the whole world upon this great moral victory.'[78]

Strong practical reasons stiffened Lincoln's resolve to stand by his emancipation policy. To renege on a carefully calculated proclamation would be to confirm the charge of irresolution. It would send out the wrong signal to the European powers, whose continuing attempts at mediation were usefully undermined by Lincoln's recasting of the conflict as a struggle over the future of slavery itself. Most of all, it was incompatible with the Union's growing dependence on black troops. Lincoln had first followed up his final proclamation by encouraging commanders to use African Americans not for combat but in garrison duties, 'leaving the white forces now necessary at those places, to be employed elsewhere'; but he shortly came to share many commanders' enthusiasm for raising and arming black regiments. 'The bare sight of fifty thousand armed, and drilled black soldiers on the banks of the Mississippi, would end the rebellion at once', he reflected to Andrew Johnson, and during the spring campaigns of 1863 he followed these words with action. After Adjutant General Lorenzo Thomas's exploratory visit to the West in April, the War Department established a special bureau for organizing 'colored troops'. Soon the courage and capability of frontline black recruits – notably in Louisiana and at Fort Wagner, in South Carolina – underscored the wisdom of Lincoln's new policy.[79]

The better the policy worked, the less likely it was that emancipation would be reversed for, said Lincoln, 'negroes, like other people, act upon motives. Why should they do any thing for us, if we will do nothing for them? If they stake their lives for us, they must be prompted by the strongest motive – even the promise of freedom.' To abandon them would be 'a cruel and an astounding breach of faith'. Democrats and conservatives in the border states and Midwest might want the proclamation retracted, seeing it as an obstacle to peace and an inhibitor of white recruitment. But Lincoln knew, as he told Grant in August, that black enlistments were becoming indispensable, 'a resource which, if vigorously applied now, will soon close the contest. It works doubly, weakening the enemy and strengthening us'. A year later Lincoln estimated that some 150,000 black seamen, soldiers and laborers served the Union. 'My enemies condemn my emancipation policy', he noted. 'But no human power can subdue this rebellion without using the Emancipation lever as I have done.' By the end of the conflict, not far short of 190,000 blacks had directly supported the Union's military effort.[80]

A similar utilitarian concern marked Lincoln's encouragement of emancipationists in the loyal slave states, where his proclamation did not apply. The weaker slavery became in the borderlands, the more forlorn the Confederates' hopes. Turning 'slave soil to free', as Lincoln said in support of the admission of West Virginia as a free state, 'is a certain, and irrevocable encroachment upon the cause of the rebellion'. Specifically, Lincoln developed pressure for compensated emancipation across the border region by endorsing the payment of bounties to loyal owners whose slaves enlisted. In Kentucky, where army officers frequently clashed with uncooperative owners, white Unionists remained chronically deaf to the appeal of voluntary emancipation, despite the stark evidence of a crumbling institution as thousands of slaves sought the sanctuary of the Union lines. It was a different tale in Missouri, where the poisonous factionalism between radical and conservative Unionists, which left Lincoln friendless, nonetheless resolved itself into an effective movement for state-wide emancipation during 1864 and early 1865. More satisfactory still was the abolition of slavery in Maryland, where Lincoln had consistently nurtured the cause. 'It needs not to be a secret', he told a state leader ahead of elections for a state constitutional convention, 'that I wish success to emancipation in Maryland. It would aid much to end the rebellion.' When voters narrowly ratified the emergent free state constitution in October 1864 Lincoln joined ecstatic free blacks in celebrating what he called 'a big thing'.[81]

Intellectual conviction sustained Lincoln's utilitarianism. Persisting in his duty of seeking the divine purpose, and sure that emancipation was God's will, he saw nothing in events to show he was wrong. Disasters, as at Fredericksburg, might mean that 'the Almighty is against us', but they did not signal God's disapproval of an emancipationist course. By the spring of 1864 the nation was well down the road to extinguishing slavery, but this was not what, three years earlier, 'either party, or any man devised, or expected. God alone can claim it.' It seemed increasingly clear that 'God now wills the removal of a great wrong, and wills also that . . . the

North as well as . . . the South, shall pay fairly for our complicity in that wrong'. In similar vein he told the English abolitionist, Eliza Gurney, 'The purposes of the Almighty are perfect, and must prevail, though we erring mortals may fail to accurately perceive them in advance. . . . [W]e must work earnestly in the best light He gives us, trusting that so working still conduces to the great ends He ordains. Surely He intends some great good to follow this mighty convulsion.'[82]

God then had so ordered events that Lincoln felt increasingly justified in giving play to his emancipationist instincts. 'I am naturally anti-slavery', he told Hodges and other Kentuckians, but he had never allowed his 'primary abstract judgment on the moral question' to overrule his constitutional obligations. In the earlier part of his presidency he had not completely smothered his antislavery inclinations: with a nuance often missed, he noted that he had 'done no official act in *mere* deference' to these feelings; the executive office conferred no '*unrestricted* right to act officially upon this judgment'.[83] But his scope for constitutional action against slavery had gradually broadened. Publicly reverting to the moral, Scripture-laced language that he had used before becoming president, Lincoln wrote down his thoughts for a delegation of Baptists, in May 1864: 'To read in the Bible, as the word of God himself, that "In the sweat of *thy* face shalt thou eat bread," and to preach therefrom that, "In the sweat of *other mans* faces shalt thou eat bread," to my mind can scarcely be reconciled with honest sincerity.' And when 'professedly holy men of the South' reinterpreted the Golden Rule ('As ye would all men should do unto you, do ye even so unto them') by asking 'the christian world to aid them in doing to a whole race of men, as they would have no man do unto themselves', they engaged in far greater hypocrisy and insult to God 'than did Satan when he tempted the Saviour with the Kingdoms of the earth'.[84]

In alluding to slavery as an abuse of labor, Lincoln can be read as promoting the wartime development of the Republicans' free-labor philosophy. Heather Cox Richardson has shown how, once in national office, the party pursued measures which effectively equated Unionism with dynamic capitalist growth and the opening of economic opportunity for ordinary American farmers, workers and small manfacturers of modest wealth. This was a program to which Lincoln himself was ready to lend his weight: like other Republicans he believed that in the United States there was nothing to fix 'the free hired laborer . . . to that condition for life', that individual energy and industry in a fluid society gave realistic hope of self-advancement, and that there was a harmony of interests between labor, as the sole creator of wealth, and capital.[85]

The Republican economic program had a hard moral core. Its proponents, Lincoln intimated, would surely be less vulnerable than the champions of slavery when brought to account on the day of judgment. 'When brought to my final reckoning, may I have to answer for robbing no man of his goods; yet more tolerable even this, than for robbing one of himself, and all that was his.' There is little in Lincoln's recorded words to suggest that he believed in an afterlife, no matter how often he brooded about death, or how much he wanted to share the common belief in a reunion with loved ones beyond the grave. More powerful in Lincoln's thought than a celestial day of reckoning was the terrestrial judgment of history. As Robert V. Bruce has shrewdly argued, Lincoln found consolation in the idea that mortals would survive not in 'Heaven' but in 'memory'. His awareness of living during momentous times and his sense of moral duty to future generations – 'through time and in eternity' – acquired an extra edge after he had issued his preliminary emancipation order. 'Fellow-citizens, *we* cannot escape history', he wrote in December 1862. 'We of this Congress and this administration, will be remembered in spite of ourselves. . . . The fiery trial through which we pass, will light us down, in honor or dishonor, to the latest generation.'[86]

Lincoln learnt from his many religious visitors that his emancipationist reading of God's will, of Scripture and of historical duty had secured for him what he described as 'the effective and almost unanamous support' of 'the good christian people of the country'. It is hard to say precisely how valuable those religious voices were in stiffening Lincoln's intellectual resolve, but they clearly brought real comfort. During the dark days of 1862, when Noyes Miner told him that 'Christian people all over the country are praying for you as they never prayed for a mortal man before', Lincoln's reply evinced more than simple politeness: 'this is an encouraging thought to me. If I were not sustained by the prayers of God's people I could not endure this constant pressure. I should give up hoping for success.'[87]

Lincoln's resolving to make emancipation a non-negotiable war aim had implications for how he would approach southern reconstruction and the restoration of loyal governments. This was a sharply contested issue and one which he knew would exercise the Thirty-eighth Congress when it convened in December 1863, for by then Grant's relief of Chattanooga in October had been added to the military successes of the summer and had misleadingly opened up the prospect of the enemy's prompt collapse. Opposition Democrats included those for whom restoration and reconciliation demanded little more than a simple – but entirely unrealistic

– amnesty for all and a return to the pre-war Union, with slavery and the southern way of life intact. More significant were the conflicting pressures Lincoln faced from the ideological poles of his own party. Conservative Republicans wanted an end to slavery, but otherwise sought a generous political settlement for southern whites, especially former Whigs and small farmers; encouraged by Montgomery Blair, some countenanced deportation to resolve the volatile issue of post-war race relations. In contrast, an increasingly assertive group of radicals wanted to see a fundamental reordering of southern life before the rebels returned. Through secession and war, they argued, the Confederate states had constitutionally disintegrated. Congress, gatekeeper to the Union by virtue of its power over its own membership, had jurisdiction over the rebel South, and should ensure that emancipation was the stepping stone to equal civic and political rights for blacks. Some, including Sumner, even favored the landless enjoying a color-blind redistribution of rebel property.

Lincoln had from the outset addressed the issue of restoration. He offered no single blueprint, since that might become a straitjacket. The issues were too sensitive, the local experience too varied, for that. But he did develop a broad approach to reconstruction, shaped by his own temperamental preference and constitutional conviction, and by military and political need. The law and the Constitution would be his guide to action, not vindictiveness or hatred. The West Virginia experience showed that reaching out to, not repelling, the Confederacy's Unionist elements was the intelligent priority. These loyalists, Lincoln believed in the early stages of the conflict, constituted a huge southern reservoir of support waiting to be channeled. They should not be blamed for the actions of the misguided minority of individuals who had overturned republican government and declared independence. In legal fact there had been no secession: the states inhabited by the rebels remained under the jurisdiction of the federal authorities and Constitution. That document gave the president, as commander-in-chief, control of wartime reconstruction policy. He was obliged to nurture local initiatives toward restoring self-government. Bottom-up republicanism and self-reconstruction by local Unionists would secure an early end to the rebellion. A lasting peace would have to be built not through revolutionary shocks but by means of moderate, constitutionally-nourished, gradual change. In this way, Lincoln judged, he had the best hope of maintaining the Union political consensus essential to victory.

Translated into practical policy, Lincoln's approach meant giving authority to local military commanders who, as the Union armies advanced, would identify and sustain kernels of loyalty and prepare the ground for elections to restored governments. Early in 1862 Lincoln appointed 'military governors' for those parts of Arkansas, Louisiana, North Carolina and Tennessee then under federal control. In three cases the experiment yielded little to celebrate, but in Louisiana – where New Orleans fell to the Union in April – the regime of Ben Butler, as commander of the city, and George F. Shepley, as military governor, promised more. Lincoln thought the state might become a model for others, and partly because of this it attracted the nation's chief attention throughout wartime discussion of reconstruction.

The presence in New Orleans of an educated and propertied free black population alongside one of the most substantial white Unionist communities in the lower South seemed to offer a viable nucleus from which to build a loyal state government. However, Louisiana loyalists were divided along a conservative-radical faultline, defined by their contrasting intentions over slavery. Needing to hold together this loyalist coalition of proslavery planters and antislavery businessmen and workers, Lincoln was reluctant to see any local policy that would frighten off the conservatives, and even after issuing his preliminary emancipation order continued to offer 'peace again under the old terms under the constitution'.[88] This, however, would depend on their moving swiftly to holding elections in the Unionist enclave. A December vote in two congressional districts saw the election of two loyalist candidates, Benjamin F. Flanders and Michael Hahn: in the warm afterglow of the final Emancipation Proclamation, congressmen agreed to admit them, suppressing their concerns about Lincoln's conservatism and his forceful use of executive power. But radical doubts deepened when Nathaniel Banks, replacing Butler, established a harsh 'free-labor' regime to control the thousands of ex-slaves whose presence portended economic chaos, social confusion and a threat to military efficiency. Was this really the meaning of black freedom?

Lincoln let Banks's contractual labor system stand. But in the battle between Louisiana conservatives, who wanted to organize the state under the pre-war Constitution, and the free-state men, the president's instincts and private encouragement favored the progressives. He told Banks in August 1863 that he did not want 'to assume direction' of the state's affairs – local self-government was a better, perhaps the only proper, tool of liberation – but that he 'would be glad for her to make a new Constitution recognizing the emancipation proclamation, and adopting emancipation in those parts of the state to which the proclamation does not apply'. Intimating his preference for a gentle evolution out of slavery, he continued: 'And while she is at it, I think it would not be objectionable for her to adopt some practical system by which the two races could gradually live themselves out of their old relation to each other, and both come out better prepared for the new.' Lincoln urged Banks to 'confer with intelligent and trusty citizens of the state' and prepare the way for a state constitutional convention that would eliminate slavery.[89] Only in December did a dismayed Lincoln discover that Banks, preoccupied by military affairs in his vast Department of the Gulf, had still not acted.

By then Lincoln had himself given a lead, setting out clearly for the first time – in his annual message to Congress on 8 December – his own statement of policy on national reconstruction. It had been almost a year since his Emancipation Proclamation, and longer still since he had had to recognize that he had seriously overestimated Unionist strength, but he had not previously pushed the logic to the point of declaring a single, overarching, federally-sponsored scheme of reconstruction which explicitly demanded an end to slavery. The political and military arguments for caution had been real enough, but so too had Lincoln's constitutional scruples, especially over an 'absolutist' assault on slavery in the Louisiana enclave and other 'exempted localities' of the proclamation. The complex geometry of reconstruction strategy led Lincoln to describe it as 'the greatest question ever presented to practical statesmanship'. But by late 1863 he was ready to broadcast his solution, emboldened by Chattanooga and fall election results which gave the administration a new and unaccustomed confidence. Sensing that he needed to give an unequivocal lead ('a rallying point') to free-state forces in Louisiana and elsewhere, and fearing that a sudden Confederate collapse might result in a reunion without emancipation, Lincoln announced a scheme of oath-taking, pardon and government reorganization in the disloyal South. When as few as 10 percent of the eligible voters in 1860 had taken an oath of future loyalty and pledged to abide by his Emancipation Proclamation and congressional acts about slavery, they could set up a state government, which he would recognize.[90]

The plan proved a political masterstroke. Lincoln enjoyed the rare treat of being feted, at least in public, by both radicals and conservatives. The latter were pleased that he offered to recognize the pre-war boundaries and laws of the disloyal states, slavery excepted, that he acknowledged local control, and that he would tolerate a gradual adjustment to freedom, raising no objections if the new governments passed laws 'consistent, as a temporary arrangement' with the freedmen's 'present condition as a laboring, landless, and homeless class'. For their part, jubilant Republican radicals celebrated the president's commitment to permanent freedom, his promise to see no slaves freed by the proclamation returned to slavery, his resort to a strict loyalty oath, and his nod toward congressional authority over the admission of members returned by newly reorganized states. An initiative that won the approval not only of Chase, Chandler and Sumner, but also Blair and Reverdy Johnson was no mean feat. Both Noah Brooks and John Hay reeled in wonderment at the arrival of 'the political millennium'.[91]

Privately, in fact, the radicals harbored doubts about Lincoln's plan, worrying that the percentage threshold was too low. Their anxieties swelled into fully-fledged hostility as they watched Lincoln's leniency toward Banks's course in Louisiana. Having firmly told the commander that he was 'master' there, Lincoln felt he had to fall in with Banks's decision to hold elections under the pre-war Constitution, even though this was neither Lincoln's original preference nor the wish of the more radical free-state leaders. Fears that proslavery forces would secure control proved unfounded, but the convention that followed the victory of the more conservative free-state men produced a constitution too cautious for the radicals locally and in Washington. Critics attacked the reformers' failure to advance beyond the promise of immediate, uncompensated emancipation and give blacks the political protection of the vote. Lincoln, though, welcomed what he judged a huge step forward, one which gave the freedmen of Louisiana greater civil and educational advantages than the blacks of his own Illinois.

Narrower political concerns during a year of a presidential election sharpened the radicals' anxiety. Once reconstructed on the Lincoln plan, the reorganized states would be free to send delegates to the Republicans' nominating convention and be represented in the electoral college. This alarmed those in the party who wanted to ditch Lincoln, for the southern beneficiaries of the Ten Percent Plan would surely lend their support to its author's bid for renomination.

In February legislators began discussion of a more stringent scheme of reconstruction, one which, in its final form, would assert congressional control of the process; end slavery; put the Confederate states under temporary military rule; impose an iron-clad oath of loyalty; make readmission conditional on the allegiance of 50 percent of the voters of 1860; and exclude from government far more Confederate officials than did Lincoln's plan. Sponsored by Henry Winter Davis and Benjamin F. Wade, the bill won the overwhelming backing of congressional Republicans when it passed on 2 July. By then Lincoln had comfortably secured his renomination, but the bill's supporters included radicals who hoped that they might still, somehow, prevent his re-election. Neither did news from the front do anything to head off the challenge to the president's policy. In Virginia, Grant was on the move from early May, aiming finally to crush the Army of Northern Virginia, but during a month's heavy fighting at the Wilderness, Spotsylvania and Cold Harbor he bled Lee's forces at a huge cost to his own, losing 60,000 men. Meanwhile, Sherman's western army made only slow progress on its advance toward Atlanta.

Lincoln 'pocket-vetoed' the Wade–Davis bill by declining to sign it before Congress adjourned. He was not, he explained, prepared 'to be inflexibly committed to any single plan of restoration' or to see 'set aside and held for nought' the free-state governments already installed in Arkansas and Louisiana, 'thereby repelling and discouraging the loyal citizens' who had set them up. He doubted the 'constitutional competency' of Congress to abolish slavery in a state. Still, he added mischievously, he was 'fully satisfied with the system for restoration contained in the Bill, as one very proper plan for the loyal people of any State choosing to adopt it'. None, of course, was in the least likely to do so. What Lincoln did not say, but understood well enough, was that the Wade–Davis plan had set an impossibly high threshold in order to prevent restoration before the war's end; his own approach, instead, was to offer generous terms as a bait to waverers to give up the rebellion.

Angered by Lincoln's veto and lacking the sense of humor to cope with his teasing, Wade and Davis responded with an ill-judged and crude 'manifesto'. Their fear that Lincoln's plan would make it far too easy for unrepentant whites to resume their control over the South through mere 'shadows of governments' prompted a furious attack on the president as a dictator and a usurper of legislative power. Their bitterness was a mark of the philosophical as well as the political tension between the most convinced radicals and the president. As well as wanting an immediate end to slavery, many of Lincoln's critics urged full political rights for African Americans (though the Wade–Davis bill had made no mention of these). Universal black manhood suffrage, as well as being morally right, would guarantee southern loyalty and a permanent post-war settlement. Lincoln, as ever, favored evolution over abrupt upheaval and took an incrementalist, inclusive approach to social change.

But Lincoln's veto did not imply any slipping of the policy ratchet, or backsliding from existing commitments. Rather, all the signs are that he was moving to more advanced ground during 1864 and 1865. Throughout the war he had made clear that his intended post-war order was a restored Union dedicated to the principles of the Declaration of Independence. He had made his first public statement of the purposes of war on the eighty-fifth anniversary of the nation's founding text, in July 1861. The 'leading object' of democratic government was 'to elevate the condition of men – to lift artificial weights from all shoulders – to clear the paths of laudable pursuit for all – to afford all, an unfettered start, and a fair chance, in the race of life'. As time passed, it became clear that the post-war order would also be a post-emancipation order, one in which blacks would be entitled to the same opportunities as whites. Lincoln had never doubted that the Declaration embraced African Americans. Having 'sloughed off' the idea of colonization during the middle months of the war, he gave growing attention to the integration of blacks as equals into the reconstructed nation.[92]

Essential to their post-war opportunity, Lincoln recognized, was access to education. Freedmen had a duty to use the 'great boon' of emancipation to improve themselves, 'both morally and intellectually', but he knew, too, that without black public schools there could be no easy or swift self-improvement. In 1862 he had been irked when his military governor in North Carolina, Edward Stanly, had engineered the closure of black schools within Union lines. Subsequently he made clear, first in Louisiana and then throughout the South, that education for freedmen must be a corollary of emancipation and reconstruction.[93]

Lincoln also moved, however cautiously, toward the radicals' terrain of suffrage and economic assistance for African Americans. The attorney-general's 1862 judgment on black citizenship, sweeping away the negative ruling of the Taney court, left no legal barrier to black voting. Gradually Lincoln, who developed a deep respect for the gallantry and ability of the uniformed blacks, came to see the benefits of involving the freedmen in the guardianship of the post-war South. In March 1864 he privately urged Michael Hahn, recently elected as Louisiana's first free-state governor, to promote a new constitution that would confer voting rights on 'some of the colored people', both 'the very intelligent, and especially those who have fought gallantly in our ranks'. They would, he judged, 'probably help, in some trying time to come, to keep the jewel of liberty within the family of freedom'. However, alert to northern popular racism, to hostility amongst the conservatives of the Union coalition, and to the ambiguity of the Constitution, Lincoln held back from what the radicals wanted, namely the federal imposition of black suffrage on the South as a non-negotiable condition of reconstruction. (Hahn made Lincoln's preference known to Louisiana's constitution-makers, but as a mere wish it lacked political force, and the convention simply left open a possibility of future legislative action.) When in the winter of 1864–65 James Ashley's Reconstruction bill sought to provide for black suffrage and jury service, the president jibbed at 'a feature that might be objectionable to some' and 'rebound like a boomerang not only on the Republican party, but upon the freedman himself and our common country'. Still, as Lincoln looked ahead, in what turned out to be the last public address of his life, he made clear that he wanted to see at least some blacks receiving the political rights enjoyed by whites. And these included thousands who had recently been no more than illiterate field-hands.[94]

As the war drew to a close, Lincoln signed a bill, first introduced by Sumner, setting up within the War Department a Bureau of Freedmen's Affairs. In doing so he acknowledged that the government had at least some responsibility for the material needs of millions of ex-slaves. His ideas about the post-war relationship between freed labor and the white employing class remained inchoate and undogmatic. There was no map to mark out the African American's route from servility to confident negotiation in the labor and property markets. Probably aware of transitional arrangements in the British West Indies, Lincoln thought seriously about some kind of short-term apprenticeship system based around money wages and continuing planter control. However, Banks's highly-regulated regime in Louisiana – where loyal planters' control over contracted black laborers looked like slavery under another name – did nothing to endear the concept of apprenticeship to the radicals, who instead sought large-scale confiscation of rebels' lands and their redistribution to the freedmen. Permanent confiscation Lincoln – lawyer and constitutionalist – could not stomach, but he found acceptable a revised Freedmen's Bureau bill which established a more limited program of seizure. The Bureau would assign and rent abandoned lands to the freedmen for a period of three years, after which the occupants might buy the title. Although the radicals had had to narrow their vision, the outcome still pleased them and for all his reservations Lincoln was prepared to put his signature to a substantial extension of federal power to meet the pressing human needs of a collapsing Confederacy.

Lincoln's gradualism served a progressive purpose. His approach to social improvement was that of a political realist who knew that for every radical action there was the real threat of a conservative counter-reaction and that thoroughgoing changes could prove self-defeating. Lincoln formulated both his emancipation and his reconstruction policies convinced not only that they were true to the Founders' values, but that they offered the best means of making progress and maintaining the momentum of change. He remained firmly attached to the new government in Louisiana as a sure guarantor of 'perpetual freedom' and as the most available means of bringing the state 'into proper practical relations with the Union'. Washington's support would 'ripen it to a complete success', inspiring both the white loyalists and the blacks. 'Grant that [the colored man] desires the elective franchise, will he not attain it sooner by saving the already advanced steps toward it, than by running backward over them? Concede that the new government of Louisiana is only to what it should be as the egg is to the fowl, we shall sooner have the fowl by hatching the egg than by smashing it?'[95]

Radicals, however, white and black, deplored what they saw as Lincoln's misreading of events. Wittingly or not, he was, they believed, trading black freedom for magnanimity toward rebels. He had entrusted the restored governments in Louisiana and Arkansas to 'wolves in sheep's clothing', lamented the *New Orleans Tribune*. 'The old spirit of slaveocracy is still alive.' But in fact, with the end of the war, Lincoln's policy was in flux. Significantly, and to the disappointment of a crowd wanting a rousing speech of triumph, his first address after the Confederate surrender at Appomattox, dealt earnestly and almost exclusively with the issue of restoration. He concluded this last address of his life with an emphatic statement that what was right for Louisiana was not necessarily the best course for all. While there were inflexible *principles* at stake in the general work of restoration, the peculiarities of each southern state meant that an 'exclusive, and inflexible plan' of reconstruction would not help. He was, he said (in a passage even more tantalizing for the historian than for those who listened), considering 'some new announcement to the people of the South' and he would not 'fail to act, when satisfied that action will be proper'. Discussion in cabinet three days later suggested that what Lincoln intended in the short term was the imposition of military control over states still without loyal governments, to be followed by political reorganization under southern Unionists. Far less certain is how his policy would have evolved over time.[96]

It does not help simply to ask what Lincoln would have done in his successor's shoes. The conditions under which Andrew Johnson pursued his reconstruction policy were markedly different from those which the assassinated president would have faced. Booth's bullet changed the political weather, releasing a spirit of vengeance against the rebel South and prompting broad-based demands for a more stringent policy. Moreover, Johnson catalyzed a new political chemistry, for as an ex-Democrat, and lacking the standing of a successful war leader, he had an entirely different relationship with southern Unionism, grass-roots sentiment in the North and congressional Republicans.

Still, it is possible to reach a few plausible conclusions on what Lincoln might have done had he lived. Events would have tested his wartime preference for self-reconstruction over imposition from Washington, and for leaving it to the reorganized governments themselves to resolve the issue of black rights. William C. Harris rightly argues that Lincoln would have exercised greater influence than Johnson over the white Unionist leadership; intervened to block the draconian and discriminatory Black Codes; rationed presidential pardons; stopped the quick return to political power of high-ranking Confederates; and pressed hard to achieve at least partial black suffrage.[97] Lincoln was too wise and too experienced to have isolated himself – as Johnson did – from the heartland of his party. And, as resurgent rebels resorted to a strategy of terror, he might even have discovered an appetite for the protective use of federal power. One thing is certain: on the issue of race, the Lincoln of 1865 had advanced well beyond his ideas of 1858. In Washington, he became the first leader to welcome blacks into the White House, to invite them to formal receptions and to incorporate them in an inaugural procession. He was, according to Frederick Douglass, 'emphatically the black mans President'.[98] If Lincoln could so clearly broaden his mind during his first term of office, then further growth would surely have occurred during his second.

Lincoln's tenderness toward the southerners led many to fear that the Union, on the verge of winning the war, would contrive to lose the peace. In fact, there was no danger that the president would abandon his stated terms of peace – the ending of all hostilities, reunion and emancipation – or be outmaneuvered by Davis into conceding an armistice. When Congress learnt the detail of his secret meeting with Confederate peace commissioners on a steamer at Hampton Roads on 3 February 1865, the record not only allayed fears of a Union sell-out but won Lincoln almost universal plaudits for his political skill. But one measure of his desire for reconciliation with magnanimity was his suggestion to the commissioners that Congress find $400 million to compensate slaveholders, in return for voluntary emancipation and immediate reunion. It was an extraordinary initiative, driven in part by the hope that it would inhibit post-war guerrilla resistance and by the calculation that it would cost the Union less than if the war dribbled on into the summer months. A stunned cabinet, understandably thinking that Lincoln's political touch had deserted him and fearing 'distrust and adverse feeling', unanimously opposed the idea, which would never have won the approval of Congress.[99] Lincoln let the plan die.

Lincoln, however, confirmed his desire for a magnanimous post-war reconciliation in the most remarkable speech of his life, on 4 March, at the ceremony for his second inauguration. The rush of events suggested that the Confederacy was speedily crumbling. A crowd of over 30,000 expected the language of triumph, or at least a tone of celebration. Instead, Lincoln delivered a short, 700-word address which avoided blame, spoke inclusively, emphasized the shared experience of the two parties to the conflict and set out a case for a lack of vengeance toward the South. His peroration stipulated the cast of mind with which the victors should approach reunion: 'With malice toward none; with charity for all; with firmness in the right, as God gives us to see the right, let us strive on to finish the work we are in; to bind up the nation's wounds; to care for him who shall have borne the battle, and for his widow, and his orphan – to do all which may achieve and cherish a just, and a lasting peace, among ourselves, and with all nations.'[100]

These scriptural cadences provided a fitting climax to a speech in which Lincoln sought to find political guidance through religious inquiry, by exploring the theological meaning of the events over which he had presided for four years. Religious themes had been largely absent, or present in only a minor key in his earlier addresses, but they so dominated the second inaugural speech that it assumed the character of a sermon. The address was brief, but rich in meaning, and pulled together as a prescription for action thoughts on God's mystery and purposes that he had developed before – in his private memorandum after Second Bull Run, in his letters to Mrs Gurney and Albert Hodges, and in his remarks to visiting evangelicals.

'All knew', Lincoln said, that the South's 'peculiar and powerful interest' in slaves was 'somehow, the cause of the war'. His sympathy for the moral predicament of the South had never blinded him to the wrongness of slavery or allowed him to feel any warmth toward those – especially religious men – who contrived an intellectual defense of it. But whatever his distaste for Confederate theology ('not the sort of religion upon which people can get to heaven' was how he had recently classified it), he cautioned against the sin of self-righteousness: 'let us judge not that we be not judged.'[101] Adopting the same reasoning that had informed his private meditation of September 1862, Lincoln moved to the same conclusion. The Union's victory, when it came, would have been secured at such cost that there was only one logical explanation: 'The Almighty has His own purposes.' Working through human history, God had delivered 'this terrible war' as His punishment to both North and South for their implication in the sin of slavery. 'Woe unto the world because of offences!'[102] (Here, by invoking the sins and responsibilities of communities and nations, Lincoln exposed his intellectual debt to the Puritan-Calvinist tradition of citizenship.) 'Fondly do we hope – fervently do we pray – that this mighty scourge of war may speedily pass away', but if God – omnipotent, inscrutable and mysterious – 'wills that it continue, until all the wealth piled by the bond-man's two hundred and fifty years of unrequited toil shall be sunk, and until every drop of blood drawn with the lash, shall be paid by another drawn with the sword, as was said three thousand years ago, so still it must be said "the judgments of the Lord, are true and righteous altogether".'[103]

Lincoln took much satisfaction in this speech. He told Thurlow Weed, that he expected it 'to wear as well as – perhaps better than – anything I have produced'. But he knew that its message was disquieting. The idea that the war was punishment for northern as well as southern sins affronted many. 'Men are not flattered by being shown that there is a difference of purpose between the Almighty and them. To deny it, however, in this case, is to deny that there is a God governing the world.' This was a truth especially humbling to himself. And humility would be his watchword as he shaped the administration's post-war purposes. During his pursuit of power he had told Republicans 'to do our duty *as we understand it*'; now, after four grueling years in office, he spoke of working 'with firmness in the right, *as God gives us to see the right*'.[104]

The abrasions of war had cumulatively wrought profound changes in Lincoln's thought and political agenda. By stages the cautious Kentucky Whig moved into the orbit of Yankee Protestant Republicanism, ready to give more sympathetic consideration – if not complete approval – to the radicals' program. He advanced toward emancipation, and a broadening of black civil and political rights, with intellectual and not merely political conviction. Religion became more important to him. His God acquired a more Calvinist, conventionally Protestant, appearance. At the same time, however, he kept his humility and his temperamental distrust of the absolutism, the pretensions to superior sanctity, and Pharisaism of those religionists who pressed him toward more radical action against the South.

Yet, ironically, the certainty of moral superiority and the tendency toward self-righteousness that Lincoln saw, and distrusted, within mainstream northern Protestantism would prove one of his most valuable instruments of power. The patriotic energy which came from Unionists' conviction that their cause was right, just, blessed and godly was essential to northern victory. Lincoln recognized that reality. As the next chapter will demonstrate, Lincoln knew that nourishing and mobilizing patriotic sentiment – on both the home and military fronts – was fundamental to his power and to Confederate defeat.

Notes

In the notes for this chapter all newspaper and manuscript citations are for 1862, unless otherwise stated.

1 *CW*, 7:282.

2 Lerone Bennett, Jr, *Forced into Glory: Abraham Lincoln's White Dream* (Chicago, IL: Johnson Publishing Company, 2000).

3 *CW*, 7:282. For Lincoln's subordination and neglect of his potentially progressive and humane Indian policy, see David A. Nichols, 'Lincoln and the Indians', in Gabor S. Boritt, ed., *The Historian's Lincoln: Pseudohistory, Psychohistory, and History* (Urbana, IL: University of Illinois Press, 1988), 149–69.

4 *DJH*, 113.

5 *DJH*, 135.

6 R.W. Thompson to AL, 22 Nov., ALP; A.G. Curtin to AL, 3 March, ALP.

7 William B. Hesseltine, *Lincoln and the War Governors* (New York: Alfred A. Knopf, 1955), 178.

8 F.B. Carpenter, *The Inner Life of Abraham Lincoln: Six Months at the White House* (Lincoln, NB: University of Nebraska Press, 1995; originally published New York, 1866), 230–1; Robert S. Harper, *Lincoln and the Press* (New York: McGraw-Hill, 1951), 96–7, 184–7, 308; *DJH*, 41; *Lincoln's Journalist*, 160, 177.

9 *Lincoln Observed*, 1–12.

10 Harold Holzer, comp. and ed., *Dear Mr. Lincoln: Letters to the President* (Reading, MA: Addison-Wesley Publishing Company, 1993), 5–35; *DJH*, 19, 39; William O. Stoddard, *Inside the White House in War Times: Memoirs and Reports of Lincoln's Secretary*, ed. Michael Burlingame (Lincoln, NB: University of Nebraska Press, 2000), xi, 13–17.

11 Carpenter, *Inner Life*, 245; Mark E. Neely, Jr, *The Abraham Lincoln Encyclopedia* (New York: McGraw-Hill, 1982), 220.

12 Carpenter, *Inner Life*, 95–6, 281; *Independent*, 20 Oct. 1864; Holzer, *Dear Mr. Lincoln*, 12; *Lincoln Observed*, 99–103, 254; *Lincoln's Journalist*, 158, 160.

13 *CW*, 4:439–40.

14 S. Camp to AL, 17 Sept. 1861, A. Harris to AL, 17 Sept. 1861, J.G. Roberts to AL, 17 Sept. 1861, H.C. Garst to AL, 18 Sept. 1861, S.W. Coggeshall to AL, 18 Sept. 1861; J.L. Williams to AL, 19 Sept. 1861, W. McCaully to AL, 20 Sept. 1861, A. Williams to AL, 11 Oct. 1861, ALP.

15 A. Peck to AL, 19 Sept. 1861, E. Wright to AL, 20 Sept. 1861, T.H. Little to AL, 17 Sept. 1861, ALP; *Lincoln's Journalist*, 159–60, 166, 189; *CW*, 5:26.

16 *CW*, 5:35–53.

17 Stephen W. Sears, ed., *The Civil War Papers of George B. McClellan: Selected Correspondence 1860–1865* (New York: Ticknor & Fields, 1989), 128; Hans L. Trefousse, *The Radical Republicans: Lincoln's Vanguard for Racial Justice* (New York: Alfred A. Knopf, 1969), 184.

18 *HI*, 684–5; *RWAL*, 430.

19 *CW*, 5:30–1, 144–6; N&H, 5:205–8.

20 *CW*, 5:144–6.

21 N&H, 5:211–14.

22 *CW*, 5:222–3.

23 N&H, 6:106–7. Cf. Cleveland Congregational Conference to AL, 18 April; New York City 16th Ward Republican Association, 6 May; H.H. Van Dyck to William H. Seward, 9 May, ALP; Allan Nevins, *The War for the Union*: vol. 2: *War Becomes Revolution* (New York: Charles Scribner's Sons, 1960), 32.

24 Nevins, *War for the Union*, 2:117; R. Johnson to AL, 16 May, P. Sturtevant to AL, 16 May, H. Ketcham to AL, 16 May, S.P. Chase to AL, 16 May, C. Schurz to AL, 16 May, ALP.

25 A.T. Stewart to AL, 21 May, A. Johnson to AL, 2 May, J.M. Wightman to AL, 23 May, C. Schurz to AL, 19 May, ALP; CW, 5:222–3.

26 Mark E. Neely, Jr, *The Fate of Liberty: Abraham Lincoln and Civil Liberties* (New York: Oxford University Press, 1991), 218–21; Sears, ed., *Papers of McClellan*, 344–5.

27 Nevins, *War for the Union*, 2:146–7; Border-state congressmen to AL, 15 July, E.M. Norton to AL, 14 July, ALP.

28 T. Ewing to AL, 2 June, A.E. Carroll to AL, 14 July, ALP; *CW*, 5:328–31.

29 J.H. Bayne to AL, 3 July, ALP.

30 *CW*, 5:318.

31 *Diary of Gideon Welles: Secretary of the Navy under Lincoln and Johnson*, 3 vols (Boston, MA: Houghton Mifflin Company, 1911), 1:70–1.

32 *CW*, 5:336–7.

33 John Niven, ed., *The Salmon P. Chase Papers*: vol 1: *Journals, 1829–1872* (Kent, OH: Kent State University Press, 1993), 343; N&H, 6:126–30; Carpenter, *Inner Life*, 21–2.

34 *DJH*, 38–9.

35 Donald, 373–4; Bennett, *Forced into Glory*, 469–503; Nicholas Parrillo, 'Lincoln's Calvinist Transformation: Emancipation and War', *Civil War History*, 46 (Sept. 2000), 242–3.

36 *CW*, 5:388–9.

37 S.H. Gay to AL, Aug. [n.d.], T. Weed to W.H. Seward, 23 Aug., O.H. Browning to AL, 17 Sept., ALP.

38 *CW*, 6:419–25.

39 J.W. White et al. to AL, 24 July, B. Bannan to AL, 24 July, T.A. Marshall to AL, 27 July, H.G. Blake to AL, 28 July, N.S. Berry et al. to AL, 30 July, J.R. Doolittle to AL, 4 Aug., Z. Chandler to AL, 8 Aug., Westchester Co, NY, War Meeting to AL, 12 Sept., S.L. Casey to AL, 4 Aug., ALP.

40 Boston Park Street Church to AL, 27 Aug.; B.H. West to AL, 27 Aug.; Milwaukee Wisconsin Congregational Church to AL, 5 Sept.; W.D. Love to AL, 5 Sept.; Miami Conference of Wesleyan Methodist Connection to AL, 6 Sept.; Cincinnati Conference of the Methodist Episcopal Church [MEC] to AL, 8 Sept.; General Conference of the

Congregational Churches of Massachusetts to AL, 12 Sept.; Indiana Conference of the Wesleyan Methodists to AL, 12 Sept.; The Congregation of Milburn, Lake County, Illinois to AL, 14 Sept.; Lamoille (Illinois) Citizens to AL, 14 Sept.; North Illinois Annual Conference of the Methodist Protestant Church to AL, 14 Sept.; North Ohio Annual Conference of the MEC to AL, 15 Sept.; W.C. McCarthy to AL, 16 Sept.; West Wisconsin Annual Conference of the MEC to AL, 18 Sept.; Genessee, NY, Presbyterian Synod to AL, 18 Sept.; R.D. Owen to AL, 17 Sept., ALP.

41 *Diary of Gideon Welles*, 1:143.

42 *Diary of Gideon Welles*, 1:142–5; Niven, ed., *Chase Papers*, 393–6.

43 *CW*, 6:28–30.

44 N&H, 6:357–66; *CW*, 5:370–5; Benjamin F. Quarles, *Lincoln and the Negro* (New York: Oxford University Press, 1962), 108–23.

45 W.B. Lowry, H. Catlin, and J.F. Downing to AL, 23 Sept., ALP. Also J.W. Stone to AL, 23 Sept., T. Tilton to AL, 24 Sept., J.M. McKim to AL, 27 Sept., G. Smith to AL, 9 Oct., F.A. Hoffman to AL, 25 Sept., I. Harris to AL, 2 Oct., J.K. Porter to AL, 27 Oct. [enclosing *Speech of John K. Porter at the Union Ratification Meeting at Glens Falls, Oct. 21* (Albany, NY, 1862), 11], ALP.

46 *RWAL*, 220.

47 N&H, 6:179–81; G.B. McClellan to AL, 7 Oct., W.D. Kelley to AL, 23 July, R. Smith to R. Yates, 13 Oct., D. Davis to AL, 14 Oct., J.W. Forney to AL, 26 Sept., ALP; *CW*, 5:436–7.

48 C. Sumner to AL, 8 Nov., J.K. Dubois to AL, 3 Dec., ALP.

49 R.P.L. Baber to AL, 22 Nov., I.N. Morris to AL, 20 Nov., C. Sumner to AL, 8 Nov., C. Schurz to AL, 8 Nov., 20 Nov., S.W. Oakey to AL, 5 Nov., W.H. West to AL, 20 Oct., M. Delahay to AL, 6 Nov., ALP; *CW*, 5:493–5; *Lincoln Observed*, 14.

50 D.S. Dickinson to AL, 9 Nov., ALP.

51 *CW*, 4:518–37.

52 Michael Vorenberg, *Final Freedom: The Civil War, the Abolition of Slavery, and the Thirteenth Amendment* (Cambridge: Cambridge University Press, 2001), 31.

53 *CW*, 5:462–3; Donald, 397.

54 *CW*, 5:534–7.

55 *CW*, 5:537.

56 S.P. Chase to AL, 28 Nov., ALP.

57 F.P. Blair, Sr, to AL, 18 Dec., T.T. Davies to AL, 20 Dec., ALP; *DJH*, 104; *RWAL*, 199–200, 496.

58 W.H. Gaines and H.S. Rowland to AL, 21 Dec., R.P.L. Baber to AL, 22 Nov., Great Falls, NH, citizens to AL, Dec., Boston Residents to AL, 5 Dec., F. Wood to AL, 8, 17 Dec., J. Barnaby et al. to AL, 8 Dec., New Bedford Mass Citizens to AL, 12 Dec., Rockland, ME, Citizens to AL, 15 Dec., T.D. Eliot to AL, 17 Dec., G.W. Cochrane and J.M. Forbes to AL, 24 Dec., J.G. Whittier to AL, 24 Dec., 1860 Electors to AL, 24 Dec., Prairie Grove, IA, Society of Friends to AL, 27 Dec., S. Cobb to AL, 27 Dec., ALP.

59 *CW*, 5:338, 431, 6:28–30; L. Tilman to AL, 8 Apr., C. Schurz to AL, 19 May, J. Leavitt et al., Petition to AL, Aug., O. Browning to AL, 11 Aug., T.A. Jenckes to AL, 11 Sept., W. Sprague to AL, 26 Sept., ALP; Quarles, *Lincoln and the Negro*, 153–4.

60 Milwaukee Wisconsin Spring Street Congregational Church, 5 Sept., ALP.

61 *CW*, 6:30.

62 J. Mitchell to AL, 1 July, ALP.

63 Quarles, *Lincoln and the Negro*, 134; *CW*, 5:503.

64 S.W. Oakey to AL, 5 Nov., ALP; Michael Burlingame, *The Inner World of Abraham Lincoln* (Urbana, IL: University of Illinois Press, 1994), 268–355; Jean H. Baker, 'Mary and Abraham: A Marriage', in Gabor S. Boritt, ed., *The Lincoln Enigma: The Changing Faces of an American Icon* (New York: Oxford University Press, 2001), 36–55; *DJH*, 194, 345–6; *Lincoln Observed*, 13–14, 43, 226, 239, 261.

65 *HI*, 156, 360, 497, 521; Nicolay, *Oral History*, 5.

66 *HI*, 156, 167, 360; *Lincoln Observed*, 209–11; Nicolay, *Oral History*, 5; *CW*, 6:535.

67 Congregational Church, General Association of Illinois to AL, 1 Aug. 1861, Linn County, Oregon, Presbyterians, 18 Sept. 1861, Hudson River New York Baptist Association to AL, 18 June 1861, J. Hesser to AL, 15 April 1861, O. Browning to AL, 18 April, 30 Sept., 8 Nov. 1861, J.F. Doolittle to AL, 18 April 1861; N&H, 5:137–8.

68 E. Nason to AL, 16 April 1861, J.L. Scripps to AL, 23 Sept. 1861, A. Church to AL, 9 June 1862, E.G. Cook to AL, 21 Sept. 1862, ALP.

69 S. Jocelyn to AL, 26 Sept. 1861, ALP.

70 Mark A. Noll, 'Both Pray to the Same God': The Singularity of Lincoln's Faith in the Era of the Civil War', *Journal of the Abraham Lincoln Association*, 18 no. 1 (Winter 1997), 11–12; Allen C. Guelzo, *Abraham Lincoln: Redeemer President* (Grand Rapids, MI: William B. Eerdmans Publishing Co., 1999), 319–21; Parrillo, 'Lincoln's Calvinist Transformation', 237–40.

71 *CW*, 4:482–3, 6:244–5; Nicolay, *Oral History*, 5.

72 *CW*, 5:278–9, 403–4.

73 Noyes W. Miner, 'Personal Recollection of Abraham Lincoln', 46–8, Illinois State Historical Society; *CW*, 5:146, 279, 419–20, 478; Niven, ed., *Chase Papers*, 1:394.

74 *Diary of Gideon Welles*, 1:143; *HI*, 167–8.

75 *CW*, 5:292, 423–4, 438–9.

76 *CW*, 6:358, 365, 409, 440.

77 *CW*, 7:51, 8:152.

78 *CW*, 7:451, 8:254–5.

79 *CW*, 6:56, 149–50, 154, 158, 239, 242–3, 342, 374.

80 *CW*, 6:374, 409, 7:51, 499–501, 506–8, 8:1–2.

81 *CW*, 6:28, 7:251; Quarles, *Lincoln and the Negro*, 219.

82 *The Diary of Orville H. Browning*, ed. Theodore Calvin Pease and James G. Randall, 2 vols (Springfield, IL: Illinois State Historical Library, 1925), 1:600; *CW*, 7:282, 535–6.

83 *CW*, 7:281 (emphases added).

84 *CW*, 7:368.

85 *CW*, 5:52–3; Heather Cox Richardson, *Greatest Nation of the Earth: Republican Economic Policies during the Civil War* (Cambridge, MA: Harvard University Press, 1997).

86 *CW*, 5:535, 537, 7:368; Robert V. Bruce, 'The Riddle of Death', in Boritt, ed., *The Lincoln Enigma*, 130–45.

87 *CW*, 6:244–45, 7:368, 535; Miner, 'Recollections', 45–6.

88 *CW*, 5:462.

89 *CW*, 6:364–5.

90 *CW*, 6:428–9, 7:50–6; *DJH*, 69.

91 *CW*, 7:55; *DJH*, 121–2; *Lincoln Observed*, 93–5.

92 *CW*, 4:426, 438; *DJH*, 217.

93 *Lincoln Observed*, 142; *CW*, 6:364–5, 7:55.

94 *CW*, 7:243; *DJH*, 253; *RWAL*, 291.

95 *CW*, 8:403–4.

96 William C. Harris, *With Charity for All: Lincoln and the Restoration of the Union* (Lexington, KY: University Press of Kentucky, 1997), 266; *CW*, 8:404–5.

97 Harris, *With Charity for All*, 265–75.

98 William E. Gienapp, *Abraham Lincoln and Civil War America* (New York: Oxford University Press, 2002), 199.

99 *Lincoln Observed*, 159–63; *Diary of Gideon Welles*, 2:237.

100 *CW*, 8:333.

101 Matthew vii 1.

102 Matthew xviii 7.

103 *Lincoln Observed*, 222; *CW*, 8:332–3.

104 *CW*, 3:550, 8:333, 356 (emphases added).

Chapter Six

The Instruments of Power: Coercion and Voluntary Mobilization, 1861–65

To experience war is to experience force, and Americans of the Civil War era knew that raw truth better than any other generation in their nation's history. If the Confederacy was subject to the greater devastation of its physical landscape, and the greater proportionate loss of life, the Union suffered its own grievous human agonies. Victory, the Lincoln administration gradually learned, would come only as the North's superiority in manpower and material resources expressed itself in the force of bullet, bayonet and shell, and in the physical destruction of the enemy – and that would mean unprecedented bloodshed on both sides.

Military coercion of the Confederacy involved political coercion on the Union home front. Few aspects of Abraham Lincoln's presidency have attracted more discussion than his use of emergency executive powers. We have seen how, after Sumter, he called up the militia, proclaimed a blockade and ordered the use of treasury funds for war supplies, all before he called Congress into special session. He subsequently sanctioned arbitrary arrests, abolished slavery by presidential proclamation, endorsed conscription and began his own program of national reconstruction. Confederates and northern political foes cried 'tyrant'. The charge was tendentious, but the nation's unprecedented crisis certainly spurred Lincoln and the executive branch into forceful, interventionist and even coercive leadership. Earlier generations had expressed fears for the future of republicanism – whether from the executive 'usurpation' of Federalists in the 1790s or from the tyranny of 'King Andrew' Jackson four decades later – but no previous administration had deployed political and military power as energetically as did the Union government during the Civil War.[1]

For all that, what is remarkable about Lincoln's success in sustaining support for the Union's formidable four-year war effort is just how little it depended on executive coercion, repression and the long arm of the War Department. The main task facing the Union administration was not how to coerce or dragoon an unwilling population into an unwanted conflict; rather it was how best to encourage, nurture and sustain a potent Union patriotism. The North's superiority over the Confederacy in manpower and materiel gave hope of eventual victory, but this would only count if the enthusiasm for war immediately following the bombardment of Fort Sumter were consolidated into a longer-term appetite for the fight. Opposition Democrats and Confederate leaders alike expected Lincoln's administration to founder on the rocks of war-weariness. In fact, popular Unionism proved remarkably resilient: voluntary enlistments provided most of the Federal troops, and Lincoln secured a handsome re-election in 1864. But patriotism required nurturing from above. Without a clear articulation of the war's purpose by the Union leadership in general, and the president in particular, it is doubtful whether the people of the North would have retained their collective will to continue so grueling a conflict. Neither James Madison in the war of 1812 nor James K. Polk in the conflict with Mexico had been entirely successful in harmonizing national sentiment behind his leadership, and by definition these had been less divisive struggles than an internecine civil war. The burden of the argument here is that one of Lincoln's greatest achievements was his articulation of a rationale for the war and its sacrifices; that its formulation and reformulation were shaped in terms which, from his reading of public opinion, he knew would resonate with mainstream Unionists and cement the war coalition; that for its dissemination his administration imaginatively exploited a formidable network of governmental and voluntary agencies; and that his presidential leadership rested chiefly on persuasion, not coercion.

Lincoln possessed considerable personal authority, but his mobilization of popular support depended only to a modest degree on loyalty to him personally, and certainly not on charismatic power, strictly defined. 'Charismatic rule', if we follow the sociologist Max Weber's analysis, has to be contrasted with the traditional authority of hereditary rulers and with the impersonal bureaucracy of 'legal authority'. Charismatic power is founded on the perceived greatness and mission in the proclaimed leader during a time of crisis and instability. Lincoln's power, however, derived from holding an established political office and working within what Weber described as the 'legal-rational' framework of control. It did not depend primarily on his personal qualities.[2] Although the events of 1861–65 represented the greatest crisis and upheaval in the republic's history, Lincoln's power came, not from challenging or subverting the routine political system or the state itself, but from acting as the defender of the constitutional *status quo*, as Unionists defined it. He emphasized and represented continuity, not radical disjunction. Had McClellan, for example, been serious about supplanting Lincoln, and replaced an elected president with an unelected military ruler (in McClellan's case, one perceived as heroic, romantic, Napoleonic and driven by a sense of mission), then a charismatic form of domination might have developed – and would certainly have been necessary, had conventional constitutional forms been overturned. But what is significant is the *resilience* of the 'rational-legal' system of republican constitutionalism during the Civil War, not its fragility.

Still, in the unprecedented – and subsequently unequaled – crisis facing the Union, the personal qualities of the Union's political leadership mattered. In Lincoln's case, those qualities, as popularly perceived, were well designed to encourage and sustain a mass mobilization in support of the Union. That mobilization would have occurred regardless of who in particular was president, but we may reasonably doubt that under other incumbencies it would have been sustained so well and for so long. Perceived as the patriot, the president of honest endeavor and the plain man who knew his people, Lincoln came to enjoy a depth of popular support belied by the chronic sniping of the Washington political classes and the querulous editorial fraternity.

Coercion, repression and executive power

Lincoln was a naturally cautious, kindly and merciful man, but the remorseless logic of his single-minded pursuit of reunion led him to an ever more uncompromising use of the levers of military and political power. Both the Confederate enemy and the disloyal elements on the home front felt a tightening noose of coercion.

While it may be anachronistic to describe the conflict in its later stages as a 'total war', the North's military policy did evolve over the course of hostilities from conducting a war of conciliation toward white civilians, into a 'hard war' against them. At first, respect for the ordinary people of the South, and the idea that they were semi-detached from their political leaders, led the administration to think they could be won back to loyalty as the Union armies advanced. But the military experiences of spring and early summer in 1862 changed that. Lincoln came to see what others had been arguing for some time: that the war could no longer be fought, as he contemptuously put it, 'with elderstalk squirts charged with rosewater'. He was probably behind the War Department's executive order of 22 July empowering commanders to seize and use civilian southerners' property for military purposes.[3] Adopting an emancipation policy marked the end of conciliation, of course, but it did not lead to an immediate assault on the South's people and economy. Only in the spring of 1863, in the western theater, were military resources seriously deployed to this end, and not until the following year did the 'hard war' concept take effect in the East. Industrial capacity and railroads were destroyed, crops seized, buildings burnt, homes plundered, animals killed and eaten, and slaves freed. Confederate loyalists, and especially slaveowners, were the intended chief targets, but all southern civilians, including slaves, felt the threat of physical violence and were liable to intimidation and humiliation. In the winter of 1864–65, William Tecumseh Sherman's notorious marches of destruction from smoldering Atlanta to the sea, and on into the Carolinas, provided the climax of this combined assault on the South's psyche, material resources, and will to resist.

A corresponding evolution in military strategy accompanied this development of a hard war policy. Here, too, Lincoln played an important role, in this case actually forcing the pace of change. As a commander-in-chief with little military experience, but one who gave hours to hard strategic thought, Lincoln has subsequently won high marks from historians. Operating from first principles, rather than the textbooks of the revered Baron Jomini and other military interpreters of Napoleonic warfare, he came to see much earlier than his commanders the best means of exploiting the Union's advantage in numbers. While McClellan planned a Jominian concentration of massive force against Richmond, Lincoln was telling his western commanders that his 'general idea' was that – since 'we have the *greater* numbers, and the enemy has the *greater* facility of concentrating forces upon points of collision' – the best way to exploit the Union's superiority was by menacing the enemy 'with superior forces at *different* points, at the *same* time'. To this strategic insight he added another: that the tracking and destroying of Confederate armies, not places, was the key to victory. 'I think *Lee's* Army, and not *Richmond*, is your true objective point', he told Joseph Hooker in the summer of 1863. 'Fight him when oppertunity offers.' He wept bitterly when Meade chose not to pursue and crush Lee's retreating forces after Gettysburg.[4]

Behind Lincoln's military aggression, stood a cold statistical ruthlessness. After the grievous defeat at Fredericksburg, where the Union lost three men for every two Confederates, Lincoln remarked 'that if the same battle were to be fought over again, every day, through a week of days, with the same relative results, the army under Lee would be wiped out to its last man, the Army of the Potomac would still be a mighty host, [and] the war would be over'. As the war entered its final phase, in the winter of 1864–65, he drew public attention to the fact that an increase in population meant that, despite the melancholy multiplying of Union graves, 'we have *more* men *now* than we had when the war *began*'.[5]

At the time of Fredericksburg, Lincoln had failed to identify any commander ready to confront what his secretary William O. Stoddard called this 'awful arithmetic', but within fifteen months he had at last found one, promoted him to the revived rank of lieutenant general, and made him his general-in-chief. In Ulysses S. Grant Lincoln had a commander whose aggressive strategy and overall plan bore striking parallels to his own. Grant understood the need to synchronize the activity of the Union forces in the eastern and western theaters; to put the destruction of the enemy's armies before occupying strategic positions; to advance across the whole front; and to turn those troops passively occupying captured territory into active raiders. He discussed his thinking with Lincoln, explaining that 'it was his intention to make all the line useful – those not fighting could help the fighting'. According to Hay, the president 'recognized with especial pleasure' his own ideas, remarking, 'Those not skinning can hold a leg.'[6]

One further element completed Grant's grand design for 1864: an assault not just on southern armies but on all of the Confederacy's war resources. Military defeat alone was inadequate. To destroy armies you had to deny them food, ammunition and other supplies. Lincoln made no protest against this determined embrace of hard war policy, though it would hand a sharp weapon to political opponents and alienate some of the administration's conservative supporters. But the policy followed logically from emancipation, which made conciliation and compromise with the armed South an impossibility. Neither he nor his commanders intended all-out savagery or wanton excess. Rather they saw a controlled and morally justified means of bringing the war to a close. When Sherman described his marches as 'not . . . war but rather statesmanship' he intended no irony or black humor.[7] And with this perception of hard war as fundamentally political in purpose Lincoln surely agreed.

The Union army's coercive role was by no means restricted to the Confederate South. Maryland and other contested border areas were transformed into armed camps, while the 'Copperhead' strongholds in the Midwest and Middle Atlantic states felt the firm hand of Union commanders empowered to make what dissenters castigated as 'arbitrary arrests'. Lincoln's sequence of *ad hoc* orders suspending the privilege of the writ of habeas corpus opened the way for a military assault on civil liberties. Early on, as we have seen, he simply suspended the writ along the Washington–Philadelphia line, later extended to New York City and points north. This allowed the military authorities to arrest obstructive and disloyal civilians without having to specify charges. Far more sweeping were Stanton's orders of 8 August 1862, authorized by the president and designed to enforce America's first ever national military draft, the Militia Act of 17 July. These orders suspended the writ across the whole country when dealing with those who discouraged enlistments, evaded and impeded the draft, or were 'in any way giving aid and comfort to the enemy, or [engaged] in any other disloyal practice against the United States'. Military and civilian officers were empowered to arrest and imprison offenders, subjecting them to martial law. Lincoln's proclamation of 24 September in effect provided a formal, if anticlimactic, presidential endorsement of the War Department's orders. One year later, in September 1863, Seward drafted for Lincoln a routine reiteration of the writ's suspension throughout the United States, while also making clear its constitutional legitimacy. For Congress had in the interim passed a Habeas Corpus Act which explicitly approved presidential suspensions and which was expected to help in enforcing an essential new conscription law, the Enrollment Act.[8]

The military arrests of civilians in loyal states thus began early on and continued for the duration of the war. Most of those arrested were deserters, draft evaders and those who encouraged them. Even Union loyalists worried about the resort to conscription, a constitutionally questionable encroachment on individual freedom, while the more extreme opponents of the administration and its 'abolition war' encouraged violent resistance to the draft. The ringleaders of protests in many communities in the lower North and the Midwest – which reached their apogee in the bloody draft riots in New York City in July 1863 – became targets of arrest. So, too, did those shady businessmen, peddlers and recruitment brokers who seized the burgeoning opportunities for plundering the public purse. In the border states, where most civilian arrests occurred, a large proportion of those targeted were blockade runners, smugglers and traders in contraband goods.

Officers' actions were rarely driven by raw partisanship, but their interventions against treason or suspected disloyalty certainly had a political impact. They suppressed newspapers careless with confidential military information, seized presses, and arrested or banished pro-Confederate editors. Their targets were mainly Democrat. Provost-marshals and other troops policed the polls at election time, to head off violence against Union voters and sometimes, in border areas, to intimidate their opponents by extorting loyalty oaths under the threat of arrest. Federal forces arrested Maryland legislators in September 1861, supposedly to prevent them voting for secession at a time of possible Confederate invasion. Smaller fry were equal targets: General Halleck arrested a Missourian simply for saying, 'I wouldn't wipe my ass with the stars and stripes'. There was a fine line between prudent political action and counter-productive intervention. Anxiety often induced misjudgments over what constituted disloyalty. Thus, the misguided arrest of a Dubuque editor, Dennis A. Mahony, turned a Union troop-recruiter into an outraged critic of the president.[9]

Most notorious of all military miscalculations was General Ambrose Burnside's arrest of Clement Vallandigham, the most influential western voice of Peace Democracy. Democrats enjoyed a potent political resurgence in the spring of 1863, during what Greeley described as 'the darkest hours of the National Cause'. With the state governors of Illinois and Indiana feeling themselves under siege, and with the lower Midwest a seeming powder keg of peace sentiment, anti-abolitionism, venomous race prejudice, separatism and covert treason, Burnside watched with alarm as the administration's provost-marshal and his deputies met serious obstruction to the new conscription law. As the energetic commander of the Department of the Ohio, but one with rather more facial hair than political gumption, Burnside issued an order banning 'the habit of declaring sympathies for the enemy'.[10] Tried not by a civil court (though these were functioning) but by military commission, Vallandigham was sentenced to imprisonment for the rest of the war. The ensuing public outcry, fierce in denouncing a tyrannical assault on free speech and constitutional liberties, was by no means restricted to anti-war Democrats, nor to the Midwestern states. A chastened administration counted the damage of what several cabinet members judged a massive and unnecessary political error.

Lincoln's subsequent robust defense of Burnside's action, in his 'Corning Letter', a public address to the leaders of a mass protest meeting in Albany, New York, made no constitutional concessions to the administration's critics. 'Strong measures', he insisted, including military arrests of civilians, were allowable under the Constitution in time of rebellion. Overestimating, as did most Unionists, the real strength of secret societies and conspiracy, Lincoln maintained that those who championed habeas corpus, liberty of speech and a free press included 'a most efficient corps of spies, informers, supplyers, and aiders and abettors' of the rebels' cause. He did not concede that military arrests should be restricted to areas of actual insurrection: they were 'constitutional *wherever* the public safety does require them – as well . . . where they may restrain mischievous interference with the raising and supplying of armies, to suppress the rebellion, as where the rebellion may actually be'. The arrest would have been wrong had it been merely a response to public criticism of political and military leaders. But Vallandigham's words were 'damaging the army' and threatening the nation's existence, by undermining the draft. 'Must I shoot a simple-minded soldier boy who deserts, while I must not touch a hair of a wiley agitator who induces him to desert?'[11]

Lincoln was not squeamish about pushing the Constitution to its limits during a wartime emergency: since the cause was just, extraordinary measures would cease with the ending of hostilities, and most of the Union public supported them. He was angered less by the knowledge that there could be innocent victims of military arrests, than by learning about obstruction to military mobilization. When judges blocked recruitment by 'discharging the drafted men rapidly under *habeas corpus*', as they did to provoke a crisis in Pennsylvania in the summer of 1863, the attorney-general found Lincoln 'more angry than I ever saw him'. Welles described him as 'very determined' and ready to send the judges packing. Chase feared civil war if the writ were suspended, but Lincoln, remarkably, ordered the military officers to ignore the state's civil courts and, if necessary, use force to protect themselves from arrest by court officers.[12]

In practice, Lincoln mixed toughness with restraint, tempering a broad reading of his constitutional power with astute political realism. He knew the propaganda damage that could be done by the martyrdom of the guilty and the arrest of the innocent. Thus, he commuted Vallandigham's sentence to banishment and subsequently chose to ignore his illegal return to the country. He backed away from a punitive response to the New York draft riots, resisting calls for a formal investigation that would have been seen as provocative. In fact, he showed no appetite for exploiting his habeas corpus policy for cheap political gain, nor did he need friends like David D. Field to tell him that 'the practice of arresting citizens without legal process' invited a violent electoral backlash. Lincoln was generally tolerant of the opposition press and took no personal initiative in imposing censorship, though for security reasons he did not question the War Department's regulating of the Washington telegraph. When Burnside suppressed the *Chicago Times*, probably the most influential Democratic newspaper in the Midwest, for 'disloyal and incendiary sentiments', the president revoked the order, only to suffer the mystified anger of the many who had cheered the general on. It was entirely in character that he should tell General Schofield only to 'arrest individuals, and suppress assemblies, or newspapers, when they may be working *palpable* injury to the Military'.[13] It was for military not electoral benefits that Lincoln sailed close to the constitutional wind.

Lincoln's circumstances gave him opportunities for using and expanding presidential power in ways of which his predecessors would never have dreamed. 'This great nation has given to you almost absolute authority', a Republican ally reflected, and his grasp on the levers of power grew firmer and more expert with the passage of time. He was no instinctive administrator – Hay described him as 'extremely unmethodical' – but his skills in political management were second to none. He gave his cabinet secretaries room for maneuver in their own departments but they knew that, when he chose, he was their master, not *primus inter pares*. He left Congress to its own devices in some areas of policy-making, notably its economic program, but he kept firm control over emancipation, reconstruction and – the Joint Committee on the Conduct of the War notwithstanding – management of the war. His grip on his party, complained one of the congressional radicals, made him 'the virtual dictator of the country'. An admiring John Hay marveled as the Tycoon – his private name for the president – developed into a 'backwoods Jupiter' wielding 'the bolts of war and the machinery of government with a hand equally steady & equally firm'. Given Lincoln's combination of aptitude and opportunities, then, what is remarkable is not that he moved into questionable constitutional terrain, but that he would not allow the argument of 'necessity' alone to settle things or to become an excuse for persecution. Loyalty to the Constitution and the laws – and to their spirit – mattered. A president who never questioned the need for democratic elections even in the midst of war, who saw an obligation to resubmit himself to the judgment of the people in 1864, and who recognized the political dangers of being labeled a tyrant, felt no great urge to kick over the constitutional traces.[14]

Once in place, however, the Union's internal security system operated routinely with little input from the president. His interventions in individual cases, whether to exercise mercy or prevent injustice, operated only at the margins, as military justice became a valued and potent buttress to the Union cause. Mark Neely has shown the impossibility of putting a precise figure on the number of civilians arrested. They ran into the tens of thousand. But these included overwhelming numbers of Confederates and suspected rebels in the contested border region, where military policing shored up public order. Beyond the border, the security system was essentially deployed as an instrument of draft enforcement, not as a weapon of party political control. Most victims were held for a short period of a few weeks in federal prisons and released without trial.[15]

For Lincoln's opponents, the long reach of the War Department's security system into the homes and lives of local communities was just one element in what Horatio Seymour, New York's Democratic governor, labeled the administration's 'centralization and meddling'.[16] Federally imposed emancipation, conscription, and a roster of economic measures heralded a centralized state. Leviathan would crush the brittle bones of the decentralized antebellum republic of which Democrats had been the architects and guardians.

Such language was tendentious, but it harbored a kernel of truth. The Whig-Republicans' wartime program of railroad construction, high tariffs on imported manufactures, homestead and land-grant laws, scientific agriculture, progressive taxation and a national banking structure, did indeed draw a line under the republic of Jefferson and Jackson, and announced the arrival of a national government pledged to a liberated commercial order. The 'slave power', with its states' rights phobia of federal energy, was dead. The Republicans' cast of mind – by inclination interventionist, statist and centralizing – embraced far more easily than did their Democratic opponents' the vigorous and coercive use of civil and military authority to suppress disloyalty and sustain the war effort.

Popular mobilization: the 'power of the right word' and the agency of party

Not coercion, but the citizen's voluntary exercise of reason, Lincoln believed, would provide the bedrock of support for the Union and ensure its armies' ultimate victory. Certain that public sentiment was 'everything', he declared from the outset that he would prosecute the war 'relying upon Providence and the loyalty of the people to the government they have established'.[17] Americans had 'a fundamental idea, going down about as deep as anything' – the survival of constitutional government – 'to rally and unite' them. And they had rational faculties with which to assess events. 'Our people are easily influenced by reason', he told a group of visiting Baltimoreans early in the conflict. Later, in the dark days of 1864 he professed his continuing faith in the people: 'Let them know the truth, and the country is safe.' He understood, of course, that loyalists traveled on an emotional roller-coaster, but he also saw the depth of patriotic ardor, whether measured in the oceans of blood spilt and, more prosaically, in the buoyant sales of war bonds and the torrents of charitable giving. He knew 'the power of the right word from the right man to develop the latent fire and enthusiasm of the masses'.[18] The 'right man' was self-evidently the one man – the president – with the platform from which to reach the whole Union.

Articulating the aims and rationale of war was essential to Union victory. Lincoln's authority as a democratic politician in antebellum America derived very largely from his campaign oratory. Yet after his nomination for the presidency he never again took to the stump and, once in the White House, he made only very limited use of a weapon that had done so much to win him the high regard of Republicans nationally. As president, he spoke in public nearly one hundred times. Mostly these were not full-blown speeches but modest remarks, often unscripted. They included short addresses to troops passing through Washington, impromptu responses to well-wishers who came to 'serenade' him with music and speeches, and statements to visiting delegations – of clergymen, border-state representatives, free blacks and others. Almost all were made in the capital. His two inaugural addresses and his speech at Gettysburg were rare, set-piece exceptions to this general picture.

We may wonder about Lincoln's reluctance to speak in public, given his proven rhetorical record, his confidence in the power of language and his reiterated certainty that Americans responded well to the truth, when logically and clearly presented. The explanation lies partly in his conventional attitude that it was not quite proper for a president to make speeches at all, and certainly not during election campaigns, when stump-speaking would smack of partisanship not statesmanship. No less influential was the pressure of presidential business, whose schedule gave Lincoln few opportunities to prepare lengthy speeches. Almost all his great addresses, as at Springfield in June 1858 and at the New York Cooper Union in February 1860, followed careful deliberation, even sustained research. Protracted, meticulous preparation and several drafts preceded his First Inaugural. Once the war began, competing demands squeezed out time for writing speeches or traveling to speak outside Washington. Since, unlike modern presidents, he used no ghost-writer (though the secretary of state wrote what he said when foreign ministers were presented) and since he feared he might be led into careless, off-hand remarks (which explains why he fretted at the approach of serenaders, who always expected a few words), we should not be surprised that he spoke so little in public and that the two most celebrated speeches of his presidency, the Gettysburg address and the Second Inaugural, were his pithiest.

Some have considered Lincoln's reticence a probable mistake, a damaging and self-inflicted wound, to be contrasted with Jefferson Davis's recourse to speaking tours to bolster Confederate morale.[19] But what Lincoln lost in this respect he more than made up for by the use of other media, by which he became a ubiquitous presence, both visually and in words. The mass-produced woodcut and lithograph carried Lincoln's image into thousands of homes, as did the newly-arrived, mass-produced photograph. Lincoln sat dozens of times for photographers, and many of the seventy or so wartime likenesses of him were reproduced in huge numbers as pocket-size photographs. The president was not a vain man and knew he was no pin-up, but he was only too ready to meet the popular demand for an easily available likeness and give those who had never seen him in the flesh a sense of personal encounter.

Equally Lincoln made often brilliant use of the written word to communicate the purposes of the administration. The most formal of the president's documents, his annual and special messages to Congress (which were forwarded from the White House, to be read out by a clerk in the legislative branch), naturally consumed much of his time and blended routine information, compact analysis of events, vigorous explanation of the administration's course and, occasionally, soaring rhetoric. Then there were the published accounts of the many less ceremonial, more informal occasions: Lincoln's meetings and interviews with groups of visitors to the White House, for which he had often a scripted response. Probably most effective of all were Lincoln's carefully crafted public letters to particular individuals or mass meetings, a device he used with increasing frequency after the slide in the administration's political fortunes in the spring of 1862. Each was skillfully designed to rally opinion or prepare it for imminent changes in policy and each addressed an issue crucial to the conduct and outcome of the war: emancipation and racial issues in his letters to Horace Greeley (August 1862), James C. Conkling (August 1863), and Albert Hodges (April 1864); conscription policy to New York Governor Horatio Seymour (August 1863); and treason, military arrests and the suspension of habeas corpus to Erastus Corning, Matthew Birchard, and other New York and Ohio Democrats (June 1863). In some cases, as with his letter to a Union mass meeting in support of Maryland state emancipation in October 1864, the immediate and chief objective was local. On the other hand, his addresses to the working men of Manchester and London sought to rally overseas opinion. Some of the letters appeared not just in newspaper columns but as widely-circulating pamphlets. Seen as a whole, the president's pronouncements warrant Phillip Paludan's conclusion that for the duration of the war 'Lincoln constantly manipulated public opinion' – albeit in the pursuit of a philosophically-enhanced and rededicated Union, in the celebration of constitutionalism and in the Whiggish, romantic belief that the statesman's role was to appeal to 'the better angels of [people's] nature'.[20]

Lincoln surely regretted being unable to give voice to his own words. He was keenly alert to matters of intonation and emphasis, evident in his private recitation of Shakespearean soliloquies and in his canny advice to an actor playing Falstaff on how to get the best out of a line. Significantly, he accompanied his letter to Conkling, designed to be read out at a Union rally, with guidance on how it should be delivered. His enforced near-silence made him all the more attentive to the quality of his prose, which he sought to imbue with color, life and energy. When, in his intended message to the special session of Congress in July 1861, Lincoln described the rebellion as 'sugar-coated', the government printer objected to what was then judged an undignified expression. Lincoln was unimpressed by the distinction his critic drew between the racy language appropriate for a mass meeting in Illinois and the prose of an historic, formal document: 'that word expresses precisely my idea, and I am not going to change it. The time will never come in this country when the people won't know exactly what *sugar-coated* means!' In his public letter to Greeley, to stress the difficulty in restoring the old Union unchanged, he had written: 'Broken eggs can never be mended, and the longer the breaking proceeds the more will be broken.' Only reluctantly did he strike out a sentence which the editors of the *National Intelligencer* considered undignified. Sometimes Lincoln's lively metaphors got the better of him: even the adoring Hay judged the letter to Conkling, with its allusion to the navy as 'Uncle Sam's web-feet', to be scarred by 'hideously bad rhetoric . . . [and] indecorums that are infamous'. However, these lapses came, not from self-conscious cleverness, classical allusions or showy erudition, but from striving to be plainly understood, and in the main Lincoln's prose was arresting, lucid and strikingly economical. For admirers like Harriet Beecher Stowe, Lincoln's was the art that concealed art. By his careful avoidance of 'fine writing', as conventionally understood, and his embrace of language that had 'the relish and smack of the soil', he reached all classes, from the most sophisticated to 'the lowest intellect'.[21]

In practice, it made no great difference whether Lincoln spoke or wrote. What really counted was that his words and ideas reached and moved the widest possible audience. Lincoln's personal exertions in defining the administration's objectives were only part of the overall exercise of tapping into the Union's deep well of religio-patriotic sentiment. In seeking out the most potent agencies to harness that opinion, the government had to look beyond its official institutions, which had been chronically weak. The most powerful and extensive of the nation's networks were voluntary associations. Pre-eminently these were two-fold:

the political party – its voluntarism supplemented and compromised by the rewards of government patronage – and the churches, with their associated philanthropic agencies. By energetically exploiting the steadfast loyalism of these institutions, a president tied to the White House was able to project himself and his cause into the heartland of the Union and beyond.

Lincoln needed no lessons in how the power of party might promote a cause.[22] His presidential victory in 1860 had depended far less on his individual appeal than on the skill with which Republican organizers had projected him as the embodiment of the party's philosophy and platform. But Lincoln's election and nominal leadership of the party did not mean that the organization, whatever its potential for war mobilization, would effortlessly fall into line behind him and then stay there. The Republicans were a fragile, decentralized coalition. There were few established Lincoln loyalists in Congress. Organizationally the party was, in practice, little more than an agglomeration of local and state bodies. Philosophically, too, it was divided, as internal conflicts over emancipation, the conduct of the war, and reconstruction would show. If the party were to become a truly effective rallying force for the administration, Lincoln had to bind it together and impose his authority on it.

For these purposes he had to hand a potent weapon: presidential patronage. There was nothing new in a president fusing his roles as party leader and chief executive by distributing government jobs to the party faithful. But Lincoln had the added bonus of controlling appointments to the thousands of new offices thrown up by the wartime expansion of the army and government departments. An experienced and skillful party manager, who possessed a potent combination of tenacity, patience and command of detail, he devoted an enormous slice of his time to disposing of these posts. It was a wearisome and even draining exercise, as he sought to avoid gratuitously upsetting the competitors for office while yet remaining even-handed toward the various party factions, including his critics. But his attentiveness and refusal to be bullied undoubtedly paid off. He built up a bank of congressional indebtedness by meeting the patronage requests of interceding congressmen, and created such highly effective cadres of supporters at state level that he easily outmaneuvered those who had hoped to prevent his running for a second term.[23]

The demonstrations of Union patriotism that immediately followed hostilities at Fort Sumter and Lincoln's call to arms would certainly have occurred without the encouragement of grass-roots Republicans, though in fact local party leaders leapt to beat the martial drum, and mobilize men and resources, in an unyielding response to secessionist defiance. But as the early enthusiasm gave way first to frustration and then to war-weariness, the need to keep before the people the purposes of the Union grew increasingly urgent. Lincoln looked to his congressmen, governors and local leaders to pursue within their constituencies the themes of his formal addresses and to sell each new statement of policy and national purpose: the Emancipation Proclamation, the use of black troops, the unacceptability of peace on the terms of 'the Union as it was'. It was an expectation only partly realized, as Republican conservatives jibbed at emancipation, while radical hardliners articulated more ambitious object-ives in less emollient language. But an influential core of party loyalists, notably amongst the Republican governors, proved their persisting worth to Lincoln as interpreters of the administration's purpose.

The key northern governors in 1861 were loyal party men. They owed their office to the party; they had been agents of national victory in 1860. As the war progressed they encouraged the president to take more power into federal hands and became themselves increasingly dependent on Washington. Without War Department funds Governor Morton of Indiana would have had to recall a Democratic legislature which, bitterly opposed to an emancipationist war, had refused appropriations. Yates of Illinois, fearing civil war in his state, asked Washington to supply four regiments. In the critical state elections of 1863, especially in Connecticut, Ohio and Pennsylvania, Lincoln's interventionism included dispensing patronage, getting troops furloughed home to vote and ensuring that government clerks were given leave (and free railroad passes) to reach the polls. Thus the demands and protectiveness of party increasingly bound state and national governments together, and their mutual dependence had huge implications for Washington's communication of the Union's purpose. For one thing, it made possible political stage-management in cultivating public confidence. After McClellan's retreat from Richmond in the sum-mer of 1862, Lincoln feared that a call for a further 100,000 men, though badly needed, would provoke 'a general panic and stampede . . . so hard it is to have a thing understood as it really is'. Instead, in a scheme involving Seward, Weed and Republican governors Morgan of New York and Curtin of Pennsylvania, Lincoln got the loyal governors to sign a memorial ostensibly emanating from them but actually drawn up by the administration.[24]

The interdependence of state and national administrations, as Eric McKitrick has famously argued, became even more salient after the mid-term electoral setbacks of 1862: Democratic gains led state Republican organizations into the energetic defense of national policy – notably in justifying emancipation as essential and consistent with the original purpose of the war – and into lambasting their opponents, now encouraged to bolder calls for peace, as traitors. In this context, Republicans read their victories in the fall elections of 1863 not simply as local successes but as a triumph for Lincoln's administration. Candidates for even the lowest offices, in asking people to vote Republican, were urging an endorsement of the war, its purposes and its leaders. Local fused with national, as ordinary citizens, male and female, gave vent to a patriotism sharpened by the sacrifices and upheavals of war. Nothing better revealed the vibrancy of the Union's civic culture than the local proliferation of *ad hoc* partisan clubs and of loyalist organizations which might disclaim a partisan intent, but in effect represented interests no different from the Lincoln administration's. Wartime elections provided the arena, and the Republican party the means, for 'continual affirmation and reaffirmation of [national] purpose'.[25]

One of the most powerful ligaments of party and its ubiquitous instrument of political persuasion was its newspaper press. Lincoln's experience in antebellum Illinois, and in the campaign of 1860, had revealed the power of the daily and weekly paper to draw its subscribers into a forceful political community. Equally, the ridicule that a hostile press heaped upon him for arriving for his Washington inaugural secretly, in disguise and by night was a salutary reminder of its power to shape opinion for the worse as well as the better. Cultivating the press thus became a wartime priority, though Lincoln took considerably more interest in using the press as a broadcasting medium for the administration than in reading it for advice. Systematic news management and the modern press conference were developments for the future, of course, and even a loyal press was not necessarily uncritical or biddable. Lincoln thought the 'vilifying and disparaging' of the administration in even the Republican press played a part in its election setback of 1862.[26] He grew 'mad enough to cry' when his letter to Conkling, despite a publishing embargo, appeared word for word in the trusted *New York Evening Post* two days before it was due to be first read at a Union meeting in Springfield, Illinois. John Hay sought unsuccessfully to get an 'outrageously unfair' Republican correspondent removed from his job with the western Associated Press.[27] Still, the president, and his White House secretaries, had at their disposal a variety of means to broadcast the administration's purposes and to reward loyalty.

Hay, for instance, acted anonymously as a political ventriloquist for the White House. Writing as a 'special correspondent' for newspapers in

New York, Washington and St Louis, he engaged in a sustained propaganda exercise for an administration which sought to bolster support within opposition strongholds, especially in the Midwest. There is no evidence that Lincoln put his young secretary up to this: zealous patriotism, admiring loyalty to his president and a platform for literary exhibitionism were inducements enough. The journalist's upbeat reports are in sharp contrast to the more sober musings of his private diary, and collectively provided as patriotic a commentary on events and as positive a gloss on the Union leadership as it was possible to find. Lincoln appears as an energetic, prudent figure, with broad vision and a genius for reading the public mood. He enjoys the support of vigorous, gifted departmental secretaries and a fundamentally united cabinet. Supposed abrasions between George McClellan and his political masters are smoothed over. Though Peace Democrats are natural targets for criticism, grumbling Republican radicals attract the sharpest barbs. Military delay and battlefield setbacks prompt no defeatism or panic. The fight for constitutional liberty in the western world will succeed, since 'God and the heaviest artillery, ... justice and a fat larder' are all on one side.[28]

Lincoln himself composed a few articles specifically for the newspapers and gave careful thought to where his public letters should first appear before they were copied Union-wide. He controlled the press's access to his private meetings, allocated lucrative government printing contracts to selected Republican papers, and rewarded loyal editors and correspondents with well-paid jobs at home and abroad. Unsurprisingly, loyal correspondents made up the presidential trainload to Gettysburg in November 1863, their place on the platform assured; hundreds of local papers subsequently printed and celebrated Lincoln's speech, in repudiation of Democratic ridicule of a 'silly, flat and dish-watery utterance'. Probably most important of all, Lincoln, though not dependably accessible to reporters, made sure his door was open when it needed to be. Frequent visitors included the young Noah Brooks, reporter for the *Sacramento Daily Union*, and Simon P. Hanscom, who enjoyed 'almost exclusive access' to the president's office. Hanscom's paper, the *Washington National Republican*, mistakenly came to be seen as the administration 'organ' – a perception that Lincoln regretted, since jealousies amongst the Washington newspaper corps were unhelpful. Even so, he remained their master, using them to moderate expectations when he thought the public too sanguine and to rally sentiment in the aftermath of defeat.[29]

Republican editors nation-wide generally continued to trumpet their Unionism in even the darkest times, but their faith in the administration itself was far from constant. Joseph Medill of the *Chicago Tribune* began an enthusiast, but Lincoln failed the editor's test of radicalism, and the paper grumbled for much of the war without actually withholding support from the president himself. Conversely, the *New York Times*, under the moderate Henry J. Raymond, remained a dependable supporter even as the war's purposes became more radical and its course more bloody: the editor's increasing regard for Lincoln himself made all the difference. No newspaperman was more loyal than James W. Forney, a Philadelphia ex-Democrat whose admiration for what he termed Lincoln's 'unconscious greatness' was no doubt underscored by the president's part in getting him elected as secretary of the Senate and in securing commissions for his sons.[30] His *Philadelphia Press* gave every appearance of being a White House organ. It staunchly defended the president's handling of civil liberties and in July 1862 made a remarkable volte-face to support emancipation, a shift which, in hindsight, suggests Lincoln's blessing.

We can also see Lincoln's handiwork in Forney's establishing a new daily paper in Washington toward the end of 1862. With the stance of the influential *New York Tribune* increasingly uncertain, as Horace Greeley oscillated nervously between support for the administration and alarmed defeatism, the president had suggested to Forney that he turn his *Sunday Morning Chronicle* into a daily. Lincoln was especially concerned at the *Tribune*'s potentially demoralizing effect on Union troops at the time when he was about to remove McClellan from command. Supported by government funds (in payment for printing federal notices and advertising) and given easy access to the White House, Forney developed a newspaper which carried a message of uncompromising Unionism daily to as many as 30,000 troops in the camps and hospitals of the Army of the Potomac. His papers would set the tone for the pro-administration press in 1864 by being the first to endorse Lincoln's renomination, when many other Republican editors doubted his ability to win. The president's opponents called Forney 'Lincoln's dog'.[31]

Cheap newspapers provided Lincoln with one means of propagandizing the Union, a flood of cheap pamphlets another. At first many titles were individually financed and produced, but from the early months of 1863 pamphlet and broadside publishing achieved extraordinary levels of coordination and activity under the direction of several new publication societies. These bodies grew naturally out of existing Union Leagues and Loyal Leagues, those extra-party associations set up to rally Union morale in the bleak winter days of 1862–63. Their models included the most impressive of all pre-war publishing and distribution agencies, the American Tract Society. In New York, Boston and Philadelphia distinguished professionals and intellectuals like Francis Lieber joined with representatives of the business classes to raise huge sums for distributing free Union propaganda and channeling editorial matter to small-town newspapers, to combat defeatism and counter the 'disloyal' press. The Philadelphia Union League's Board of Publications, the largest and most efficient of these societies, raised tens of thousands of dollars toward the wartime production of well over a hundred different pamphlets and broadsheets, and distributed over a million items of literature in army camps and on the home front.[32]

Naturally enough, the publication societies put the president's own words to their patriotic purposes. But Lincoln intervened directly himself. Wanting to ensure that his Corning letter, of which he was particularly proud, was not merely reproduced in friendly newspapers, he had it printed and sent to Republicans across the country on the frank of his private secretary. This kept the chief executive personally immune to charges of squalid electioneering but indicated the importance he attached to the letter's circulation. The recipients included Francis Lieber, who wrote to assure the president that the Loyal Publication Society of New York would run off 10,000 copies. Around half a million of what another New Yorker described as 'the best Campaign document we can have in this state' were produced for voters and for soldiers in the field.[33]

In that letter, as indeed elsewhere, Lincoln pursued the same intelligent political strategy that he had adopted from the outset, one which equated the Union–Republican party with inclusive, 'large-tent' patriotism and dressed the opponents of the administration in the clothes of narrow, illegitimate faction. Corning and his fellow protesters had consciously chosen to call themselves 'Democrats', Lincoln noted with regret, 'rather than "American citizens"'. He lamented that, in a 'time of national peril' they had chosen not to engage 'upon a level one step higher than any party platform; because I am sure that from such [a] more elevated position, we could do better battle for the country we all love, than we possibly can from those lower ones', where habit, prejudice and 'selfish hopes of the future' diverted energies into wasteful partisan warfare. 'But since you have denied me this', he added skillfully, 'I will yet be thankful, for the country's sake, that not all democrats have done so.' And, with that, he gathered the latter-day heirs of Andrew Jackson into the folds of the Union party.[34]

Making Republicans and Unionists one, defining them not as a conventional party but – in Lincoln's public words to Conkling – as a patriotic home for all 'noble men, whom no partizan malice, or partizan hope, can make false to the nation's life': this was how the Republicans managed 'to delegitimise the opposition' and simultaneously allow Democrats the political leeway to support the administration but avoid the guilt of party betrayal.[35] Lincoln and his party brilliantly managed to denigrate partisanship as the weapon of traitors and their fellow-travelers, while yet garnering the advantages of a continuing two-party system.

The fall elections of 1863 marked the high point to date of this strategy of non-partisan partisanship. The patriotic Union Leagues, with their membership rituals, oaths to the flag and the Bible, and mass meetings, may not have enjoyed formal links with the administration party, but in every essential respect they functioned as a force of electoral mobilization. In the key states the Leagues' energies fused with those of the formidable publication societies and the more conventional party organizers, to seek the electoral benefits of the upturn in the Union's military fortunes in the summer and fall. Etiquette stopped Lincoln from openly campaigning but, whereas in 1862 he was sure his unpopularity made him a political liability, he now took a much more active interest in the Union–Republican canvasses, aware of their significance for his chances of re-election in 1864. He was not disappointed. Vallandigham's defeat in the Ohio gubernatorial race and Curtin's victory in Pennsylvania provided the administration with especially heartening successes. They suggested the disabling effect on the anti-administration forces of laboring under the tag of 'rebel sympathizers', while showing how the Republicans' claim to patriotism and conservatism could bind many who still thought of themselves as Democrats into the Union coalition.[36]

Popular mobilization: churches and philanthropic organizations

The churches and the benevolent organizations they sustained can claim to have been the first truly effective national networks in the United States. More consistently than any other governmental or voluntary agency in the early republic they drew ordinary people into an arena extending beyond their locality and state. Being a member of a church usually meant being part of a denominational connection whose preachers and press gave members a taste of the world beyond, mobilizing them in pursuit of ambitious benevolent causes, national and international in scope. At the outbreak of civil war this network of churches and related philanthropic, reform societies gave the North a potent weapon. Recruiting the clergy and lay leaders as active advocates of the Union cause would give the administration direct access to the nation's largest complex of subcultures. In particular, it would harness the forces of evangelical Protestantism – the millions of Methodists, Baptists, Presbyterians,

Congregationalists and others, who together formed the most formidable religious grouping in the country.

Lincoln had not needed the election of 1860, with its unprecedented fusing of religion and politics, to remind him that the American experiment of separating church and state had done little to blunt the political appetites of the clergy and their members. He could equally have been in no doubt about the subsequent rallying of the northern churches to the cause of Union. Bombarded by the resolutions of ecclesiastical bodies, besieged by religious deputations, and in regular receipt of the New York *Independent*, the most influential of all religious papers, Lincoln and his White House secretaries were well equipped to gauge the shifts in religious opinion. Northern clergy, divided before the war over slavery, now united in defense of the Union, as the 'higher law' minority of radical antislaveryites found common cause with 'law and order' conservatives. Much of their analysis, even their words, echoed Lincoln's own. Secession constituted rebellion and treachery when urged, as by Confederates, without good cause. It was an act of national suicide and anarchy, for its underlying principle destroyed all government. (Wisconsin Methodists rehearsed the *argumentum ad absurdum*: 'Wisconsin may secede from the Union. . . . So this county may secede from Wisconsin, this township from the county, and this village from the township; and the fast boy who steals his father's purse may secede.') To destroy the American Union was to end a glorious and historically unique experiment in political and religious freedom, one revolving around government by the people, 'the best form of government on earth'. The Union's failure would resonate beyond the current time and place, for to sustain republicanism was to fight for 'the peace of future ages . . . for free government in our land and in all the lands for all ages to come'.[37]

Thus the Union was not just politically significant: it had meaning for the romantic and spiritual sensibilities of Americans. Protestants prized it as the vehicle for God's unique role for America within human history. The 'acute millennial consciousness' of North American Protestants, carried to the New World by the original Puritan settlers and successively passed down to each new generation, gave the new nation a powerful sense of being God's instrument in the coming of His Kingdom. Its physical geography and natural resources indicated the oneness that God had intended for it. For the first seven decades of the Republic's existence most Protestants believed that the fusion of evangelical piety and republican government would have such a powerful moral effect that the Kingdom of God would be inaugurated by persuasion alone, without the need for arms. But southern secessionists, in an act of destruction that challenged God's Providence, had changed all that. And whereas in the antebellum generation, the call to defend the Union had been the cry of northern conservatives eager to find common ground with southern churches, it now became, in James Moorhead's words, a cry 'infused with a new moral significance. . . . The holy Union that Northerners defended was no longer the compromise-tainted object of earlier years; it was democratic civilization in collision with an alien way of life.'[38]

If the majority of Protestants accepted the government's initial definition of the war exclusively as a struggle to re-establish the Constitution and laws, there were those like Thomas Eddy who predicted from the start that the 'logic of events' would transform it into an assault on slavery. With contrabands filling the Union camps, making the government further complicit in slavery, it seemed clear to one Methodist bishop, Leonidas Hamline, that 'the North, under the present war regimen, has become responsible for slavery as never before, and must, under military rule, pronounce the slaves free, or God will not allow us to suppress this rebellion'. Through 1862 even cautious evangelicals warmed to emancipation and the use of black troops as divinely-proffered means of ending the suffering and restoring the Union. American history, the culmination of world history, would resolve the battle between Antichrist and the Christian order; between southern slavery, feudalism and the Cavalier mentality on one side and freedom – Yankee and Puritan – on the other. Slavery was 'waiting at Armageddon for the hosts of righteousness to march out and put him to final rout'. When it came, the Emancipation Proclamation appeared to purify the war and the nation, opening the way to victory. Exultant Wisconsin Wesleyans reminded Lincoln of God's assurance that 'if we take away from our midst the yoke . . . our light Shall break forth as the morning Our health Shall Spring forth Speedily and the glory of the Lord Shall be our reward'.[39]

Lincoln, as president, acted as a typical New England Whig in his easy acceptance of religion's role in public affairs. He worked hard to keep open two-way channels with religious leaders, especially evangelicals, and to deal sensitively with them, aware not only of their power but also of the deep reservoir of goodwill on which he could draw. If it is not clear how far Lincoln's cultivation of their company had to do with his own spiritual quest, there is no doubt that those contacts provided him with a way of reaching potent opinion-formers. In informal conversations at the White House he met the full denominational gamut of religious visitors who arrived confident of a catholic welcome from a president known for his non-sectarian tolerance and religious humility. Some came to lecture, some to deliver homilies, some to seek appointments, others merely to pay respects or renew acquaintance. They included the strategically placed, including editors of mass-circulation papers like Henry Ward Beecher and Theodore Tilton, denominational leaders like Matthew Simpson and distinguished abolitionists like William Lloyd Garrison. There were representatives of the chief wartime philanthropic bodies, particularly Henry Bellows and George H. Stuart of the United States Sanitary Commission, the most formidable and practical of the agencies devoted to the medical care and well-being of soldiers in the field.

Lincoln also held more formal meetings with delegations from particular denominations (Friends, Presbyterians, Baptists, Methodists, and others), from particular localities (notably the visit of leading Chicago clergy in September 1862), and from particular causes (including Sabbatarians, Sons of Temperance, Covenanters seeking a Christian amendment to the federal Constitution, and the US Christian Commission). On occasions humor threatened to get the better of him, as when he told a delegation of temperance reformers that battlefield losses could not be blamed on the demon alcohol 'as the rebels drink more & worse whiskey than we do'. Some failed to understand the political value of these meetings, seeing only an oppressed president deferring weakly to pressure groups. 'I wish that Halleck would put a Guard on the White House to keep out the Committees of preachers, Grannies and Dutchmen that absorb Lincoln's time and thought', grumbled William T. Sherman.[40] In fact, Lincoln turned these meetings to his political advantage, commonly responding to his visitors' formal addresses with his own carefully crafted words.

There were other ways of reaching out to the influential religious element, not least through presidential patronage, which offered a means of stroking the institutional egos of churches, especially those which complained of neglect or discrimination. Inclusive Unionism, Lincoln understood, meant opening the door to Jewish army chaplains (just as it prompted him to overturn Grant's ban on 'Jew peddlers', because it proscribed 'an entire religious class, some of whom are fighting in our ranks').[41] It also meant special attention to the Methodists, who had for some time felt that their nation-wide power had been undervalued in Washington. Now, in recognition of the Church's sheer numbers and reputation for full-blooded Unionism, Secretary of War Edwin Stanton showered army contracts on Methodist laymen. He also, in 1863, put at Bishop Edward Ames's disposal those 'secessionist' southern Methodist meeting houses in vanquished areas lacking a loyal ministry. When Lincoln found out, he called on Stanton to rescind the order, unhappy at the blurring of the line separating governmental and ecclesiastical jurisdiction.[42] Even so, the essential trust between the administration and the Methodist bishops was not compromised: important here was Lincoln's willingness to honor many of Bishop Simpson's requests for political offices for his co-denominationalists, the most notable being the appointments through James Harlan as Secretary of the Interior.[43]

But Lincoln's most powerful weapon was the spoken and written word. In speeches designed specifically for religio-philanthropic audiences, as with his addresses to fund-raising sanitary fairs and denominational groups; in proclaiming days for fasting and thanksgiving; in set-piece speeches which, if not usually cast in religious language, appealed to the better side of human nature and called on a deep moral understanding of America's meaning (as in his salvationist rhetoric of rebirth at Gettysburg) – in all these ways Lincoln spoke a language which persuaded the public that the administration was under the guidance of a man who recognized his dependence on Divine favor. It was a common experience for observers to perceive in Lincoln what George Peck called a capacity for reverence and 'deep religious feeling'. 'I should be the veriest shallow and self-conceited blockhead upon the footstool', the pious Noah Brooks reported Lincoln as saying, if 'I should hope to get along without the wisdom that comes from God and not from man.' Jonathan Turner shrewdly commented that both president and people 'seem . . . to imagine that he is a sort of half way clergyman'.[44] In fact, as Lincoln's remarkable Second Inaugural Address revealed, the president's understanding of the Almighty's role in Union affairs was far more subtle than that of many professional theologians. But it revealed a president capable of a meaningful engagement with the nation's Christian leaders.

Thus Lincoln went a long way toward satisfying those who cast him as an instrument of the divine will. Well before he had inspired them with his emancipation order, New School Presbyterians told him, 'When we look at . . . the wonderful way in which this people have been led under your guidance, we glorify God in you.' Later, as freedom became a reality, African Americans saw the president-emancipator as an Old Testament prophet. At a fast-day gathering near the White House, an old preacher 'with a voice like a gong prayed with hands uplifted "O Lord command the sun & moon to stand still while your Joshua Abraham Lincoln fights the battle of freedom"'. 'Up our way', a visitor from Buffalo told the president at a White House reception, 'we believe in God and Abraham Lincoln.' Hay recorded William D. Kelley's remark that 'the Lord has given us this man to keep as long as we can'. And a Chicago Methodist believed he had located 'the true theory & solution of this "terrible war"' in the vivid remark of one of the city's lawyers: '*You may depend upon it, the Lord runs Lincoln.*'[45]

The administration's efforts achieved their reward. Cadres of mainstream Protestants in effect acted as ideological shock troops, putting their full-blooded Unionism at the service of patriotic politics and encouraging even some previously apolitical clergy to become an arm of the Republican party. They regarded silent prayers for the president as a necessary duty but one secondary to more vocal support. And, driven as it was by love of country, they saw loyalty to the administration not as grubby politics but as obedience to the claims of St Paul on behalf of established government. A Wisconsin loyalist reflected that 'God has happily, for us, broken up our whole system of politics, and set us free from the reproach of preaching politics . . . , for politics and the gospel are now one, and what God hath joined together let no man put asunder'. Only cheap, godless partisans felt the lure of the old ways. 'What a terrible thing this "Party Politics" must be!' exclaimed another northwesterner. 'It seems to me that the Breckinridge prong of the Democracy would sustain its party, and support its measures, if by so doing it set adrift this great Ship of State . . . to the Devil, or to the nearest port of entry.'[46]

Church meetings fused the sacred and the secular, the patriotic and the partisan. Congregations sang 'America' and the 'Star-Spangled Banner' and cheered the sanctified stars and stripes that fluttered over their buildings. The most widely circulating Protestant newspapers, including the *Independent* and the cluster of regional *Christian Advocates* which gave Methodist editors such a commanding platform, remained staunchly loyal. A network of potent clerical speakers took to the rostrum and pulpit. Bishop Matthew Simpson, who criss-crossed the country as an 'evangelist of patriotism', was unsurpassed in his power to melt an audience to tears or rouse it to the heights of passionate enthusiasm for the war-torn flag. There was nothing coincidental about the president's engaging Simpson to substitute for him at the Philadelphia Sanitary Fair.[47] Lincoln had no need to take the stump himself when he could rely on a ready-made army of speakers willing to act as his proxy.

Hostile pockets of conservative, even southern-oriented, churches in the lower North launched virulent assaults on the administration's 'puritan meddling', but more immediately irritating for national authorities was the chorus of dissident radical voices within the Unionist ranks of evangelical Protestantism. Such preachers and religious writers as George B. Cheever, Charles G. Finney, William Goodell, Theodore Tilton and – intermittently – Henry Ward Beecher acted as the self-appointed conscience of the Union, convinced that, unprompted, Lincoln would fall sadly short of the mark. Even religious editors and spokesmen of a more moderate and forgiving mien had their anxieties over aspects of national policy and practice, but they were generally hesitant about launching direct attacks on the president and his administration, taking to heart the scriptural command to speak well of civil rulers. Thomas Eddy, often using his *Northwestern Christian Advocate* to press for more radical measures, never doubted the honest intentions of government officers and feared the corrosive effect of political criticism on public morale. The Chicago editor came close to real anger only when confronted with news of revelry and dancing in Mrs Lincoln's White House in the winter of 1862: he advised Lincoln to read the story of King Belshazzar's feast, confident his readers needed no reminding of the ruler's untimely end. But in the main Eddy and other Protestant leaders remained loyal to the maxim: 'It is not wise to destroy confidence in our rulers.'[48]

Collectively evangelicals worked to prepare the nation for sacrifice in an extended and gigantic war. Press and pulpit steeled women to the knowledge that victory would cost the lives of thousands of sons, brothers and husbands; reassured young men that there was a sweetness in dying for their country and its noble, millennial cause; and prepared all for a protracted war that would impose a massive financial burden. They speculated on God's likely purposes in allowing battlefield defeats. They boosted popular morale during the lowest ebb of Union fortunes, in 1862 and early 1863. They echoed the government's calls for troops, endorsed the introduction of conscription, and became recruiting agents themselves. Female evangelicals, through Relief Associations, Soldiers' Aid Societies and the Sanitary Commission, raised funds, produced uniforms, and prepared quilts and other supplies. Ministers defended the administration's suspension of habeas corpus, and welcomed strong-arm action against draft resisters and dissenters who overstepped the limits of legitimate opposition. Border evangelicals like Robert J. Breckinridge and William G. Brownlow stiffened the spines of middle-state Unionists. Chaplains and agents of the Christian Commission – as well as of the more secular Sanitary Commission – moved beyond simple benevolence to inspire the serving men of the Federal armies with the high purposes of the Union. The Episcopalian bishop, Charles P. McIlvaine, and the Catholic archbishop, John Hughes, as well as Henry Ward Beecher, served as administration agents in rallying support in Europe.[49]

It is no overstatement, then, to suppose that the combined religious engines of the Union – and the motor of evangelical Protestantism in particular – did more than any other single force to mobilize support for the war. In fusing a defense of lawful government against sinful rebellion with a vision of a new moral order they gave heightened meaning to loyalty. The administration knew their value. Whereas Jefferson Davis and the southern leadership had to break with their section's conventional political culture when they chose to deploy religion for overtly political ends (which they did, it has to be said, with the zeal of the recent convert), Lincoln had no such intellectual embarrassment. He simply rejoiced in what he described to a group of Baptists in the spring of 1864 as 'the effective and almost unanamous support which the Christian communities are so zealously giving to the country'.[50]

The Union army as a moral force

Paradoxical as it may seem, the North's most potent physical force, the Federal army, also acted as a moral or non-coercive force, energizing Unionism and rallying support for the administration. The senior Francis P. Blair was quite right in telling Lincoln, 'We must look to the Army as a great political, as well as war machine.'[51] Northern soldiers constituted a mighty weapon whose informal operations on the home front were less easily measured than the battlefield impact of their bullets, shells and bayonets but which in their own way worked to stiffen patriotism. They were mostly volunteers, even after the introduction of conscription: of the total of some two million who served in Union colors fewer than 50,000 were draftees. Most either were or came to be staunch Republicans, loyal, even devoted, to Lincoln, and dedicated to the political and moral values symbolized by the flag under which they served; they generally voted the Union ticket at elections and exercised a pervasive influence over their families and home communities.

Lincoln himself needed no instruction in the army's moral authority and he knew the political damage that would follow if the loyal public thought the administration were not the truest friend of its fighting men. Thus he persisted with McClellan, Frémont and other generals for longer than was militarily wise out of a concern, he explained, not to 'shake the faith of the people in the final success of the war'.[52] Likewise he saw the importance of forging the strongest of bonds between himself and his common soldiers, not simply because it was the commander-in-chief's duty to sustain their morale as a fighting force, but because he knew that through them he would exercise an influence over the confidence of the broader public.

Lincoln's words circulated in the army camps at least as freely as they did amongst the civilian population, especially through newspapers and pamphlets aimed specifically at soldiers. But as their commander and president, Lincoln was determined to be seen as well as heard, despite his having mostly to be stationed in Washington. Unlike Jefferson Davis, who was rarely glimpsed in person by his own troops, Lincoln made himself remarkably visible to his. He acknowledged new regiments as they marched past the White House on their way to serve. He took part in several great reviews of McClellan's massed forces in 1861 and 1862, watching their embarkation for the Peninsula venture and meeting them at Harrison's Landing after the campaign's ignominious collapse. In the spring of 1863 he made a morale-boosting visit of several days to Hooker's Army of the Potomac, accompanied by his family (with editor Brooks in tow), and reviewed 60,000 men. With Grant headquartered at City Point in the summer of 1864, Lincoln made an unannounced two-day visit, riding through the ranks and talking at length with the men. He (as did Mary Lincoln) visited hospitals, both in the field and in Washington, shaking hands with the wounded and thanking them for their patriotic sacrifice. This could be a grim duty, though it filled Lincoln's undoubted psychological need to do something to mitigate the bloodbath of war. The president's hospital visits also provided some unexpected moments of emotional release through moments of dark humor – as when he encountered a leg-less soldier laughing at a pious visitor who had just given him a tract on the iniquity of dancing.[53]

Additionally, Lincoln had close-quarter meetings with his serving men in Washington. Quite apart from his offering impromptu remarks to particular units passing by the executive mansion, he met very many Union volunteers individually. Early in the war he earnestly promised his troops that he would take care of them, urging even the lowliest privates to bring their problems and grievances to him. He and his secretaries found themselves bombarded by letters and speculative visitors, as soldiers and their families sought help in cases that most often related to sickness, pay, furlough or military punishment. Lincoln held perhaps 2,000 or more private interviews with Union soldiers.[54] This was a tiny proportion of the enlisted men, but it did not take long for the impressions of those who had seen or met the president to be broadcast throughout the close-knit regimental communities that made up the Federal army.

By these means Lincoln became a powerful virtual presence amongst his men. What they saw and generally admired was the common touch of a president who lacked airs and graces, who remained accessible, approachable and amiable, and who mixed charm with good humor, joke-telling and easy familiarity. He 'aint proud', thought one; 'he belongs to the common people', judged another. His quaint, awkward, even ugly physical appearance and manner generally served to reinforce the sense of his ordinariness and lack of affectation. Some found him comical – on horse back in coat-tails and stove pipe hat he cut a ludicrously elongated figure – but his ungainliness only increased the affection. 'His riding I can compare to nothing else than a pair of tongs on a chair back', reported a Pennsylvanian, 'but notwithstanding his grotesque appearance, he has the respect of the army.'[55]

Even more important in cementing the soldiers' trust was their widespread belief that Lincoln made their well-being his chief concern. First-hand reports of the president's sympathy crackled swiftly through the mass medium of the army's ranks. They told of his concern for the wounded, his provision of field and hospital chaplains, his finding government jobs for disabled veterans and amputees, and his support for the work of the soldiers' aid organizations (though he had initially shared the War Department's skepticism over the value of these civilian bodies). His reputation for kindliness burgeoned as he agonized over the hundreds of court-martial cases that ended up on his desk. Having ordered that no soldier should be executed for any crime without his first reviewing it, Lincoln sought to avoid the 'butchery' of capital sentences whenever possible and early in 1864 commuted all such sentences in cases of desertion (what he called his 'leg-cases') to imprisonment for the war's duration. That his troops saw a president ever more physically ravaged by the grind of office naturally sharpened their sense of a leader who shared their trials, anxieties and sorrows. Watching him in the biting wind during the review days of April 1863, men recognized a fellow-casualty of the war, 'thin and in bad health'. As one soldier put it, in terms widely echoed, 'He is to all outward appearances, much careworn, and anxiety is fast wearing him out, poor man.'[56]

Lincoln thus came to be personally loved and admired, as Jefferson Davis never was. Understandably cautious as he was about dismissing McClellan, when the time came to do so in the fall of 1862 he was confident that he enjoyed the trust of the rank and file, even if his stock was low amongst the Democrats in the general's officer corps. Whatever the 'headquarters bluster' – as Schurz called it – and the indignation of some volunteers, few blamed Lincoln personally for the change of command.[57] Thereafter the president became the unchallenged recipient of most soldiers' loyalty. To the common terms of endearment – 'Old Abe', 'Uncle Abe' – a new one was added. The commander-in-chief who referred to the Union troops as 'my boys' and whose paternalistic devotion inspired such confidence came increasingly to be called 'Father Abraham'.

The soldiers to whom Lincoln became a father-figure had grown to young manhood in highly politicized and democratic local communities whose inhabitants were instilled with an active sense of civic duty. James

McPherson and Joseph Allan Frank have justly described the Union's volunteers as 'citizen-soldiers'. However much human feelings – loyalty to comrades-in-arms, a generalized sense of duty and honor, a concern to carry on the fight on behalf of their slain fellows, and a desire to punish the enemy – helped carry soldiers through their bloody ordeal, the Union's troops were no less energized by the political meanings they attached to the struggle. Soldiers read newspapers, set up debating societies that mirrored the lyceums of their home communities, and discussed the larger issues at play in the war. The camps, according to an Illinoisan, were 'filled with grave reasoners'; after the war Ulysses S. Grant was quite clear that the Union had benefited from having armies 'composed of men who were able to read, men who knew what they were fighting for'.[58] African-American troops naturally brought their own ideological fervor to a struggle for universal emancipation and black rights. But white troops, too, shared a firm grasp of the political significance of the conflict.

Thus when Lincoln's fighting men thought about their president they conjured up more than a personally sympathetic figure. He became, too, the embodiment of the nation's cause. Soldiers saw in the Union a set of political and moral principles, secured by the sacrifices of the revolutionary generation, and which now made the republic what one described as 'a beacon of hope to the nations of the world'. When the armies observed Washington's birthday and listened on 4 July to the public reading of the Declaration of Independence, they affirmed their faith in republican liberty and 'the best government ever organized by man'. At the same time, deep state, local and personal allegiances reinforced this devotion to abstract principles: the Union's power partly derived from its being, in one historian's words, 'the family writ large'.[59] As its head and cogent expounder of its meaning, Lincoln was truly 'Father Abraham'.

The unified political purpose that Lincoln encouraged amongst his troops by arousing 'their slumbering patriotism', as one private put it, was challenged but not fundamentally compromised by his role as the Great Emancipator. The president recognized that the army was not a political monolith, that slavery was a divisive issue and that an emancipation policy would alienate many serving men. The proclamations of 22 September 1862 and 1 January 1863 were indeed seen as an expression of 'niggerism', especially amongst volunteers from the lower North and the western states. 'Ask any solder what he thinks of the war', one reported. 'He will answer, "I don't like to fight for the damned nigger." It's nothing but an abolition war, and I wish I was out of it.' A captain wrote bitterly, 'Old Abe Lincoln is a god damned shit and if I had to choose between him and Jeff Davis, I don't know who I'd vote for. I hope to sink in hell if I ever have to draw my sword to fight for the negroes.' But Lincoln calculated that, on balance, a policy of emancipation would do more good than harm within the ranks. According to James Stradling, a cavalry sergeant who visited the White House in March 1863, the president expected his troops to wake up to the military benefits of an assault on slavery and of the use of blacks in front-line service. Lincoln's belief that the proclamation would serve to inspire, not alienate, the common soldier proved well founded. If an Indiana sergeant spoke with uncommon force when he said 'he was in for emancipation subjugation extermination and hell and damnation' if they would bring the war to a speedy end, his underlying sentiment was common enough amongst ordinary soldiers. Pragmatic calculation fused with abolitionist idealism to create a swelling tide of pro-emancipation sentiment from the spring of 1863, drowning out the shrinking minority of antis who nursed a bitter sense of betrayal.[60]

Union soldiers did not keep their views to themselves. The bonds between northern communities and 'their' regiments – symbolized by the flag which each departing unit received in patriotic civic rituals and which it subsequently carried into battle as a potent emblem – remained extraordinarily powerful throughout the war. Even the developing emotional gap, described by Gerald Linderman, between battle-scarred troops and the people back home could not destroy the mutually sustaining reciprocities of army camp and domestic community. For their part, home localities provided their volunteers with emotional and practical succor, bolstered their morale, articulated the meaning of war and held hostage their soldiers' reputations. In return soldiers actively encouraged a 'fireside patriotism' on the home front. They worked directly, through private correspondence and letters to newspapers, and in public meetings, church services, sanitary fairs and other fund-raising occasions. But they also effected an influence at a remove, through the patriotic army reports of journalists, agents of the Sanitary and Christian Commissions, and others whose wartime activity took them into the field. And through their deaths, and the community mourning that followed, Union troops prompted large questions about the political and religious meaning of the war. Thus it was that a New York captain could tell his wife, 'It is the soldiers who have educated the people . . . to a just perception of their duties in this contest.'[61]

From the pens and mouths of thousands of Federal soldiers came a message of the justice of the Union cause, of the nation's being on God's side and of the religious significance of the struggle for republican government. As an Ohio corporal explained late in the war, there was a '*big Idea*' at stake, namely 'the principles of Liberty, of Justice, and of the Righteousness which exalteth a Nation'. One wrote to his wife, 'Every day I have a more religious feeling, that this war is a crusade for the good of mankind.' Men wrote on stationery bearing printed verses that fused the religious and the patriotic: 'For right is right, as God is God / And right will surely win; To doubt would be disloyalty – / To falter would be sin.' The Federal army, then, functioned as a surrogate pulpit. Soldiers explained that Lincoln's administration could 'claim the divine blessing' because of its 'manifest desire . . . to do what is right for the sake of right'. Echoing Lincoln and the jeremiads of Protestant preachers, they also presented the war as a punishment for the Union's chronic sins of national pride, neglect of God and black enslavement. But the cause itself was not wrong, and the army itself, not only in the words of its own men but in the potent images of Julia Ward Howe, became a symbol of Christian triumph. In the resounding 'Battle Hymn of the Republic' the Union forces carried the unsheathed sword of the Lord; their watchfires in the 'hundred circling camps' stood as altars; their 'burnished rows of steel' announced the gospel; they, like Christ, died 'to make men free'.[62] Union soldiers – responding to the trumpet call of a wrathful, judgmental God – were engaged in a millennial struggle for both national and religious salvation.

At the same time, the Union army exercised its enormous moral and political authority more prosaically, sustaining the administration by encouraging enlistments, invigorating the Republican–Union party and demonizing the peace opposition. Soldiers broadcast in their home communities their contempt for the cowardly and selfish who sought to avoid service: 'Are they afraid of a little danger of hardship?' asked one volunteer. 'If they are, they are not fit to be called *free Americans*.' The 1863 Conscription Act won the warm support of serving men. 'All men in the Army believe in the Draft', declared a New York officer. 'I think that some of them do not believe in much else beside the President and Drafting.' As well as encouraging recruits for the front line, many soldiers sought to beef up the administration party at home, by calling on wives, sisters and other womenfolk to expand their notions of civic duty. 'I know ladies are not usually interested in such matters [as politics]', wrote an army surgeon to his wife ahead of state elections in 1863, 'but the time has come when they as well as the sterner sex must put a shoulder to the wheel.'[63]

Extreme circumstances – treachery on the home front – demanded extraordinary measures of this kind. Troops 'choked with rage' at

Copperhead opponents of the war. 'I believe I *hate* them worse than the *rebels* themselves', wrote one. Soldiers urged home-front loyalists to control 'every Fop Editor of a Penny Sheet' who warred against the administration's emergency measures. Whenever they heard a 'traitor letting loose his sympathizing slang, they should *bust his crust*'. Peace men 'have no rights *But to be hung*'. At times, indeed, soldiers' burning anger turned moral force into physical coercion. Southern and central Illinois in the early weeks of 1864 witnessed daily 'affrays' between Peace Democrat residents and furloughed volunteers: 'that the soldiers would take but little copperhead lip before proceeding to knock the tories down is hardly a matter of surprise', a loyalist editor reflected. Soldiers helped divide local communities to a degree not seen since the Revolutionary era, sure that, as a gathering of Iowans insisted, 'in this crisis there can be but two classes of men "Patriots and Traitors"'.[64]

The soldiers' role as sustainers of the Union administration achieved its most practical expression at the polls. The experience of war served only to confirm the political loyalties of those who had been Republicans at the outset. 'If people expect me to come home less a Republican than I went out they will be disappointed', an Ohio private told his wife as the second year of war drew to a close. 'I may not then support Abraham Lincoln as ardently as I did but Republicanism does not consist in the support of Abraham Lincoln.'[65] At the same time, large numbers of the 40 percent or so of troops who in 1860 had cast Democratic ballots responded to the rise of Copperheadism and calls for a negotiated peace by cutting their traditional ties and actively sustaining the Union–Republican ticket in the watershed state elections of 1863. Troops tactically furloughed by Lincoln's War Department lieutenants swept Curtin to power in Pennsylvania and John Brough in Ohio. As Lincoln looked ahead to the presidential election year of 1864, he could take much comfort from knowing that he had in his army not only a staunchly loyal political force but one which would play its part in energizing and mobilizing the wider Union public.

The election of 1864: 'the second birth of our nation'

Probably the greatest test of the ability of Lincoln's administration to rally popular support came in the summer and fall of 1864. That year's presidential election followed months of turbulence in public opinion. If by November the outcome appeared a foregone conclusion, that had certainly not been the case in the steamy days of summer, when Union hopes fell to one of their lowest points in the war. John Hay acknow-ledged those swirls of opinion when in June he reflected, 'In the stress of this war politics have drifted out of the hands of politicians & are now more than ever subject to genuine popular currents.' Even so, Lincoln maintained his faith in the fundamental loyalty of the 'honest . . . masses': he was sure, he told the Congregationalist minister Edward N. Kirk, that they would never consent to disunion. But they could be misled into believing that reunion might be realized by means other than war. His administration's task was to keep the hard reality before them. 'Let them know the truth, and the country is safe.'[66]

Following the etiquette of the day, Lincoln avoided brashly soliciting a return to office, but by the fall of 1863 his ambition had become clear enough. His desire for re-election was understandable in human terms: however oppressive the burdens and cares of office, he conceded that 'it would be a very sweet satisfaction' to win the approval of his fellow citizens. But he could invoke a public interest, too: 'swapping horses in the middle of the stream' would be risky and destabilizing, and the endorsement of his policies would put a large nail in the coffin of the Confederacy.[67]

His hopes would depend to a large degree on factors beyond his direct control, for public confidence was intimately connected with battlefield success. Though Lincoln had real faith in Grant and Sherman, and in their plans for a broad-front spring offensive into the Confederate heartlands, he could not be sure how quickly they would press on to a signal victory; he could also reflect, as Nicolay put it, that 'our Spring campaigns . . . have so generally been failures that people are begin-ning to feel superstitious about them'.[68] But whatever the military con-tingencies, there was still much the president could do, and rather than allow inertia to stifle all action, Lincoln busied himself with the election throughout the year, working to ensure an efficient harnessing of the agencies of home-front mobilization: party, churches and army. Of these, the most problematic was his party, which was riven by factionalism in Washington and beyond.

Lincoln had to address these party divisions well before the election campaign, for there would be no re-election without renomination. He knew he faced opposition from a minority within most of the state par-ties, mainly from radicals who doubted his commitment to the rights of freedmen in the post-war order, but also from those who thought that he was simply not up to the job. Chase – radical, ambitious, confident of his intellectual superiority and enjoying an independent power-base through his command of Treasury Department patronage – posed the chief threat.

In February Senator Samuel C. Pomeroy called on the party to ditch Lincoln and adopt Chase, but his circular letter provoked a sharp backlash, not least since the war at last appeared to be going well. Many state Republican organizations came out strongly for Lincoln, and even Ohio (the Treasury secretary's home state) endorsed the president. Chase unpersuasively denied advance knowledge of the circular and shortly announced he was not a candidate for his party's nomination.

Republican intrigues against Lincoln did not end there. As Nicolay dyspeptically remarked, various other names were floated by a few malcontents who wanted to establish 'the nucleus of a little faction in opposition to Lincoln, but there is not the remotest prospect that their eggs will hatch'.[69] One name was Grant, who actually had no wish to challenge the incumbent and whom Lincoln brought to the capital to be ceremoniously promoted to general-in-chief. Another was Frémont, who was more open to overtures of this kind but who lacked any real power-base outside the Missouri community of antislavery radicals and German Americans. At Cleveland on the last day of May these westerners joined with a section of organized abolitionism, represented by Wendell Phillips, and a cluster of Democrats to nominate Frémont on an independent ticket designed to siphon off Republican votes. Few Lincolnites, and certainly not Lincoln himself, betrayed serious alarm at a movement – the Radical Democracy – lacking a broad base of public support.

By the time the Republicans gathered at Baltimore in early June Lincoln's nomination was a foregone conclusion. His men dominated the party's national executive and controlled the state delegations, largely made up of federal office-holders who owed their jobs to the president. For months Lincoln had exhausted himself in pursuit of Republican harmony, intervening as mediator in factional conflicts within several states, and much of the goodwill he enjoyed in the party at large derived from a belief that he was well suited to hold it together: even antislavery radicals acknowledged the benefits of his '*patriotic* policy' of uniting 'men of varying shades of sentiment upon a policy radical enough *to destroy slavery*, conservative enough *to save the nation*'.[70] At the same time, even those who disliked Lincoln saw that he enjoyed a warmth of support amongst ordinary voters and soldiers that exceeded his standing with his party's leaders.

The convention, meeting on Lincoln's doorstep, pursued the president's agenda. Following the Army of the Potomac's horrendous recent losses in the Wilderness and at Spotsylvania the mood was generally sombre, darkening further as delegates began to learn of yet more slaughter, at Cold Harbor; yet Grant's bull-dog grit, as Lincoln termed it, and remarkable determination to keep pushing forward to destroy the enemy and capture Richmond – at whatever cost – provided its own hope and grisly inspiration.[71] Delegates unanimously renominated Lincoln and rallied behind a platform which, at Lincoln's insistence, nailed its colors proudly to an emancipation amendment to the Constitution, endorsed the vigorous prosecution of the war, celebrated the fighting men, black as well as white, and demanded the Confederates' unconditional surrender. To this explicit emphasis on liberty (a stunning riposte to the more tentative stance of Frémont's Radical Democrats) the convention married an equal stress on the party's non-partisan and inclusive Unionism: they would campaign not as Republicans but as a broad-based National Union party. To reinforce their appeal to conservatives and to border-state men, delegates chose to nominate for vice-president not the New England incumbent, Maine's Hannibal Hamlin, but the Tennessee loyalist, military governor and War Democrat, Andrew Johnson. Lincoln refused to give even a private indication of his personal preference but many of those who swept Johnson on to the ticket did so in the firm belief that they were following the president's wishes.

Developments in the short term served only to reinforce the sense of Lincoln's firm control. After yet another episode in which Chase provoked a dispute with the president over patronage appointments, the secretary of the Treasury proffered his resignation, now for the third time. It proved once too often. Lincoln, safely renominated and exasperated by Chase's ill-judged attempt to assert his authority, accepted the resignation, telling the secretary that they had 'reached a point of mutual embarrassment' that threatened the public good. For a replacement Lincoln turned to William Pitt Fessenden of Maine, a sound party man, widely respected in Congress yet no threat to the president. Then, soon afterwards, Lincoln pocket-vetoed the Wade–Davis bill: to a measure which showed that some radicals continued to oppose his re-election, he gave a party leader's unequivocal response, underscoring his authority and reassuring the moderates and conservatives of the National Union coalition that the administration would not be the prisoner of congressional radicals.

Yet during the days of high summer, in July and August, the mood in the party grew darker, increasing the pressure on Lincoln to reconsider his position. The stalemate in Virginia continued, with Grant now besieging Petersburg after the unprecedented slaughter of May and June; Sherman, defeated at Kennesaw Mountain, continued at only a snail's pace toward Atlanta; Jubal Early's Confederate raids from the Shenandoah on Washington and other targets, though endangering few lives, inflicted humiliating political damage. With the Union's coffers depleted and another draft imminent, opposition Democrats played on a deepening war-weariness to demand negotiations to end the conflict.

Calls for peace extended well beyond the ranks of the usual Copperhead suspects, who maintained that only the administration's intransigence over emancipation prevented a settlement. Greeley, dreading a future stained by 'new rivers of human blood', learnt that Confederate diplomats were at Niagara Falls on a peace mission. He urged the president to negotiate. Lincoln realized that this was not a serious overture from Jefferson Davis but a ploy to cause political mayhem and swing an election which gave the Confederacy its best hope of independence. Yet he knew, too, that the public mood would not excuse any missed opportunities for peace. Cunningly, he appointed the reluctant Greeley as his envoy to Niagara Falls, correctly believing that nothing would come of a meeting with men who, it unsurprisingly transpired, had been given no power to negotiate. He also set his political terms so high – in a letter 'To Whom It May Concern' – that he knew they would be unacceptable: peace proposals, he insisted, must be based on reunion and 'the abandonment of slavery'. But in setting conditions which appeared fiercer than the Emancipation Proclamation, Lincoln not only gave a political weapon to the opposition, but prompted howls from those National Union party conservatives, and especially War Democrats, committed to reunion alone as the war's goal.[72]

The party's demoralization reached its nadir during mid and late August. Joseph Medill, editor of the *Chicago Tribune*, was just one who feared that 'thanks to Mr. Lincoln's blunders & follies we will be kicked out of the White House'. Alarmed at the implications of a Copperhead victory, well-to-do Republicans sold their greenbacks – federal paper currency unredeemable for precious metal – and bought land. The 'diseased restlessness' of 'growling Republicans', John Hay reported from Illinois, had left the party prey to 'the elements of disorganization that destroyed the whigs'. Nicolay showed a similar contempt for the 'croakers' and 'weak-kneed d—d fools' who had fallen into 'a disastrous panic – a sort of political Bull Run' and who thought that salvation would come only by replacing Lincoln with a new candidate.[73] Radical Republicans, including Tilton of the *Independent* and Greeley, met in New York to plan a new convention, at Cincinnati in late September, which would choose a new standard-bearer – perhaps Ben Butler, or Chase, or even Grant.

Four days later, on 22 August, the party's national chairman, Henry Raymond, told Lincoln that only 'the most resolute and decided action on the part of the Government and its friends' could prevent the key states of Illinois, Indiana, and Pennsylvania – and so the country – 'from falling into hostile hands': a peace commission to Richmond, specifying reunion but not emancipation as the basis of negotiations, would alone persuade the Union's doubters that the administration was not deliberately protracting the war in order to secure abolition. Lincoln dallied with the idea, believing that Davis would myopically turn down the proposal and so reinvigorate northern Unionism. But on reflection he chose to reject what would have appeared an ignominious surrender, 'worse than losing the Presidential contest'. And that contest did indeed look to be lost. In a despairing private memorandum of 23 August he deemed it 'exceedingly probable that this Administration will not be re-elected': in that case he must 'so co-operate with the President elect, as to save the Union between the election and the inauguration', for Lincoln knew that the Democrats' nominee – even if a Union loyalist like McClellan – would be bound by a platform that would open the door to *de facto* Confederate independence.[74]

Yet even in the darkest days Lincoln resisted all thought of withdrawing from the race, convinced it would produce not a Republican victory but party confusion and in-fighting. Denying that he had been 'seduced by . . . the lust of power', he caustically asked if those who charged him with hurting the common cause had 'thought of that common cause when trying to break me down?' His supporters around the country voiced their alarm. 'You have the hearts of the *people* and will have *their votes*', Samuel Carey wrote. 'Your withdrawal would disintegrate the union party & destroy us. A victory by Grant & Sherman will secure you every electoral vote in the Union and we will elect you at all events.'[75]

It was a prescient judgment, for on 2 September Sherman would capture Atlanta – the Confederates' workshop and a bridgehead for controlling the Gulf states – and a little later Sheridan would crush Early's forces in the Shenandoah. In fact, the spirits of Union men had begun to lift even before then, when the Democrats adopted a 'surrender platform' at their Chicago convention: nominating McClellan as presidential candidate could not disguise Vallandigham's inky thumbprints on a program which deemed the war a failure and called for a truce as a step toward ending the conflict 'on the basis of the Federal Union of the States'. However, it was mainly the breakthrough on the battlefield that effected what Nicolay described as 'a perfect revolution in feeling', for most Republicans agreed that the Atlanta victory alone 'ought to win the Presidential contest for us' and they turned to that campaign 'hopeful, jubilant . . . and confident of success'.[76]

The party now drew together. A flood of reports told the White House that Republican Cassandras – the 'parcel of sore headed, disappointed, impracticable politicians', as one of Lincoln's Illinois associates dismissed them – had been silenced. One of those 'soreheads', the *Independent*'s Theodore Tilton, promised Nicolay that the 'sudden lighting up of the public mind' would surely heal divisions. 'Rather than have Chicago and McClellan triumph', he declared, 'I would cheerfully give up my life, with only an hour's preparation for death. My hands are tired with writing private letters, far & near, counseling all my friends to unite on Mr. Lincoln.' The plans for a new convention collapsed, as state governors emphatically endorsed the president. Only Frémont's candidacy stood in the way of electoral unity. Probably through the efforts of Senator Chandler, concerned like other radicals that a split vote would open the door to McClellan and 'treachery', a deal was brokered by which Frémont would withdraw if Montgomery Blair left the cabinet. Lincoln liked his postmaster general and admired his administrative ability but knew he was an increasing liability. Blair's deep conservatism on racial issues and hot-blooded propensity for making personal enemies had alienated the party's radicals, notably in his own Maryland and in Frémont's Missouri. 'Blair every one hates', Henry Wilson told Lincoln, 'tens of thousands of men will be lost to you or will give a reluctant vote on account of the Blairs.' Frémont pulled out on 17 September and six days later Lincoln wrote to the loyal Blair requesting his resignation, which was duly forthcoming.[77]

Throughout the two months of serious campaigning Lincoln, like McClellan, made few appearances in public, and cultivated an impression that he was remote from the action: he told Francis Carpenter, 'I cannot run the political machine; I have enough on my hands without *that*. It is the *people's* business, – the election is in their hands.' But he was busy enough behind the scenes, trying to keep the party focused, intervening on behalf of incumbent Republicans in congressional races, striving to heal local conflicts in fractious key states, notably Pennsylvania and Missouri, and aiming to neuter hostile editors like Bennett of the *New York Herald* by dangling the prospect of a government post. Lincoln's concessions to both conservatives and radicals reinforced the unifying effect on the party of the Chicago outcome: even Wade and Davis took to the stump, as did Chase, aglow in hope that he might replace the ailing chief justice, Taney. The president kept in touch not just with Raymond and the party's national executive committee but with local leaders, taking a deep interest in the activities of the Union Leagues and valuing no less than anything their work as propagandists.[78]

Gratifyingly for the White House, the campaign drenched the electorate in an unprecedented torrent of publications, produced at unheard-of expense. Whatever the frictions between the powerful state committees and the Union Congressional Committee, between the localities and the center of a loose-jointed, largely decentralized organization, the party's organizers supplied literally millions of printed items. Underpinning the party's propaganda battle were the hundreds of small-town daily papers, whose proudly independent editors had sustained Lincoln even during the hard days of summer, reflecting a telling depth of support for the president amongst local subscribers. These editors encouraged the efforts of the myriad local Wide Awake and Union clubs, chided members into ever more energetic canvassing and document-distribution, and carried throughout their neighborhoods uplifting reports of public meetings, spectacular marches and horse-drawn patriotic tableaux.[79]

No less significant than the administration's faith in the agency of party was their rallying of institutional Protestantism. Lincoln himself seized every reasonable opportunity to harness to his chariot of re-election the patriotism of religious bodies. A striking instance occurred in May. The supreme body of the Methodist Episcopal Church, meeting in Philadelphia, appointed five ministers to deliver an address to the president and assure him of the denomination's continuing support for the Union and its war aims. One of the party, Granville Moody, knew the president and met him in advance. Lincoln, with his party's nominating convention only weeks away, saw a chance to stage-manage the occasion and asked Moody to leave a copy of the address. When the deputation arrived the next morning they were ushered in by the secretary of state and received 'with great courtesy' by the president and senior cabinet members. The president stood 'straight as an arrow' as he listened to the Methodists' statement and then took from his desk the brief response that he had prepared overnight. In five short sentences he thanked them, endorsed their sentiments, ensured that other churches would take no offense by his singling out Methodists for praise, and then flatteringly described them as 'the most important of all' denominations: 'It is no fault in others that the Methodist Church sends more soldiers to field, more nurses to the hospitals, and more prayers to heaven than any.' After a brief, informal conversation the ministers withdrew, much impressed with Lincoln's generous, high-toned remarks. Returning to their Conference the next morning, proudly clutching a signed copy of the president's words to show their colleagues, they were taken aback to discover that a full account of the meeting had already been published in the daily papers. The White House had telegraphed the news the previous day; the story had gone into type in Philadelphia even before the committee had left Washington. Lincoln's reply was designed not just for his five visitors but for the other 7,000 ministers and nearly one million members of the largest, most influential church of the land. Lincoln had left nothing to chance.[80]

By early September the majority of the North's active Protestants were evidently committed to Lincoln's re-election. Though a group of alienated radicals, many of them liberal Protestants, took a lead from Anna Dickinson, Wendell Phillips and other unyielding critics of the administration, far more significant was the binding of Garrison's wing of abolitionism and its newspaper presses into the National Union coalition. They joined mainstream evangelicals to form a broad front of political activists. Lincoln had good reason at this time to remark to a Congregationalist minister, 'I rely upon the religious sentiment of the country, which I am told is very largely for me.' Indeed, the final two months of the campaign witnessed the most complete fusing of religious crusade and political mobilization in America's electoral experience.[81]

The Kentucky Presbyterian, Robert Breckinridge, who chaired the party's Baltimore convention in June, was only one of hundreds of ministers who adorned National Union platforms and took to the stump. In Chillicothe, Ohio, Granville Moody opened the party's campaign with a three-hour speech liberally interspersed with hymn-singing, prayer and Scripture readings on the duty of loyalty. Thomas Eddy drove himself to exhaustion as he engaged in an unending round of ward and camp meetings, election speeches, political sermons, addresses to troops and – as a Methodist newspaper editor – of religio-political journalism. The National Union Committee employed Henry Ward Beecher to speak in the final stages of the campaign. Matthew Simpson, at the request of local Republican organizers, delivered his celebrated war speech – a setpiece *tour de force* – at the New York Academy of Music just a few days before the poll, in the presence of the *Tribune* and the city's other newspapers: though avoiding conspicuous partisanship, the bishop left no one in any doubt that his celebration of national greatness amounted to a passionate call to sustain the 'railsplitter . . . President'.[82]

The Union Leagues printed and circulated many of these political sermons. Religious tract society agents distributed campaign literature. Religious newspapers called on churches to become Republican clubs. Gatherings of ministers, in Baptist and Congregational associations, Presbyterian synods and Methodist conferences more or less explicitly told their members to vote the Lincoln ticket. They 'should march as churches in our processions, as churches to the polls', insisted the New York

Independent. Gilbert Haven called on Methodists 'once more [to] march to the ballot-box, an army of Christ, with the banner of the cross, and deposit, as she can, almost a million votes for her true representative'.[83]

Encouraging this interplay of religion and politics were Lincoln's calls for days of national prayer and thanksgiving, which he called on several occasions during the war. He had on several earlier occasions reached out to the devout in this way. As well as providing an opportunity for ministers to rally support for the continuing struggle, these services gave the hundreds of thousands who attended a consciousness of belonging to a single community united in sacrifice and aspiration. By a short proclamation Lincoln could use one of his most supportive networks to secure a national charge of adrenalin. He chose his occasions with deliberation, as his political opponents understood. In 1864 he hesitated over appointing a day of fasting and humiliation during the low point of summer, fearing its impact on popular morale, and left it to Congress to take the initiative. But after the successes at Mobile and Atlanta he moved swiftly to proclaim Sunday 10 September a day of thanksgiving. In this he was effectively licensing every minister to wave the Union–Republican flag from the pulpit. Opposition Democrats, sensing a blend of low political cunning and the 'Phariseeism of New England', cried foul when Union clergy read to their congregations a proclamation which attributed the turn of events to God's intervention and asked for prayers 'that He will continue to uphold the government of the United States against all the efforts of public enemies and secret foes'. Then, on 20 October, Lincoln issued a further Proclamation of Thanksgiving: with the election under three weeks away he pointedly wrote of the Union's hope, under 'our Heavenly Father', of 'an ultimate and happy deliverance' from the trials of war, and the triumph of 'the cause of freedom and humanity'.[84]

Through platform, pulpit and printed page, Republican party activists rallied a public overwhelmingly devoted to restoring the Union. Issues of principle would dominate, but campaign discourse necessarily included celebrating Lincoln's presidential qualities and countering the carping of those who deemed him unfit for his job. The president's Republican critics detected vacillation, timidity, weakness, and a lack of the 'overshadowing ability' that marked, for instance, Chase's handling of national finances or Grant's military command. Lincoln himself judged he was most vulnerable on the score of his personal leadership and generally even those who listed his virtues also conceded his shortcomings, fallibility, and lack of brilliance. But if few claimed greatness for Lincoln, almost all extolled his personal integrity, kindliness, honesty of purpose, political candor and fair dealing, refusal to bear grudges, and – above all – his persevering and unbending Unionism. These qualities took on added lustre when set alongside the sombre portrait that National Union men sketched of McClellan: the vain, opportunistic, cowardly and two-faced nominee of a schizophrenic party.

Union party campaigners, then, were hardly exponents of a cult of personality. Yet they benefited from a widely shared perception of Lincoln as a moral agent, whether as an honest, plain man of the people or as the human means by which a higher power had delivered emancipation. John Gulliver, the Congregational minister of Norwich, Connecticut, in a widely circulated public letter, praised him for his stern antislavery resolve throughout the turns and twists of war: 'Slow, if you please, but *true*. Unimpassioned, if you please, but *true*. Jocose, trifling, if you please, but *true*. Reluctant to part with unworthy official advisers, but *true* himself – *true as steel!*' And on the night of Lincoln's re-election a fellow clergyman displayed a transparency over his door: 'The angel of the Lord called unto Abraham out of heaven a second time.' Harriet Beecher Stowe and others helped wrap Lincoln, the southern-born westerner of unorthodox belief but now the friend of fast-days and national thanksgivings, in the mantle of high-principled New England Puritanism.[85]

Faint echoes of the 1840s still sounded, though. According to one of Lincoln's Treasury officials, Lucius E. Chittenden, 'there were sullen whisperings that Mr. Lincoln had no religious opinions nor any interest in churches or Christian institutions'. The president was not helped by his apparent ambivalence toward the National Reform Association, an interdenominational body established in 1863 to secure a Christian amendment to the Constitution, recognizing the nation's dependence on God. The Association had initially enjoyed the support of mainstream evangelicals who thought that the unamended Constitution explained why the Emancipation Proclamation had not brought about any improvement in the Union's fortunes. Lincoln himself seemed to give its representatives a sympathetic hearing. But the movement's popularity slowly waned as a variety of radical evangelicals, Jews and non-Christians expressed their opposition, and as the Union secured battlefield success. When Lincoln failed to act purposefully, Thomas Sproull, the editor of the *Reformed Presbyterian and Covenanter*, denounced the president as a deist who had never distinctly recognized Christianity and had 'refused to honor the Son'. Sproull appealed to all 'who believe in Christ' to prevent the infidel's return to office.[86]

However, Lincoln's re-election depended far less on his satisfying public curiosity about his private standing with God than on the depth of popular commitment to the Union and on convincing people that the Republican–Union candidate was the nation's only realistic guarantor. An evangelical banker, Joseph B. Maxfield of Brooklyn, wrote to the president as polling-day approached to ask urgently if the Lincoln who publicly acknowledged God in his proclamations was also 'rejoicing in hope of eternal life through the precious blood of Christ'. But the president's answer would not affect his vote: Maxfield had 'learned to love [Lincoln] as a man' and looked to him 'as being under God – the nation's hope'.[87] The great achievement of the Union party's campaigning was to harness this deep-rooted nationalism through an appeal to both high purpose and political realism.

Familiar secular and religious themes were sharpened, heightened and interwoven in the rhetoric of the campaign, as political and church presses, often indistinguishable, and embracing Lincoln's own vision, gave meaning to the struggle for national existence. The battle to preserve popular self-government against 'the pretentious rule of an aristocratic class' set Christian civilization against barbarism; the war to suppress an unholy rebellion against 'the best, most equitable, most righteous, most benevolent government' had, through sacrifice, given birth to a more devout, elevated, unselfish and God-fearing patriotism. The nation's past was the history of the providential handing down of a priceless heritage from the revolutionary Fathers to the current generation. The nation's present showed the continuing marks of God's favor: burgeoning philanthropy, religious revivals, the yoking of 'wives, daughters and sweethearts' in the common pursuit of the Union cause, and the leading of the Union's Christian soldiers out of the Wilderness. The purified nation of the future would pursue an 'onward march to material prosperity and empire', battling 'the leagued foes of Freedom and Republicanism all round the world'.[88]

By 1864 most Republicans were committed to a restored Union, shorn of slavery and economically transformed. They soft-pedaled the emancipation theme during the campaign, alarmed as Democrats seized on Lincoln's 'Niagara manifesto' as evidence that antislavery bigotry alone prevented peace. But the issue of the slaves' freedom was hardly absent. Given the broad-based racial antipathies and stereotyping amongst the Union electorate, Republicans tended to emphasize the pragmatic before the principled benefits of the administration's policy. Emancipation provided the means of victory: only the 'black warriors' whom his proclamation had secured for the Union armies now stood between the rebels and Confederate independence, Lincoln insisted, in a widely circulated interview. Emancipation also promised economic benefits to ordinary working men, 'the bone and sinew' of the country, since the death of a socially hidebound, aristocratic South would open the way for general education, skilled wage labor, freedom to help oneself, technological and industrial progress, social mobility, class harmony, and nation-wide prosperity. And, if Lincoln was right that slavery had caused the war, then only emancipation would bring permanent peace to a reunited country.

Yet more often than not, even in the moderate heartlands of Republicanism, these pragmatic considerations were framed by a Protestant language that signaled a deeper meaning. This cast emancipation as atonement for sin, a means of national redemption, an honoring of God's purposes and a working out of the principle of the equal brotherhood of man under the universal fatherhood of God. Few would have quarreled with the *Chicago Tribune*'s verdict that 'this is in its profoundest aspect, a religious contest . . . a war for Christian civilization, for God's pure truth'. What, following national redemption, 'shall prevent the American Union from being, henceforth the crowning national work of the Almighty, the wonder of the world?'[89]

An election which promised to inaugurate 'the second birth of our Nation' could not, National Union leaders insisted, be a conventional party struggle. 'Remember', urged the national executive committee, 'that the contest is not one for party ascendancy' but for the government's survival.[90] With life-long 'genuine' Democrats prominent at local and national level, gracing public platforms and chairing meetings, the Union party proved brilliantly successful in presenting itself as a unique cross-party vehicle of nationalism and in characterizing its opponents as 'pseudo', 'humbug' or 'bastard' Democrats, a factious coalition of disunionist traitors, peace-plotters, foreign financiers and naive McClellanites.

The Democrats' Chicago platform, with its call for an armistice and a convention of states, provided an easy target for 'patriot' opponents: a ceasefire for negotiation, quite apart from implicitly conceding the Confederacy's separate nationality, would give the rebels time to regroup and rebuild, demoralize the North and bring a dishonorable peace that would see 'the Potomac and the Ohio washing our southern shores'. After recent successes the Union stood 'just on the eve of victory', facing an exhausted foe and leaving Jeff Davis desperate to win through the ballot box what he had failed to achieve on the battlefield. War, dreadful though it was, insisted Unionists, offered the sole honorable course, for only by crushing the South's capacity to resist would American nationality be established 'on a basis as unyielding and eternal as the Rock of Ages'. The impious treason of the Chicago men mocked the legitimate tradition of Christian pacifism. As one Lincolnite put it, 'while nearly every pulpit in the land gives its utterances in favor of war, the cry from the dram-shops and all the purlieus of vice is peace! peace!'[91]

Unionists had a no more effective emblem of the moral legitimacy of war than the nation's soldiers – martial Christianity personified – who became a ubiquitous campaign presence. McClellan had been nominated to scoop the soldiers' vote but whatever loyalty fighting men might feel for their old commander generally could not outweigh their trust in Lincoln's steadfastness and their contempt for what one called 'the cor-ruption, concession, and damnation policy of the Democracy'. Officers addressed National Union rallies. Ex-prisoners of war told of Confederate inhumanities. Wounded men and amputees provided graphic reminders of the nation's debt to past and present heroes. Scores of ordinary sol-diers graced political platforms. Military bands and escorts accompanied snaking processions of Wide Awakes. Regiments marched by the White House to deliver a salute and occasionally prompt a reply from the pres-ident. Collectively they offered an unequivocal message: the 'true road to peace' lay through hard fighting till the rebellion was put down. Only a Union vote would honor the bloody sacrifices of 'Father Abraham's boys in blue'.[92]

Ever-present troops did as much as anything to reinforce the overall thrust of the Union party's rhetoric, that voters faced a simple, life-and-death choice in a crisis of unique historical significance. In the cross-roads of history they must choose between good and evil, between legitimate authority and anarchy, between 'the life or degradation of the nation'. Defeat for Lincoln on 'the day of national judgment' would mean 'the hands on the dial of Civilization will be set a century backward'. Worse, 'failure now is failure forever': 'We may write "Ichabod" on the wall of its Temple of Liberty – "The glory is departed."'[93]

Democrats ridiculed such apocalyptic rhetoric as a smokescreen to hide Lincoln's tragic blend of incompetence and revolutionary dogmatism. They lambasted emancipation, racial revolution, national 'consolidationism' and the threat to individual liberties (underscored by a September draft) as malign Puritanical meddling, and promised instead 'the Union as it was, the Constitution as it is, and the nigger where he was'. It was a message which might have worked before Atlanta changed the country's mood. In the party's strongholds of the lower North, Midwest and upper South an anti-war, lilywhite, anti-Yankee message played well amongst some agrarian groups, the mass of small producers and urban immig-rants. But the improving military situation exposed a party divided between the minority Copperhead element and those who rejected any hint of compromise with the rebels. Unable to articulate a consistent message, in danger of appearing unpatriotic, and failing to make most voters see race and not nationality as the key issue, Democrats remained in the eyes of political centrists more of a protest movement than a viable alternative administration.

Rhetorical strategy, organizational effort and the judicious furloughing of troops brought Lincoln's party stunning success in the state elections in October. The victory in Pennsylvania, which Lincoln awaited anxiously 'because of her enormous weight and influence', and even more in Indiana, where a Copperhead administration would have provided 'a grand central rallying point for . . . lurking treason', removed any real doubt about a National Union victory a month later and demoralized the opposition.[94] On 8 November Lincoln and Johnson took the electoral votes of all but three of the twenty-five states in which the contest was fought.

Even so, McClellan was not crushed: although he took only New Jersey and the slave states of Delaware and Kentucky, he won a respectable 44 percent of the four million votes cast. A solid core of Democratic voters, committed to the Union but not to emancipation, kept it a viable and competitive force in the free states of the middle Atlantic seaboard and the Midwest. In some areas McClellan won with a bigger vote than his party had secured in 1860. These were mainly cities and mining counties with a large proportion of Irish and other foreign-born laborers anxious about inflation, the power of capital and being drafted into a war for the negro. 'Pat casts his vote (or votes) on the side which he is told is hostile to "naygurs"', Greeley judged, 'and struggles to roll back a threatened inundation of free black labor from the South.'[95]

By contrast, Lincoln's strength lay chiefly amongst native-born farmers, but he also did well amongst the skilled workers and professional middle classes of the cities. New England and areas of Yankee settlement remained strongholds, but the party now took a grip in places where it had once been quite weak, including Baltimore and Philadelphia. In the lower North and border states the appeal to conservative Unionists of the Fillmore–Bell–Everett stamp proved even more successful than it had four years earlier, and Everett himself campaigned for the president's re-election. As in 1860, Lincoln made inroads into the German vote in Missouri, Illinois and Wisconsin, having taken pains to ensure they were targeted in their own language. And, true to the promise that (as one volunteer told the president) 'the Soldiers vote will be all on one side', Lincoln benefited from a four-to-one advantage amongst the fighting men. While not crucial to his overall victory, it certainly gave him the edge in a handful of states.

Most remarkable of all was the political fusion of most of the core elements of northern Protestantism with the Republican–Union party. 'There probably never was an election in all history into which the religious element entered so largely, and so nearly all on one side', rejoiced the editor of the nation's chief Methodist newspaper, expressing the widespread belief of most party activists. The big evangelical denominations, and the small, radical antislavery offshoots, together with the Quakers, Unitarians and other liberal Protestant groups, swung behind Lincoln even more firmly than in 1860. McClellan unsurprisingly retained the Democrats' hold on most Catholic voters; Protestant editors universally lamented the 'rebel sympathy' of the newly-naturalized Irish Romanists in particular. Democrats probably also won a majority of Episcopalian and Old School Presbyterian voters, as well as antimission Baptists and Disciples in the lower Midwest. But most Protestants found their center of gravity securely within a Union party that seems to have tugged many Baptists and Methodists, and even Old School Presbyterians, from Democratic moorings. In a celebratory editorial, written in the grey dawn after election day, Theodore Tilton attributed Lincoln's victory to 'nothing less than an over-ruling Divine Hand outstretched to save the Republic'. More prosaically we can see it as in large part the result of an extraordinary mobilization of Union opinion by those who saw themselves as God's agents: the leaders of the Protestant churches.[96]

Lincoln regarded his re-election, both process and outcome, as a defining episode of the war, one which thoroughly vindicated his faith in 'the people'. He rejoiced with Hay that a 'quiet and orderly' election had revealed the essentially non-coercive genius of the Union's free institutions and the nation's capacity to function even in wartime 'without running into anarchy or despotism'. During the darkest days of the conflict, he had been sure that the nation would endure if its survival were to depend on ordinary men and women's loyalty to its ideals and institutions. When, briefly, it had seemed that a peace candidate might triumph in 1864, he had not doubted the continuing depth of popular Unionism, nor had he given any thought to canceling or postponing an election which embodied the constitutional and republican values for which the war was being fought, and through which the voices of nationalism could express themselves. He knew, as a fellow Illinoisan put it, 'that we are not to expect the Union to be saved by any one in particular, but by the whole people. . . . They must save it – the wise common sense of the people rather than the craft of its leaders, the organic wisdom of the nation rather than the cunning of astute politicians.'[97]

What would have followed a victory for McClellan on the Chicago platform is a matter of uncertain speculation. Nicolay, along with so many others, thought it would see peace bought 'at the cost of Disunion, Secession, Bankruptcy and National Dishonor, and an "ultimate" Slave Empire'.[98] McClellan himself would no doubt have opposed a permanent separation, but it is not clear how he would have prevented it had he been driven to concede an armistice. Either way, universal emancipation would have been an improbable outcome: whether a Democratic peace brought a reunified nation or a fractured Union, it would surely have seen slavery still legally protected in parts of North America.

In the event, the Republican–Union victory kept the door open for the triumph of a quite different vision for the nation, one articulated by both Lincoln and a myriad of local activists. It was based on a deep sense of America's historical significance and providential role, and on a continuing commitment in the present and future to a set of ideas based less on blood and race than on ideals of equality and freedom. One of Lincoln's great political achievements was so to define these national ideals and elevate the Union cause as to harness the energizing forces of Yankee Protestant radicalism, without at the same time frightening off more conservative Unionists. In emphasizing, as historians have so much, Lincoln's shrewd holding together of a broad Union coalition and his pragmatism in keeping conservatives on board, there is a danger of undervaluing the significance of the more radical elements in the amalgam. Lincoln knew that for most of the time, given the problems facing any third party in a two-party political system, radicals had little option but to stick with the Republicans. But he also recognized the destructive power of defeatism and war-weariness, and the need to harness enough of the radicals' vision to keep Union loyalists energized and inspired. He needed the radicals, just as they needed him. Over time he showed enough of those who were ready to listen that he was, in Congressman William Kelley's words, 'the wisest radical of them all'.[99]

Notes

1 James G. Randall, *Constitutional Problems under Lincoln* (rev. edn, Urbana, IL: University of Illinois Press, 1951); Mark E. Neely, *The Fate of Liberty: Abraham Lincoln and Civil Liberties* (New York: Oxford University Press, 1991); Herman Belz, *Abraham Lincoln, Constitutionalism and Equal Rights in the Civil War Era* (New York: Fordham University Press, 1998), 17–43.

2 Ian Kershaw, *Hitler* (London: Longman, 1991), 10–11 and *passim*, offers a brilliant analysis of the quintessence of charismatic authority.

3 *CW*, 5:346; Mark Grimsley, *The Hard Hand of War: Union Military Policy toward Southern Civilians 1861–1865* (Cambridge: Cambridge University Press, 1995), 87.

4 *CW*, 5:98, 6:257.

5 William O. Stoddard, *Inside the White House in War Times: Memoirs and Reports of Lincoln's Secretary*, ed. Michael Burlingame (Lincoln, NB: University of Nebraska Press, 2000), 101; *CW*, 8:151.

6 *DJH*, 193–4.

7 Grimsley, *Hard Hand of War*, 171–4, 182, 213.

8 Neely, *The Fate of Liberty*, 52–3; *CW*, 5:436–7, 6:451–2.

9 Neely, *The Fate of Liberty*, 14–18, 58, 64.

10 Donald, 419.

11 *CW*, 6:260–9.

12 *Diary of Gideon Welles: Secretary of the Navy under Lincoln and Johnson*, 3 vols (Boston, MA: Houghton Mifflin Company, 1911), 1:432; Howard K. Beale, *The Diary of Edward Bates 1859–1866* (Washington, DC: Government Printing Office, 1933), 306; *CW*, 6:460; Neely, *The Fate of Liberty*, 69–71.

13 D.D. Field to AL, 8 Nov. 1862, ALP; Mark E. Neely, Jr, *The Abraham Lincoln Encyclopedia* (New York: McGraw-Hill, 1982), 57; *CW*, 6:492.

14 S.W. Oakey to AL, 5 Nov. 1862, ALP; *HI*, 331; Allen C. Guelzo, *Abraham Lincoln: Redeemer President* (Grand Rapids, MI: William B. Eerdmans Publishing Co., 1999), 363; Michael Burlingame, ed., *At Lincoln's Side: John Hay's Civil War Correspondence and Selected Writings* (Carbondale, IL: Southern Illinois University Press, 2000), 54.

15 Neely, *The Fate of Liberty*, 113–38.

16 Guelzo, *Abraham Lincoln*, 383; H. Seymour to AL, 3, 21 Aug. 1863, ALP.

17 *RWAL*, 195.

18 *CW*, 5:424. The words, though not Lincoln's, were ones to which he enthusiastically assented.

19 David Donald, *Lincoln Reconsidered: Essays on the Civil War Era* (2nd edn, New York: Random House, 1961), 57–60; William E. Gienapp, 'Abraham Lincoln and Presidential Leadership', in James M. McPherson, ed., *'We Cannot Escape History': Lincoln and the Last Best Hope of Earth* (Urbana, IL: University of Illinois Press, 1995), 77–8.

20 Phillip Shaw Paludan, *'The Better Angels of Our Nature': Lincoln, Propaganda and Public Opinion in the North During the American Civil War* (The Lincoln Museum, Fort Wayne, IN, 1992), 12, 17 and *passim*.

21 *DJH*, 128; Neely, *Abraham Lincoln Encyclopedia*, 68; F.B. Carpenter, *The Inner Life of Abraham Lincoln: Six Months at the White House* (Lincoln, NB: University of Nebraska Press, 1995; originally published New York, 1866), 126–7; N&H, 6:152–3; Burlingame, ed., *At Lincoln's Side*, 54; *Chicago Tribune*, 16 Jan. 1864.

22 Eric L. McKitrick, 'Party Politics and the Union and Confederate War Efforts', in William Nisbet Chambers and Walter Dean Burnham, eds, *The American Party Systems: Stages*

of *Political Development* (2nd edn, New York: Oxford University Press, 1967), 117–51, presents a powerful case for the value of party to the Union cause. Mark E. Neely, 'The Civil War and the Two-Party System', in McPherson, ed., *'We Cannot Escape History'*, 86–104, offers a cautionary note.

23 Allan G. Bogue, *The Congressman's Civil War* (Cambridge: Cambridge University Press, 1989), 31–40, 51.

24 William B. Hesseltine, *Lincoln and the War Governors* (New York: Alfred A. Knopf, 1955), 198–200, 314–15, 319–39.

25 McKitrick, 'Party Politics and the Union and Confederate War Efforts', 148–9, 151; Adam I.P. Smith, 'The Presidential Election of 1864: Party Politics and Political Mobilisation during the American Civil War' (PhD thesis, University of Cambridge, 1999), 18.

26 *CW*, 5:494; H.C. Bowen to AL, 2 Dec. 1862, ALP.

27 *Lincoln Observed*, 64–6, 245; *DJH*, 127, 332 (the corrrespondent was Whitelaw Reid).

28 *Lincoln's Journalist*, 296.

29 *Lincoln Observed*, 1–11, 50–2, 66, 69–70, 104, 113, 245; Robert S. Harper, *Lincoln and the Press* (New York: McGraw-Hill, 1951), 173–5, 221, 282–9.

30 *DJH*, 78, 146.

31 John W. Forney, *Anecdotes of Public Men*, 2 vols (New York: Harper and Brothers, 1873, 1881), 1:283; Harper, *Lincoln and the Press*, 109–12, 175, 179–84.

32 Frank Freidel, ed., *Union Pamphlets of the Civil War*, 2 vols (Cambridge, MA: The Belknap Press of Harvard University Press, 1967), 1:1–24.

33 *CW*, 6:264; Neely, 'The Civil War and the Two-Party System', 93–4.

34 *CW*, 6:267–8.

35 Smith, 'The Presidential Election of 1864', 53–4.

36 *DJH*, 129; Smith, 'The Presidential Election of 1864', 88–100.

37 *Northwestern Christian Advocate*, 13, 28 Aug., 16 Oct. 1861.

38 James H. Moorhead, *American Apocalypse: Yankee Protestants and the Civil War 1860–69* (New Haven, CT: Yale University Press, 1978), x, 39. See also Peter J. Parish, 'The Instruments of Providence: Slavery, Civil War and the American Churches', in W.J. Sheils, ed., *Studies in Church History: vol. 20: The Church and War* (Oxford: Blackwell, 1983), 291–320.

39 Moorhead, *American Apocalypse*, 96–104, 112; *Northwestern Christian Advocate*, 12 June, 4 Sept. 1861; Victor B. Howard, *Religion and the Radical Republican Movement 1860–1870* (Lexington, KY: University Press of Kentucky, 1990), 11–67; John R. McKivigan, *The War against Proslavery Religion: Abolitionism and the Northern Churches 1830–1865* (Ithaca, NY: Cornell University Press, 1984), 183–201; West Wisconsin Annual Conference of the Wesleyan Methodist Connection of America to AL, 11 Oct. 1862, ALP. The conservative Charles Hodge presents a shimmering example of how the fear of Union defeat worked to blur the line between abolition as legitimate end and emancipation as morally justified means. Charles Hodge, 'The General Assembly', *Biblical Repertory and Princeton Review*, 36 (July 1864), 538–51.

40 *DJH*, 89; *CW*, 6:486–7; Brooks D. Simpson and Jean V. Berlin, eds, *Selected Correspondence of William T. Sherman, 1860–1865* (Chapel Hill, NC: University of North Carolina Press, 1999), 500–1.

41 I. Leeser to AL, 21 Aug. 1862; Board of Delegates of American Israelites to AL, 6 Oct. 1862, 8 Jan. 1863, ALP.

42 The issue was neither new nor unique to Methodism. The case of S.B. McPheeters had troubled Lincoln since late 1862. This pro-Confederate Presbyterian minister had been forced from his St Louis pulpit by Unionist troops, though he had not preached rebellion from the pulpit. Lincoln disapproved and countermanded the order. Lewis G. Vander Velde, *The Presbyterian Churches and the Federal Union, 1861–1869* (Cambridge, MA: Harvard University Press, 1932), 305–24.

43 M. Simpson to D.P. Kidder, MEC Bishops' Autographs and Portraits, United Library, Garrett-Evangelical Theological Seminary, Evanston [hereafter IEG]; Donald G. Jones, *The Sectional Crisis and Northern Methodism: A Study in Piety, Political Ethics and Civil Religion* (Metuchen, NJ: Scarecrow Press, 1979), 36, 40, 42; Robert D. Clark, *The Life of Matthew Simpson* (New York: Macmillan, 1956), 224–35. When the delegation of Methodists met Lincoln in May 1864, Ames, in an informal moment, turned the conversation to the issue of the southern Methodist churches, but Lincoln avoided a direct response.

44 George Peck, *The Life and Times of Rev. George Peck D.D.* (New York: Nelson and Phillips, 1874), 380; *Lincoln Observed*, 145; Howard, *Religion and the Radical Republican Movement*, 71; Noyes W. Miner, 'Personal Recollections of Abraham Lincoln', Illinois State Historical Society.

45 E. Nason to AL, 16 April 1861, O.H. Browning to AL, 30 April 1861, ALP; N&H, 6:322–3; *HI*, 602; *CW*, 7:535–6; Burlingame, ed., *At Lincoln's Side*, 135; *DJH*, 132; D.H. Wheeler to D.P. Kidder, 14 Dec. 1863, Kidder Papers, IEG.

46 *Northwestern Christian Advocate*, 2 Oct. 1861; C.B. Trippett to D.P. Kidder, 7 July 1863, Kidder Papers, IEG.

47 George Crooks, *The Life of Bishop Matthew Simpson of the Methodist Episcopal Church* (London: Wesleyan Methodist Book Room, 1891), 377–86; J. Matthew Gallman, *Mastering Wartime: A Social History of Philadelphia during the Civil War* (Cambridge: Cambridge University Press, 1990), 148–51.

48 *Northwestern Christian Advocate*, 8 Jan., 12 Feb., 13 Aug. 1862.

49 George M. Fredrickson, 'The Coming of the Lord: The Northern Protestant Clergy and the Civil War Crisis', in Randall M. Miller, Harry S. Stout and Charles Reagan Wilson, eds, *Religion and the American Civil War* (New York: Oxford University Press, 1998), 110–30; Moorhead, *American Apocalypse*, 129–72; David B. Cheseborough, ed., *God Ordained This War: Sermons on the Sectional Crisis, 1830–1865* (Columbia, SC: University of South Carolina Press, 1991), 6–8, 83–122.

50 *CW*, 7:368.

51 F.P. Blair, Sr, to AL, 18 Dec. 1862, ALP.

52 *Lincoln Observed*, 237.

53 *Lincoln Observed*, 35–45, 92, 107, 235–6, 238.

54 William C. Davis, *Lincoln's Men: How President Lincoln Became Father to an Army and a Nation* (New York: The Free Press, 1999), 130.

55 Davis, *Lincoln's Men*, 54, 56–7, 68, 134–5.

56 Davis, *Lincoln's Men*, 141.

57 Davis, *Lincoln's Men*, 87.

58 J.M. Palmer to D. Davis, 26 Nov. 1862, ALP; James M. McPherson, *What They Fought For, 1861–1865* (Baton Rouge, LA: Louisiana State University Press, 1994), 4–6; Joseph Allan Frank, *With Ballot and Bayonet: The Political Socialization of American Civil War Soldiers* (Athens, GA: University of Georgia Press, 1998).

59 Reid Mitchell, *Civil War Soldiers* (New York: Viking Penguin, 1988), 11–12, 16–17, 20–1.

60 Davis, *Lincoln's Men*, 99, 101; *RWAL*, 429; McPherson, *What They Fought For*, 62.

61 Gerald Linderman, *Embattled Courage: The Experience of Combat in the American Civil War* (New York: The Free Press, 1987), 216–29; Frank, *With Ballot and Bayonet*, 166–8; McPherson, *What They Fought For*, 5–6.

62 McPherson, *What They Fought For*, 43; Steven E. Woodworth, *While God is Marching On: The Religious World of Civil War Soldiers* (Lawrence, KS: University Press of Kansas, 2001), 98–9, 107, 110–11.

63 Frank, *With Ballot and Bayonet*, 170; Davis, *Lincoln's Men*, 107; Robert Hubbard to wife, 25 Feb. 1863, Letters of Robert Hubbard, Civil War Manuscripts Collection, Yale University Library, quoted in Adam I.P. Smith, 'Partisan Partisanship: The Northern Political Experience during the Civil War' (unpublished paper), 16–17.

64 Davis, *Lincoln's Men*, 106; Frank, *With Ballot and Bayonet*, 171–3; *Chicago Tribune*, 8 Feb. 1864; Frank, *With Ballot and Bayonet*, 173.

65 Davis, *Lincoln's Men*, 107.

66 *DJH*, 208; *RWAL*, 278.

67 *RWAL*, 418, 506; *Lincoln Observed*, 66–8.

68 Michael Burlingame, ed., *With Lincoln in the White House: Letters, Memoranda, and Other Writings of John G. Nicolay, 1860–1865* (Carbondale, IL: Southern Illinois University Press, 2000), 139.

69 Burlingame, ed., *With Lincoln in the White House*, 131.

70 Smith, 'The Presidential Election of 1864', 109.

71 Carpenter, *Inner Life*, 283.

72 *CW*, 7:435, 451.

73 Burlingame, ed., *At Lincoln's Side*, 92–3; Burlingame, ed., *With Lincoln in the White House*, 151–4.

74 H.J. Raymond to AL, 22 Aug. 1864, ALP; *CW*, 7:514.

75 *RWAL*, 393–4; S.F. Carey to AL, 1 Sept. 1864, ALP.

76 Burlingame, ed., *With Lincoln in the White House*, 157–8.

77 J. Conkling to AL, 6 Sept. 1864, T. Tilton to J.G. Nicolay, 6 Sept. 1864, H. Wilson to AL, 5 Sept. 1864, ALP.

78 Carpenter, *Inner Life*, 275; J.W. Forney to AL, 14 Sept. 1864, ALP; *DJH*, 229–30, 359.

79 See, for example, *The Scioto Gazette* [Chillicothe, OH], 1 Nov. 1864; *Chicago Tribune*, 18, 19 Oct. 1864.

80 Granville Moody, *A Life's Retrospect: Autobiography of Rev. Granville Moody, D.D.*, ed. Sylvester Weeks (Cincinnati, OH: Cranston and Stowe, 1890), 441–5; Peck, *Life and Times*, 378–81; Crooks, *Life of Bishop Matthew Simpson*, 396.

81 Howard, *Religion and the Radical Republican Movement*, 68–89; James M. McPherson, *The Struggle for Equality: Abolitionists and the Negro in the Civil War and Reconstruction* (Princeton, NJ: Princeton University Press, 1964), 260–86; *RWAL*, 446.

82 *Scioto Gazette*, 20 Sept. 1864; T.M. Eddy Diary, IEG.

83 *Independent*, 27 Oct. 1864; Gilbert Haven, *Sermons, Speeches and Letters on Slavery and Its War: From the Passage of the Fugitive Slave Bill to the Election of President Grant* (New York: Carlton and Lanahan, 1869), 481–2.

84 *CW*, 7:533–4, 8:55–6; Joel H. Silbey, *A Respectable Minority: The Democratic Party in the Civil War Era, 1860–1869* (New York: W.W. Norton, 1977), 75–6. Davis called nine days of national fasting. Cheseborough, *God Ordained this War*, 226.

85 *Independent*, 1 Sept., 27 Oct., 3 Nov. 1864; Clark, *Life of Matthew Simpson*, 240–3. Mark Hoyt, a wealthy Methodist layman and Union–Republican party activist, judged that Simpson's speech, just five days before the presidential ballot, would 'give ample time for it to produce its result on the election'. Jones, *The Sectional Crisis and Northern Methodism*, 42–3. Gulliver's panegyric to Lincoln in the columns of the *Independent*, he explained in a letter to the president in the dark days of August, was designed to counteract 'the present vacillating feverish state of feeling in the Republican party toward you'. The article prompted cries of 'hoax' from Democrats, but the Yankee clergyman was real enough. His church deacons included Governor William A. Buckingham; his acquaintances numbered Theodore Tilton, who urged Gulliver to let him publish the article immediately on the heels of the Democratic convention. J.P. Gulliver to AL, 26 Aug., 12 Sept. 1864, ALP.

86 L.E. Chittenden, *Recollections of President Lincoln and His Administration* (New York: Harper and Brothers, 1891), 446–51; William Sutton, 'Seeing through a Glass Darkly: Abraham Lincoln and the Northern Evangelical Clergy, 1860–1865' (unpublished typescript, University of Illinois, 1985), 24–5; Moorhead, *American Apocalypse*, 141–2.

87 J.B. Maxfield to AL, 21 Oct. 1864, ALP.

88 *Northwestern Christian Advocate*, 12 Oct. 1864; *Chicago Tribune*, 8 Nov. 1864.

89 *Chicago Tribune*, 4 Aug., 28 Sept. 1864.

90 *Chicago Tribune*, 19 Oct. 1864.

91 *Christian Advocate and Journal*, 25 Aug., 27 Oct. 1864; Address of the National Union Executive Committee, *Chicago Tribune*, 19, 22 Oct. 1864.

92 R.E. Fisk to J. Hay, 22 Sept. 1864, ALP; Burlingame, ed., *With Lincoln in the White House*, 158 (summarizing Grant's views as set out in the *New York Times*); *Northwestern Christian Advocate*, 26 Oct. 1864.

93 *Christian Advocate and Journal*, 11 Aug., 27 Oct. 1864; *Harper's Weekly*, quoted in *Northwestern Christian Advocate*, 14 Sept. 1864; *Chicago Tribune*, 19, 20 Oct., 8 Nov. 1864.

94 *DJH*, 40–1.

95 *Northwestern Christian Advocate*, 23 Nov. 1864.

96 *Christian Advocate and Journal*, 17 Nov. 1864; *Independent*, 17 Nov. 1864; *Northwestern Christian Advocate*, 23 Nov. 1864; *Zion's Herald*, 24 Sept. 1864; *Chicago Tribune*, 4 Nov. 1864; Howard, *Religion and the Radical Republican Movement*, 88–9; Dale Baum, *The Civil War Party System: The Case of Massachusetts, 1848–1876* (Chapel Hill, NC: University of North Carolina Press, 1984), 91, 95–100; Stephen L. Hansen, *The Making of the Third Party System: Voters and Parties in Illinois, 1850–1876* (Ann Arbor, MI: UMI Research Press, 1980), 142–3; *Independent*, 10, 17 Nov. 1864.

97 *DJH*, 252; *Northwestern Christian Advocate*, 2 Nov. 1864.

98 Burlingame, ed., *With Lincoln in the White House*, 157.

99 *DJH*, 196. Cf. M. Sutliff to AL, 4 Sept. 1864, ALP.

years on the circuit no doubt contributed to this shrewdness in judging people, while his formidable memory meant that, as one admirer put it, he 'seemed to have read the character, and to know the peculiarities of every leading man in Congress and the country'. Even Bennett of the *New York Herald*, hardly a sycophant, paid tribute to the president's 'shrewd perception of the ins and outs of poor weak human nature', which 'enabled him to master difficulties which would have swamped almost any other man'.[5]

Though most Unionists believed Lincoln lacked the brilliance and nobility that they felt the presidency demanded in a time of crisis, his personal strengths served the administration well: over the long haul which no leadership committed to restoring the Union could have avoided, Lincoln's tenacity, patience, shrewdness in personal dealings and unblinking focus on essentials more than offset his lack of administrative experience and his inefficient, unbusinesslike ways. It was easy to underestimate him – though from that he derived unexpected advantage. In the pre-war court-room, in Swett's memorable metaphor, anyone 'who took Lincoln for a simple-minded man would very soon wake up with his back in a ditch'. In wartime, the Union's competing egos only slowly woke up to the full reality of the quaint president's increasing control and authority.

While treating Congress with relative deference, rarely using the presidential veto, and giving his cabinet secretaries considerable autonomy in their own particular spheres, Lincoln jealously guarded the president's power in key domains. As head of the executive branch, he alone would define the war's goals and set the means of achieving them. As commander-in-chief, he would not cede all authority to his generals; indeed, learning from the chronic failings of McClellan, he strengthened his grip on the strategic reins. As the leader of his party, he saw its value as an instrument of popular mobilization, while equally understanding the dangers of partisan narrowness in a conflict which needed the Union's 'discordant elements', as he termed them, to be bound firmly together.[6] And, as the nation's representative and political figurehead during what he defined as 'a people's war', he put his faith in his own proven sensitivity to public opinion.

Through this formidable, if unspectacular, combination of personal qualities, political authority and diagnostic ability, Lincoln sustained what proved to be a stunningly effective overall strategy. Historians have rightly made much of his caution, especially in the earlier phases of the war, as he knitted border conservatives, residual Whigs and War Democrats into the Union coalition. Rather less has been made of Lincoln's understanding of the need to inspire and energize the North, and to inoculate it against the most virulent strains of war-weariness and defeatism, by articulating an ideal of the nation that spoke to a higher patriotism and an expanded vision of the Union. He did this on his own terms and not the radicals', but the vision that he offered in the later stages of the conflict owed far more to New England Protestantism and 'Yankeedom' than it did to his cultural roots in the border and lower North. Lincoln's growing religious seriousness as president is worthy of note, but what is more important in explaining his political achievement is his effective channeling of the forces of mainstream Protestant orthodoxy, the most potent agents of American nationalism.

The Lincoln presented here, then, was an energetic, active president. His commonly-noted fatalism induced not political passivity but an under-standing that the individual politician would fail if he tried to swim against or resist the larger tide. 'Lincoln's whole life was a calculation of the law of forces, and ultimate results', Swett maintained. 'The world to him was a question of cause and effect.'[7] This did not encourage inertia in a man for whom 'work, work, work' was 'the main thing'. Rather, it meant identifying and promoting the means by which the larger forces at play could be advanced. Convinced that the Union both should and could be saved, and sure that slavery's days were numbered, Lincoln seized his historical moment as the instrument of a providential purpose.

*

Four years' active leadership gave Lincoln few opportunities for even brief relaxation – let alone recuperation – from the burdens of office. Work itself was not a great strain, though: it was the fits of grief that proved most disabling. Willie's death stabbed at his heart; the mounting slaughter in the field brought on deep depression. During the first bloody week of the Wilderness campaign he scarcely slept. Carpenter described a man in torment, pacing to and fro, 'his hands behind him, great black rings under his eyes, his head bent forward upon his breast, – altogether such a picture of the effects of sorrow, care, and anxiety as would have melted the hearts of the worst of his adversaries'. Yet Lincoln had strat-egies for survival, fashioned during a lifetime punctuated by bouts of despair – what he called the 'hypo'. He had been particularly afflicted by melancholia as a younger man, notably over romantic attachments, and had come to learn an empowering lesson: each attack would pass in time. 'You can not now realize that you will ever feel better', he told a bereaved young woman. 'And yet it is a mistake', he added, revealing his own therapy: 'You are sure to be happy again.'[8]

Relief also came from his well-developed sense of the ridiculous. Lincoln used humor as his recreational drug. What others derived from a glass of wine or a pleasurable meal, Lincoln got from hearty laughter. He relished humorous writing and delighted in David Ross Locke's comic creation, Petroleum V. Nasby. He loved anecdotes and jokes, refined and vulgar. He used them sometimes as political camouflage but at other times as a refuge, contagiously leading the laughter. Forney deliberately took proven raconteurs with him on his visits to the White House to lighten the president's gloom. Those who lacked a sense of humor were a trial to him: of one cabinet member, probably Chase, he complained – in words borrowed from Sydney Smith – that 'it required a surgical operation to get a joke into his head'. When during the dismal days of 1862 he was rebuked by a senator for embarking on a humorous story, he protested poignantly, 'I say to you now, that were it not for this occasional *vent*, I should die.'[9]

But Lincoln was fundamentally too serious-minded to find refuge in levity alone. Much of his love of Shakespeare derived from the dramatist's extraordinary insights into human psychology and from his meditations on political power and its transience, burdens and griefs. 'He read Shakespeare more than all other writers together', recalled Hay, who listened for hours, evening after evening, as Lincoln read to him from his favorite plays: *Hamlet*, *King Lear*, the histories and, especially, *Macbeth*. His relish for the speeches of flawed legitimate monarchs like Lear and Richard II, and of the usurping rulers Richard III, Macbeth and Claudius, cannot be plausibly explained by some sublimated tyrannical impulse in himself. Rather, the experience of these Shakespearean heads of state, whose ambition had won them 'the hollow crown', spoke to the condition of a man whose restless desire for the highest office in the Union had delivered a fearful, bone-wearying duty. His particular fascination with Claudius's soliloquy, beginning 'O, my offence is rank', in which the murderous king struggles honestly and despairingly with his conscience, and which Lincoln considered 'one of the finest touches of nature in the world', may well have had to do with his own (at times crushing) sense of responsibility, if not guilt, for the onset of a murderous war. Shakespeare – particularly through his great comic creation, Falstaff – brought Lincoln the joy of laughter, too, but it was above all for 'companionship in melancholy' that the overburdened president turned to his favorite dramatist.[10]

There was one venue above all where Lincoln could be sure of an escape into laughter or unreal tragedy: the theater. At Ford's or at Grover's, with family and friends, he could hope to find a refuge from office-seekers and the pestering clamor of the White House, and – as Noah

Brooks put it – might 'unfix his thoughts from cares and anxieties'. He attended all kinds of entertainment, from opera to minstrelsy, from Shakespeare to popular but undistinguished comedy. It was to one of the latter, *Our American Cousin* at Ford's Theater, that Lincoln prepared to go on the evening of Good Friday, 14 April 1865. Five days earlier Robert E. Lee had surrendered his army to Grant at Appomattox Court House, less than a week after the fall of the Confederate capital. In these twilight days between war and peace – with Joseph E. Johnston's forces still at large but vulnerable in North Carolina, with the Union public jubilantly expecting an imminent end to the conflict, and with the president encouraging ideas of national reconciliation based on loyalty, clemency and political rights to certain classes of blacks – Lincoln recovered a boyish cheerfulness which startled Mary. 'We must *both*, be more cheerful in the future', he told her on the afternoon of his final visit to the theater; 'between the war and the loss of our darling Willie – we have both, been very miserable'.[11]

From his knowledge of the stage Lincoln would have known that in classic tragedy the victims are imprisoned by circumstances of their own creating and from which they render morally impossible their own escape. Innumerable historians have implicitly adopted just that fatalistic mode in telling and retelling the events of Lincoln's last Good Friday, alert to the president's chronic and incorrigible laxness over his personal safety; to his desire not to be cut off from the public by an imperial guard; to his deafness to the pleas of Stanton and Hill Lamon (his usual bodyguard, but absent that day) not to go out that night – an occasion made all the more dangerous by its being generally known that he and Grant would share the state box.[12] That a theater-loving president bent on non-punitive peace should have been slain by a notable Shakespearean actor casting himself as the guardian of the Old South layered the tragedy of assassination with heavy dramatic irony. John Wilkes Booth and his fellow conspirators had earlier aimed to kidnap Lincoln in exchange for Confederate prisoners of war but, with the war virtually at an end, with his band of accomplices dwindling, and driven by racial venom to pre-empt Lincoln's reconstruction policies, Booth turned in desperation to a theatrical act of self-styled tyrannicide. His cruel bullet into the back of the president's head released Lincoln from the burdens of office, sent Mary spiralling into inconsolable grief, aroused white-hot feelings of vengeance across the Union, and plunged the Confederate South into paroxysms of fear over the price it might have to pay.[13]

In too small a bed in a cramped room across the street from the theater, Lincoln lingered for a further nine hours after the shooting, never regaining consciousness. The doctors who clustered around the bed to which he had been carried were surprised by his resilience *in extremis*, but eventually – at 7.22 a.m. on Saturday 15 April 1865 – he passed from life into history and memory.

*

When a distraught Edwin Stanton, present at Lincoln's death, remarked, 'Now he belongs to the ages', it is unlikely that he realized just how swiftly and thoroughly his all-too-human friend and ally would be transformed into an iconic, mythic figure. Lincoln's unique achievements – as president and commander-in-chief of the victorious Union in a fratricidal war, as the preserver of American nationhood, and as the author of the emancipation edict – would themselves have guaranteed his historical celebration and acclamation. But the manner and suddenness of his death opened the door to his apotheosis, or deification.

A million or more grieving people turned out to pay their respects as Lincoln's body, after a military funeral, was taken to lie in state in the Capitol and was then slowly carried on a special funeral train back to Springfield, along the 1,600-mile route that the president-elect had taken to Washington in 1861. Stunned at the loss of a man they had come to think of as a friend or a brother or a father, millions more looked to their religious and civic leaders to put a profound collective sorrow into words. In their myriad black-edged editorials and sermons, the clergy sought to articulate the mixture of misery, anger and bewilderment felt across the North. They extolled Lincoln's personal traits and accomplishments with a degree of unanimity unknown during his lifetime. Some earlier critics remained silent and a very few even risked life and limb to utter a discordant note, but mostly those who had once hurled brickbats now fashioned eulogies. In celebrating Lincoln, the kind, the gentle, the honest, the witty, the sagacious, the unselfish and the representative man they drove from view the shrewd and guileful politician, and the man of flesh and blood and human foibles. Lincoln's greatness – even 'grandeur', as Joseph Thompson saw it – raised him to an equality with, and even superiority to, George Washington himself. He was, in Bishop Matthew Simpson's words, 'no ordinary man': the nation had come to see that God had prepared him through life for the ordeal that lay ahead and that 'by the hand of God' he had been 'especially singled out to guide our government in these troublesome times'.[14]

A contemporary journalist immediately understood the significance of what was at work: 'It has made it impossible to speak the truth of Abraham

Lincoln hereafter.' The iconic figure who took a place in American memory would become a constant impediment to historians trying to catch the essence of the man beyond. Moreover, there have been not one, but multiple, American *memories*. David Blight has shone a brilliant light on the competing folk narratives of the Civil War in the half-century after Appomattox. Lincoln, naturally, was incorporated (alongside Frederick Douglass, William Lloyd Garrison and others) into the heroic African-American script of emancipation. But implicitly the president who had intended 'malice toward none' could be slowly incorporated, too, into a script of national 'reconciliation' which marginalized and downgraded the black race: gradually in the South 'the Black Republican' Lincoln became, for some at least, the charitable Lincoln whose death had deprived the Confederacy of a southern-born ally.[15]

The Lincoln delineated in the present study is a man who, politically gifted though he was, earns the label 'exceptional' chiefly because of the office he held and the singular circumstances in which he held it. Lincoln is best understood, not as the extraordinary figure of the iconographers, but as a man of his times, politically wise but capable of misjudgments, too, and powerful largely because he was representative and, as such, deeply familiar with his people and his context. This gave him a real feel for the direction of events. Thus, he came to see that a party committed to quarantining slavery was capable of securing the highest office in the land; he realized that he had the qualities – and good fortune – to fit that party's prescription of its ideal candidate; he rightly sensed that his own outrage at southern secession was widely enough shared to make defense of the Union politically practicable; and he understood that his power as a war president depended above all on his harnessing the potent force of popular nationalism.

Problematic as his deification may be for the historian, Lincoln's instant elevation to the pantheon had its own public significance and demonstrated that – thanks to his martyrdom – he continued to exercise remarkable political power even in death. Desperate to understand their cruel bereavement, most Union loyalists were convinced that the assassination had a meaning, however opaque, and that 'the permissive hand of God' had allowed a temporary evil 'for His own wise and holy ends'. The Almighty had deemed His agent's work on earth completed: having guided the nation safely through its era of crisis, Lincoln would have been too lenient and merciful for the next stage, the era of Reconstruction.[16]

Lincoln's martyrdom derived particular potency from its Christian, vicarious character. A chorus of voices claimed the murdered president for the church. It was, they agreed, a shame that he had made no public profession of faith, but it would have come, in time. Some clutched at the implausible report of a tearful Lincoln telling how, when he visited the heroes' graves at Gettysburg, 'I gave myself to God, and now I can say that I do love Jesus.' Speaking at the Springfield interment, Matthew Simpson reassured his mass audience that at least Lincoln 'believed in Christ the Saviour of sinners; and I think he was sincere in trying to bring his life into harmony with the principles of revealed religion'.[17]

Lincoln's religious credentials and role as liberator of an enslaved people cast him as a latter-day Moses (though one who had freed even more slaves than the Old Testament leader, 'and those not of his kindred or his race'); he had taken 'this Israel of ours' over 'the blood-red sea of rebellion' and like Moses, had been allowed to see, but not enter, the Promised Land. More compelling still were the Christ-like characteristics of the murdered president. Vicarious sacrifice for his people on Good Friday succeeded a Palm Sunday in which Lincoln had in humble triumph entered the Confederate capital of Richmond: 'As Christ entered Jerusalem, the city that above all others hated, rejected, and would soon slay Him . . . so did this, His servant, enter the city that above all others hated and rejected him, and would soon be the real if not the intentional cause of his death.' A theater may have been 'a poor place to die in', but the president had gone out of a sense of duty, 'not to see a comedy, but to gratify the people'. God had taken Lincoln, 'the Saviour of his country', from the American people, just as He had taken Moses and Jesus when their tasks were done. In future, urged Gilbert Haven, his death should be commemorated not on the calendar date, but on every Good Friday, as 'a movable fast' to be kept 'beside the cross and the grave of our blessed Lord, in whose service and for whose gospel he became a victim and a martyr'.[18]

The profoundest historical consequences of Lincoln's assassination, then, had less to do with his removal from the fraught politics of Reconstruction (we may reasonably wonder, if there had been no murder, whether the exhausted Lincoln would naturally have lived out his second term), than with the sanctification of American nationalism.[19] As they mourned, Americans were encouraged to discover in Lincoln's death a millennial promise that fused the secular and the sacred. Through 'Black Easter' the Almighty was unfolding a plan that would secure the Kingdom of God and a purified nation. A Brooklyn Presbyterian rejoiced that 'A martyr's blood has sealed the covenant we are making with posterity', guaranteeing 'the rights of men, the truth of the Gospel, the principles of humanity, the integrity of the Union, the power of Christian people to govern themselves, the indefeasible equality of all creatures of God . . . , no matter what may be the color of their skin'. Likewise George Dana Boardman, a Philadelphia Baptist, read in Lincoln's death a glorious promise of the nation's future greatness. Had he lived into old age 'no nation would have been born of him'. But an inscrutable providence had allowed 'the glorious seed' to die 'that it might ... bring forth much fruit. ... I see springing from the tear-wet bier of Abraham Lincoln the green and tender blades which foretell the birth of an emancipated, united, triumphant, transfigured, immortal Republic.'[20]

Many Americans thus drew from Lincoln's assassination what Henry Ward Beecher described as 'a new impulse of patriotism'. Matthew Simpson felt powerfully the nation's duty 'to carry forward the policy . . . so nobly begun . . . to give every human being his true position before God and man; to crush every form of rebellion, and to stand by the flag which God has given us'. The slain president's cause – 'to decide whether the people, as a people, in their entire majesty, were destined to be the government, or whether they were to be subject to tyrants or aristocrats, or to class-rule of any kind' – was close to resolution. 'If successful, republics will spread in spite of monarchs, all over this earth.' Echoing Lincoln's sense of the nation as 'the last best hope of earth', the interpreters of his death deemed God to be saying 'to all the nations of the earth, "Republican liberty, based upon true Christianity, is firm as the foundation of the globe"'.[21]

Thus Lincoln, through his life and death, bequeathed an enhanced and ambitious nationalism to his successors. How subsequent political generations harnessed that force lies well beyond the scope of this study. Lincoln cannot be held responsible for the way in which they chose to deploy the power they inherited. But his was a model which offered some check on the arrogance of power. While he was certainly not reluctant to wield political authority, his practical policy grew from a strong sense of moral purpose, and his course as president was shaped not by impulsive, self-aggrandizing action or self-righteousness, but by deep thought, breadth of vision, careful concern for consequences and a remarkable lack of pride.

Notes

1 Nicolay, *Oral History*, 83.

2 Gideon Welles, *Lincoln and Seward. Remarks upon the memorial address of Chas. Francis Adams, on the late William H. Seward, with incidents and comments illustrative of the measures and policy of the administration of Abraham Lincoln* (New York: Sheldon & Company, 1874), 32; *HI*, 167.

3 F.B. Carpenter, *The Inner Life of Abraham Lincoln: Six Months at the White House* (Lincoln, NB: University of Nebraska Press, 1995; originally published New York, 1866), 148–9; *DJH*, 132.

4 *CW*, 6:538; *HI*, 166; John W. Forney, *Anecdotes of Public Men*, 2 vols (New York: Harper and Brothers, 1873, 1881), 1:176.

5 Forney, *Anecdotes of Public Men*, 1:39; Robert S. Harper, *Lincoln and the Press* (New York: McGraw-Hill, 1951), 322.

6 *HI*, 165.

7 *HI*, 162.

8 Carpenter, *Inner Life*, 30–1; *CW*, 6:16–17.

9 *Reminiscences of Carl Schurz*, 3 vols (New York: The McClure Co., 1907–08), 2:91; Forney, *Anecdotes of Public Men*, 1:86; Carpenter, *Inner Life*, 149–53, 278.

10 Michael Burlingame, ed., *At Lincoln's Side: John Hay's Civil War Correspondence and Selected Writings* (Carbondale, IL: Southern Illinois University Press, 2000), 137; Don E. Fehrenbacher, *Lincoln in Text and Context: Collected Essays* (Stanford, CA: Stanford University Press, 1987), 157–63.

11 *Lincoln Observed*, 250; Justin G. Turner and Linda Levitt Turner, *Mary Todd Lincoln: Her Life and Letters* (New York: Alfred A. Knopf, 1972), 284–5.

12 Carpenter, *Inner Life*, 62–7. In fact, Grant and his wife declined the invitation to attend.

13 Leaping from the Lincolns' box, Booth broke a leg and rode off in great pain, to take refuge with Confederate sympathizers. Twelve days later he was tracked down and shot by Union cavalry. Several of his band of accomplices – who failed in their assigned roles as assassins of the secretary of state and the vice president – were brought to trial and hanged. Subsequent theories, which have embraced in the plot the Confederate leadership and high-ranking Unionists (including Edwin Stanton), are as groundless as they are sensational.

14 David B. Chesebrough, *'No Sorrow like Our Sorrow': Northern Protestant Ministers and the Assassination of Lincoln* (Kent, OH: Kent State University Press, 1994), 16–17; *Northwestern Christian Advocate*, 10 May 1865.

15 Merrill D. Peterson, *Lincoln in American Memory* (New York: Oxford University Press, 1994), 21, 191; David W. Blight, *Race and Reunion: The Civil War in American Memory* (Cambridge, MA: Harvard University Press, 2001), 369.

16 *Northwestern Christian Advocate*, 10 May 1865; Chesebrough, *'No Sorrow like Our Sorrow'*, 67.

17 Chesebrough, *'No Sorrow like Our Sorrow'*, 30; *Northwestern Christian Advocate*, 10 May 1865.

18 Chesebrough, *'No Sorrow like Our Sorrow'*, 16, 33–6, 39, 68–9; Gilbert Haven, *The Uniter and Liberator of America: A Memorial Discourse on the Character and Career of Abraham Lincoln delivered in the North Russell Street, M.E. Church, Boston, Sunday, April 23, 1865* (Boston, MA: James P. Magee, 1865), 4, 30.

19 Harriet Beecher Stowe reported Lincoln as telling her, 'Whichever way it ends, I have the impression that I shan't last long after it's over.' *RWAL*, 428. Chase, Stanton and Seward were all dead within eight years of the war's end.

20 Chesebrough, *'No Sorrow like Our Sorrow'*, 76–7.

21 *Northwestern Christian Advocate*, 10 May 1865; Chesebrough, *'No Sorrow like Our Sorrow'*, 74, 106; Thomas Reed Turner, *Beware the People Weeping: Public Opinion and the Assassination of Abraham Lincoln* (Baton Rouge, LA: Louisiana State University Press, 1982), 45.

Chronology of Lincoln's Life

1809	February 12	Born near Hodgenville, Hardin County, Kentucky, son of Thomas and Nancy Hanks Lincoln
1811	Spring	Family moves to a farm on Knob Creek, ten miles north
1816	December	Family moves to Spencer County, Indiana
1818	October 5	Mother dies of 'the milk sickness'
1819	December 2	Father marries Sarah Bush Johnston of Elizabethtown, Kentucky
1828	January 20	Older sister, Sarah, dies in childbirth
	Spring	Takes a flatboat to New Orleans
1830	March	Family moves to Macon County, Illinois
	Summer	Delivers his first political speech
1831	April–July	Second flatboat trip to New Orleans
	July	Settles in New Salem
1832	April–July	Serves in Black Hawk War and is elected captain
	August 6	Defeated in election for Illinois state legislature
1833	January	Buys a general store with William F. Berry
	May 7	Appointed postmaster (and serves for three years)
1834		Supplements income by work as assistant surveyor Begins to study law
	August 4	Elected to Illinois House of Representatives
	December 1	Begins first term in state legislature
1835	March	Sells personal possessions to pay off debt
1836	August 1	Re-elected to state legislature (second term)
	September 9	Receives law licence
1837	March 1	Formally enroled as a lawyer and permitted to charge legal fees
	March 3	With Dan Stone enters protest in the legislature against slavery
	April 15	Moves to Springfield and becomes John T. Stuart's junior law partner
1838	August 6	Re-elected to the state legislature (third term)

1840	August 3	Re-elected to the state legislature (fourth and final term)
1841	January 1	Breaks off engagement with Mary Todd
	April	Dissolves partnership with Stuart and becomes Stephen T. Logan's junior partner
1842	September 22	Challenged by James Shields to a duel
	November 4	Marries Mary Todd
1843	August 1	Birth of their first son, Robert Todd Lincoln
1844	December	Forms legal partnership with William H. Herndon, dissolving his connection with Logan
1846	March 10	Birth of Edward Baker Lincoln (Eddie), second son
	August 3	Elected to US House of Representatives from the Seventh Congressional District of Illinois
1847	December 3	Takes his seat in Congress
1849	March 4	Completes his congressional term
1850	February 1	Eddie dies from pulmonary tuberculosis
	December 21	Birth of William Wallace Lincoln (Willie), third son
1853	April 4	Birth of Thomas Lincoln (Tad), fourth son
1854	May 30	Kansas–Nebraska bill signed into law
	October 16	Peoria speech
	November 7	Elected to Illinois state legislature
	November 27	Gives notice that he will resign to seek US Senate seat
1855	February 8	Narrowly defeated for senator in the state legislature
1856	February 22	Joins those organizing the Republican party in Illinois
	May 29	Speaks at Republican state convention and is nominated a presidential elector
	June 19	Runner-up in Republican national convention ballot for vice-presidential nominee
1858	June 16	Nominated for US Senate by the Republican state convention; 'House Divided' speech
	August 21– October 15	Debates publicly with Douglas
	November 2	Republicans' plurality in state election fails to prevent Douglas's re-election to Senate
1860	February 27	Address at Cooper Union, New York
	May 9–10	State Republican nominating convention at Decatur instructs delegates to support Lincoln at national convention in Chicago

	May 18	Nominated for president by the Chicago convention
	November 6	Elected president
	December 20	South Carolina passes ordinance of secession
1861	February 11	Leaves Springfield for Washington
	March 4	Inaugurated as sixteenth president
	April 12	Confederate forces bombard Fort Sumter
	April 15	Issues call for 75,000 volunteers
	April 19	Proclaims a blockade
	April 27	Suspends writ of habeas corpus along the Philadelphia–Washington military line
	July 4	Special message to Congress
	July 21	First battle of Bull Run
	August 6	First Confiscation Act
	September 12	Revokes Frémont's proclamation
	November 1	Appoints McClellan to command of US Army
1862	February 6	Capture of Fort Henry
	February 16	Capture of Fort Donelson
	February 20	Son Willie dies
	March 6	Special message to Congress on compensated emancipation
	April 6–7	Battle of Shiloh
	April 25	Union capture of New Orleans
	May 19	Revokes Hunter's proclamation
	May 31–June 1	Battle of Seven Pines
	June 25–July 1	Seven Days' Battles
	July 12	Meets border-state representatives
	July 17	Second Confiscation Act
	July 22	Submits draft emancipation proclamation to cabinet
	July 23	Names Halleck general-in-chief
	August	Institutes militia draft under Militia Act of 17 July
	August 29–30	Second battle of Bull Run
	September 17	Battle of Antietam
	September 22	Issues preliminary Emancipation Proclamation
	September 24	Issues proclamation suspending writ of habeas corpus throughout the Union
	October–November	Union–Republican losses in state elections

	November 5	Removes McClellan and appoints Burnside as commander of the Army of the Potomac
	December 13	Battle of Fredricksburg
1863	January 1	Issues final Emancipation Proclamation
	January 25	Replaces Burnside with Hooker
	May 1–4	Battle of Chancellorsville
	May 6	Arrest of Vallandigham
	May 18	Siege to Vicksburg begins
	June 28	Replaces Hooker with Meade
	July 1–3	Battle of Gettysburg
	July 4	Fall of Vicksburg
	July 13–16	Draft riots in New York City
	September 19–20	Battle of Chickamauga
	October–November	Union–Republican gains in state elections
	November 19	Gettysburg Address
	November 23–25	Battle of Chattanooga
	December 8	Issues Proclamation of Amnesty and Reconstruction
1864	February 20	Pomeroy Circular published, promoting Chase for president
	March 10	Assigns Grant to command of all Union armies
	May–June	Grant's Virginia offensive
	June 8	Renominated for presidency by National Union convention
	June 19	Siege of Petersburg begins
	June 30	Accepts Chase's resignation from cabinet
	July 4	Pocket vetoes Wade–Davis bill
	July 18	Appoints Greeley to peace mission
	August 5	Battle of Mobile Bay
	August 29	Democratic convention nominates McClellan for president
	September 2	Atlanta falls to Sherman
	September 17	Frémont withdraws from presidential contest
	September 23	Asks Blair to resign
	November 8	Re-elected president
	November 16	Sherman starts march to the sea
	December 15–16	Confederate defeat in battle of Nashville
	December 22	Sherman occupies Savannah
1865	January 31	Congress passes Thirteenth Amendment
	February 3	Attends Hampton Roads Peace Conference

March 4   Delivers second inaugural address
April 4   Visits Richmond, two days after the Confederate evacuation
April 9   Lee surrenders at Appomattox Court-house
April 11   Delivers his last speech
April 14   Shot by John Wilkes Booth at Ford's Theater
April 15   Dies at 7.22 a.m.
May 4   Buried in Springfield

Further Reading

No short bibliography can possibly do justice to the rich and ever-growing trove of scholarly writings about Abraham Lincoln, let alone about the political era in which he lived. What follows is chiefly designed as a guide to some of the best and most influential works relating to Lincoln himself, and offers a fuller indication of the studies on which I have drawn than can be gleaned from the citations for each chapter.

Biographies

Amongst the shelf of modern one-volume biographies, three in particular stand out. Benjamin P. Thomas, *Abraham Lincoln: A Biography* (New York: Alfred A. Knopf, 1952) is a superbly crafted work of synthesis and was the first biography to benefit from the opening of the Abraham Lincoln Papers in the Library of Congress in 1947. Beautifully written, and offering a masterclass in the art of compression and story-telling, is David Herbert Donald, *Lincoln* (New York: Simon & Schuster, 1995), though it overstates the president's 'passivity'. Allen C. Guelzo, *Abraham Lincoln: Redeemer President* (Grand Rapids, MI: William B. Eerdmans Publishing Co., 1999) treats Lincoln's Whiggish ideas and personal beliefs with unusual but compelling seriousness. Beyond these, two succinct biographies are noteworthy: Mark E. Neely, *The Last Best Hope of Earth: Abraham Lincoln and the Promise of America* (Cambridge, MA: Harvard University Press, 1993) and William E. Gienapp, *Abraham Lincoln and Civil War America* (New York: Oxford University Press, 2002), which is especially good on Lincoln's presidential leadership.

Of the several multi-volume lives, two demand particular attention. If few today have the stamina to digest all ten volumes of John G. Nicolay and John Hay's 'official' work, *Abraham Lincoln: A History* (New York: The Century Co., 1890), and if its obvious bias and life-and-times approach appear limiting, it still remains an essential source, one characterized by scholarship and real candor. The finest multi-volume modern biography is James G. Randall, *Lincoln the President* (4 vols, New York: Dodd, Mead, 1945–55), completed by Richard N. Current, which follows a 'Revisionist' line and presents Lincoln as a liberal and realist in vexatious conflict with the Radical Republicans.

1: Inner power, 1809–54

Essential for Lincoln's early life in Kentucky and Indiana, for his young manhood in New Salem and for his non-political life in Springfield are the mass of recollections which William Herndon elicited after Lincoln's death, though in many cases it is a matter of fine judgment whether they offer a searchlight or a distorting mirror. The material informed William H. Herndon and Jesse W. Weik, *Herndon's Life of Lincoln*, ed. Paul M. Angle (Cleveland, OH: The World Publishing Company, 1942) and is superbly set out in Douglas L. Wilson and Rodney O. Davis, eds, *Herndon's Informants: Letters, Interviews, and Statements about Abraham Lincoln* (Urbana, IL: University of Illinois Press, 1998). Walter B. Stevens, *A Reporter's Lincoln*, ed. Michael Burlingame (Lincoln, NB: University of Nebraska Press, 1998) and Michael Burlingame, ed., *An Oral History of Abraham Lincoln: John G. Nicolay's Interviews and Essays* (Carbondale, IL: Southern Illinois University Press, 1996) provide additional recollections.

For the New Salem period Benjamin P. Thomas's useful *Lincoln's New Salem* (Springfield, IL: Abraham Lincoln Association, 1934) should be read in conjunction with Douglas L. Wilson, *Honor's Voice: The Transformation of Abraham Lincoln* (New York: Alfred A. Knopf, 1998), a shrewd and original book which is also revelatory about Lincoln's early years in Springfield. There are further insights in Douglas L. Wilson, *Lincoln before Washington: New Perspectives on the Illinois Years* (Urbana, IL: University of Illinois Press, 1997) and valuable social context in Kenneth J. Winkle, *The Young Eagle: The Rise of Abraham Lincoln* (Dallas, TX: Taylor, 2001). Lincoln's economic ideas and his Whig perspectives are the subject of Gabor S. Boritt, *Lincoln and the Economics of the American Dream* (Memphis, TN: Memphis State University Press, 1978), Olivier Fraysse, *Lincoln, Land, and Labor, 1809–1860*, trans. Sylvia Neely (Urbana, IL: University of Illinois Press, 1994), Daniel Walker Howe, *The Political Culture of the American Whigs* (Chicago, IL: The University of Chicago Press, 1979), Joel H. Silbey, '"Always a Whig in Politics": The Partisan Life of Abraham Lincoln', *Papers of the Abraham Lincoln Association*, 8 (1986) and Guelzo's biography.

Lincoln's political career before 1850 is the subject of Paul Simon, *Lincoln's Preparation for Greatness: The Illinois Legislative Years* (University of Oklahoma Press, 1965; repr. Urbana, IL: University of Illinois Press, 1971); Donald W. Riddle, *Lincoln Runs for Congress* (New Brunswick, NJ: Rutgers University Press, 1948); Donald W. Riddle, *Congressman Abraham Lincoln* (Westport, CT: Greenwood Press, 1979) and Paul Findley, *A. Lincoln: The Crucible of Congress* (New York: Crown Publishers, 1979).

Of the many works which consider Lincoln's temperament and personality, and his understanding of religion, the following warrant particular attention: Michael Burlingame, *The Inner World of Abraham Lincoln* (Urbana, IL: University of Illinois Press, 1994); Charles B. Strozier, *Lincoln's Quest for Union: Public and Private Meanings* (New York: Basic Books, 1982); William J. Wolf, *The Almost Chosen People: A Study of the Religion of Abraham Lincoln* (Garden City, NY: Doubleday, 1959); Hans J. Morgenthau and David Hein, *Essays on Lincoln's Faith and Politics*, ed. Kenneth W. Thompson (Lanham, MD: University Press of America, 1983); Allen C. Guelzo, 'Abraham Lincoln and the Doctrine of Necessity', *Journal of the Abraham Lincoln Association*, 18 (1997); and Robert V. Bruce, 'The Riddle of Death', in Gabor S. Boritt, ed., *The Lincoln Enigma: The Changing Faces of an American Icon* (New York: Oxford University Press, 2001).

2: The power of opinion, 1854–58

Don E. Fehrenbacher, *Prelude to Greatness: Lincoln in the 1850's* (Stanford, CA: Stanford University Press, 1962) remains the outstanding work on Lincoln and the political upheaval wrought by the Kansas–Nebraska Act: it has rightly achieved the status of a classic. Also helpful in placing Lincoln within the evolving Republican coalition are Don E. Fehrenbacher, *Chicago Giant: A Biography of Long John Wentworth* (Madison, WI: American History Research Center, 1957), Mark M. Krug, *Lyman Trumbull: Conservative Radical* (New York: A.S. Barnes and Co., 1965) and Edward Magdol, *Owen Lovejoy: Abolitionist in Congress* (New Brunswick, NJ: Rutgers University Press, 1967). The wider national context of party realignment is best pursued in two magisterial works: Michael F. Holt, *The Rise and Fall of the American Whig Party: Jacksonian Politics and the Onset of the Civil War* (New York: Oxford University Press, 1999) and William E. Gienapp, *The Origins of the Republican Party, 1852–1856* (New York: Oxford University Press, 1987). The state setting is delineated in Stephen L. Hansen, *The Making of the Third Party System: Voters and Parties in Illinois, 1850–1876* (UMI Research Press, Ann Arbor, MI, 1980).

Lincoln's oratorical style and engagement with the public are pursued in Waldo W. Braden, *Abraham Lincoln: Public Speaker* (Baton Rouge, LA: Louisiana State University Press, 1988). Of the several scholarly editions of the Lincoln–Douglas debates the most imaginative is Harold Holzer, ed., *The Lincoln–Douglas Debates: The First Complete Unexpurgated Text* (New York: Harper Collins, 1993), which exposes the unedited reality behind the polished texts that appeared in the friendly partisan press. Harry V. Jaffa, *Crisis of the House Divided: An Interpretation of the Issues in the Lincoln–Douglas Debates* (Chicago, IL: The University of Chicago Press, 1959, 1982) is a political philosopher's exploration of the principles and continuities underpinning Lincoln's political thought; David Zarefsky, *Lincoln, Douglas, and Slavery: In the Crucible of Public Debate* (Chicago, IL: The University of Chicago Press, 1990) offers a rhetorical analysis of the candidates' arguments. William Lee Miller, *Lincoln's Virtues: An Ethical Biography* (New York: Alfred A. Knopf, 2002) rightly emphasizes Lincoln's devotion to a moral standard while yet remaining an effective democratic politician.

3: The power of party, 1958–60

The Republican party that elected Lincoln is contrastingly delineated in Eric Foner, *Free Soil, Free Labor, Free Men: The Ideology of the Republican Party before the Civil War* (New York: Oxford University Press, 1970); Richard H. Sewell, *Ballots for Freedom: Antislavery Politics in the United States 1837–1860* (New York: Oxford University Press, 1976); Michael F. Holt, *The Political Crisis of the 1850s* (New York: John Wiley and Sons, 1978); and William E. Gienapp, 'The Republican Party and the Slave Power', in R.H. Abzug and S.E. Maizlish, eds, *New Perspectives on Race and Slavery in America* (Lexington, KY: University Press of Kentucky, 1986). Lincoln's increasingly evident appetite for the presidency and the 1860 campaign itself are the subjects of William E. Baringer, *Lincoln's Rise to Power* (Boston, MA: Little, Brown, 1937) and Reinhard H. Luthin, *The First Lincoln Campaign* (Cambridge, MA: Harvard University Press, 1944). The maneuvers at the Chicago convention are further examined in Willard L. King, *Lincoln's Manager: David Davis* (Cambridge, MA: Harvard University Press, 1960). For the Democrats' predicament, see in particular Robert W. Johannsen, *Stephen A. Douglas* (New York: Oxford University Press, 1973). The most helpful analysis of the voting patterns is William E. Gienapp's essay, 'Who Voted for Lincoln?', in John L. Thomas, ed., *Abraham Lincoln and the American Political Tradition* (Amherst, MA:

University of Massachusetts Press, 1986), 68–72. The religious dimension of the campaign is set in wider context in Richard J. Carwardine, *Evangelicals and Politics in Antebellum America* (New Haven, CT: Yale University Press, 1993) and William E. Gienapp, 'Nativism and the Creation of a Republican Majority in the North before the Civil War', *Journal of American History*, 72 (1985).

4: The limits of power, 1860–61

Phillip Shaw Paludan's *The Presidency of Abraham Lincoln* (Lawrence, KS: University Press of Kansas, 1994) offers a fresh and incisive examination of Lincoln's term of office and its immediate antecedents. James M. McPherson, *Battle Cry of Freedom* (New York: Oxford University Press, 1988) and Peter J. Parish, *The American Civil War* (New York: Holmes and Meier, 1975) provide the two most readable and authoritative single-volume treatments of the conflict. Each of these is relevant to the subject of this and later chapters, as is Allan Nevins, *The War for the Union* (4 vols, New York: Charles Scribner's Sons, 1959–71).

David M. Potter's *Lincoln and His Party in the Secession Crisis* (New Haven, CT: Yale University Press, 1942, 1962), Kenneth M. Stampp, *And the War Came: The North and the Secession Crisis* (Baton Rouge, LA: Louisiana State University Press, 1950) and William E. Baringer, *A House Dividing: Lincoln as President Elect* (Springfield, IL: Abraham Lincoln Association, 1945) are indispensable for understanding Lincoln's options and actions in the months that climaxed in hostilities at Fort Sumter. Harry V. Jaffa, *A New Birth of Freedom: Abraham Lincoln and the Coming of the Civil War* (Lanham, MD: Rowman & Littlefield, 2000) examines Lincoln's political thought, as expressed in this crisis of the Union, and places it in a wide philosophical context. On the Sumter crisis itself, Richard N. Current, *Lincoln and the First Shot* (Philadelphia, PA: J.B. Lippincott, 1963) provides a compelling analysis.

The significance of the border states, and Lincoln's strategy toward them, are the subject of William E. Gienapp, 'Abraham Lincoln and the Border States', in Thomas F. Schwartz, ed., *'For a Vast Future Also': Essays from the Journal of the Abraham Lincoln Association* (New York: Fordham University Press, 1999) and William W. Freehling, *The South vs. The South: How Anti-Confederate Southerners Shaped the Course of the Civil War* (New York, Oxford University Press, 2001). Lincolnians' efforts to cement Democrats into the war coalition are addressed in Joel H. Silbey, *A Respectable Minority: The Democratic Party in the Civil War Era, 1860–1869* (New

York: W.W. Norton, 1977) and Christopher Dell, *Lincoln and the War Democrats: The Grand Erosion of Conservative Tradition* (Rutherford, NJ: Fairleigh Dickinson University Press, 1975). Lincoln's grappling with the international dimension of the conflict and his determination to keep the European powers from intervening is the focus of Howard Jones, *Union in Peril: The Crisis over British Intervention in the Civil War* (Chapel Hill, NC: University of North Carolina Press, 1992).

For this period of the presidency, as for the later years, historians are especially dependent on the pens and historical self-awareness of Lincoln's secretaries. Probably the single most valuable source for Lincoln in the White House context is Hay's diary, now available in a fine modern edition: Michael Burlingame and John R. Turner Ettlinger, eds, *Inside Lincoln's White House: The Complete Civil War Diary of John Hay* (Carbondale, IL: Southern Illinois University Press, 1997). Hay's sparkling newspaper commentaries, dating chiefly from the early presidency, are in Michael Burlingame, ed., *Lincoln's Journalist: John Hay's Anonymous Writings for the Press, 1860–1864* (Carbondale, IL: Southern Illinois University Press, 1999). Important, too, are Michael Burlingame, ed., *At Lincoln's Side: John Hay's Civil War Correspondence and Selected Writings* (Carbondale, IL: Southern Illinois University Press, 2000) and Michael Burlingame, ed., *With Lincoln in the White House: Letters, Memoranda, and Other Writings of John G. Nicolay, 1860–1865* (Carbondale, IL: Southern Illinois University Press, 2000), as well as Burlingame's edition of Nicolay's interviews and essays, noted earlier.

5: The purposes of power, 1861–65

Lincoln's views on race are considered in Don E. Fehrenbacher, 'Only his Stepchildren: Lincoln and the Negro', *Civil War History*, 20 (1974) and George M. Fredrickson, 'A Man but Not a Brother: Abraham Lincoln and Racial Equality', *Journal of Southern History*, 61 (1975). They are also the subject of Lerone Bennett, Jr, *Forced Into Glory: Abraham Lincoln's White Dream* (Chicago, IL: Johnson Publishing Company, 2000), which is more an uncomfortable polemic than a balanced historical analysis, and turns Lincoln into a white supremacist. Gabor Boritt has explored in several publications the complexity and evolution of Lincoln's thinking about colonization, most recently in 'Did He Dream of a Lily-White America? The Voyage to Linconia', in Gabor S. Boritt, ed., *The Lincoln Enigma: The Changing Faces of an American Icon* (New York: Oxford University Press, 2002). Lincoln's approach to Indian issues is addressed in David A. Nichols,

Lincoln and the Indians: Civil War Policy and Politics (Columbia, MO: University of Missouri Press, 1978). Jean H. Baker, *Affairs of Party: The Political Culture of Northern Democrats in the Mid-Nineteenth Century* (Ithaca, NY: Cornell University Press, 1983) indicates the gulf between Lincoln's views and those of vehement Democratic racists.

There is yet no definitive treatment of Lincoln and emancipation, but the several helpful studies available include John Hope Franklin, *The Emancipation Proclamation* (New York: Anchor, 1965) and Benjamin F. Quarles, *Lincoln and the Negro* (New York: Oxford University Press, 1962). The portrait painter F.B. Carpenter in *The Inner Life of Abraham Lincoln: Six Months at the White House* (Lincoln, NB: University of Nebraska Press, 1995; repr. of 1866 edition) reports his conversations with Lincoln, on which historians of emancipation have been especially dependent. James M. McPherson, 'Who Freed the Slaves?', in his *Drawn with the Sword: Reflections on the American Civil War* (New York: Oxford University Press, 1996) and Ira Berlin, 'Who Freed the Slaves? Emancipation and Its Meaning', in David Blight and Brooks D. Simpson, eds, *Union and Emancipation: Essays on Politics and Race in the Civil War Era* (Kent, OH: Kent State University Press, 1997) offer contrasting answers to their common question. Lincoln's contribution to the process that turned the Emancipation Proclamation into the Thirteenth Amendment is examined in Michael Vorenberg's deeply researched *Final Freedom: The Civil War, the Abolition of Slavery, and the Thirteenth Amendment* (Cambridge: Cambridge University Press, 2001).

The religious workings of Lincoln's mind in wartime are explored in Nicholas Parrillo, 'Lincoln's Calvinist Transformation: Emancipation and War', *Civil War History*, 46 (Sept. 2000); Mark A. Noll, 'Both Pray to the Same God': The Singularity of Lincoln's Faith in the Era of the Civil War', *Journal of the Abraham Lincoln Association*, 18 (Winter 1997), 11–12; Ronald C. White, Jr, *Lincoln's Greatest Speech: The Second Inaugural* (New York: Simon & Schuster, 2002); and Guelzo's biography. Garry Wills, *Lincoln at Gettysburg: The Words that Remade America* (New York: Simon & Schuster, 1992) is a brilliant work, but one which imposes on Lincoln's short speech more than it can reasonably bear.

Lincoln's plans for reconstruction and his relations with the Radical Republicans can be pursued in Hans L. Trefousse, *The Radical Republicans: Lincoln's Vanguard for Racial Justice* (New York: Alfred A. Knopf, 1969); Herman Belz, *Reconstructing the Union: Theory and Policy during the Civil War* (Ithaca, NY: Cornell University Press, 1969); Peyton McCrary, *Abraham Lincoln and Reconstruction: The Louisiana Experiment* (Princeton, NJ: Princeton University Press, 1978); LaWanda Cox, *Lincoln and Black*

Freedom: A Study in Presidential Leadership (Columbia, SC: University of South Carolina Press, 1981). Taking issue with these is William C. Harris's wide-ranging study, *With Charity for All: Lincoln and the Restoration of the Union* (Lexington, KY: University Press of Kentucky, 1997), which emphasizes the essentially conservative purposes of Lincoln's restorationist policy. For the larger context, Eric Foner, *Reconstruction: America's Unfinished Revolution 1863–1877* (New York: Harper & Row, 1988) is indispensable.

6: The instruments of power, 1861–65

Lincoln's respect for the Constitution, his use of the coercive power of the state, and his record on civil liberties are the subject of two outstanding studies: James G. Randall, *Constitutional Problems under Lincoln* (rev. edn, Urbana, IL: University of Illinois Press, 1951) and Mark E. Neely, *The Fate of Liberty: Abraham Lincoln and Civil Liberties* (New York: Oxford University Press, 1991). Also helpful are several essays in Don E. Fehrenbacher, *Lincoln in Text and Context* (Stanford, CA: Stanford University Press, 1987) and Herman Belz, *Abraham Lincoln, Constitutionalism and Equal Rights in the Civil War Era* (New York: Fordham University Press, 1998). The centralizing and nationalizing tendencies of the war are discussed in Richard Franklin Bensel, *Yankee Leviathan: The Origins of Central State Authority in America, 1859–1877* (Cambridge: Cambridge University Press, 1990) and Heather Cox Richardson, *Greatest Nation of the Earth: Republican Economic Policies during the Civil War* (Cambridge, MA: Harvard University Press, 1997).

Lincoln's relationship with his generals, his military understanding, and the development of a hard war strategy are best pursued in T. Harry Williams, *Lincoln and His Generals* (New York: Alfred A. Knopf, 1952), a sparkling gem of a book; Gabor S. Boritt, ed., *Lincoln's Generals* (New York, Oxford University Press, 1994); and Mark Grimsley, *The Hard Hand of War: Union Military Policy toward Southern Civilians 1861–1865* (Cambridge: Cambridge University Press, 1995). Lincoln's enthusiasm for the possibilities of new technology is the subject of Robert V. Bruce, *Lincoln and the Tools of War* (Indianapolis, IN: Bobbs-Merrill, 1956).

The argument that party conflict helped the Union survive is set out in Eric L. McKitrick, 'Party Politics and the Union and Confederate War Efforts', in William Nisbet Chambers and Walter Dean Burnham, eds, *The American Party Systems: Stages of Political Development* (2nd edn, New York: Oxford University Press, 1967). It is provocatively rebutted by

Mark Neely in *The Union Divided: Party Conflict in the Civil War North* (Cambridge, MA: Harvard University Press, 2002). The story of Lincoln and the wartime Republican party can be approached from a variety of angles. The best studies include Harry J. Carman and Reinhard H. Luthin, *Lincoln and the Patronage* (New York: Columbia University Press, 1943); Kenneth M. Stampp, *Indiana Politics during the Civil War* (Bloomington, IN: Indiana University Press, 1945, 1978); William B. Hesseltine, *Lincoln and the War Governors* (New York: Alfred A. Knopf, 1955); Dale Baum, *The Civil War Party System: The Case of Massachusetts, 1848–1876* (Chapel Hill, NC: University of North Carolina Press, 1984); Robert J. Cook, *Baptism of Fire: The Republican Party in Iowa, 1838–1878* (Ames, IA, 1994); and Lex Renda, *Running on the Record: Civil War Era Politics in New Hampshire* (Charlottesville, VA: University Press of Virginia, 1998). Adam I.P. Smith's forthcoming book on the North's wartime political experience (New York: Fordham University Press) will be an important addition to this list.

The most assured and grounded study of mainstream Protestantism in the wartime Union is James H. Moorhead, *American Apocalypse: Yankee Protestants and the Civil War 1860–69* (New Haven, CT: Yale University Press, 1978). The role of the United States Sanitary Commission in rallying broad-based support for the Union is well examined in Jeanie Attie, *Patriotic Toil: Northern Women and the American Civil War* (Ithaca, NY: Cornell University Press, 1998). Union soldiers' motivation and politics are addressed in Reid Mitchell, *Civil War Soldiers* (New York: Viking Penguin, 1988); James M. McPherson, *For Cause and Comrades: Why Men Fought in the Civil War* (New York: Oxford University Press, 1997); Joseph Allan Frank, *With Ballot and Bayonet: The Political Socialization of American Civil War Soldiers* (Athens, GA: University of Georgia Press, 1998); William C. Davis, *Lincoln's Men: How President Lincoln Became Father to an Army and a Nation* (New York: The Free Press, 1999); and Steven E. Woodworth, *While God is Marching On: The Religious World of Civil War Soldiers* (Lawrence, KS: University Press of Kansas, 2001).

The 1864 election is the subject of David E. Long, *The Jewel of Liberty: Abraham Lincoln's Re-election and the End of Slavery* (Mechanicsburg, PA: Stackpole Books, 1994). Although he probably understates the extent of treason amongst wartime dissidents, Frank L. Klement has done more than anyone to shed light on the anti-war Democrats and the 1864 climax of the peace movement: see, especially, *The Copperheads in the Middle West* (Chicago, IL: The University of Chicago Press, 1960) and *The Limits of Dissent: Clement L. Vallandigham & the Civil War* (1970; repr. New York: Fordham University Press, 1998).

Conclusion: power in death

William Hanchett, in *The Lincoln Murder Conspiracies* (Urbana, IL: University of Illinois Press, 1983), provides a cool-headed examination of Lincoln's assassination and its subsequent interpretation and re-interpretation. Contemporary reactions to Lincoln's death are considered in Thomas Reed Turner, *Beware the People Weeping: Public Opinion and the Assassination of Abraham Lincoln* (Baton Rouge, LA: Louisiana State University Press, 1982) and David B. Chesebrough, *'No Sorrow like Our Sorrow': Northern Protestant Ministers and the Assassination of Lincoln* (Kent, OH: Kent State University Press, 1994). The evolving place of Lincoln and of the Civil War in the nation's psyche is the focus, respectively, of Merrill D. Peterson, *Lincoln in American Memory* (New York: Oxford University Press, 1994) and David W. Blight, *Race and Reunion: The Civil War in American Memory* (Cambridge, MA: Harvard University Press, 2001).

Reference

Finally, two indispensable reference works deserve special mention: Earl Schenck Miers, ed., *Lincoln Day by Day: A Chronology 1809–1865* (3 vols, Washington, DC: Lincoln Sesquicentennial Commission, 1960) and Mark E. Neely, Jr, *The Abraham Lincoln Encyclopedia* (New York: McGraw-Hill, 1982).

Index

abolitionism, 116, 206, 282, 288, 298n39; abolitionists, 20, 21, 52, 77, 84, 95, 98, 211, 212, 270; perceptions of southern sinfulness, 104. *See also* antislavery; churches; Lincoln

abolitionists, 20, 21, 52, 77, 84, 95, 98, 211, 212, 270

Adams, Charles Francis, 143, 177

Adams, Henry, 142

Adams, John Quincy, 204

African Americans. *See* blacks; Emancipation Proclamation; race; slavery

Albany Evening Journal, 120

Altoona (Pennsylvania) conference, 211

American Colonization Society, 22

American nationalism, 101, 291, 292, 295, 296, 306, 310, 311, 312. *See also* Unionism

American party. *See* Know Nothing party

American republicanism, 26, 65, 80, 82, 222, 232, 248, 268–9, 277; republican constitutionalism in Civil War, 249–50

American Revolution, 145, 219, 277

'American System', 12, 13, 15

American Tract Society, 80, 265

Ames, Edward, 108, 270, 299n43

Anderson, Robert, 153, 155, 159, 172, 174

Andrew, John A., 111, 194

Antietam, battle of, 210, 225

antislavery: and moral certainty, 66; pressure on Lincoln, 193, 206, 218; radicalism, 52, 94, 121–2, 124, 174–5, 282. *See also* abolitionism; churches; Whig party

Appomattox, Virginia, 239, 307

aristocracy, 101, 118, 291, 292; anti-aristocratic sentiment, 100, 169

Arkansas: and secession, 167, 187n31; in Civil War, 171, 215; restored government in, 233, 236, 239

armistice, 240, 296

Army of Northern Virginia, 236

Army of the Potomac, 180, 201, 208, 212, 226, 251, 265, 275, 282

Arnold, Isaac, 36, 160

arrests, military, 161, 169, 213, 248, 252–4, 256, 259. *See also* courts-martial; habeas corpus; martial law

Ashley, James, Reconstruction bill, 237–8

Ashmun amendment, 20

Associated Press, 263

Atlanta, Georgia, 236, 251, 283, 285, 289, 293

Atlantic slave trade, 78, 93, 116, 205

Bacon, Leonard, 29, 41n46

Baker, Edward D., 8, 9, 54, 55, 220

Baldwin, John B., 155

Ball's Bluff, battle of, 181

Baltimore, Maryland, 103, 168–9, 294; 1864 Republican convention in, 282, 288